KV-486-845

eils il library

LEEDS BECKETT UNIVERSITY
LIBRARY
DISCARDED

Leeds Metropolitan University

17 0590082 2

Cases on Consumer–Centric Marketing Management

Vimi Jham
Institute of Management Technology, UAE

Sandeep Puri
Institute of Management Technology, India

A volume in the Advances
in Marketing, Customer
Relationship Management,
and E–Services (AMCRMES)
Book Series

BUSINESS SCIENCE
Reference
An Imprint of IGI Global

Managing Director:	Lindsay Johnston
Production Manager:	Jennifer Yoder
Publishing Systems Analyst:	Adrienne Freeland
Development Editor:	Myla Merkel
Acquisitions Editor:	Kayla Wolfe
Typesetter:	Erin O'Dea
Cover Design:	Jason Mull

LEEDS METROPOLITAN
UNIVERSITY
LIBRARY

1705900822
MK-B
CC-143027
9.4.14
658.8343 CAS

Published in the United States of America by
Business Science Reference (an imprint of IGI Global)
701 E. Chocolate Avenue
Hershey PA 17033
Tel: 717-533-8845
Fax: 717-533-8661
E-mail: cust@igi-global.com
Web site: http://www.igi-global.com

Copyright © 2014 by IGI Global. All rights reserved. No part of this publication may be reproduced, stored or distributed in any form or by any means, electronic or mechanical, including photocopying, without written permission from the publisher.
Product or company names used in this set are for identification purposes only. Inclusion of the names of the products or companies does not indicate a claim of ownership by IGI Global of the trademark or registered trademark.

Library of Congress Cataloging-in-Publication Data

Cases on consumer-centric marketing management / Vimi Jham and Sandeep Puri, editors.
    pages cm
  Includes bibliographical references and index.
  Summary: "This book presents a collection of case studies highlighting the importance of customer loyalty, customer satisfaction, and consumer behavior for marketing strategies"--Provided by publisher.
  ISBN 978-1-4666-4357-4 (hardcover) -- ISBN 978-1-4666-4358-1 (ebook) -- ISBN 978-1-4666-4359-8 (print & perpetual access) 1. Marketing--Management--Case studies. 2. Customer relations--Case studies. 3. Customer services--Case studies. 4. Consumer behavior--Case studies. I. Jham, Vimi, 1968- II. Puri, Sandeep, 1972-
  HF5415.13.C335 2014
  658.8'343--dc23
                                2013011319

This book is published in the IGI Global book series Advances in Marketing, Customer Relationship Management, and E-Services (AMCRMES) (ISSN: 2327-5502; eISSN: 2327-5529)

British Cataloguing in Publication Data
A Cataloguing in Publication record for this book is available from the British Library.

All work contributed to this book is new, previously-unpublished material. The views expressed in this book are those of the authors, but not necessarily of the publisher.

Advances in Marketing, Customer Relationship Management, and E-Services (AMCRMES) Book Series

Eldon Y. Li
National Chengchi University, Taiwan &
California Polytechnic State University, USA

ISSN: 2327-5502
EISSN: 2327-5529

MISSION

Business processes, services, and communications are important factors in the management of good customer relationship, which is the foundation of any well organized business. Technology continues to play a vital role in the organization and automation of business processes for marketing, sales, and customer service. These features aid in the attraction of new clients and maintaining existing relationships.

The Advances in Marketing, Customer Relationship Management, and E-Services (AMCRMES) Book Series addresses success factors for customer relationship management, marketing, and electronic services and its performance outcomes. This collection of reference source covers aspects of consumer behavior and marketing business strategies aiming towards researchers, scholars, and practitioners in the fields of marketing management.

COVERAGE

- B2B Marketing
- CRM and Customer Trust
- CRM in Financial Services
- CRM Strategies
- Customer Relationship Management
- Data Mining and Marketing
- E-Service Innovation
- Ethical Considerations in E-Marketing
- Legal Considerations in E-Marketing
- Online Community Management and Behavior
- Relationship Marketing
- Social Networking and Marketing
- Web Mining and Marketing

IGI Global is currently accepting manuscripts for publication within this series. To submit a proposal for a volume in this series, please contact our Acquisition Editors at Acquisitions@igi-global.com or visit: http://www.igi-global.com/publish/.

The Advances in Marketing, Customer Relationship Management, and E-Services (AMCRMES) (ISSN 2327-5502) is published by IGI Global, 701 E. Chocolate Avenue, Hershey, PA 17033-1240, USA, www.igi-global.com. This series is composed of titles available for purchase individually; each title is edited to be contextually exclusive from any other title within the series. For pricing and ordering information please visit http://www.igi-global.com/book-series/advances-marketing-customer-relationship-management/37150. Postmaster: Send all address changes to above address. Copyright © 2014 IGI Global. All rights, including translation in other languages reserved by the publisher. No part of this series may be reproduced or used in any form or by any means – graphics, electronic, or mechanical, including photocopying, recording, taping, or information and retrieval systems – without written permission from the publisher, except for non commercial, educational use, including classroom teaching purposes. The views expressed in this series are those of the authors, but not necessarily of IGI Global.

Titles in this Series

For a list of additional titles in this series, please visit: www.igi-global.com

Transcultural Marketing for Incremental and Radical Innovation
Bryan Christiansen (PryMarke, LLC, USA) Salih Yıldız (Gümüşhane University, Turkey) and Emel Yıldız (Gümüşhane University, Turkey)
Business Science Reference • copyright 2014 • 394pp • H/C (ISBN: 9781466647497) • US $185.00 (our price)

Progressive Trends in Knowledge and System-Based Science for Service Innovation
Michitaka Kosaka (Japan Advanced Institute of Science and Technology, Japan) and Kunio Shirahada (Japan Advanced Institute of Science and Technology, Japan)
Business Science Reference • copyright 2014 • 522pp • H/C (ISBN: 9781466646636) • US $185.00 (our price)

Innovations in Services Marketing and Management Strategies for Emerging Economies
Anita Goyal (Indian Institute of Management (IIM), Lucknow, India)
Business Science Reference • copyright 2014 • 331pp • H/C (ISBN: 9781466646711) • US $185.00 (our price)

Internet Mercenaries and Viral Marketing The Case of Chinese Social Media
Mei Wu (University of Macau, China) Peter Jakubowicz (The Chinese University of Hong Kong, Hong Kong) and Chengyu Cao (Tsinghua University, China)
Business Science Reference • copyright 2014 • 351pp • H/C (ISBN: 9781466645783) • US $175.00 (our price)

Cases on Consumer-Centric Marketing Management
Vimi Jham (Institute of Management Technology, Dubai) and Sandeep Puri (Institute of Management Technology, Ghaziabad)
Business Science Reference • copyright 2014 • 362pp • H/C (ISBN: 9781466643574) • US $175.00 (our price)

DISSEMINATOR of KNOWLEDGE

www.igi-global.com

701 E. Chocolate Ave., Hershey, PA 17033
Order online at www.igi-global.com or call 717-533-8845 x100
To place a standing order for titles released in this series,
contact: cust@igi-global.com
Mon-Fri 8:00 am - 5:00 pm (est) or fax 24 hours a day 717-533-8661

Editorial Advisory Board

Bruce Chien-Ta Ho, *National Chung Hsing University, Taiwan*
Nagendra V. Chowdary, *Aegis Global Academy, India*
Vinita Sahay, *Indian Institute of Management, India*
Kalyan De, *L M Thapar School of Management, India*
G.C. Tripathi, *Institute of Management Technology, India*
Roma Mitra Debnath, *Institute of Management Technology, India*
Gunjan Malhotra, *Institute of Management Technology, India*
Vishal Talwar, *London School of Management and Economics, UK*
Jayanthi Ranjan, *Institute of Mangement Technology, India*
Eric Van Genderen, *Institute of Management Technology (IMT), UAE*

List of Reviewers

Sujana Adapa, *University of New England Business School, Australia*
Sonali S. Gadekar, *MET's Institute of Management, India*
Eric Viardot, *EADA Business School, Spain*
Necia Boone, *University of Phoenix, USA*
Tugba Ucma, *Muğla Sıtkı Koçman University, Turkey*

Table of Contents

Detailed Table of Contents

Tugba Ucma, Muğla Sıtkı Koçman University, Turkey
Ali Naci Karabulut, Muğla Sıtkı Koçman University, Turkey
Ali Caglar Uzun, Muğla Sıtkı Koçman University, Turkey

This case talks about Turkey's consumer market, for understanding the behaviours
of the Turkish consumers that are different in terms of cultural variables, by taking
advantage of mental accounting.

Bhavna Bhalla, Institute of Management Technology, India

This case talks about Turkey's consumer market, for understanding the behaviours
of the Turkish consumers that are different in terms of cultural variables, by taking
advantage of mental accounting.

Bhawana Sharma, Jaipur National University, India
Tulika Sood, Jaipur National University, India

This Case Study is based on Relationship Marketing focusing on a service Industry
i.e. Insurance Industry. It talks about a sales representative not only needs to be
professional but also he needs to bond well with all his clients in order to be able
to meet their expectations as required therefore, any Employee who is loyal to his
organization as well good in his PR skills is sure to reach the ladder of success.

This case examines the necessity of these functions in order to bring delight in the minds of the customer and give them an experience as a whole. The case outlines few failures which results due to poor planning in the strategy of a new product launch. The case also throws light on the distance which is generated between the sales force and the company.

This case is about the technology component integrations in the marketing strategy of U-Globe organization – a travel service provider organization to assess their customer satisfaction.

This case is set in the Middle East, and centers around the two main concepts of: 1). Customer-centric business practices, and 2). Ethical healthcare behavior, respectively. The case goes on to talk about healthcare industry that has the added challenge of needing to offer customized products/services that not only address the needs/wants of customers, but must do so in an ethical and sensitive way.

This case study about illustrates the effectiveness of pursuing a customer centric marketing approach in order to achieve long term strategic success and market leadership in the fashion industry.

The following case on the product "Fair & Lovely" gives a background of the market for fairness creams in India and focuses on different aspects of behavior of women as consumers of this product.

The case focuses on Mirza International Limited which was originated from a small Tannery business in India. The company management, however, is now at a crossroads with regard to more aggressive approach international brand building for its product and strategic decisions thereof. This case aims to address these issues regarding smaller company's internationalization and marketing there off.

This case talks about Delhi Bank having a very low customer base and many customers have shifted their accounts to other banks because of dissatisfaction with the bank and in the last 6 months number of customers are reduced to 2875 from 2900. Branch is having allocation of 1.50 Crores only for loan disbursements during Jan-March, 2011 period but the loan applications are for 2.20 crore. There are six applicants with different backgrounds and this amount cannot be increased. Bank manager Siddhant, needed to take the call for final disbursements.

This case study is prepared for the informative purpose, as it will provide the Literature over Facebook and the technologies it is using. It also include the technology change and the shortcomings that Facebook was facing and how developers resolve them.

This case study focuses on mid-size hotel industry in India. It will analyze the extent to which the pricing strategies are adopted in order to optimize revenues.

This case study provides information related to the Australian retail-banking sector and specifically about the Australian internet banking environment.

This case is about political Lobbying in the telecom industry in India.

This case talks about the strong marketing strategy, development of the retail chain, and a change in the philosophy and style of sale of products which led totThe growth in this sector could also be attributed to striking the chord with the consumer and challenging the buying power of the consumer.

This case talks about the various underlying issues relating to the fraud that took the industry observers, market players and regulators by surprise and shock. It also talks about the implications to the future of Wealth Management, with special reference to India, in the greater interests all the stakeholders, particularly the investors at large.

The case study provides an overview about Duke and Duchess Technology Centers as well as Triumph Management Company, products and services, competition, management structure, leadership styles, and recent challenges.

This case talks about challenges faced by a pharmaceutical company of high attrition of new hires and took the initiative of revamping its employee on-boarding program.

Foreword

Teaching through cases has been a preferred mode of teaching in management schools for a fairly long time. One of the problems management faculty face is finding cases that are exciting, relevant to their subjects, and topical. This requires a constant influx of new cases. Since only a few faculty members in a few schools write them, it is difficult to find what you need.

I am very happy that my faculty colleagues at IMT have chosen to publish this edited collection of cases that will be useful to those faculty who teach customer-oriented courses. In most business schools, a large number of students elect to take courses in marketing. This collection contains material useful to almost every area within marketing including CRM, consumer behavior, and many related areas such as technology used in customer interface (cloud computing) or strategic management, which also has an impact on management of customers and their retention.

While an individual faculty member can choose what he wants to out of this collection, it is possible that multiple faculty members from a Business School will find some of their needs fulfilled through the collection of cases from diverse countries that this book contains. Students may also find this a useful reference to learn more about the subjects covered.

Here is to wishing the authors of this edited volume and the authors of individual cases great success with this unique endeavour. IMT has always been at the forefront in encouraging such creative ventures, and will continue to do so.

Rajendra Nargundkar
IMT Ghaziabad, India

Rajendra Nargundkar *chairs the position of Director at IMT Nagpur and Sr. Dean Academics at IMT Ghaziabad. He earned his Doctoral from Clemson University after completing PGDM from IIM Bangalore. An engineer from Osmania University, he is a keen researcher and an avid writer. His current research interests embrace World-class customer service, G to C Services and Business School Branding. His publications include a number of papers in high order international journals and cases of remarkable distinction. He has also authored and co-authored a number of books in Marketing.*

Preface

There are many bestselling books, celebrity seminars and trainings in the market that speak of the importance of a customer, but the poor customer is still not treated well. Customer oriented marketing has become a vital aspect in business as it contributes greatly to the success of the organization. The study of customers helps organizations to improve their marketing strategies by understanding issues such as consumer behavior, customer satisfaction, customer loyalty, relationship marketing, customer centricity, and more. This book is designed to provide instructors with concrete, active learning tools and examples that can be implemented in the classroom. This book is a collection of cases on customer centricity in the field of marketing management. It discusses the prominent issues of marketing related to the customers.

The distinctive feature of the book remains its focus on the concept of customer centricity. In today's complex, high tech environment, the customer-centricity approach can offer high touch and great competitive advantage to an organization. Great companies apprehend this and they are building their value proposition around what really matter to customers and then structuring their products and services accordingly. Becoming customer-centric means having a holistic view of an organization from the outside-in rather than the inside-out that is, through the perspective of the customer rather than the marketer.

The traditional marketing concept tends to be more short-term oriented. The customer centricity, by contrast, de-emphasizes the functional role of marketing. It enlarges the market meaning not only to the key market players, direct, and indirect customers, but also to online market players, distributors, competitors, influencers, and other stakeholders. It conditions that every department in an organization is responsible for customer centricity by enhancing customer value. In this hyper competitive, global, deregulated, and deeply reformed by the information technology revolution, customer centricity is the only way for a firm to achieve its objective of profit and growth.

To explore the nature of business organizations and its application in management education, business schools throughout the world are increasingly adopting the case methodology for teaching. In the fields of marketing, there exists a need for real life management cases. This book fills an important need in this context by focusing on real life management issues in this unique challenging environment. The book is an edited collection of 22 cases in the area of marketing and strategy focusing on the role and importance of customers and related strategies. Different marketing experts and researchers all over the world have contributed cases for this book.

Special effort is made to include more cases with coverage on a.) the 'solution-information-value-access' approach as the best way to create customer centricity; b.) on Customer Relationship Management as IT has reformed the ways to manage one-to-one relationships with customers; c.) on the emergence of new approaches like marketing analytics, predictive analytics and regain management; d.) finally, on presenting a global perspective with the majority of cases drawn from the global scene.

This book explores the nature of business organizations and its application in management education. It is written for professionals who want to improve their understanding about real life issues and policies related to customers. It covers the major management areas including: Cloud computing, consumer behaviour, customer centricity, customer experience management, customer lifecycle management, customer loyalty, customer relationship management, customer satisfaction, customer trust, internal marketing, marketing analytics, regain management, and relationship marketing.

Tugba Ucma's case, "Understanding Consumer Behavior through Mental Accounting: Evidence from Turkish Consumers," is based on understanding the behaviors of the Turkish consumers that are different in terms of cultural variables by taking advantage of mental accounting.

Bhavna Bhalla in her case, "What Went Wrong?," explores the successful interview strategy and selection criterion for the post of a market representative. The scope of discussion covers the flow from preparation to execution to be successful in any interview.

The "Case Study on Relationship Marketing," by Bhawana Sharma and Tulika Sood, is focused on the insurance industry where the very essence of marketing for Insurance products to clients is entirely based on relationships. A sales representative not only needs to be professional, but also needs to bond well with all his clients in order to be able to meet their expectations and move up the ladder by achieving targets with customer retention, loyalty, and word of mouth.

In "A Line in Water: A Case of Customer Relationship Management," Chandra Shekhar Padhi casts light on the distance which is generated between the sales force and the company. The distances occur due to various factors like resistance to change by the sales force, pressure from higher management on strategic compliance, and inefficient communication strategy between the two. The case helps in understanding the fragile bridge which connects the higher management of the company to the sales team on field.

Ooi Chien Shing, Seng Kah Phooi, and Ang Li-Minn in their case, "The Realization of Customer Satisfaction with Technology Integrations," discuss the technology component integrations in the marketing strategy of U-Globe organization–a travel service provider organization-to assess their customer satisfaction. They have explained and compared the customer satisfaction tools used by the organization as well as the management concerns in conducting these customer satisfaction assessments. They have provided recommendations and solutions to show the possible ways in solving the existing problems and improving the way of assessing customer satisfaction by integrating the appropriate technology.

In the case study, "Always Trust the Customer: How Zara has Revolutionized the Fashion Industry and Become a Worldwide Leader," Eric Viardot discusses the revolution of the fashion industry by Zara and how it became a worldwide leader. This case study illustrates the effectiveness of pursuing a customer centric marketing approach in order to achieve long term strategic success and market leadership in the fashion industry.

"Consumer Behavior Perspective for Fairness Creams: A Case of Fair & Lovely," by Yasser Mahfooz, Faisal Mahfooz, and Ahmed A. Al-Motawa gives a background of the market for fairness creams in India and focuses on different aspects of behavior of women as consumers of this product.

Gautam Dutta's case "International Branding at Mirza International: Dilemma Unsolved" focuses on the dilemma often faced by medium sized firms from Asia in entering developed country markets in terms of branding or generic product development strategy. This case aims to address these issues regarding smaller company's internationalization and marketing thereof. The case illustrates the differences in brand building that exists in a big multinational company and in smaller companies while internationalization.

Sandeep Puri and Jayanthi Ranjan in their case on "Delhi Bank of India: Dilemma of a New Bank Manager," explore the dilemma of a bank manager struck with decreasing customer satisfaction and retention. The Dwarka Branch of the bank is not doing well and has a very low customer base with many customers shifting their accounts to other banks. The branch has an allocation of only ₹1.50 Crores for loan disbursements for the period of January through March 2013, but the loan applications are for ₹2.20 crore. There are six applicants with different backgrounds and this amount cannot be increased.

Case "Facebook: An Application of Cloud Computing" by Lokesh Sharma is prepared for the informative purpose, as it provide the literature over Facebook and the technologies it is using. It also includes the technology change and the shortcomings that Facebook was facing and how developers resolved them. There are detailed explanations in this case chapter.

Nidhi Chowdhry in her case study, "Price Effectiveness in Hotels: Case Study Comparing Strategies Adopted by Mid-Size Hotels in New Delhi," compared the strategies adopted by mid-size hotels in New Delhi focus on mid-size hotel industry in India and analyzed the extent to which the pricing strategies are adopted in order to optimize revenues.

Pardeep Bawa in his case, "Indian Luxury Car Market Changing Lanes: A Case of BMW India," explores the factors responsible for growth of the Indian luxury car market with special reference to BMW's growth to the number one position in India in just three years with the help of cars customized for Indian infrastructure conditions, an aggressive distribution strategy, pricing designed in lieu of competition and the Indian customer, and a very comprehensive and smart promotional efforts.

Pradeep Kautish in his case on "Niche Marketing Strategies for Business Growth: An Experiential Journey," discussed suggest that the consumer behavior is the sum total to a range of political, economic, technical, and social environmental influences which is dynamic in nature. The art of adapting to the changing environment may sound easy, but these changes are not visible to the insensitive eyes. His case deals with the decision dilemma of a management professional who is in the process of deciding about acquiring a niche marketing company and the case narrates about four companies with the marketing strategies they employ for market share.

Rajeev Sharma in his case on "Marketing of Tobacco Products in Australia: Dealing with the Emerging Regulations," explores the role and responsibility of governments in regulating such goods and services. The Australian Federal Government has recently introduced a bill into the parliament which aims to lay down very stringent guidelines and restrict the promotional options for tobacco product marketing in Australia. This real and evolving case study looks into the challenges faced by the marketers.

Shreya Dhingra in her case study, "Concentra BPO: The Falling Customer Satisfaction," reflects upon the relationship between employee satisfaction and customer satisfaction. This case study explains how a company can increase a customer's satisfaction just by understanding and treating their employees as the first customers of the organization to be served.

The case study, "Customer Experiential Management at High Five Hotels Pvt. Ltd, Nashik," by Sonali Gadekar and Sushil Gadekar is based on experiential marketing and presents various innovative promotional strategies followed in the hospitality industry. The ultimate outcome and the results after applying this 'experiential techniques' were excellent in terms of financial returns as well as customer satisfaction.

Sujana Adapa and Fredy Valenzuela in their case study on the "Customer's Ambidextrous Nature of Trust in Internet Banking: Australian Context," provide information related to the Australian retail-banking sector and specifically about the Australian internet banking environment. This case provides information related to the ambidextrous nature of the trust component and how the aforesaid affects the consumer's perception levels towards the adoption/non-adoption of internet banking in the Australian context.

S. Jayachandran in his case on "Should Corporate Political Lobbying Come under Scanner by Regulatory Mechanism? Vaishnavi Corporate Communication and 2G Spectrum Scam: A Political Lobbying Case" raises four criticasl points for discussions regarding marketing facilitating agents, public relations, marketing strategy, and lobbying as the backdrop of the changing marketing environment.

The case "Tata GoldPlus: Adoption of Customer Oriented Strategy for Penetrating Market Opportunity," by Salma Ahmed, evaluates the strategy adopted Tata Gold Plus to make its position in the market and explores the opportunities and strategies required to retain market shares and remain at the top in its domain.

Suresh Chandra Bihari in his case, "When Citi was Found Sleeping," discusses the incidence of a high profile branch in India where several depositors and high-net worth individuals were duped in a fraud engineered by their Global Wealth Manager. The clients were offered super normal returns and were lured by the Relationship Manager who enjoyed a special relationship of trust and confidence with the clients. The clients were cheated understandably for their lack of understanding of the nuances of the product but the greater issue at stake was the onerous practices of Wealth Management by Banks in India and the lack of regulatory control in this fast developing area that allowed the incident to happen in the first place.

Necia Boone's case study "Triumph Charter School Service Provider" provides an overview about the company, its products and services, competition, management structure, leadership style, and challenges.

Shalini Kalia, Neha Mittal, and Rohit Arora in their case, "Maximizing Employee On-Boarding: A Study in a Pharmaceutical Company," explore the gaps in on-boarding process of a pharmaceutical company faced with the challenge of high attrition of new hires.

The book is targeted to a different audience—primarily MBA students, professionals, and researchers working in the field of marketing management in various disciplines. The book is expansive in its coverage, including relative emphasis on customer relations integrated marketing communication, sales and service management, consumer research, and marketing analytics. Moreover, the book provides insights into practical aspects of marketing in any organization. This book can also be recommended with other books for courses like: CRM, Consumer Behavior, Retail Management, Sales Management, Product Management, and Marketing of Services.

Vimi Jham
Institute of Management Technology, Ghaziabad and Dubai

Sandeep Puri
Institute of Management Technology, Ghaziabad and Dubai

Chapter 1
Understanding Consumer Behavior through Mental Accounting:
Evidence from Turkish Consumers

Tugba Ucma
Muğla Sıtkı Koçman University, Turkey

Ali Naci Karabulut
Muğla Sıtkı Koçman University, Turkey

Ali Caglar Uzun
Muğla Sıtkı Koçman University, Turkey

EXECUTIVE SUMMARY

By setting out from similar studies, this study falls within international literature. The intention is to measure, in connection with Turkey's consumer market, in order to understand the behaviors of the Turkish consumers that are different in terms of cultural variables. The operability of this international theory is achieved by taking advantage of mental accounting. In seeking the essential objective of the research, a working group formed from two subgroups in order to manifest the decisiveness in the purchasing decisions of individuals, as well as the effects of the mental accounting theories. The first subgroup is formed by 100 university students whose ages are varied between 18 and 30. The second group forms from the same number of students at the same age range. According to the results of analysis carried out in the direction of the collected data from the sub groups, the consequences of this

DOI: 10.4018/978-1-4666-4357-4.ch001

Copyright ©2014, IGI Global. Copying or distributing in print or electronic forms without written permission of IGI Global is prohibited.

study support the results of the other a priori study in the literature. The greatest consequence of this research is the reactions developed in the expenditures and savings of the consumers subsequent to the formed sunk costs become varied with in terms of the independent "budget" variable.

1. INTRODUCTION

To be able to create value in the sense of marketing, it is required to structure all marketing offer from the consumer's perspective, properly. Prior to the business enterprises pass to production and marketing processes, they should determine the elements of very high concern in terms of the consumer and develop thereof by putting their products on so as to gain favor as parallel to these elements. In this context, in order to be capable of to describe which objectives originate consumer behaviors, and why/how that has been progressed come into being as a marketing problem for which response in multidisciplinary scale is sought. The specified problem constitutes the outlet of this study because the economical decision making process that lies at the bottom of the theories, which aim at explaining consumer behaviors in literature, requires interdisciplinary study.

As it is known, there are a lot of internal and external factors that effect purchasing behavior of consumer and these factors give shape to the process of making a decision by customer in interaction one another. Especially being under the influence of the environmental stimulant of today's customer all the more for every passing day leads to an increasing variety at the buying behaviors as well and it's possible that causes inconsistency, maybe at the consumption behavior of individual. This diversity condition in the factors mover and shaker to consumer behavior is the principal factor that makes the necessity of predictability by explaining the consumption behavior difficult. Therefore, developing models capable of achieving explanatory & realistic information became the priority target of a good number of theorists who work in regards with marketing by looking at the consumption behaviors from more integrated approaches.

The oldest model among those is the one that has been developed by psychologist Kurt Lewin. The model proposed by Lewin, within the context of explaining the consumption behavior, is a fundamental and important model, in terms of leading to the other models. According to this, human behavior is developing under the interaction of personal factors and environmental factors. This model is known as the "black box model" or the "stimulus–response model" in literature. Figure 1 gives the appearance of the model (İslamoğlu & Altunışık, 2008).

William J. McGuire is one of the theorists who defines consumer decisions as information processing and groups the factors that have influence on consumer selections in three ways: the external factors, the internal directive factors, and the internal dynamic factors (McGuire, 1976). McGuire expresses that consumers who need the information for being able to decide whether to buy or not have processed in eight phases, known as: exposure, perception, comprehension, agreement, retention, retrieval, decision making, and action (1976). However, he realized this information processing under the conditions of "a situation of uncertainty where information is lacking or ambiguous for many dimensions" (McGuire, 1976).

Engel et al who define the decision making process of consumers as a problem solving process similar to the McGuire's "information processing," have described the external factors that effect consumer as the "environmental influences" and internal factors as the "individual differences." According to this, these wide range factors complicating the decision making process of consumers, originate with the environmental influences such as culture, social class, personal influence, family, situation, and the individual differences such as consumer resources, motivation, knowledge, attitudes, personality, values, and lifestyle. The consumer resources, one of the individual factors that effects consumer decision, are traced under three subtitles: 1.) money, 2.) time and 3.) information reception–processing capabilities (Engel et al., 1993).

In addition to this, economic resources–such as income or wealth–in the literature were the first variables to be analyzed in the study of consumer behavior, with studies traced back as far as 1672. The first with a reasonable statistical basis was published by Ernest Engel in 1857. For this study's theoretical base, the relationships between income and expenditures became popularized as Engel's Laws of Consumption. They contained propositions about the relationship between income and proportion spent on categories such as food, clothing, lodging, education, health, recreation, and so forth (Engel et al, 1993).

It is pointed out by the mentioned models that, the effect of economical resources owned by a consumer is absolute on buying behavior. But, bearing in mind the complexity of the decision making process of consumers and the variety of the factors influence this process, it is not possible to be able to clearly forecast the rate of power and determination under different conditions which are of primary concern. Therefore, the literature of psychology, economics, and finance all propose various theories at this juncture on the explanation of buying decision. There is no

Figure 1. The "Black Box Model" of Kurt Lewin

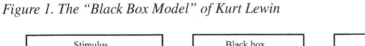
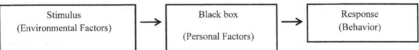

| Stimulus (Environmental Factors) | → | Black box (Personal Factors) | → | Response (Behavior) |

doubt that the buying decisions of individuals would be affected at different levels and under different conditions from these economic factors. For example, when a consumer would consume his/her budget by searching the product component that would gain maximum favor. This is envisaged by Alfred Marshall who constructed the classical economic theory, with the appendages of the "marginal spending" and "marginal benefit" (Marshall, 2009). When will the rational behavior and measurable benefit at the consumption expenses will be superseded by the hedonic (pleasure, fun), esthetic (beauty), emotional (happiness, surprise, poignancy), and symbolic (self-identity, self-exploration, self-expression) (Srinivasan, 1987: 96-100)? Or, when would individuals create their own mental accounting systems? And how they would decide on their expenditures? By collecting their economic activities in the mental accounting theory, which is based on how the individuals organize and manage their financial decisions, developed by Thaler and Shefrin' in (1981), this falls within the foundation of the study. Again, when would consumers prefer the uncertainty and risk alternatives over the greater income expectation as it is envisaged by the prospect theory developed and suggested by Kahneman and Tversky (1979) based on the mental accounting? Or when will consumers decide on buying, as foreseen by the expected utility theory, would spend according to the rational decision making model that determines what kinds of peculiarities they have to use?

It is possible to increase the questions at the basis of the theories explaining economical behavior. In this study, however, the response is sought for the specified questions, within the scope of the mental account theory that is one of the most essential paradigms of the last period especially in the field of the behavioral finance. Put in terms of Turkish consumers, the status of the mental account theory in respect to the decision of individual on whether or not to buy constitutes the primary objective of the study. In order to measure primary objective, it is analyzed that at the buying decisions of consumers, what will be the direction the economical factors can be developed, where any sunk cost has been realized, and the findings are introduced together with the other studies that fall within the literature as comparative.

2. LITERATURE REVIEW: CONCEPTUAL UNDERPININGS OF MENTAL ACCOUNTING THEORY

The researches implemented for more than twenty one years on decision theory, make the two paradigms a current issue. One of these is mental accounting, and the other is reason-based choice (Kivetz, 1999). Under the circumstances, falling short of the forecast consumer behaviors, especially concerning the classic economy theories becomes effective. In the face of the deficiency of the classic economy theories in this connection, for the intention to describe consumer behaviors from economical standpoint, the mental accounting theory that has been developed by Thaler (1980, 1985, 1990, 2008) explains behavioral factors in the decision making process through mental accounting. The research with case study of and based on the mental accounting theory that has been initiated by Thaler (1980, 1985), have been continued later on by Tversky and Kahneman (1981), Prelec and Loewenstein (1998), Heath and Soll (1996), and Gourville and Soman (1998). All of which, extended Thaler's (1980, 1985) work to develop the theories of prospective accounting, mental budgeting, and payment depreciation of the sunk cost effects (Ramphal, 2006).

In this study, it is focused on the mental accounting theories. Over here, the cause lies behind the development of theory becomes effective. Thaler and Shefrin (1981) specify that the individuals have organized their financial decisions as is in organizations and then they created their own mental accounting systems, by setting off their dependants. According to this theory, the individuals gather all their decisions, and optimize their consumption choices. In this way, they decide on spending by collecting their activities in the mental accounts in this context (Milkman & Beshears, 2009). According to this theory, the assets/products of individual are collected in three mental accounts. These accounts are: current income, current assets, and future income (Karlsson et.al., 1997). This explains the fundamental aim of the mental accounting study of choice/preference psychology (Thaler, 1999: 184). Understanding the operation of the mental accounting systems carries weight in terms of how and to what extent the preferences of the individuals are affected from psychological factors. Generally, the rules of the mental accounting are subjected to changes due to the psychological effects.

In which category a purchasing transaction would be included depends on whether merging the conclusion of this transaction with the conclusions in the other categories or keeping them separate and the frequency of assessments of accounts can affect the attractiveness of the options perceived. An important conclusion of these psychological effects refutes the substitution theory of economy. The money in a mental account can not substitute with the money in another account. Due to the negative assertions being brought onto the validity of the substitution theory, the concept of the mental accounting is welcomed as an important economical and psychological fact (Thaler, 1999).

In terms of estimating individual decisions, especially, under the uncertainty medium, explanation of the mental accounting in the preference of a consumer with behavioral basis lies at the root of this theory (Thaler, 2008). All in all, this new model is used together with the models of cognitive psychology and micro economy. It is started to the development of this model with the mental coding combination of gains and losses. Accounting systems affect the decisions in unexpected forms. This situation is used for the intention to forecast consumer behaviors. In each behavior type, the mental accounting system contains the application of a simple economical principal by individual (Thaler, 2008).

By handling the principals of the mental accounting theory, the concept of prospective accounting that has been developed by Prelec & Loewenstein (1998: 10), describes how individuals are in tendency to use their own mental account for each economical transaction. The mental evaluation process comprises the sensed benefit of consumer and cost together. That is to say, contrary to the new classical economical theories, the components of cost benefit in the prospective accounting interact (Ramphal, 2006). Within the direction of these explanations, the mental models of individuals can be summarized in Figure 2.

The mental model specified by Soman (2004) summarizes the mental process, performing cost benefit analyses of individuals during taking consumption decision thereby. On the other hand, in the studies carried out by selecting the mental accounting theory as the baseline, the concept of sunk costs that is used frequently can be effective in terms of the buying decision of individual. In the direction of implemented explanations, the consumer behaviors in Turkey are explained & forecasted in this study by selecting the mental accounting theory as the baseline. In this way, the validity of mental accounting theories in Turkey is being tested against the international literature.

3. METHOD

When Thaler (1990) put his theory forward firstly, he has investigated the issue of why of individuals use the mental accounting. All in all, he found that the cognitive processes have been shortened in respect to the mental accounting on the behaviors during decision making of individuals and stated that they made decision making processes simpler.

The aim of the present study is to use the methodologies of previous studies (Tversky & Kahneman, 1981; Prelec & Loewenstein, 1998; Heath & Soll, 1996;

Figure 2. The role of mental representations in judgment and decision making

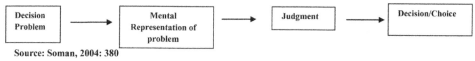

Source: Soman, 2004: 380

Gourville & Soman, 1998; Ramphal, 2006) to determine or investigate whether the theories of mental accounting exist among Turkish consumers or mental accounting theories can be used to explain for consumer behavior in Turkey. The questions of the study in this direction are as follows:

RQ1: Explanation of the buying decisions of individuals through the instrumentality of the mental accounts; does it make different in terms of the "monthly income" variable?

RQ2: Explanation of the buying decisions of individuals through the instrumentality of the mental accounts; does it make different in terms of the independent variable of "gender"?

RQ3: Can the buying decisions of individuals be explained through the instrumentality of the mental accounts?

RQ4: Do sunk costs effect the buying decisions of individuals?

3.1. Unit of Analysis and Data Collection

The analysis units of the research are the consumers in Turkey. The sampling of the research comprises of two sub-groups. The root cause of execution of the research by sub-groups is to bring the effects of the mental accounting theories, the decisiveness of individuals in taking buying decision, into public view.

While the first subgroup formed from 100 university students whose ages are varied between 18 and 30, the second group forms from the same number of students at the same age range. For the participants, two questionnaires have been prepared. Both questionnaire samples are enclosed. As the questionnaire was given to the first subgroup, there were scenarios prepared by selecting the mental accounting theories as the baseline and it is interrogated that whether or not the preference of consumer is differentiated by these scenarios. At the preparation of these scenarios, the studies of Tversky and Kahneman (1981), Prelec and Loewenstein (1998), Heath and Soll (1996), Gourville and Soman (1998), and Ramphal (2006) were taken advantage of. They specified in the foregoing years beside the researchers, and three scenarios oriented to determine the effects of prospective accounting, mental budgeting, and sunk costs formed from three sections. In addition to this, it was given place to demographic properties in the measuring instrument and the questions in regards with monthly budget. In the questionnaire prepared for the consumers in the second group, the questions pertain to demographic variables and income. Two questions requested consumers to make a selection between two alternatives. In the questions, the second group consumers were asked to make a choice between these questions without giving place to the scenarios in respect to the mental accounting theories.

Thus, at the same time it was gauged that what degree these alternatives were preferred by consumer without any mental accounting effect.

30 university students per group were selected for the pilot application of the developed measuring instrument. As the directions of the responses indicate, it was ensured that the expressions in the scenarios were still simplified. After, randomly selected sub groups having 100 persons per group, measuring instrument were applied. By taking advantage of mental accounting theories, the responses of 100 participants whom the first questionnaire were applied thereto in the first sub group were subjected to assessment. But, the responses of only 82 participants of the second sub group have been obtained as appropriate for analysis. By starting out from the achieved data, first of all the reliability and validity levels of the questionnaire were measured, and then they were subjected to statistical analysis. All in all, the responses in regards to the research questions have been obtained by testing the hypothesis indications that the behaviors of Turkish consumers, which were accepted at the beginning, can be described with the assistance of the mental accounting theories.

3.2. Findings and Discussion

As per the achieved data the demographic peculiarities in regards to the participants of the first sub group are as follows: 58% of the participants are male, while 42% are female. The average age of the first sub group is 20. 41% of the participants of the second sub group are male, while the 59% thereof are female. The average age of the second sub group is 21. The average monthly budget of the first and second groups is ₺567,13.

In the first scenario introduced to the participants who fall within the first sub group, two house alternatives both have the same properties one another, have been introduced as follows:

- First House
  - **Rent:** ₺300
  - **Deposit:** ₺300
- Second House
  - **Rent:** ₺250
  - **Deposit:** ₺400

It was requested from the participants to decide to rent the second house for one year, but then they assume that they have lost ₺400 that were reserved for deposit. Under the circumstances the participants were asked which house they would prefer with the reason of this preference.

In the scenario given, the second house is the rational choice in the sense of the consumer, since and from the point of view of the annual cost for the first house is ₺3900, while the same for the second house is ₺3400. The aspect of the responses taken in the frequency analysis is after ₺400 losses; 18% of the participants preferred the first house, while 82% preferred the second house. As per the obtained results, 18% of the participants make a selection irrationally by growing away from rationality. In addition to this, while the ones who have preferred the second house rationally, defined the reasons they have preferred this house as long term profitability, the other 18% ones who made irrational choice by growing away from rationality defined the reason of their choice as despondency. When this situation is evaluated in terms of mental accounting theories, it may be pronounced that the ones who have preferred the first house of which total cost is ₺500 more, did not post the ₺ 400 lost into the future income mental accounting item that is one of the mental accounting item of Thaler and Shefrin (1981) and grown away from rationality.

It is not in question that the house choices of the participants in this scenario differentiate in point of the independent budget (t = 1.260, p > .05) and gender (Chi – square = 1. 469, df = 4, p > .05) variables.

In the second scenario given to the first sub group, the information in respect to alternatives having the same properties for the houses to let again is as follows:

- First House
    - **Rent:** ₺300
    - **Deposit:** ₺300
- Second House
    - **Rent:** ₺250
    - **Deposit:** ₺300

As it is seen the rational preference over here is the second house due to its monthly rent is ₺50 cheaper. But, it was requested from the participants to assume that they have already come to an agreement for renting the first house, while they have uninformed on the second house alternative yet, and paid ₺300 deposit to the landlord. Then, it was requested from the participants to assume that they have faced for the second house alternative and under the circumstances, they have been asked whether or not they would prefer the second house of which rent is cheaper, for the sake of giving up ₺300 they have already given as deposit.

In the scenario given, the annual cost of the first house is (300 x 12) + 300 = ₺ 3900, and the annual cost of the second house is (300 x 12) + 300 = ₺3900, including also an additional extra cost of deposit lays bare that the second house is a rational choice from the viewpoint of consumer. The prospect of the responses received in the frequency analysis is in the direction of the 42% of the participants preferred the first house, while 58% preferred the second house. According to the results achieved, it is seen that 42% of the participants made a selection by growing away from rationality. Nevertheless, while the 58% section giving rational decision defined the reason of they have preferred the second house was profitability, the other 42% that has grown away from rationality said the reason they preferred the first house was because they did not have to pay a deposit and would not to take great pains thereto. When the conclusion is assessed in terms of mental accounting theories, the rational choice was not preferred by the 42% of the participants as a consequence of the ₺300 deposit of the first house, which is paid as extra because it has not been recognized mentally by the participants. In that case, it may be pronounced that, the ₺300, over paid by the ones who have preferred the second house was entered up into the future income mental accounting item, that is one of the mental accounting items of Thaler and Shefrin (1981), and they did not decide in the direction of rationality.

It is not in question that the house choices of the participants in this scenario differentiate in point of the independent variables as budget ($t = .810$, $p > .05$) and gender (Chi – square $= 0. 453$, df $= 4$, $p > .05$).

The third scenario falls within the first sub group is like this; You think about going to a concert of the artist you really like in different city. The price of concert ticket is ₺100 and the cost of one way transportation is ₺50.

Variation 1: Assume that, after buying the concert ticket, the said one way transportation expense has been increased to ₺100. Do you still go to the concert?

Variation 2: You have bought both of round trip transportation tickets ₺50. But, after you have reached the city where the concert is, you learned that the concert tickets were sold out, but you may still get one from the black market for ₺200. Do you still go to the concert?

In the first case, while the 53% of the participants responded as they would still go to concert; the remaining 47% said that they decided not to go.

In the second case, despite the sunk cost is ₺100 by being as the same of the first case, while only 34% of the participants responded as they would go to the concert, the remaining 66% said that they would withdraw from the concert.

This finding bears a resemblance to the Broadway play scenario employed by Kahneman and Tversky (1979) in their performance. In other words, although there is a 40 dollar loss in both cases in the work of the authors, the finding of "most people are not volunteer to buy a new ticket in place of the lost one, but they are eager to pay the extra 40 dollars when s/he has lost 40 dollars from his/her pocket." In both cases in this study, notwithstanding ₺100 loss exists, it is similar with trend of "being volunteer to buy travel ticket but not to buy concert ticket". At the same time, that strengthens the thesis of "the money in a mental account does not supersede the money in another one" (Thaler, 1999).

It is not in question to differentiate in the first condition of the scenario where the participants go to the concert in point of the independent variables as budget (t = .505, p > .05) and gender (Chi – square = 1.756, df = 2, p > .05), in the second condition, it is also not in question to differentiate in point of the independent variables as budget (t = 1. 278, p > .05) and gender (Chi – square = 2. 339, df = 2, p > .05).

As it is seen in the whole findings above, it is not in question to differentiate, the decision making trend being constituted after any sunk cost, according to the independent variable of budget. But without giving any sunk cost scenario, it was determined that the responses given to the following two questions asked to the second sub group have been differentiated as per the budget variable.

Question 1: *Which alternative do you prefer between the following houses to let?*

- First House
    - **Rent: ₺300**
    - **Deposit: ₺300**
- Second House
    - **Rent: ₺250**
    - **Deposit: ₺400**

Question 2: You think about going to a concert of the artist you really like in different city. Let's assume the price of concert ticket is ₺100 and the cost of one way transportation is ₺50. Would you still go to the concert if the total cost of the concert would be ₺300, instead of ₺200?

According to the conclusions (t = 2.200, p > . 003) of the independent t test of the responses given to the first question, it is seen that is differentiated according to the independent variable of budget. In other words, the responses given to this question in the second sub group where there is no cost effect, underwent a change according to the income level of the participants. The participants who have higher budget favored more the first house of which rent is higher.

Again, according to the conclusions (t = 2.484, p > . 008) of the independent test of the responses given to the second question, it is seen that differentiation occurred according to the independent variable of budget. In other words, the responses given to this question in the second sub group where there is no cost effect of sunk cost differed according to the income level of the participants. The participants who have a higher budget stated that they would not give up going to concerts where the cost thereof has been increased as well.

As it is seen from the research findings, there are significant differences between the first and second sub groups at their preferences for both accommodations that are an obligatory necessity and going to concert that are a hedonic expense. The participants with higher income level of the second sub group who were asked for their direct preferences behave quiet differently compared to the participants who have a lower income level. In other words, the consumers who have high income level also have at their accommodation high expenditures as a consequence of the mental accounting calculations which they made subsequently to sunken cost return to rationality. Saving trends were developed for entertainment expenses.

CONCLUSION

In this study, by setting off similar works that fall within the international literature; which benefit from the mental studies for understanding the behaviors of the Turkish consumers who are different as far as at the cultural variables are concerned, the workability of this international theory is measured in terms of Turkey's consumer market. Within the scope of this study that has been implemented with the intention of testing the validity of the mental accounting theory in Turkey, a consequence of the measurements carried out to put forward the effects of the theory in respect to the purchasing decisions of individuals, a set of some important and expressive findings were reached.

The answers of the individuals who have been attended in the area investigation to the attitude related questions bring up to some conclusions, which support the validity of some hypothesis in the mental account such as;

1. Individuals may perceive the same costs at different magnitude under different conditions,
2. Individuals may lose their abilities of rational thinking and making a selection, under some demoralization,
3. A value found in a mental account can be insufficient to substitute another value having the same amount in another mental account.

The findings obtained by this study are also important in terms of manifesting a new condition. They also support the previous studies in the mental accounting literature. This situation indicates that the responses, developed by consumers at their expenditure and savings following the constituted sunk costs, are being differentiated from the viewpoint of the independent variable of the "budget."

REFERENCES

Engel, J. F., Blackwell, R. D., & Miniard, P. W. (1993). *Consumer behavior* (7th ed.). Chicago: Harcourt Brace.

Gourville, J. T., & Soman, D. (1998). Payment depeciation: The behavioral effects of temporarily separating payments from consuption. *The Journal of Consumer Research, 25*(2), 160–174. doi:10.1086/209533.

Heath, C. & Soll. (1996). Mental budgeting and consumer decisions. *The Journal of Consumer Research, 23*(1), 40–52. doi:10.1086/209465.

İslamoğlu, A. H. & Altunışık. (2008). *Tüketici davranışları*. İstanbul: Beta Publications.

Kahneman, D. & Tversky. (1979). Prospect theory: An analysis of decision under risk. *Econometrica, 47*(2), 263–291. doi:10.2307/1914185.

Karlsson, N., Garling, T., & Selart, M. (1997). Effects of mental accounting on intertemporal choice. *Göteborg Psychological Reports, 27*, 1–17.

Kivetz, R. (1999). Advances in research on mental accounting and reason–based choice. *Marketing Letters, 10*(3), 249–266. doi:10.1023/A:1008066718905.

Marshall, A. (2009). *Principles of economics* (8th ed.). New York: Cosimo Publications.

McGuire, W. J. (1976). Some internal psychological factors influencing consumer choice. The University of Chicago Press Journal of Consumer Research, 2(4).

Milkman, K. L. & Beashers. (2009). Mental accounting and small windfalls: Evidence from an online grocer. *Journal of Economic Behavior & Organization, 71*(2), 384–394. doi:10.1016/j.jebo.2009.04.007.

Prelec, D. & Loewenstein. (1998). The red and the black: Mental accounting of savings and debts. *Marketing Science, 17*(1), 4–28. doi:10.1287/mksc.17.1.4.

Ramphal, S. (2006). *Mental Accounting: The Psychology of South African Consumer Behaviour*. (Unpublished Master's Thesis). Pretoria, South Africa, University of Pretoria.

Soman, D. (2004). Framing, loss aversion, and mental accounting. In Koehler, D. J., & Harvey, N. (Eds.), *Blackwell Handbook of Judgment & Decision Making*. Hoboken, NJ: Blackwell Publishing Ltd. doi:10.1002/9780470752937.ch19.

Srinivasan, T. C. (1987). An integrative approach to consumer choice. *Advances in Consumer Research. Association for Consumer Research (U. S.), 14*, Retrieved from http://www.acrwebsite.org/volumes/display.asp?id=6661.

Thaler, R. H. (1980). Towards a positive theory of consumer choice. *Journal of Economic Behavior & Organization, 1*, 39–60. doi:10.1016/0167-2681(80)90051-7.

Thaler, R. H. & Shefrin. (1981). An economic theory of self control. *The Journal of Political Economy, 89*(2), 392–406. doi:10.1086/260971.

Thaler, R. H. (1985). Mental accounting and consumer choice. *Marketing Science, 4*(3), 199–214. doi:10.1287/mksc.4.3.199.

Thaler, R. H. (1990). Anomalies: Saving, fungibility, and mental accounts. *The Journal of Economic Perspectives, 4*(1), 193–205. doi:10.1257/jep.4.1.193.

Thaler, R. H. (1999). Mental accounting matters. *Journal of Behavioral Decision Making, 12*, 183–206. doi:10.1002/(SICI)1099-0771(199909)12:3<183::AID-BDM318>3.0.CO;2-F.

Thaler, R. H. (2008). Mental accounting and consumer choice. *Marketing Science, 27*(1), 15–25. doi:10.1287/mksc.1070.0330.

Tversky, A., & Kahneman, D. (1981). The framing of decisions and the psychology of choice. *Science, 21*(1), 453–458. doi:10.1126/science.7455683 PMID:7455683.

APPENDIX 1

First Subgroup's Questionnaire

Dear Participant,

The entire questions in this questionnaire aim at to value some attitudes at the buying behaviors of individuals. The responses you have given shall not be assessed personally and be kept secret, and will not be used in anywhere except this scientific study. Thanks for your kind participation.

What is

     age (...................)
     gender (.................)
     monthly personal budget (..................)

Question 1: You look for a leasehold house and there are two alternatives as below:

- First House
  - **Rent:** ₺300
  - **Deposit:** ₺300
- Second House
  - **Rent:** ₺250
  - **Deposit:** ₺400

Let's assume that you have preferred the Second House between these alternatives, but you have lost ₺400 that was reserved for deposit by you, while you go to rent the house. Under this new case, which alternative you prefer? a) First House or b) Second House

Why?...

Question 2: You look for a leasehold house. There are two alternatives, which have identical one another in respect to all characteristics, under the following conditions, in the same site.

- First House
  - **Rent:** ₺300
  - **Deposit:** ₺300

- Second House
  - **Rent: ℭ250**
  - **Deposit: ℭ300**

Let's assume that while you are unaware from the Second House alternative yet, you already came to an agreement to rent the first house and paid ℭ300 deposit to landlord and you can not get that money back. On such an occasion, if you met with the second house alternative, do you prefer this second house of which rental is cheaper at the expense of renouncing your claim to get ℭ300 deposit back and to pay another ℭ300 as well. a) Yes or b) No

Why?...

Question 3: You think about to go a concert of the artist you like too much, in different city. The price of concert ticket is ℭ100 and the cost of one way transportation is ℭ50.

Variation 1: Let's assume that the cost of one way transportation that was ℭ50 after you have bought the concert ticket increased to ℭ100 for those particular dates. You have no choice to sell your concert ticket to somebody else. Would you still go to the concert? a) Yes or b) No

Variation 2: You have bought both of round trip transportation tickets ℭ50. But, after you have reached the city where the concert is given, you have learned that the price of concert tickets which were ℭ100 have been run out of and the only possibility and chance you may get it from black market by paying ℭ200. Do you still go to the concert? a) Yes or b) No

APPENDIX 2

Second Subgroup's Questionnaire

Dear Participant,

The entire questions in this questionnaire aim at to value some attitudes at the buying behaviors of individuals. The responses you have given shall not be assessed personally and be kept secret, and will not be used in anywhere except this scientific study. Thanks for your kind participation.

What is

Your age? (.................)
Your gender? (.................)
Your monthly personal budget? (.................)

Question 1: You look for a leasehold house and there are two alternatives as below:

- First House
    - **Rent:** ₺300
    - **Deposit:** ₺300
- Second House
    - **Rent:** ₺250
    - **Deposit:** ₺400

Which alternative you prefer? a) First House or b) Second House

Question 2: You think about to go a concert of the artist you like too much, in different city. The price of concert ticket is ₺100 and the cost of one way transportation is ₺50. Would you still go to the concert if the total concert cost would be ₺300 instead of ₺200? a) Yes or b) No

Chapter 2
What Went Wrong?

Bhavna Bhalla
Institute of Management Technology, India

EXECUTIVE SUMMARY

This case is about the interaction that takes place between Chetan and Bhagat. Chetan is a freelance trainer who grooms the corporate trainees on various aspects of communication and soft skills. He also takes sessions on successful interview strategy and selection criterion for the post of market representative. Bhagat, one of his acquaintances, needs feedback for the interview that he just appeared for. During the conversation he puts forward what he did during the day to understand the nitty-gritties of the interview. The context of this conversation is to understand where Bhagat faltered. The scope of discussion covers the flow from preparation to execution to be successful in any interview.

CASE DESCRIPTION

On 27 December, 2012, Chetan, age 45, a consultant to many MNCs, was reading the editorial section of a local newspaper when he came across an article that was talking about dos and don'ts of being a successful candidate for an interview. This article was relevant to those who aspire for the role of a market representative. While reading, he recalled his own experience of conducting so many mock interviews and discussing the concepts with the participants. When he was in middle of his thoughtful reading, Bhagat knocked on his door. He was there to discuss with Chetan what went wrong with him during the interview that he had the same day.

DOI: 10.4018/978-1-4666-4357-4.ch002

Copyright ©2014, IGI Global. Copying or distributing in print or electronic forms without written permission of IGI Global is prohibited.

CHETAN'S BACKGROUND

Chetan was HR head of an organization, called "People's Dreams," that served in the area of personality development and creative skills enhancement. His constant engagement with responsibilities like hiring the new talent and training them to be effective human beings, along with effective managers, made him aware of the intricacies of the interview process, the stages, and the evaluation process. He had a name for himself in the training field and was often approached by people seeking guidance to improve their chances of being successful in an interview. Of course, they were not there to learn the theory of interviewing, but to practice the principles effectively.

Bhagat was one of his acquaintances and he often approached Chetan for tips and feedback.

BHAGAT'S STORY

On meeting Chetan, Bhagat narrated the entire sequence of events which occurred when he appeared for the interview that morning. He told Chetan that he received this interview call from "Princetech Media" the day before. The Recruitment Head of the organization told him about the three levels of the interview–the first level will screen his candidature, the second level will grill him further (his performance at this level will determine his selection), and the third level will finalize his selection or cancellation. The recruitment head also told Bharat that they are looking for a candidate who possesses good communication skills, is creative, is an effective team player, and is willing to devote more time for official chores beyond the usual office hours. Since this was an unexpected call which he had less time to prepare for he got very anxious and lost focus after the call. This morning when he got up, he found no water or electricity which further enhanced his anxiety. That was a bad thing to start the day with, he thought. Gradually when he brought himself back to his senses, he found that his CV is not updated. He updated it, but then the problem was having its updated version's print-out. Another problem hit him. The interview was scheduled to start at 10:00 am which he managed to reach and hence appeared on time. However, after the third level of interview, he was feeling very exhausted and in that exhaustion did not greet the panel members while leaving the board room. Also, he thought that since the interviewers were very casual and open that they would not mind his actions. However, now upon introspection of what happened during the day, he was not able to judge his own performance and found himself too low. He wanted to know about his mistakes that may have hampered his performance. Chetan was listening to him patiently till now. Once Bhagat was through with his talk, Chetan thought of asking some questions to have better idea about how the day went by for him.

INTERACTION BETWEEN CHETAN AND BHAGAT

Chetan: Bhagat, what is making you feel low about the whole situation?

Bhagat: Sir, I don't know what it is, but I know my performance this morning was not even satisfactory. I was ready for this opportunity, but it came so suddenly that I did not get enough time to prepare. Why didn't the company inform me of this interview earlier? I would have prepared better.

Chetan: Hmm, do you remember what kind of preparation you did? I mean, I know you had mentioned some in your story, but I want to listen to the story that you have not narrated.

Bhagat: I think you are talking about my appearance and the way I presented myself at the interview. Well, I dressed myself with a properly ironed red formal shirt and black trousers. I carried all the documents with me, but the certificates were not in sequence owing to a last minute CV update. I reached the venue on time after travelling in a local bus for half an hour. These days it is so hot that my shirt was all wet with sweat.

Chetan: Okay! Do you remember what happened during the first level of the interview? It was the screening stage, right? It must have been quite rigorous then.

Bhagat: Oh, yes! It was pretty tough. Though the panel members were quite friendly, the questions that they asked were general in nature. I did not know most of the answers so I guessed. They were nodding and smiling throughout when I was answering which gave me much needed confidence that I was doing well. At the end they said, "Though we are calling you for the second round of the interviews, we would like to see more of you and less of what you have said in this interview." I did not understand why they had said that.

Chetan: Did they ask you about your area of specialization that they may put you in, if selected?

Bhagat: No, but they did ask about the sales target and role of marketing in media services. Since I was not prepared with such a question, I was taken aback and therefore did not answer.

Chetan: What happened during the second stage?

Bhagat: The same thing was repeated, but this time I did not guess for the answers. This time, since I knew the answers, I was speaking well. However, I have problems with my speaking skills, that is. Though I knew the content, I had problems in expressing those. My throat was choked because of nervousness. It took the maximum time and I felt that they were stressing me with their rapid fire questions.

Chetan: *Did you repeat these things in the third round as well as I sense? Or the experience was different in the third stage?*

Bhagat: *I think the third stage did not go as per my expectations. They asked me about my knowledge of the organization, the job profile offered, the expected salary, et cetera. I had applied to their call some four months back so it was quite difficult to recall the details. This difficulty was further multiplied with the day's busy schedule and back to back interview sessions. In that exasperation I even forgot to greet them at the end of the interview. Now when I am recollecting, I am not able to judge my overall performance, despite being called for all the three stages of the interview.*

(A long silence)

Chetan: *Ok! Would you like to add to this description anything that you can now recall?*

Bhagat: *(After further introspection) Yes! When I was answering they were jotting down something to which I tried to peep at while replying. They didn't notice that, but I guess one of the panel members was observing me throughout. He was there in all three levels as if he was scrutinizing me thoroughly. Before I left he said, "Something needs overhauling in your personality," which actually is a cause of bother for me now.*

CHETAN'S RESPONSE

Chetan had a serious look even after interaction was finished. He was thinking about his first interview when he had a similar experience. He wanted to advise Bhagat straightaway, but thought that he probably needed some innovative guidance to understand what went wrong on that day. He decided something and asked Bhagat to come the next day in the same way as if he is going for an interview. The next day when Bhagat came, Chetan guided him to make him understand what was wrong with his approach and learn the correct way. The attitude which Bhagat needed, but did not have any idea about, before this practical session, was finally clarified by the end of the day.

Chapter 3
Case Study on Relationship Marketing

Bhawana Sharma
Jaipur National University, India

Tulika Sood
Jaipur National University, India

EXECUTIVE SUMMARY

A paradigm shift has occurred in the concepts of marketing from the production concept to the societal concept. A prominent concept today is the customer concept, which aims to build loyalty and lifetime value by creating, maintaining, and enhancing relationships with the customer by addressing individual customer needs. Relationship marketing is a bifurcation from the customer concept, which seeks to earn and retain long-term preferences, business, and ultimately, a marketing network. In relationship marketing, both parties collaborate on identifying needs to fulfill. Immediate sales are not of prime concern in this model. Organizations should understand the fact of when–and how–to use relationship marketing. The five R's of Relationship Marketing are Relationship, Realization, Response, Relevance, & Respect. This case study addresses relationship marketing focusing on a service industry (i.e. Insurance Industry). A Sales representative needs to bond well with all his clients in order to be able to meet their expectations as required. Therefore, an employee with good PR skills is sure to climb the ladder of success. The protagonist in the case study, Mr. Sahil Sharma, an Employee of AFRO-INDIA Insurance Ltd., guides and trains his entire team to build, maintain, and enhance their relationship with their clients. This will not only make the clients loyal to the organization, but also will also make them brand ambassadors through word of mouth.

DOI: 10.4018/978-1-4666-4357-4.ch003

Copyright ©2014, IGI Global. Copying or distributing in print or electronic forms without written permission of IGI Global is prohibited.

BACKGROUND OF THE CASE

Afro-India Insurance Ltd is an insurance company with a market presence across India. It has completed ten years in the Indian market with a market share of 25%. With 22 Life Insurance Companies in India vying for a piece of the market share, the competition for sustainment is tough in a region where the customers have little to no idea about life insurance policies. The customers in India are adamant of the fact that to invest in a product like life insurance whose benefits can only be reaped after death is a waste. Therefore, the question which arises here is that, how is it then possible to gain market share and attract customers? And further, what is there to make these customer prospects into consumers?

Insurance being a pure service, it is required that all of the frontline staff involved in customer interaction should and must be trained in soft skills. They need to be aware of the importance of understanding the customer perceived service quality so that they may meet or exceed the desired expectation of the customers. This in turn will enhance the final service delivery process by making the customer loyal.

A case study on the life insurance industry is our study. This case study will enable readers to understand the various ingredients in retaining customers by delighting them through exceeding their expectations in delivering the services.

CASE DESCRIPTION

Mr. Praveen Sahai joined AFRO-INDIA Insurance Co. as Branch Manager-Direct Channel, Jaipur Branch, with a team of 12 Sales executive reporting to him directly. He had a very laid-back attitude and used to go to any heights to meet the monthly targets. The entire team working under him was less motivated and did not appreciate his working style. He was very authoritative and did not value clients or customer retention. According to him once a deal is struck and you have sold him the life insurance policy there should be no looking back. Instead, he thought it better to concentrate on the next deal. This attitude of his has made the working conditions of all sales executive working at AFRO-INDIA miserable. Moreover, the existing clients would never give any referrals for they themselves have not been receiving the right service. Mr. Praveen's only motive was to make his team work in the way he wanted so he could meet deadlines and targets.

Mr. Sahil Sharma, a sales executive who is a part of the team under Mr. Praveen Sahai, got promoted to Branch Manager-Direct Channel due to his excellent performance with 150% target achievement. The Vikaspuri-Delhi branch was allotted to him for his operations. Therefore, he had to leave Jaipur and start all over again in Delhi. As the Dehli branch was new to him, he first tried to acquaint himself with all the staff members from the lowest level (peon), all the way through operations staff and colleagues and up to HR. The very motive behind him getting to know everybody in the branch was so he could look to someone for any kind of help.

His next goal was to recruit a team of 12 Sales Executive under him. Mr. Sahil did it with ease as he got all the support from the HR team and built a strong team under him. When a new Sales Executive joined him, he specifically ensured that:

1. He made the Sales Executive easy with the work place.
2. He trained him with the philosophy that insurance selling is all about relationship building.
3. The very first call that you take with a client need not mean that he will take the policy. Nevertheless, the motive should be to create such a rapport with the prospect client that any time in the future he opts for a life insurance policy he has no other option but you.

This attitude of Sahil made all his team members work with zeal and constant motivation. He himself tries to attend one opening call with his all team members so that they understand the meaning of relationship building. For he knows very well that if one client who is a prospect now, is converted into a consumer he/she can become a brand ambassador for the company. This is possible, however, only if the customer perceives that his expectations have been met. All was well at Delhi. Sahil's team was meeting the deadline of the targets. At the same time, Mr. Praveen was facing acute pressure from his team members and the clients in Jaipur. He could not cope with the situation and resigned from his present position of BM. The management now took a very wise and important decision of transferring Sahil from Delhi to Jaipur to handle the entire situation.

This call from the Management side was a boon for Sahil as he could return to his hometown after almost one and a half years in Delhi and be with his son and wife. However, at the same time, it came as a shock to the entire team at Delhi-Vikaspuri which was very apprehensive of the new boss who would be heading them.

CHALLENGES

The team at Jaipur knew the working style of Sahil as he was amongst them and was promoted to the position of BM from Sales Executive. All the team members were very comfortable working under him. In fact, they idolized him for his genuine working style.

The very first day at the Jaipur office, he met all of his team members and tried to locate the exact problem that they were facing in selling life insurance policy. Some of the problems are highlighted below as per discussion:

1. Mr. Praveen laid emphasis only on selling the product rather taking pains in knowing the want and need of the prospective customer.
2. He used aggressive marketing skills whereas insurance, being a service industry, required more soft skills.
3. He did not make his team understand the concept of after sales service, which is utmost and prerequisite in the insurance sector.
4. He did not teach his team about relationship building with clients taking into consideration the Five R's.
5. Praveen did not value customer retention. Instead, he focused only on one time sale.
6. The Nature of Praveen, being very aggressive, was not compatible with any person in the branch.
7. A blunder Praveen committed was he did not understand when–and how–to use relationship marketing.

Sahil took to account all problems and tried to inculcate in the team members that "customer is the king" and it is no longer enough to satisfy customers, we must delight them. So it is more important to build a relationship, maintain a relationship, and enhance a relationship with a prospect client or consumer rather than selling the product. Next, he traveled with all his team members to the calls and within a month, a drastic change could be seen. All those clients who had earlier shunned AFRO-INDIA Insurance due to unruly and unprofessional behavior of Praveen started again investing and taking life insurance policies due to the genuine and professional attitude of Sahil.

The consistent performance of Sahil in terms of customer retention and customer loyalty gave him a promotion to territory manager. Moving up the ladder within a span of five years from a mere sales person to the position of TM and for his loyalty towards the organization he was felicitated.

Sahil still interacts with all his clients who have taken policies from him when he was a sales executive. Today around 50 sales executive, 10 SDM's and 5 BM's, are working under him. Anytime he finds himself and his team short of target, he can go to any of Clients with whom he has created and maintained a long relationship.

CONCLUSION

The marketing of insurance products to all the clients during his work tenure was not only professional, but also allowed Sahil to bond with all his clients and he was therefore able to meet their expectations as required. Therefore, any employee who is loyal to his organization as well as in possession of good PR skills is sure to climb the ladder of success. Sahil definitely knows that long-term relationship builds good will in the market, which is why he guides and trains his entire team to build, maintain, and enhance their relationship with their clients. This will not only make the clients loyal to the organization but also will become a brand ambassador through word of mouth. Therefore, he uses this relationship marketing as a promotional tool rather than marketing tool.

Chapter 4
A Line in Water:
A Case of Customer Relationship Management

Chandra Shekhar Padhi
Great Lakes Institute of Management, India

EXECUTIVE SUMMARY

According to C. K. Prahlad and Venkatram Ramaswamy, "The competence that customers bring is a function of the knowledge and skills they possess, their willingness to learn and experiment, and their ability to engage in active dialogue." This case examines the necessity of these functions in order to bring delight in the minds of the customer and give them an experience as a whole. The case outlines few failures which results due to poor planning in the strategy of a new product launch. The case also casts light on the distance which is generated between the sales force and the company. These distances occur due to various factors like resistance to change by the sales force, pressure from higher management on strategic compliance, and inefficient communication strategies between the two. The case helps in understanding the fragile bridge which connects the higher management of the company to the sales team on field.

It was evening and the cloudy sky had brought an early darkness. As Hemant Kumar, the regional sales manager of a leading automobile company in India looked into his weekly sales report, he thought that his career is also in the same state. Three months back his company had launched a new product in the market. The strategy looked impressive and innovative and at the time the execution was going as planned. Still, he thought that he had not been able to deliver as per the plan and this was

DOI: 10.4018/978-1-4666-4357-4.ch004

Copyright ©2014, IGI Global. Copying or distributing in print or electronic forms without written permission of IGI Global is prohibited.

obviously not desirable. The whole process started with a huge noise and high acceleration, but as the things started to gain momentum, Hemant felt as if it lacked the punch it needed.

Hemant had passed his engineering and campus recruitment. The day he joined the automobile industry was his birthday. That was eleven years ago. Hemant had climbed the ladder fast and had been a great person to work with. He was hardworking and capable, and he always achieved his targets above expectations. This brought him promotions, handsome bonuses, and respect from every direction. He maintained good relationship with dealers by encouraging them and solving their problems (Appendix 7). All this has brought him the desk upon which he now looked with a confused glare.

He got up and looked through the window. He thought of his current actions and realised that he was only drawing lines in water. He sipped the warm coffee and looked into the crimson sky and searched for rays of hope.

ORGANIZATION BACKGROUND

The automobile market has been growing at a fast pace for the past 10 years. After liberalization many new multinational companies started coming into India. The domestic companies were able to shield themselves by superior knowledge of customer priorities and concerns and due to greater reach into the various cities. However, now the scenario had changed and not only did the multinational companies produce tailor-made products, but they have also gained access to the market by joint ventures.

With competition increasing day by day, the economic slowdown was the new problem. People are no longer willing to invest in luxury items. Even with good financing schemes, people were keeping the idea of buying a vehicle in low priority. With people not ready to invest, the insecurity had forced many fresh orders to be cancelled. The security forfeited is nothing in comparison to the damage done if the vehicle is already in assembly, especially if it is to be produced in rare colors.

Suppliers of automobile companies used to purchase raw material in bulk on credit terms & transfer the cost benefits in order to remain preferred suppliers to automobile companies. The volume of transactions gave marginal profits, but still secured business. Now the manufacturers had reduced their orders since the setups were low. This led to inventory pileup and ate up whatever was left of the profit.

The manufacturer was not at ease either. They had to keep producing the minimum at breakeven volumes. Employees were forced to take leaves and high finished goods inventory was left. Whereas the manufacturers were shutting down the production for days, the sales wing was in deep pressure to deliver targets despite customer pockets getting smaller.

The dealer was in the most uncomfortable chair in the system. In the whole buying process, after taking the booking amount, the dealer takes money from financial institutions in order to buy the vehicle from the factory. According to one of the dealers:

The booking amount which we take is much less than what is the money we take at risk from banks. The vehicle itself takes around at an average 12-14 days to reach and all this time and till we get the money from customer we bear the cost of the costly cars. If we don't sell a vehicle in the same month, including those that are displayed, then the profit margin reduces to nil. The sales team also now delivers in an incentive mindset which is an added cost to every sale (Appendix 2).

The dealer also had to invest in local advertising campaigns, as well as vehicle test drives. With all this they still had to maintain the standards of the company.

SETTING THE STAGE

The company had made a huge effort in bringing out the product. QFD (Quality Function Deployment) was deployed throughout the whole process. Customers in various cities were reached and the needs were identified, which were then summed up in designs and models. These were made with about 80 colors and 5 variants. The executive boards selected 6 colors and 3 variants. The offering created a new perspective niche in the market. The companies already existing models have gone through regular upgrades and were nearing the end of growth stage. A new model was in drastic need for business to go on. The company having being targeting the cities stressed features of looks, design, and style with handsome performance and efficiency. The vehicle was able to carry around 8-9 people comfortably and can go for outdoor outings and rough rides of adventure. In the same time the company pitched the vehicle to be a family vehicle. With both the customer segments needs met, the vehicle created a new niche of product offering, which was highly marketed to create general awareness and curiosity in consumers.

The whole vehicle was marketed based on its product offering. The advertisement campaign consisted of two parts. One was pre-launch advertisement and other was post-launch advertisement. The pre-launch advertisement was designed as to generate curiosity and was aired a couple of weeks ahead of launch.

A team of young operations people were trained for two weeks in the head office and sent to area offices around the country to help gather data and help in knowledge sharing about the product. The regional sales teams were made and people were assigned tasks. The whole teams of cross-functional departments were coordinated by head office by regular mailings and video conferencing.

At the dealership end, a team of dedicated sales force was formed to carry on the sales activity of the new product. They were given training on product specifications and features. They were also educated about the potential competitor brands and their advantages and disadvantages. Then, the company came up with a new concept of giving a "unique buying experience." which aimed at having a minimum level of facilities for customers and similar promotion by everyone. In order to do so, the company prepared a sales pitch which was to be repeated by every sales person and also promoted a culture of confidence throughout the dealerships. Lastly, the company supplied the dealerships with POS (Point Of Sale) materials to attract attention of customer. The advertising materials included standees and banners (Appendix 6).

The dealerships dedicated a group of sales representatives to do cold calls to previous customers. The customers were called and asked for test drives at their mentioned locations. The previous customers were prioritized according to their response and called again and given information regarding the product and pursued them for conversions. Various industrialists and wealthy people were called for a grand launch at regional head offices and a good market was expected (Appendix 4).

CASE DESCRIPTION

The execution was done and, as planned, the orders started to flow in. The software of the dealership management program was of great help (Appendix 1). The dealer after taking the signing amount was putting the order through the software which was then automatically added to the master schedule for production. The customers were committed a lead time of 30 days where as the dealerships were committed a delivery within 21 days and instructed to give the news of early delivery to customer as a matter of delight. The behavior of sales force, the schedule of test drive, the cleanliness and decorum of the dealership, the positioning of display vehicles, and customer behavior were closely audited everyday with monthly senior management visit to every dealership which reinforced discipline (Appendix 3). Apart from that, proper documentation and record keeping was given due diligence so as to avoid confusion.

The cold calls continued and the sales speech was told to every customer on phone as well as to the walk in customers. But soon problem started as stated by a dealer's relationship manager:

The customer started complaining of repeated calls. Since company insisted on re-peating the same sales speech, every time the customer was called the reps started repeating the same thing again and again. It irritated the customers. The sales speech was also lengthy which was almost for three minutes, the customers used to hang up or interrupt in-between. This instilled a notion that the speech is useless. After we repeatedly informed to authorities the sales speech was reduced to one minute only for the telephone conversations

The training module was extensive and the sales representatives were told to perfect the speech by practice. The sales representatives had a different perspective about the whole process:

The company thinks the sales to be just a process but it is actually an art. Every customer is not the same. Every customer is not patient enough and they interrupt in between. This makes us forget the sales speech and we say the features accord-ing to our own way. We cannot tell to customers "wait let me remember my sales speech". We all have our own way of selling the product.

With an increase in orders the production was ramped up, but still the delivery dates started stretching. Dealers were supposed to give customer delight by delivering the product sooner, but rather they had to call again to the customers to inform the delay. The company said: *We had to concentrate on growing our market in major metropolitan cities. Therefore we admit there was a supply crunch in some parts.* With increasing delay the customers started coming to dealership in person to en-quire. Initially most of the customers were previous customers hence relationship maintenance was essential so customers were given the display vehicles if it was of desired color so as not to forfeit commitment and to maintain the existing rela-tions. The lack of display vehicles in dealerships resulted in sales person resorting to brochures to explain the vehicle without physical feel of the vehicle. Only one test drive vehicle per dealership created busy schedule for onsite and offsite customers. Many customers started returning from dealership without even seeing the product.

The new product created lots of doubts about the features. These were collected and suitable answers to those queries of customers were circulated to every dealer-ship. The sales force started complaining that

the product features which were hyped in actual terms was as modest as other competitor cars and the customer is educated enough to know it apart from that the customers will not wait for company to revert, it's us who has to revert then and there. The company does not release white variant giving reason of losing the model to taxi segment, but at the same time it is election season and white vehicles are on demand. Customers want the primary color and we only have lame excuses to offer.

With all these problems looming in, the competitors were able to deliver the vehicles at a much faster rate. Customers started getting vehicles from alternate company dealerships in committed time. The vehicles were also delivered the same day.

This forced the customers to opt for other easier alternatives and they started taking back orders. The scheme of return of signing amount, if not delivered in due date, forced the dealers to return the money and to take the burden of finding another customer for the same vehicle. People were offered alternate colors with an option of getting vehicles faster. As a result customer dissatisfaction had risen and the sales had been badly affected (Appendix 5).

THE CURRENT CHALLENGES FACING THE ORGANIZATION

The whole order of the system was becoming chaotic and difficult to control. There is still hope that something can be done to improve the image of the company and with it: the sales. The relationships with customers have to be improved and measures needs to be adopted in order to ensure repeat business from existing customer and also to attract new business. The major customers who were in good relationship with Hemant complained of poor and irritating ways of marketing the product. Hemant's thought is still floating in the ripples trying to figure out a way to draw the line in water.

REFERENCES

Dyche, J. (2001). *The CRM handbook: A business guide to customer relationship management*. New York: Addison-Wesley Professional.

Pralahad, C. K., Ramaswamy, P. B., Katzenback, J. R., Lederer, C., & Sam, H. (2002). *Harvard business review on customer relationship management*. Boston: Harvard Business Press.

Sewell, C., & Brown, P. B. (2002). *Customers for life: How to turn that one time buyer into a lifetime customer*. New York: Crown Business.

APPENDIX 1

Figure 1. Dealer side management portal sample

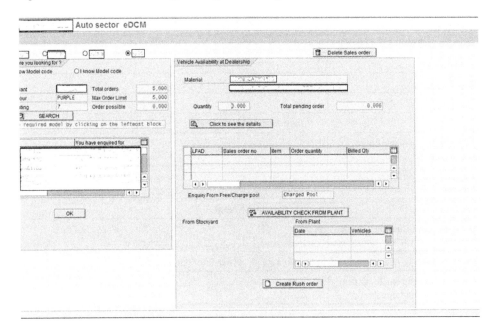

APPENDIX 2

Table 1. Interest structure of dealership financing sample

Sr. No.	Bank/NBFC	Amount	Rate
1	SBI	85% (On Road Cost)	11.75% to 12.25%
2	Axis Bank	80% (On Road Cost)	12.25%
3	HDFC	90%	13.65%
4	ICICI Bank	85%	15.50%
5	Kotak Bank	80%	14%
6	Magma	85%	16.25%
7	Cholamandalam DBS	85%	16 to 18%
8	MMFSL	90%	18%

APPENDIX 3

Table 2.

	Shriram Motors	Remarks
Show Room Exterior and Interior Signages		Dealership is under construction
Main Signage	N	
Internal Signages	N	
Hoarding (if applicable)		
Customer/Valet Parking		
Valet parking available board prominently displayed	N	
Trained Vallet Person available in uniform	N	
Welcome Stamp		
Stamping on all Customer Hand	N	The Kit hasn't reached the dealership
Display Area Ready as per the Theme		
A well decorated vehicle (as per vehicle display policy)	N	To arrive, area identified in the dealership
Backdrop and Floor	N	To arrive
Talkers	N	To arrive
Branding	N	To arrive
MP 3 Talkers	NA	Non metro dealership
Music	N	Provision not available
Brochure/Leaflets/Price Display Board		
Availability of Brochure/Leaflets at dealership	N	To arrive
Electronic price board in place	N	To arrive
POS Material/Display Stands		
Brochure Display Stands prominently displayed	N	Dealership under construction
Paint Shade Stand prominently displayed	N	
Vehicle Specification Stands prominently displayed	N	To arrive
POS Displayed	N	To arrive

continued on following page

Table 2. Continued

	Shriram Motors	Remarks
Furniture, Interiors, and Housekeeping		
Sales desk	N	
Housekeeping in General	N	Two sofa sets will be put up.
LCD Display System		
AV's played on LCD TV (as available)	N	Will be setting it up
Accessories Display in Place		
Initial Kit	N	To arrive
Test Drive Kit	N	To arrive
Accessorized vehicle on display	N	To arrive
Camera and Instant Photo for All Test Drives		
Digital camera available at dealership	Y	
Printer available at dealership	Y	
Staff well aware about operations of the process	Y	
Photographs given to customers coming for Test drives	N	To be done
Delivery Area		
Demarcated, Decorated with standard checkered backdrop	N	Area identified
Showroom Timings Extended/Sunday Open - 3 Months Post Launch (9am -10pm)		
New timings of showroom prominently displayed at showroom	N	
Timings being communicated vide advertisements etc.	N	
Policy		
New vehicle display policy being adhered to		
Capitalisation policy being adhered to		
Showroom floor area management policy being adhered to		
Vehicle Booking policy being adhered to		

APPENDIX 4

Figure 2. Cost estimation for launch

Venue		Cost	Tax %	Tax amount	Total cost / pax	Pax	Total Cost
Spring field	High tea	150	0.125	18.75	168.75	55	9281.25
	Dinner	550	0.125	68.75	618.75	140	86625
	Snacks	120	0.125	15	135	140	18900
						Drinks	25000
						Hall charge	35000
						Décor	30000
							204806.25

Venue		Cost	Tax %	Tax amount	Total cost / pax	Pax	Total Cost
Reish	High tea	750	0.275	206.25	956.25	55	52593.75
	Dinner	1350	0.275	371.25	1721.25	140	240975
	Snacks	500	0.275	137.5	637.5	140	89250
						Drinks	35000
						Décor	30000
							447818.75

Venue		Cost	Tax %	Tax amount	Total cost / pax	Pax	Total Cost
Raj	High tea	700	0.361	252.7	952.7	55	52398.5
	Dinner+snacks	1050	0.361	379.05	1429.05	140	200067
						Drinks	35000
						Décor	30000
							317465.5

APPENDIX 5

Figure 3. Sales statistics for three months

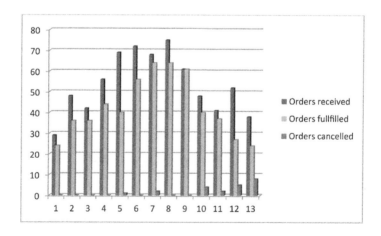

APPENDIX 6

Table 3. Dealership readiness data sample

Dealer	Place	Funds Arrangements Details	Infrastructure Stage	Manpower Stage	Remarks
Shriram motors	Kolkata	Assuming 30 vehicles stock, Rs 2.5 Crores from own fund	Ready	4 exclusive to be recruited	Interviews in process, to be closed by Nov 30th
AR Automobiles	New Delhi	Wants Rs 100 lacs from ABN. Rest to be arranged through own funds.	Ready	3 exclusive to be recruited	Interviews scheduled for Nov 10th
CSP motors	Chennai	Rs 100 lacs from ABN.	Ready	2 exclusive to be recruited	Interviews to start next week, to be closed by Nov 30th
Maya Automobiles	Mumbai	ABN Amro, Rs 50 lacs extra, above the current limit of Rs 200 lacs. Applied for additional Rs 40 lacs from Allahabad bank.	Ready	2 exclusive to be recruited. SM already recruited for personal channel	Interviews in process, to be closed by Nov 30th
DP Associates	Bengaluru	Applying on own for Rs 250 lacs from Allahabad bank	Ready	3 exclusive to be recruited and 1 SM	Interviews completed. Final selection to be over by Nov 30th
Captain Kariyappa Pvt Ltd	Sikkim	Rs 150 lacs to be recommended from SCB	Ready	3 exclusive to be recruited	To decide on this dealer

APPENDIX 7

Table 4.

Roles and Responsibility of Regional Sales Manager
Revenue generation
Target achievement
Developing team members
Company's representative in the HQ
Exploring new territories
Motivator
Customer relationship Builder
Brand Builder

Chapter 5
The Realization of Customer Satisfaction with Technology Integrations

Ooi Chien Shing
Sunway University, Malaysia

Seng Kah Phooi
Sunway University, Malaysia

Ang Li-Minn
Edith Cowan University, Australia

EXECUTIVE SUMMARY

This case is about the technology component of integrations in the marketing strategy of U-Globe Organization–a travel service provider organization to assess their customer satisfaction. The general information about the company is firstly provided in organization background. It is then followed by the stage setting which describes the current technology utilization and management practices of the organization. In the case description the customer satisfaction tools that are used by the organization are explained and compared, as well as the management concerns in conducting these customer satisfaction assessment. The limitation or challenges with their current approach in technology related ways to realize the satisfactions are also discussed. At the end of the case, the recommendations and solutions are provided to show the possible ways in solving the existing problems and improving the way of assessing customer satisfaction by integrating the appropriate technology.

DOI: 10.4018/978-1-4666-4357-4.ch005

Copyright ©2014, IGI Global. Copying or distributing in print or electronic forms without written permission of IGI Global is prohibited.

ORGANIZATION BACKGROUND

History of the Organization

U-Globe Travel International Ltd. is an international travel services provider with specialization its management system. It was founded by U. Gary Charlwood, who used to work as a tour guide in Europe. The company was established in 1979 in British Columbia, Canada. The first agency was opened in the year of Personal Computer (PC) launched by IBM when most of today's common technology components did not exist. In the 1980's the organization started franchising in America and Canada. It then expanded to European countries in the 1990's and Australia, Asian, African, and Middle eastern countries in the 2000's.

With the rapid improved communication technology and internet, every industry has been revolutionized. The travel agency experienced its greatest transformation as well and now there is more mobility and freedom for travelers today than ever before. Majorly in western countries, the organization has franchised 750 locations within 30 years.

Type of Organization and Products/Services Provided

As a travel service provider organization, the main target customers are the mid-size enterprise (SME) and any vacation traveler. They comprise locations in more than 60 countries under a famous and reliable brand, common system, and services standards.

The services that provided by the organization can be categorized as follows:

- **Travel Consultation:** Based on their professionalism and years of experience in this field, the organization provides the best fares and travel guides to the customers' business company trips. This service also covers the analysis of the travel expenses and trip arrangements so that customer can have effective cost management.
- **Business Travel Tools:** In major business travel planning, status of reservation and fare charged are the most concerned points by customers. The organization offers the service in finding the options and fares which saves customers' time in searching through website pages or contacting to each destination.
- **Vacation Planning:** The companies also provides wide-ranging vacation travel services such as transportations, hotel reservations, cruises, adventure travel, honeymoons and all inclusive package tours. Their professional travel consultants and destination specialists are ready to help customers in choosing the best available options.

Strategic Planning

There is a lot of competition between the similar services providers in the travel management share market. To stand out from these organizations, U-Globe requires good strategic planning to stay aligned with or surpass them. Thus, the organization invents a lot of efforts to gain high brand recognition and customer's positive impression by delivering promotions, advertisement, direct marketing, various communication tools, and online supports to secure and retain the existing customers.

In term of technology, U-Globe utilizes exclusive technology to conduct their business management, marketing, cost budgeting, transactions, financial analysis, and control efficiently. Besides, to maintain or improve the quality assurance, a quality control system is also used frequently to ensure the accuracy and best fares for every reservation of customers. U-Globe also prepares the latest technology solutions to the customers and these are fully supported by their regional team. The technology solutions are always customized to maximize their efficiency and profitability in business activities.

To enhance the revenue of the organization, U-Globe not only emphasizes their Customer Relationship Management (CRM), they also build strong relationships with their suppliers in the travel industry. The suppliers include those who provide 24-hour traveler rescue support and conduct carbon offset program. The organization practically set up a Preferred Supplier Program to deliver performance through uncertain market shares. With the enhanced revenue and profit, the supplier relationships delivers special benefits which are able to indirectly build better or maintain customer relationships.

Since this organization's main delivered services are in consultations and solutions provided by the agents, the professionalism of their consultancy is required to be maintained or improved in terms of skill and knowledge. U-Globe updates their information regarding customer's traveling experience based on the internet and consumer travel reviews. The organization can indirectly be acknowledged with information about the offered products from their own and competitors. In addition to information updating, U-Globe also conducts skill development and training programs to enhance the employee's selling skills, effective use of technology solutions, service delivery, service recovery, relationship and business activities with suppliers, and service/product training. Remarkable performance from the staff also will be rewarded in order to maintain the motivation in enhancing their performance.

With this strategic planning throughout the years, in combination with the sales volume from all the franchises around the world, the organization earned around 5.0 billion dollar in the recent annual sales.

SETTING THE STAGE

In the stage setting, we focus on the technology utilization and its advancements, management practices, and related roles of internal staffs that involved in this case.

Technology Utilization and Advancements

As a customer-centric organization, U-Globe aimed to serve customers seamlessly through new channels. Few approaches for advancements have been conducted by the organization to extend the capability of the utilized technology component to provide better customer-centric marketing management. One of the approaches is integrating the technology in communication tools. This gives more options and opportunity of interactions between the customer service teams and customers so that better customer services can be conducted. The utilizations are including:

- Telephone and Video Chat

Before the invention of personal computer, telephone is their only device can be relied to approach customers and other agents/partners at a long distance. Since the establishment of this travel organization, telephone has been still playing an important role in the communication tool. With the improvement of online technology, an alternative voice telecommunication tool has developed as computer application – which mostly called as video conferencing software. This application can provide user information in visual and audio during video chatting or conferencing. In year 2011, U-Globe started integrating this tool in customer service to communicate with customers. This benefits the customer in replacing non-verbal visual cues of communication ways, and ability to share visualized data such as photos or maps in their company.

- Company Website

The website not only provides the general information about the company's services, it also gives customers the convenience to find regional agents' contact methods so that the customer can choose their most preferred ways to approach the organization.

LEEDS METROPOLITAN UNIVERSITY LIBRARY

- Email

Email has become one of the most important communication tools to be used, especially for businesses, in the past decade. U-Globe provides the option to contact them through email based on customer's concern in different categories: general question/feedback, media, marketing, and corporate sales.

- Social Media

Facebook and Twitter are two of the most popular social networks since 2009. Facebook, for instance, claimed to have at least 901 million active users in year 2012(Hachman, 2012). So, U-Globe took this technology advantage to create its own fan-page to enhance the interaction with customers. It is an effective method of the company's marketing strategy because the organization is able to get more exposure to the customers who "like" their fan-page in Facebook and promote their latest update at customer's Facebook *News Feed*.

- Global Booking Engine

Because many business travel accounts are stored accordingly to their fellow agencies based in 60 different countries, it is hard to manage their data and account. Recently, U-Globe launched a web-based global booking engine to ease the data management and centralize all the access to customer's account.

Management Practices

The management practice of this company is to ensure the consistent best-in-class customer service and actual day-to-day accomplishments of the operations. As a customer-centric organization, they focus on the main customer commitments in their management practices as stated in the following paragraphs.

Firstly, the company always portrays the professionalism in their business to the customers. Thus, all the agents were trained extensively to be the certified travel professionals, who emphasize delivering excellent customer service and quality assurance.

Quick response to the customer is a good practice in customer service. So, in communication with customers through email, telephone, or fax, the company is required to have a short waiting time for answering and responding to any issues or problems raised by customer.

Thirdly, since the company is delivering services such as travel consultancy, it is important to have the efficient management for customers when undergoing a business trip or other services. So, in collaboration with the franchises in more than 60 countries, customers can rely on every agency in these different locations.

Besides, reservations from customers are quality assured by the company. This is to avoid wrong date/tickets/hotel reservations and meet customer demands and requirements correctly. To ensure the accuracy of their services, U-Globe company always confirms all the given travel information and itinerary in documents to be error-free.

To stay competitive in this business, the company is required to promise their customer the best fare when planning their trips or other related services. So, one of the customer commitments from the company is to consistently investigate and update themselves with the latest fares or promotions from all relevant channels. With experience and professionalism in finding and researching the information from various channels, the company can manage the travel costs efficiently.

Lastly, to maintain or improve the quality of their services, the performance of existing customers and potential customers are closely monitored by the company so that any problems faced by these customers can be addressed immediately. In addition, every complaint from customers will go through the service recovery which resolves any dissatisfaction about the delivered services.

CASE DESCRIPTION

This case is about the satisfaction realization with technology integrated tools that have been used by the U-Globe organization. In this section, the concern points from management and organization are described. It is followed by how the organization utilized the technology components to assess customer satisfaction.

Management and Organizational Concerns

Customer satisfaction is one of the main sources to acknowledge the companies about the quality of their products or service and the customer's loyalty (Hill & Alexander, 2006). As a telecommunication service provider with millions of subscribers, it is unavoidable to have different level of satisfactions from them. For instance, customers normally tend to approach the company and show their dissatisfactions when their received products and services did not meet the expectations. The approaches can be through phone calls, online survey, or online feedback with text. There are few main concerns in management and organizational perceptive(Uniglobe, 2011):

- Telephone and email response time

Short time taken to respond to customer reflects excellent customer service because customers can feel how much the organization cares about their customers. So, in terms of satisfaction, U-Globe is concerned about customers' impressions in the response time.

- Booking accuracy

It is unavoidable to have some emergencies happened during the customer's business travel. However, it is the organization's responsibility to conduct flight ticket, transportation arrangement, and hotel room reservations accurately in order to reduce the possibilities in failing customer's business trip plan. This may affect customer loyalty with the organization.

- Provision of options and alternatives based on travel needs

As travel consultants prepare the options of trip packages for customers, it is important to have at least one of them ready. Otherwise, the agents need to prepare the alternative plans for the customers based on their preferences. This reflects the quality of the customer services and is the main key to closing a deal. Thus, if a customer is able to make his/her decision within the first few options, this indicates the satisfactions on the services.

- Overall services

Overall services refer to the customer impression from the moment he/she approaches the organization staff or consultant until the endpoint of the delivered service.

Technology Components

Since the past decades in the area of marketing, there have been a high number of innovative ways of integrating technology components into their implementations of business strategies. Through various media facets, from traditional television to recent social media website, organizations keep finding ways to improve effectiveness and reduce expenses in conducting advertisement and promotion of their products over the years. One of the largest improvements or advantages delivered is the different communication process from one way communication to two-ways communication (Kerin, Hartley, & Rudelius, 2013). This transforms the "end-path" of the connection (between company and customer) which from traditional media such as television or magazine advertisement that ends with the received customer, to social media such as Facebook and Twitter that does not end with any individual receiver.

This improved communication process not only gives the organization a faster and more convenient way to approach their customers, but it also provides the advancement of survey tools at the same time. The differences of these most commonly used technology-integrated survey tools can be summarized in Table 1.

U-Globe applied these survey tools to obtain customer satisfaction. An online survey is conducted annually in October through email and travel itinerary to have the customer rate based on their service quality on a scale of 1 to 5. The concern points in this survey include customer satisfaction on organization response time, booking accuracy, overall services, and so on. For video chat, telephone call, and online feedback, the agents will response to the customer as soon as possible upon reception. Solutions to the customer's dissatisfactions are also promised to be given shortly after they are acknowledged.

Table 1. Comparison of advantages and disadvantages for the four most commonly used survey tools in U-Globe company

	Advantages	**Disadvantages**
Telephone Call	• Customer and company are able to give immediate response	• Customer may need to pay for the telephony services
Video Conferencing	• Free • Customer and company are able to give immediate response • Customer can watch the consultant presentation choose to display their own face during the conversation	• Both customer and company sides need to have basic requirement of video conferencing such as web-camera and microphone
Online Survey	• Free • Easier and more convenient to administer compare to the paper survey • Straight forward to assess customer satisfaction based on the questions and satisfaction scales set by the company	• Difficult to have customers recalled of their experiences • Customers have high possibilities not telling the truth • Required good and helpful question development
Online Feedback	• Free • Customer saves time and energy • Social media is popularly used recently	• Not suitable if the customer's complaint need immediate response from company • Emotions are hard to be identified by company from text • Normally is set up with a language only

CURRENT CHALLENGES FACING THE ORGANIZATION

As mentioned previously, the organization conducted customer satisfaction online survey annually. Although they obtained a remarkable satisfaction results from customers, the data may be not accurate as the customers have a high possibility of failing to remember their experience and simply complete the survey based on their overall impressions. Without the specific customer information based on the real experiences, it is hard for the organization to track their mistake and revise for improvements in their services or marketing strategies.

Thus, one of the current challenges that can be concluded from this problem is the immaturity of technology's adaptation in the organization to address customer needs. In the stage setting section, the technology utilizations of U-Globe organization are listed out and most of them are applied in communication with customer. The reason of identifying the challenge as immaturity of technology adaption is because there is less data integration with the available technology components, especially those that are able to interact with customers. For instance, during a conversation with customer, the service agents or consultant provided few options of trip packages to the customer. When discussing and describing each option to customers, they will portray their satisfactions on the services. However, these satisfaction levels have been overlooked by the organization because using manpower to analyze every conversation with customers is difficult and time consuming. The organization only can rely on the professionalism of service agents to close a deal or solve their problems. There is less technology adaption in their communication tools that can assist the agents and the marketing management team to determine the customer satisfactions.

SOLUTIONS AND RECOMMENDATIONS

There is a recommendation for adapting systems into their existing technology components to help them in facing the challenge. Firstly, based on the communication tools that utilized by U-Globe Company which are video conferencing, telephone call, and online feedback in social media or email, different data can be captured as shown in Figure 1.

As shown in Figure 2, the captured data from the communication tools that are used by the organization can be in image, speech signal, and text. Typically in most organization, this data is stored in databases for future analysis after capturing and the related customer-centric applications normally focus in integrating these data with 3 levels: data warehousing, reporting, and analytics (Al-Shammari, 2009). However these stages are not always cost-effective because a high volume of data

Figure 1. Captured data from different communication tools

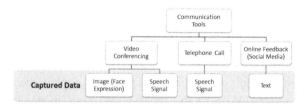

needs to be stored before the analysis is performed. So it is recommended to use the captured data and apply analysis to extract important information simultaneously. In this case, automated emotion recognition system and automated text content analysis tool can be adopted to solve the problems.

Automated Text Content Analysis Tool

The automated text content analysis tools have been widely utilized by many organizations in the past three years because of the rising popularity of social media. A lot of complete commercial software with similar features is ready in the market today. Business organizations just need to get the services from the software company. One of the most popular pieces of software for this automated text content analysis tool is Get Satisfaction (2012). It provides services to enhance the customer relationship with organization by collecting and analyzing the text feedbacks across all available social media that related to the organization.

Automated Emotion Recognition System

The image and/or speech signal data that is obtained from telephone talk and video chat is able to further extract the information contained in it as well. Although there

Figure 2. Process flow of the information and data between customer and consultant over the communication platform with integrated audio-visual emotion recognition

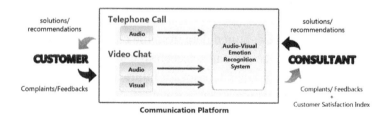

is research that is able to perform content analysis using speech recognition through the images and speech from video, it is too complex to be integrated and the analysis result is not promising (Ezzat, Gayar, & Ghanem, 2010).

For telephone call and video chat, it is recommended to have instant analysis on the customer satisfaction. During conversation through these communication tools, when the travel consultant is giving options or consultations to the customers, customers could have different satisfactions level based on their preferences. Emotional states are more directly related to satisfaction from customers compared to other information forms extracted from image and speech (Kasiran & Yahya, 2007). Using the automated emotion recognition system, the consultants or agents are able to assess customer satisfaction based on their emotions. Alternative solutions can be then given to the customer. The process flow can be visualized as shown in Figure 2:

The automated emotion recognition system consists of five main stages:

Stage 1: Audio and/or Visual Data Input

Since the system is suggested for both telephone and video conferencing communication tools, it is optional to have audio and/or visual data be obtained. Once this data is obtained, the system is expected to have a sufficient temporary storage to save them.

Stage 2: Data Pre-Processing

After getting this data from the communication tool, the data is pre-processed in order to standardize the obtained information. For instance, the images that contained face expression of customers require the whole face unit to be detected and segmented. On the other hand, the certain time range of signals needs Voice Activity Detector (VAD) to identify the segments of time range that contain the existence of a human voice (Cho & Kim, 2011).

Stage 3: Emotion Feature Extraction

Feature extraction plays an important role in most of the pattern recognition system. At this stage, feature extraction techniques are required to extract the important components that related to emotional states from the pre-processed data. Popular techniques that normally used for the emotion recognition system are Principal Component Analysis (PCA) and Linear Discriminant Analysis (LDA)(Li & Oussalah, 2010; Zhang, Lei, Chen, Chen, & Chen, 2010).

Stage 4: Emotion Classification

Classification is the stage that the extracted components can be classified to their corresponding emotional stage. The popular techniques for classifications are including k-Nearest Neighbors, Neural Network, and Hidden Markov Model (HMM) that using distance measuring (Zhan, Chen, & Zhang, 2006), identical structure of biological neurons (Chen, Cowan, & Grant, 1991), and probability algorithm to model sequential data (Moni & Ali, 2009) respectively.

Stage 5: Customer Satisfaction Index Calculation

Once the emotion is acknowledged from the output of the previous stage, calculation of customer satisfaction index is the final stage to relate the emotional state to customer satisfaction. Similar to the satisfaction scale in the survey paper, the simple calculation of the satisfaction indexes can be defined by the organization to categorize the different emotion states in different customer satisfaction level.

Another benefit of using this automated system in communication tools is tracking the calculated results based on different issues. Example of this outcome is shown in the Table 2 where all the information is automatically generated by the system except the comment column that requires the agents to input manually regarding the discussed issues during the time period.

CONCLUSION

In conclusion, the integration of technology in U-Globe Organization to assess customer satisfaction is included in this case. From the technology utilization in the company, many communication tools have the potential to be further enhanced or

Table 2. Example tabulated result from the integrated emotion recognition in video conferencing

Date	Agent	Ref. Number	Conversation Start Time	Conversation End Time	Customer	Emotion States	Satisfaction Level (0-100)	Comment
12/6/2012	ABC	00001-1	09:18:47	09:22:41	EFG	Neutral	54	
12/6/2012	ABC	00001-2	09:28:46	09:32:11	EFG	Happy	78	
12/6/2012	ABC	00002-1	09:50:16	09:52:11	GHI	Happy	81	

integrated to be used to improve their service quality. Thus, instead of relying on the existing online survey to collect satisfaction information from customers annually, this case is suggesting more possible ways to have the realization of customer satisfaction in real time.

REFERENCES

Al-Shammari, M. (2009). Capturing data from customers Customer Knowledge Management: People, Processes, and Technology (169-190). New York: Information Science Reference.

Chen, S., Cowan, C. F. N., & Grant, P. M. (1991). Orthogonal least squares learning algorithm for radial basis function networks. *IEEE Transactions on Neural Networks*, *2*(2), 302–309. doi:10.1109/72.80341 PMID:18276384.

Cho, N., & Kim, E.-K. (2011). Enhanced voice activity detection using acoustic event detection and classification. *IEEE Transactions on Consumer Electronics*, *57*(1), 196–202. doi:10.1109/TCE.2011.5735502.

Ezzat, S., Gayar, N. E., & Ghanem, M. M. (2010). Investigating analysis of speech content through text classification. In *Proceedings of Investigating Analysis of Speech Content through Text Classification*. Paris: IEEE Press. doi:10.1109/SOCPAR.2010.5686000.

GetSatisfaction. (2012). *Get satisfaction anywhere*. Retrieved from http://getsatisfaction.com.

Hachman, M. (2012). Facebook now totals 901 million users, Profit slip. *PCMag.com*. Retrieved from http://www.pcmag.com/article2/0,2817,2403410,00.asp.

Hill, N., & Alexander, J. (2006). *Handbook of customer satisfaction*. New Delhi: Gower.

Kasiran, Z., & Yahya, S. (2007). Facial expression as an implicit customers' feedback and the challenges. In *Proceedings of Computer Graphics, Imaging, and Visualisation*. Bangkok, Thailand: IEEE Press. doi:10.1109/CGIV.2007.40.

Kerin, R., Hartley, S., & Rudelius, W. (2013). *Marketing*. New York: McGraw-Hill.

Li, J., & Oussalah, M. (2010). Automatic face emotion recognition system. In *Proceedings of the IEEE 9th International Conference on Cybernetic Intelligent Systems*. Reading, UK: IEEE Press.

Moni, M. A., & Ali, A. B. M. S. (2009). HMM based hand gesture recognition: A review on techniques and approaches. In *Proceedings of the 2nd IEEE International Conference on Computer Science and Information Technology*. Washington, DC: IEEE Press.

Uniglobe, T. I. (2011). *Nine in Ten business travel clients give uniglobe high marks for service quality*. Retrieved from http://corp.uniglobetravel.com/site/viewhome.asp?aid=39086&sit=314&vty=ARTICLE&tid=21030&sessionid=.

Zhan, Y., Chen, H., & Zhang, G.-C. (2006). An optimization algorithm of k-nn classification. In *Proceedings of the Fifth International Conference on Machine Learning and Cybernetics*. Dalian, China: IEEE Press.

Zhang, S., Lei, B., Chen, A., Chen, C., & Chen, Y. (2010). Spoken emotion recognition using local fisher discriminant analysis. In *Proceedings of the IEEE 10th International Conference on Signal Processing* (ICSP). Beijing: IEEE Press.

Chapter 6
Intensive Care

Eric Van Genderen
Institute of Management Technology (IMT), UAE

EXECUTIVE SUMMARY

Customer-centric organizations are those firms that seek to gain a strategic advantage by focusing on the customer (as opposed to the firm, product line/service(s), processes, financial statements, etc), thereby more effectively offering goods/services that meet the needs and wants of the customer. As an industry, healthcare has the added challenge of needing to offer customized products/services that not only address the needs/wants of customers, but must also do so in an ethical and sensitive way. Patients availing the products/services of healthcare professionals, more-often-than-not, require psychological support in addition to the requisite physical care and/or treatment. It has been well established that one's psychological state has dramatic impact on the physical and vice versa. This case is set in the Middle East, and centers around the two main concepts of: 1). Customer-centric business practices, and 2). ethical healthcare behavior, respectively. The case, itself, is closely based on the author's first-hand experience. Identifying information has been modified so as not to reveal the identities of the institution, managing enterprise, or employees.

ORGANIZATION BACKGROUND

The Royal Women's Infirmary is located in a major city in the Middle East and has been operating for more than three decades with a current labor force of over 1,000 employees (nearly 20% of which are doctors and nurses). The Royal Women's Infirmary specializes in the areas of obstetric and neonatal care. With the capacity to

DOI: 10.4018/978-1-4666-4357-4.ch006

Copyright ©2014, IGI Global. Copying or distributing in print or electronic forms without written permission of IGI Global is prohibited.

handle well over 200 inpatients, a large ICU, outpatient care, and specialty clinics, the infirmary is viewed as being large by Middle East standards. As is common for hospitals seeking to maintain international standards, the Royal Women's Infirmary is a 'jointly commissioned' venture, owned by the local government, and managed/operated by a Western specialist organization. Due to growth, the Royal Women's Infirmary recently expanded its Neo-natal and Urgent Care units, in addition to its ambulatory services.

SETTING THE STAGE

Like most organizations, the Royal Women's Infirmary has 'mission' and 'vision' statements, which they proudly display to the public. These statements speak of 'compassion' and 'family centeredness'. The infirmary further declares 'core values' including: 'care and compassion,' 'ownership and accountability,' 'respect and cultural sensitivity,' 'integrity,' 'commitment to quality,' a holistic and patient-centered approach,' 'quality,' and so forth.

The Royal Women's Infirmary maintains memberships in several international healthcare organizations, not the least of which is the University Healthcare Consortium (UHC). The UHC was formed in 1984 (Chicago), for the self-stated purpose of:

Providing the lens through which the organization assesses all it does, UHC's mission is to create knowledge, foster collaboration, and promote change to help members succeed.

Moreover, the UHC's vision maintains an objective to:

...help members attain national leadership in health care by achieving excellence in quality, safety, and cost-effectiveness. (About university hospital consortium, n.d.)

Although the international healthcare industry represents great potential for profitability; especially in the private sector, Western healthcare professionals have been guided, for centuries, by a code of ethical conduct known as the 'Hippocatic oath'; see the sample of a modern version below:

I swear to fulfill, to the best of my ability and judgment, this covenant:

I will respect the hard-won scientific gains of those physicians in whose steps I walk, and gladly share such knowledge as is mine with those who are to follow.

I will apply, for the benefit of the sick, all measures [that] are required, avoiding those twin traps of overtreatment and therapeutic nihilism.

I will remember that there is art to medicine as well as science, and that warmth, sympathy, and understanding may outweigh the surgeon's knife or the chemist's drug.

I will not be ashamed to say "I know not", nor will I fail to call in my colleagues when the skills of another are needed for a patient's recovery.

I will respect the privacy of my patients, for their problems are not disclosed to me that the world may know. Most especially must I tread with care in matters of life and death. If it is given to me to save a life, all thanks. But it may also be within my power to take a life; this awesome responsibility must be faced with great humbleness and awareness of my own frailty. Above all, I must not play at God.

I will remember that I do not treat a fever chart, a cancerous growth, but a sick human being, whose illness may affect the person's family and economic stability. My responsibility includes these related problems, if I am to care adequately for the sick.

I will prevent disease whenever I can, for prevention is preferable to cure.

I will remember that I remain a member of society with special obligations to all my fellow human beings, those sound of mind and body as well as the infirm.

If I do not violate this oath, may I enjoy life and art, be respected while I live and remembered with affection thereafter. May I always act so as to preserve the finest traditions of my calling and may I long experience the joy of healing those who seek my help (Lasagna, 1964).

Like many professional codes of ethics, the Hippocratic oath is not legally binding to those who have taken it, but rather represents an ethical and philosophical framework for the healthcare industry, within which healthcare professionals can practice, whilst recognizing certain limits to their skills, abilities, and knowledge, as well as maintaining focus on their overall professional objective–the health and well-being of the patient.

CASE DESCRIPTION

It was the eve of February 16. The doctor was pale and anxious as she repeated the instructions to Kathy and Derek that they were to 'go straightaway to the critical care unit at the Women's Royal Infirmary, as Kathy was in grave danger of prematurely delivering the baby.' As they left their local clinic, both parents were frantic and bewildered. What was happening? How could this be the case? The two had only recently returned from a restful vacation, during which time, a family friend, an obstetrician, had carefully examined Kathy, concluding that her pregnancy was progressing well.

Kathy was just over 22 weeks pregnant, and both parents had relaxed considerably having quite uneventfully completed the first trimester of Kathy's pregnancy. Two years earlier, Kathy had given normal birth to a healthy baby boy. Kathy and Derek were already purchasing baby clothes and accessories for their soon-to-be baby girl. The grandparents had been notified, visits were being planned to see the new baby–upon arrival–and a short list of possible names had been meticulously assembled. In short, Kathy and Derek were eagerly anticipating the arrival of their daughter.

The night of February 16, Kathy had noticed 'spotting', and decided to pay a visit to the physician overseeing her pregnancy, who was conveniently located at a medical clinic next door to their residence. Upon initial examination, the doctor had become quite anxious. Further examination seemed to exacerbate the OB's expression to one of obvious alarm. Both Kathy and Derek were in shock, not fully comprehending the nature of the situation, although picking up on the tacit and overt indications of distress, resulting in the physician's instructions to go directly to the urgent care admittance at the Royal Women's Infirmary–which they did.

Upon entering the urgent care unit of the infirmary, Kathy and Derek went straight to the registration and admissions desk, operated by two foreign nurses and a local administrator. The head nurse read through the referral prepared by the clinic, and advised the administrator that the patient was in 'urgent need of assessment and admittance.' The local administrator insisted on having all forms filled, and proceeded with them to the finance office to complete the admission paperwork, returning only to request Kathy's insurance card.

As was common within the region, Kathy and Derek were covered by insurance provided (by law) by Derek's employer, which in this case, was the local federal government (the Ministry of Education). Medical facilities utilized the insurance cards to ensure that the policy matched the individual availing the services, but also sent copies to the insurance company in question, for the purpose of claiming reimbursement for services rendered. The inability of a healthcare service provider to produce a copy of the beneficiary's insurance card, would lead to a rejection of the claim by an insurance company.

Derek and Kathy explained to the administrator that Kathy was insured by Derek's work, the federal government, but that the insurance company 'FedInsure Ltd.' had yet to supply them with new cards, since their policies had been renewed on January 1 of that year. To this, the local administrator quite abruptly stated that 'without the insurance card, Kathy would need to leave the hospital.' Derek suggested that the administrator might consider having the accounts department simply phone the 24-hour contact line for FedInsure and verify that Kathy was insured. At this, the local woman disappeared back to the accounts office.

In the meantime, Kathy was beside herself, while the nurses, quite appalled and anxious, conversed between themselves, agreeing that there was no time to lose, and that the matter of the insurance card should not take precedence over the urgent care required by Kathy. Derek was simply attempting to console his wife, agree with the nurses, and fully comprehend what was taking place. Here they were, in danger of losing their baby, standing in an urgent care facility, squabbling with a local administrator over a card the insurance company had not yet dispatched. The entire situation seemed senseless.

After a few minutes, the local woman returned, maintaining that 'Yes, the insurance company had confirmed Kathy's coverage, but that she and the accounts' supervisor had agreed that without the card–Kathy would not be admitted to the infirmary.' At this point, Derek and the two nurses interjected, while Kathy erupted in hysteria sobbing, 'Where can I go? What am I to do–and what will become of my baby? Do you expect me to go home in this condition?' The atmosphere was strained with tension, sobbing, pleading, and concern, as Derek and the nurses urged the administrator to reconsider this unthinkable position, to which the local woman replied 'You will need to leave now. I have other work to do. Peace be with you.'

Outraged, Derek pointed out that this situation was absurd. Kathy was fully insured; as had been verified, she and the baby were in critical condition, and nearly two hours had expired since leaving the clinic for the Royal Women's Infirmary, seeking urgent attention. The local woman calmly requested that security escort Derek and Kathy to the parking area, as they would not be seen due to their not having Kathy's insurance card. As the security officer timidly approached the two, Kathy sobbed to the local woman, 'Do you care nothing for me and my baby? Don't we matter at all?'

Before the woman could answer, Derek took control of the situation, clarifying to the woman that Kathy was insured, and therefore had the full right to be admitted and treated, and therefore, under no circumstances, would he and his wife leave the hospital. Derek emphasized the critical nature of his wife's condition, urging the local woman to admit her and worry about bureaucratic trivialities later. It was at this point that a small man wearing sports attire quietly approached the heated conversation; just in time to hear the administrator, once again, give the directive for the security guard to escort Kathy and Derek off the infirmary premises.

With a look of confusion, and a quiet voice, the man asked what was going on, and why was the administrator requesting security to remove Derek and Kathy from the hospital? Derek quickly updated the gentleman, at which point the man introduced himself as being Dr. James Lander, the recently appointed Chief Medical Officer (CMO), from Canada, in charge of operations. Dr. Lander then focused on the local administrator asking why Kathy had not yet been assessed by a triage physician, to which the woman calmly replied that 'the accounts' supervisor had agreed with her that Kathy should not be seen, since she did not have her insurance card with her.'

At this point, Derek interjected with an irritated voice, that the administrator had verified Kathy's insurance, yet still refused to let her be seen by a doctor. Dr. Lander then took charge, saying, 'This is an absurd situation. Insurance cards can be produced later. From the referral I have read, this patient needs immediate assessment by the triage doctor on duty, and admittance into our urgent care unit.' At which point, the two nurses sped Kathy in a wheelchair to the triage doctor's unit. The triage doctor, Dr. Patel, was of Asian origin, with many lines of experience on her brow. Dr. Patel examined Kathy, and immediately called the urgent care inpatient unit, indicating that a patient was being admitted from triage with the condition of 'inevitable miscarriage.'

Overhearing this conversation taking place at her bedside, Kathy, again, became hysterical. As tears streamed down her face, she exclaimed, 'My baby, my baby, don't let my baby die!' To this, Dr. Patel calmly told her that,'We can only wait for it to happen, and help you through–but a miscarriage is inevitable. I have seen this so many times. Your cervix has opened 4.5 centimeters my dear.' At this, the hysteria became worse. Derek consoled his wife, telling her that things may improve, and not to lose hope, while simultaneously feeling enraged that an experienced doctor would be so insensitive.

Kathy was next wheeled to the urgent care inpatient ward, where she was met by the head nurse, assigned nurse, and duty physician. Derek continued speaking softly to Kathy, telling her that everything would be fine and just to relax and think positively. However, Derek's own mind was becoming increasingly alarmed. Why weren't they doing anything to prevent the baby from moving further down, or at least to close or block the cervical opening? Why was nothing even being *attempted*? Derek felt helpless, and the medical professionals around him seemed to simply be waiting for them to lose their baby girl. Derek felt outraged, but spent the next few hours alleviating Kathy's fears, until she finally fell asleep, and he could go home and attempt to get a little rest himself.

A few hours later, Derek was rudely awakened by an authoritative voice on the other end of his mobile phone, 'Mr. Derek this is Reem calling from the insurance claims office at the Royal Women's Infirmary Your wife, Kathy, has still not shown her insurance card, and we have made it clear that if we do not receive it by noon today, she will be required to pay the entire amount owed–plus a deposit on the estimated future treatment–or be discharged from the hospital.' Derek's anxiety returned as he attempted to politely explain that there was no reason to threaten, and further, that he had only been home for a few hours, and fully intended to contact the insurance company and see what could be done about the card, given that it had still not been sent to his employer. However, as he spoke, Reem commanded from the other end of the phone 'Noon Mr. Derek–or your wife will be discharged.'

Adrenaline raced through Derek's veins as he frantically phoned the HR specialist at his office at the Ministry of Education. Derek explained the situation to the administrator, who confirmed that the insurance cards for the company still had not been received by FedInsure Ltd. The HR administrator then gave Derek the name and contact phone number for the authority's account manager, whom Derek contacted right away. The account manager apologized for being several weeks late in issuing the cards for the ministry, but mumbled that he had been on annual leave, and that there had been no one available to take on his incomplete accounts. Derek related the situation with concerning his wife, and the account manager assured him that he would have both of their insurance cards ready by the next day. 'No! You are already 6 weeks late with the cards, and if I do not produce my wife's card at the hospital by 12-noon, they will discharge her, and she will be delivering our baby at home.' At this, the account manager promised he would at least have Kathy's card ready within the hour. 'One hour!' Derek repeated. 'I shall be at your office to collect the card in exactly one hour!'

Foregoing breakfast and a shower, Derek hailed a taxi and started across the city to FedInsure, dialing Kathy at the hospital as he rode. Kathy answered the phone in tears. 'They are going to make me leave the hospital! An administrator has called me three times. I told her we were insured, but haven't received the cards from the insurance company–but she doesn't care. They want the card, or they are going to make me leave!' Derek attempted to persuade her that this was not going to happen, and that he was on his way to collect her card, and that he would then go directly to the hospital and sort out the issue once and for all. 'Once I have taken your card to the insurance claim office at the infirmary, I am going to make a serious complaint to the administration. The customer care at the Royal Women's Infirmary has been an absolute nightmare.' The account manager at FedInsure, true to his word, had the card ready and waiting for Derek when he arrived. With a sigh of relief and 'shukran' (Arabic for 'thank you'), Derek was in another taxi, and racing towards the Royal Women's Infirmary.

Recollecting his wife's awful state, and the rude and threatening discourse to which he had awoken, Derek wasted no time upon arrival at the infirmary finding the insurance claim office. Upon entering, Derek demanded to know who had called him in the morning. The three individuals stood and stared for a moment, before one after another, they all three denied having made any calls to Derek. At this, Derek openly displayed his mobile phone, with the direct phone number glaring at the three of them. Two administrators looked at the third, at which point Derek exclaimed 'Here is the card. You owe both my wife and me a serious apology after your abusive threats. Where do you think you are working–an automobile repossession firm?' The woman merely looked at Derek with a bewildered face, before leaving the room with the comment that she 'had only been doing her job.' Derek reported this incident to the local administrative coordinator in charge, who took it all somewhat lightly, but promised to have a word with the employee.

Turning his attention back to Kathy and the baby, Derek went straightaway to her room, only to find her still panicked over the insurance card, and to learn from the attending nurse that Kathy's cervix had dilated another .5 centimeters since being admitted the night before. Both Derek and Kathy were losing hope of Kathy's condition improving–or even stabilizing. Derek had a conversation with the 'lead physician' and Dr. Lander, which amounted to nothing more than an attempt on their part to prepare them for the worst. Derek presented his confusion as to why the medical staff wasn't trying anything, acknowledging that he, himself, had no expertise when it came to healthcare, but also imploring that there must be something they could try. The two doctors just looked at each other, before insisting that there really was nothing that could be done at this stage except wait. 'Don't worry,' one of them said, 'It will be all over within another day or so.' Worrying was about the only thing Derek *could* do–apart from keeping his wife company and attempting to ease her anxiety.

A couple of hours later, the attending physician came into the room, quickly read through Kathy's chart, asked her how she was feeling, and told her to prepare herself mentally, because the miscarriage was 'inevitable,' and that the post-natal specialist would be in to see her in the morning, to speak with her about survival rates, resuscitation, and so forth. This was all Kathy and Derek could bear. Kathy burst out weeping and Derek confronted the doctor, 'Are you God? Do you believe you have the right to decide what is unquestionably going to happen–and what isn't? Do you, as a medical doctor think it is professional to use terms such as 'inevitable'? How is my wife meant to maintain hope and optimism when she is constantly told that a miscarriage is 'inevitable'? Is it even ethical for you or any other staff member to accept the situation as being 'inevitable'? Such acceptance undoubtedly affects decisions, judgment, and performance.' The doctor was shaken, and obviously didn't know how to respond–so she quickly exited the room.

Derek spent several hours attempting to calm himself, and restore his wife's confidence that they at least might have a chance of stabilizing her, and saving the baby. But, his attempts were futile. 'I have heard it enough times. There is no use in holding onto false hopes. I am going to lose the baby and there is nothing that can be done,' wailed Kathy. At this point, Derek was extremely concerned about Kathy's mental state-as well as her physical condition–and resolved to spend the rest of the night with her in the infirmary. Derek and Kathy narrated the past events to each other, searching for a clue as to what had gone wrong, but it was no use. No level of analysis or retrospection was going to change their situation. As desperate as he felt, Derek still maintained an optimistic outlook when speaking with his wife, but her perspective had changed. She just kept repeating, 'If I am going to lose the baby, I just want it all over with. I don't want to just keep waiting, not knowing for how long…'

On the morning of February 18, the physician on duty made her rounds. An examination of Kathy revealed no further dilation, resulting in the doctor informing Kathy and Derek that Kathy's situation was stable for the moment. The physician then indicated that the postnatal specialist was busy with several patients in one of the other wards, but would be visiting Kathy sometime in the afternoon. Derek decided to utilize at least part of the time to share some of his concerns with Dr. Lander; given his position as the Chief Medical Officer. Derek presented three main points to Dr. Lander that were central to his displeasure concerning the treatment his wife was receiving at the Royal Women's Infirmary:

1. The incidences concerning Kathy's medical insurance card.
2. The medical staff members' continued usage of the term 'inevitable miscarriage', rather than employing a more professional approach by using medical terminology to describe the condition.
3. The nonchalant manner in which the medical staff was treating Kathy's situation; specifically, not attempting any kind of preventive measures, in favor of simply waiting–as they expected a miscarriage–sooner or later.

The CMO listened patiently and acknowledged the three points. He went as far as to agree fully with Derek concerning the first two points, but assured him that the hospital was doing everything possible–but that there really was nothing that could be done apart from simply monitoring Kathy and the baby at this point. Derek emphasized to Dr. Lander how the continued usage of the term 'inevitable miscarriage' had destroyed his wife's hope, by psychologically conditioning her to accept that the baby would be miscarried–and most probably lost. Derek continued that such behavior on the part of any healthcare worker was unprofessional, unethical, and could place the infirmary at risk of litigation.

The CMO showed genuine concern, but was careful not to accept any legal responsibility on behalf of the hospital, in favor of apologizing and acknowledging that as the new Chief Medical Officer at the Royal Women's Infirmary, there was much work to be done in order to 'raise the standards of the institution to those in the West.' Dr. Lander seemed to open up under the circumstances, describing in detail the high standards required by the federal Ministry of Health, when it came to the hiring of doctors and nurses, paying special attention to qualifications, the origin of the qualifications, and the experience of doctors and other medical staff. 'The Ministry of Health has made it very difficult for us to hire the doctors and nurses we require, because of their high standards.' Derek couldn't help thinking that he wished the requirements were even *more* rigorous, considering their own current experience with the Royal Women's Infirmary.

Regarding the first point, the CMO supported Derek's position, stressing that 'Back in North America, doctors would be expected to employ medical terms that address the condition, as opposed to using prognoses, heavily laden with prejudgments.' Dr. Lander further agreed with Derek that the role of healthcare professionals was to support the psychological wellbeing of the patient in addition to the physical. The CMO assured Derek that this point was one of many he intended to incorporate into the professional training and protocol for the Royal Women's Infirmary. Derek felt a bit better following his conversation with the CMO, then turning his attention back to Kathy, returning to her room where he found her getting some much needed rest. He took the opportunity to relax a little as well.

Both Derek and Kathy were hoping for some positive news from the post-natal specialist. The Royal Women's Infirmary was known for its excellent facilities in the region for dealing with premature births and had a reputation for being able to successfully deal with 'premies' with a high survival rate. However, with the arrival of the postnatal specialist, the anxiety in Kathy's room rapidly rose. Quite clinically and matter-of-factly, the doctor explained how, statistically, the probability of an infant's survival after birth gradually rose throughout the pregnancy, giving examples of different ages as calculated by weeks of gestation. He went on to add that 'The policy at the Royal Women's Infirmary was to not resuscitate a prematurely born infant if the baby was not either at the weight of 500 grams, or 23 weeks old.' He went on to add that, 'a less developed fetus would, most likely, not survive, and even if it did, it would probably have severe physical and/or mental problems.'

Both Derek and Kathy were horrified at what they were being told. Derek, not believing he could have heard the specialist correctly, asked the doctor directly, 'So, if I am understanding your correctly, if our baby is not quite 23 weeks AND weighs less than 500 grams, the hospital will not assist her to live?' This the doctor confirmed, and went on to mention that at present, Kathy's fetus weighed approximately 420 grams, and was only 22 weeks and 3 days old. Therefore, should Kathy's baby be born within the next 72 hours, and be unable to survive on its own, that the infirmary would have no choice but to let things take their natural course. The post-natal specialist then completed his visit with a brief wish for Kathy and Derek's success in this situation–and departed. Hearing all of this enraged Derek, and sent Kathy back into fits of tears, wailing, 'Why can't this all just be over with?' Derek stayed with Kathy through dinner, and into the late hours of the evening, until his wife finally drifted off to sleep.

The next morning, February 19, Derek, bright and early, was at his computer, desperately searching the Internet for information concerning gestation periods, premature births, and survival rates, when he came across a very interesting article about a prematurely born infant in the United States, who was younger than their child, weighed less, and who had been successfully delivered and cared for. With a newly found sense of victory and hope, Derek seated himself at the computer, and typed a letter to Dr. Lander:

Dear Dr. Lander,

Further our conversation concerning the use of the term"inevitable", I thought I would share the article below. This baby was born at roughly the same age as ours is now-only weighing much less than ours. I would like assurances that your medical staff will give our baby every opportunity to survive-even if born at or around 23 weeks.

Born at just 22 weeks-Amilla is not yet allowed home
By NICK McDERMOTT
February 2007

A girl born after just under 22 weeks in the womb-among the shortest gestation periods known for a live birth-will remain in a hospital a few extra days as a precaution, officials said.

Amillia Taylor, who weighed less than 10 ounces (283 grams), had been expected to be sent home this week. However, routine tests indicated she was vulnerable to infection, said Dr. Paul Fassbach, who has cared for the baby since shortly after she was born.

"She has been fine," Fassbach said, but doctors are being extra cautious "now that she's going into the world."

Doctors say she is the first baby known to have survived after a gestation of fewer than 23 weeks. But full-term births usually come after 37 to 40 weeks. Amillia was just 9 1/2 inches long and weighed less than 10 ounces when she was delivered by Caesarean section. She now weighs 4 1/2 pounds.

She has suffered respiratory and digestive problems, as well as a mild brain hemorrhage, but doctors believe the health concerns will not have major long-term effects.

"Her prognosis is excellent," said Dr. Paul Fassbach, who has cared for Amillia since her second day.

Amillia was conceived in vitro and has been in an incubator since birth. She will continue to receive a small amount of supplemental oxygen even after she goes home.

Her parents Sonja and Eddie, from Homestead, Florida, were visiting friends in Miami when Mrs Taylor went into labour at just over 19 weeks pregnant, having conceived by IVF. Doctors attempted to delay the birth but eventually were forced to carry out an emergency caesarean.

Amillia Taylor weighed just under 10oz and was only 9 1/2 inches long at birth Dr Guillermo Lievano, who delivered Amillia, said he was not expecting her to survive.

"I was prepared for the worst and prepared to break the bad news to the mother."

Amillia responded to treatment, however. During two months in an incubator, she even had plastic surgery after her left ear was partially torn off during the delivery.

"I'm still in amazement," said Mrs Taylor, 37, a teacher. "I wanted her to have a chance and I knew in my heart that she was going to make it."

"It was hard to imagine she would get this far. But now she is beginning to look like a real baby. Even though she's only 4lb now, she's plump to me."

Ten ounces of determination: Amillia was little longer than this pen William Smalling, neo-natologist at Baptist Children's Hospital in Miami, said: "She's truly a miracle baby. We didn't even know what a normal blood pressure is for a baby this small." Amillia's incredible story will reignite the debate over Britain's abortion laws, which campaigners say must be updated in the light of recent medical advances. Babies can still be aborted for non-medical reasons at up to 24 weeks. Recent evidence shows that, of those born at 25 weeks, half of them manage to live.

Source: http://www.dailymail.co.uk/health/article-437236/Born-just-22-weeks-- Amilla-allowed-home.html#ixzz0fvcOQQdv

Kindest regards,
Mr. Derek Sullivan

(No acknowledgement or response was ever received by Derek.)

Derek arrived at the Royal Women's Infirmary just in time to join his wife for breakfast. Kathy seemed to be in good spirits–all things considered. Derek and Kathy were introduced to a new duty nurse, who proved to be very experienced and especially sensitive to their situation and concerns. Over the next several hours, the RN took a special interest in Derek and Kathy, and they in her. She agreed with them that there were some serious problems at the infirmary, but assured then that she would do her best to assist them in any way she could. Just having a professional individual who genuinely cared seemed to lift Derek and Kathy's senses of confidence and even hope that things still might work out positively for them and their child. Lunch was brought, and both Derek and Kathy slumbered much of the afternoon, and into the evening. Just after 9 pm, Derek was suddenly awoken by Kathy's calls for help. Their days of anxiety and stress had just turned into a catastrophe–Kathy's cervix had started bleeding.

For three hours, the bleeding was on-and-off. The head nurse was systematically changing Kathy's bandages and monitoring the baby. Just after midnight on February 20, the fetal sack was exposed to the point that it was obvious there would be no reversing the situation. The post-natal specialist was busy in the incubation unit, so the miscarriage was handled by the head nurse, assisted by the duty nurse. At 22 weeks and 5 days, Kathy and Derek's baby was delivered–but did not survive the natural birthing process. No option of a C-section (Caesarean section) was ever given by the medical staff. The vital signs of the infant were normal, prior to the birthing process. But bruising, caused by the passing of the baby through the cervical canal, could be clearly seen on the back of its tiny body. The duty nurse brought Kathy and Derek a tiny sweater for the motionless baby, along with a small Bible, and left them alone to begin the grieving process. Derek and Kathy could do nothing more than to gaze at their little lost one–and weep together.

AFTERMATH

Within hours of the tragic loss of their little girl, Derek and Kathy were pestered by the administration of the hospital to produce a valid and attested marriage certificate, as 'intimate' relations and births outside of marriage were illegal within the region. Further, burial of the child had to be arranged. As Derek and Kathy had no experience or contacts for shipping the small corpse back to their country, they opted to have the hospital provide the service–not knowing that once the release form had been signed, the infirmary would not divulge when, where, or how the service would be carried out. Derek was given two weeks compassionate leave by his employer, during which time he visited the CEO of the Royal Women's Infirmary, feeling that he, Kathy, and the baby had not received the kind of treatment they deserved, or was the norm for a world-leading healthcare management company from the West. The CEO was reluctant to admit any improprieties from the infirmary's side, and when Derek mentioned possible litigation, the CEO seemed to threaten him by retorting that, 'You should know that this is a government owned hospital, and in this region, anything owned by the government is protected.' Derek then pointed out that he could always sue the company in its home country, to which the CEO responded, 'Good luck, but don't plan on working in this region any longer.' At which point the CEO briskly indicated that he was meeting somebody for lunch and left the building.

Kathy and Derek never got over the loss of the child, feeling that things could have been different had the Royal Women's Infirmary given them better treatment. As much as Derek and Kathy wanted a second baby, the whole experience had damaged Kathy's self-confidence to the extent she no longer believed in her own physical ability to produce another healthy child. Needing his employment, and not knowing how to go about it–especially from abroad, Derek never took legal action against the international healthcare management company; although he continues regretting this decision. Several months later, Derek and Katy met a couple, through a friend, who were currently having a similar experience with the Royal Women's Infirmary. Like Derek and Kathy, the couple had experienced a complication with the pregnancy, and had rushed to the urgent care unit during the night–also, not having their health insurance card with them. However, in this case, the CMO did not happen to stop by and intervene. Instead, the pair were escorted off the hospital premises. During the process, the woman's water broke, and they nearly lost the twins she was carrying. Luckily, her husband was able to withdraw enough cash from an ATM machine to appease the local administrator, who eventually allowed the woman to be admitted into the hospital.

REFERENCES

About university hospital consortium. (n.d.) The University Hospital Consortium's official website. Retrieved from http://www.cancernz.org.nz/reducing-your-cancer-risk/.

Lasagna, L. (1964). *Evolution of medical ethics: Hippocratic oath modern version*. Retrieved from https://owlspace-ccm.rice.edu/access/content/user/ecy1/Nazi Human Experimentation/Pages/Hippocratic Oath-modern.html.

Chapter 7

Always Trust the Customer:
How Zara has Revolutionized the Fashion Industry and Become a Worldwide Leader

Eric Viardot
EADA Business School, Spain

EXECUTIVE SUMMARY

This case study illustrates the effectiveness of pursuing a customer centric marketing approach in order to achieve long term strategic success and market leadership in the fashion industry. The case study provides the most significant elements of Zara's history. Then it describes the competitive environment. Next it reveals how Zara has set up a unique, lean, and agile supply chain strategy in order to deliver new products on a very frequent basis and faster than any of its competitors, as fashion customers expect constant changes. Then the case study details the customer centric marketing strategy, with the use of customers as the source of the inspiration for fashion design, the central role of the stores to build a very high level of trust with its customers, which is used by Zara to make a distinctive brand strategy. Finally, the case study discusses the new challenges that Zara customer centric marketing strategy is meeting when confronted with the expansion on the Chinese market and the online market.

DOI: 10.4018/978-1-4666-4357-4.ch007

Copyright ©2014, IGI Global. Copying or distributing in print or electronic forms without written permission of IGI Global is prohibited.

On this nice day of June 13, 2012, Pablo Isla, CEO of Inditex was enjoying the presentation of the last result of the company about the first quarter of 2012. The revenues were up by 27% compared to the same quarter in 2011, beating the forecast of the analysts by more than 13%; Net margin was also up and even better, for the first time ever, was equal to that of archrival H&M at 14.1%. This was just the confirmation that Inditex, with its flagship brand, was now the unconditional world-wide leader in the apparel industry.

Furthermore, in the latest edition of the Global RepTrak™ 100, a study measuring corporate reputations worldwide Zara was the only Spanish brand in the ranking, confirming the extremely good image of the company. Zara, the oldest brand – or concept as described by Inditex was the most important for the group. With 1830 stores in 84 countries, Zara represented 65% of the revenues but almost 80% of the margin.

BACKGROUND

The amazing success of Zara-and Inditex-is closely linked with his founder, Amancio Ortega Gaona. He began his career in 1963 as a clothing manufacturer. The business grows steadily over the decade until Ortega owns several factories, which distribute their merchandise to other European countries.

In 1975, Amancio Ortega opened the first Zara store on a street in downtown La Coruña, Spain in 1975. The expansion strategy which made a small Spanish clothing firm into the undisputed worldwide leader in apparel can be described in three phases: First came the national development in Spain, then the international expansion in Europe and in the US and Latin America (1988-2003), and finally the global surge in Asia and the rest of the world. There were about 1750 Zara stores in 80 countries. Zara was also extremely successful in China and online Zara shop was planned to be launched in summer 2012 for the winter season opening in China.

As illustrated in Figure 1 the rise of Zara and Inditex has been extraordinary. From 1991 to 2003, Zara sales grew more than 12-fold from €257 million to €3.220. From 2003 to 2008, the company managed to double its size. By August 2008, sales edged ahead of Gap, making Inditex the world's largest fashion retailer and Zara the worldwide leading brand in the apparel industry. From 1991 to 2011, the compound average growth rate is about 18.5%, meaning that Zara has managed to double its size almost every 4 years! This commercial success reflects the importance of growth in the Zara culture. The founder Ortega likes to repeat that "a company that does not grow will die." Ortega stepped down as CEO in 2011 leaving the place to Pablo Isla, but he is still very involved in the strategic decision of the company.

THE INDUSTRY AND THE COMPETITION

In the apparel industry, Zara global's main competitors are H&M, Gap, & Benetton.

Hennes & Mauritz AB, also known as H&M, is an apparel and accessory store founded in 1947 in Sweden known for offering the latest fashion trends. H&M is the world's second biggest-selling clothing retailer and it has proven to be a very aggressive competitor for Zara. H&M specializes in taking advantage of the season's latest looks inspired by design houses around the world and providing women, men, and children contemporary clothing styles at low prices. Targeting the 18 to 34-year-old market, the company manufactures affordable, stylish clothing. H&M operates more than 2,500 stores in 43 countries, with more than 200 stores in the U.S. Its brand has a strong recognition worldwide.

Gap built its iconic casual brand on basics for men, women, and children first in providing jeans, khakis, and T-shirts which had become the standard fashion in the U.S. in the 1990's from hip teens to suburban moms to Sharon Stone, who wore a Gap turtleneck to the Oscars in 1995. The group expanded with the urban chic chain Banana Republic and chic at a discount Old Navy. The diversification was initially successful but entered in trouble in the mid 2000's as the brands went too deep in their concept and frustrated the clients who switched to fresher competitors. Gap experienced a decrease in revenues and market share as well as financial losses. Since then, it seems that Gap struggles to recapture customers who have abandoned

Figure 1. Inditex sales and net income from 1975 to 2011

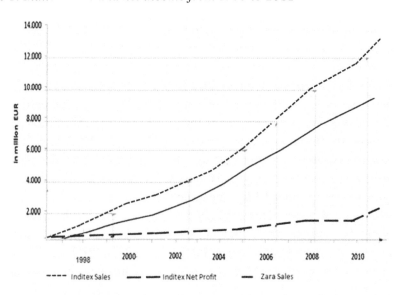

Source: Inditex annual reports and documents compiled by the author

it though it has some hit products like the Perfect Black Trousers in 2010 or the special collections in collaboration with Stella McCartney. In 2011, Gap operates about 3,200 stores worldwide. It has sold more than 150 stores in the US because of the competition of specialty retailers like Abercrombie & Fitch and low price fashion specialists like H&M and Zara.

Benetton, created in 1965 in Milano, Italy, has always emphasized brightly colored knitwear. It achieved prominence in the 1980s and 1990s for its controversial advertising. Benetton's model is based on an integrated production model with an outsourced go-to-market organization. All the production is sold through a network of more than 6,500 franchised stores in 120 countries generating over €2 billion. While Benetton was fast at certain activities such as dying, it had long production cycle time as it is it looked for its retailing business to provide significant amount of orders before starting its manufacturing operations. This model has proven ineffective to keep up pace with the accelerated high fashion pressure by Gap, then H&M, and now Zara. The company has recently reorganized and is getting significantly faster in fabrication and store delivery.

The apparel industry is still very fragmented geographically. Thus, Zara is also facing many local champions such as American Apparel (US), Kookai (France), Next (UK), C&A (Germany-Belgium), Uniqlo (Japan), or Lojas Renner (Brazil).

ZARA BUSINESS MODEL: BUILT TO BE FAST

Fashion customers expect constant changes so new product have to be available on a frequent basis (Bruce and Daly, 2006). Thus fashion companies are using time as a factor of competitive differentiation. And on that matter, one of the characteristics of Zara is its ability to be the fastest among its competitors. The typical retailer needs an average of six months to design a new collection and then another three months to manufacture it. But the average time for a Zara concept to go from idea to appearance in store is 2 to 3 weeks. In 2008, when considering the time from creation to delivery, Zara was 12 times faster than Gap and five times faster than H&M (the second best in class in the apparel industry).

Furthermore, Zara is not only faster but also "fresher", as it is also able to offer ten times more unique products, as the collection are changing every three weeks. In 2011, Zara had created around 40,000 new designs and had sold worldwide roughly 900 million garments.

Such amazing results are made possible by the unique approach of the supply chain. Zara is able to be so alert because it is vertically integrated and it has a deep symbiosis with its-mostly locals-suppliers; it is also making a very effective use of the technology for just-in-time manufacturing, and finely it has set up a world class logistics to swiftly deliver its products to the stores.

While H&M has 900 suppliers and no factories, nearly 60% of Zara's merchandise is produced in-house in 23 highly automated factories which are located in Galicia, a remote location in North West Spain with no special tradition in clothing.

Zara attempts to keep its offering simple, with usually just three sizes and three colors. The raw material is bought in large volume to save cost. The cloths are cut by computer-guided cutting tools which follow the patterns made from selected designs. About half of the clothes are made undyed so the firm can respond quickly if there are some fashion shifts at mid-season. The dyes come from Zara's own subsidiary and the dying is performed by robots. Inventory optimization models help the firm determine how many of which items in which sizes should be delivered to stores during twice-a-week shipments, ensuring stores are stocked with just what they need.

Then the prepared fabric pieces are sent to local subcontractors for the sewing of the garments to using seamstresses in cooperatives. In this part of Spain, Zara is usually their only client. They have worked with Inditex so long they are not even written contracts. They receive a flat fee per type of garment, and they operate on short lead times and fast turnaround. They are all located close to the main central facility of Zara in La Coruña, meaning that Zara has a better control on transportation delays and quality management and "sunk cost" (Popp, 2000; Hines, 2001) than if it was sourcing overseas.

Zara relies also on third parties in low-cost manufacturing locations, mostly in Turkey and Asia, for its "staple," collection items with minimal fashion content, such as t-shirts, jeans, lingerie, and woolens. They usually have a longer shelf life than the fashion driven garments and this outsourcing policy is made in order to save costs. Those items represent 40% of the total volume but only 15% of the total value of Zara products.

Zara has been a forerunner in developing a Quick Response (QR) supply chain where product specifications are finalized very closer to delivery. The goal is to reduce excess stocks and risk associated with forecasting (Birtwistle et al., 2003) as companies acknowledge that QR can result in forecast accuracy as high as 95 percent (Mattila et al., 2002) adjust to the ever changing taste of its "fashionistas", Zara manufactures only 15 to 20 percent of production before the season begins. 50 percent is made at the start of the season and the remainder is manufactured in-season. In comparison, most of the other apparel companies are committing 80% to 90% of their production in advance of the season.

Furthermore, Zara has managed to change the timing of the collection. Luis Lara, a former commercial Director at Zara, says, "the season used to start in September, but we moved it to August, and then to July so we could get more information from the customers about their desires and incorporate them earlier in our production planning."

All the items are then sent to one of the nine distribution centers located in Spain with a total of more than 1,000,000 square meters. The biggest one is in La Coruña and sizes 500,000 square meters, about the size of 65 soccer fields. The facilities move about 2.5 million items a day, with no item staying in-house for more than 72 hours. Using renewable energy systems, the logistics centers are heavily automated with ceiling-mounted racks and customized sorting machines. All garments are ironed in advance, packed on hangers, attached with security and price tags, and finally sorted out to be prepared for shipping.

All the shops that can be reached overnight all over Europe (about 75 per cent of deliveries) are served by the firm's trucking fleet powered by biodiesel. Farther destinations (about 25 per cent) are supplied by chartered cargo flights from Air France-KLM Cargo and Emirates Air. Flights are coordinated so that after the outbound shipment of Inditex products, the return legs are loaded with raw materials and half-finished clothes items from locations outside of Spain. "This system enables a product to get from the distribution centers to the European stores in an average of 24 hours, 48 hours in America and Asia" (AR 2010). Shipments tend to have almost zero flaws, with 98.9 per cent accuracy and under 0.5 per cent shrinkage.

This well organized machine has not been built from scratch: It has been made along a trial and error process. The only difference with the competition is that Zara has learnt faster from its own errors than the rest of the apparel makers. The lesson for Zara is summarized by Ortega: "To be successful, you need to have five fingers touching the factory and five touching the customer", meaning that the company must control what happens to its product until the customer buys it.

This very integrated and sophisticated production and logistics model has been designed not to be fast *per se* or in order to beat the competition. It has been conceived by M. Ortega and then constantly refined during Zara expansion with only one goal. To better serve the customer and to adapt quickly to its new desires and expectations. And the location in Spain, a country which is not known for being the cheapest as far as the labor cost are concerned, participates to the same customer oriented philosophy. Says Pablo Isla, the CEO, "Proximity sourcing is extremely relevant to us, to be able to react during the season and to maintain flexibility."

For the same reason, there is a strong emphasis on communication within Zara. "An on-going and fluid relationship between store, personnel, design teams is essential for being able to react to changes in customer desires with new products in store as quickly as possible" (Annual Report 2010).

Thus Zara´s supply chain can be described as "leagile" (Van Hoek, 2000; Bruce et al., 2004) as it combines the lean and agile supply chain management to respond to changing markets (Naylor et al., 1999; Abernathy, 2000). With such a configuration, the use of information technology is essential to share data for fast and accurate data in order to improve the visibility of the requirements. On that matter, Zara relies on its own information technology system, which is completely proprietary and far from the standards of the IT market. In fact, Zara's IT infrastructure is relatively simple but completely in line with the needs of the company. This, means that for the same level of performance- or even better-its IT expenditure is less than one-fourth the fashion industry average (Sull & Turconi, 2008).

FASHION FOR CUSTOMERS

It is often said that Zara is about Fast Fashion, but actually Zara is about Customer-Centric Fashion. Zara is fast because fashion shoppers like to change and Ortega was the first to create a company which listen to its customers and which does not try to impose a model created by some "iconic" or "creative" designers. Zara´s total orientation to the customer is the origin of its fabulous development. "The customer is the engine for all our activity. It is the star of our business model" states the official presentation of the company in the 2011 annual Report.

Amancio Ortega says: "the customer must continue to be our main centre of attention, both in the creation of our fashion collections and in the design of our shops, of our logistical system and of any other activity." The strategic supremacy of customers in Zara business model is engrained in the mission and vision of the company: "Zara is in tune with its customers, who help it give shape to the ideas, trends and tastes developing in the world. This is the secret to its success among a wide range of people, cultures and generations, who, despite their differences, all share a special fondness for fashion."

The typical Zara customer as identified by the company is a person who is up to date with the latest developments in the fashion industry and wants fashionable, trendy, and unique outfits at affordable prices. There is no geographic, demographic, or economical element in this understanding of the customer. Years ago, the typical Zara customer would have been described as the Chica Zara, the typical Spanish woman between 25 to 40 years old. But today the Zara shopper can be a man, a woman, a teenager, or even a child, located in every place of the world where fashion is important, typically large cities where people do have a reasonable purchasing power and an appetence for style and mode.

One key consequence of the customer centricity of Zara business model is that Ortega has turned the basic rules of fashion upside down. Since the time of "haute couture" in France and then Italy, the business has been dominated by powerful – and often- talented designers who were "deciding" what would be the fashion of the year. Top designers of today such as Tom Ford, John Galliano, Stella McCatrney or Ralph Lauren are influencing the trends in fashion. They work also for retailers which are using their design to manufacture massively the same model, outsourcing the materials and the manufacturing, before piling the clothes in thousands of distribution outlets while spending millions of euros or dollars to advertise their product and influence the consumers and drive it to the shop.

"Zara does not sell high-cost, aspirational fashion that needs a massive marketing and advertising campaign behind it to sell the 'dream'. They are about being realistic and achievable," says Nancy Georges retail strategist and author of the recent book, *7 Powerful Ways to Boost Retail Profit*. Zara sells accessible, wearable, and instant fashion that the customers have either seen the look on the catwalk and can't afford it, or they want new fashion at a mid-range price. Zara was described once by a Goldman analyst as "Armani at moderate prices". Zara's garments look like high fashion, but are significantly less expensive. The quality of the product is good and if Zara's offering is sometimes referred to as clothing to be worn six to ten times; it is due to the ever changing tastes of Zara customers not because of the poor quality of the items.

Using its customers as a source of ideas and inspiration, Zara is skilled at picking up the latest trends in fashion. Its team of almost 300 young and unknown designers creates designs based on the latest styles from the catwalk and other fashion hotspots, which are effortlessly adjustable to the mass market.

For instance, stories abound about the fact that some years ago after Madonna's first concert date in Spain during a recent tour, her outfit was copied by Zara designers. By the time she performed her last concert in Spain, some members of the audience were wearing the same outfit (Kumar & Linguri, 2006). In 2003, when the Crown Prince of Spain announced his engagement to Letizia Ortiz, she wore a white trouser-suit for the occasion. In just three weeks, the same white trouser-suit was available in all European Zara shops where it was snatched up by hundreds of European women.

On an average, Zara generates an amazing 40,000 items a year versus 2,000 to 4,000 items presented at other large chains like H&M and Gap. And those products fit extremely well with the fashion conscious customers of Zara. Take a recent testimonial about Zara from Liz Jones, one of the leading fashion trend setters in the UK press: "The brand has executed all the key trends extremely well. The bags are brilliant as are the shoes. When once there were rows and rows of black courts, there are myriad funky flats on offer and peep-toe platforms in hot pink and orange. The accessories beat Marks & Spencer hands down. Yes, Gap does swimwear better, M&S does better undies, Banana Republic does better workwear, and Cos does simple sporty separates extremely well, but if you are looking for a few pieces to take on holiday, there are colorful kaftan shirts, drawstring silk or linen trousers, and wacky T-shirts...." Those are the typical comments of Zara's clients.

With its global expansion, Zara pays close attention to catering to the various climates and weather-based trends of each geography. Some apparel retailers recycle their European or North American seasonal collection six months later in Australia, South Africa, or South America. But Zara produces separate collections targeted specifically for its northern and southern hemisphere stores.

Once the garments are made, Zara send them out quickly to all its stores in the world. As the CEO, Pablo Isla comments: "The vertical integration of our production system allows us to place a garment in any store around the world in a period between two to three weeks." Actually, if an item is demanded by enough customers, it can be in their Zara stores to accommodate that request within 10 days.

This unique combination of a large number of customer driven references and the ability to manufacture and delivered them quickly provides another unique and valuable competitive advantage to Zara: its ability to have a new collection every three weeks in the store. This is extremely appealing to "fashionistas". Actually, Zara has global average of 17 visits per customer per year, much higher than the average five to six annual visits to its competitors.

With this fast fashion model Zara manages to create a climate of exclusivity, opportunity, and scarcity, which is exactly what fashion shoppers are looking for. It brings customers into stores to see what is new, what they must not miss, and what they must own before it's gone forever. What is truly extraordinary is that Zara was the first fashion apparel to come with this new disruptive approach.

For instance, when Zara opened its first store in the United kingdom, on the trendy London's Regent Street, shoppers went browsing without shopping, thinking they would come back later to buy during a discount sale. Then the store assistants explained that the collections were changed every two weeks, and the style liked by the customer would very likely not be available later or even ever. Thus, if they wanted something, they had to buy it now. Customers got the message and Regent Street became one of Zara's most profitable stores while more stores opened in the UK.

Some customers are getting so hooked to the Zara style that they get up early at the date when the next collection is delivered by the "Zara truck" in order to be the first to enjoy the wider choice of the new offer that may not last long. And when they enter the store they know the newest items arrive on black plastic hangers before store staff transfer items to wooden hangers afterward. In some cases, there are stores which are running out of stock. However, Zara does not view this as a negative since it reinforces the shoppers' perception of the uniqueness of their purchase.

Zara's objective is not that consumers buy a lot, but that they buy often. To do so they have to find something fresh every time they enter the store. Hence Zara changes its designs very quickly and offers only limited quantity during a restricted amount of time. An additional benefit of producing in small quantities is that Zara saves on cost, should a design not be very well-received.

Zara customer centric model is to be responsive to fashion items that are selling well during the season, and to discontinue those that are not. Says Jesus Echevarria, Director of Communication: "There is no point in sticking to one set of designs if customer feedback is that certain pieces are not popular. We only want to put pieces in-store that customers are happy with, and that suit their current and changing styles and taste."

With such a policy of scarcity and just-in-time, Zara does not have to rely heavily on discount prices like its competitors: Zara's unsold items account for only 10% of the total stock while the average for the industry is between 17 to 20%.

Another expression of Zara commitments to its customer is to apply the Inditex own standards of health and safety described as "Clear to Wear" and "Safe to Wear" which have been put in place since 2006 and are in a constant evolution. Those standards are in accordance with the most demanding regulation at the world level. For instance, the group realized more than 70,000 chemical analyses per year and has set up a whole array of statistical evaluation tools. The company describes those standards as being part of its corporate DNA and their compliance is absolutely mandatory for the suppliers. The corporate motto on that matter is that a safe product begins with responsible design and ends with the correct marketing procedures.

Clear to Wear standards guarantee that all Zara products do not involve any risks for the health and safety of the clients. Most notably, the company seeks the elimination or the regulation of the use of substances of legally limited uses which, if they are present in the product above certain levels, might be harmful.

Safe to Wear standards are designed to prevent Zara products for presenting problems for the physical safety of customers. They are related to lace and cords in small pieces in clothing for kids under 3 years old, clothing for users under fourteen years old, objects with pointed or sharp edges, and inflammability of garments.

THE IMPORTANCE OF THE STORE AS THE POINT OF CONTACT WITH THE CUSTOMER

The store is the cornerstone of the Zara Customer centric approach. The store is where the company´s business model starts and ends, with the customer as its main asset.

In January 2012, Zara reported 1,830 stores in 84 countries, with a net addition of 113 new stores in 2011. The company was planning to open between 125 and 130 new stores in 2012, in other words, one new store every 3 days!

Everything is made at the store to welcome the fashion customers. This includes a privileged location in main cities, meticulously planned show windows and a uniquely conceived architecture inside and out, a precise product coordination, and an excellent customer service.

Privileged Locations

Like for any retail business, location is a key success factor in order to get the maximum traffic of prospects and customers. In the case of Zara, this is even more critical as the store is the only way where Zara is connecting with its customers. This is due to the fact that since its creation and contrary to the rest of its competitors, Zara has never invested in advertising especially at the level of brand building. Its brand strategy is based only on word-of-mouth which reinforces the sense of exclusivity and scarcity. Zara products are never advertized: the customer has to enter the store to see them. If they like the collection they will tell to their friends and social relations to hurry before it goes out of stock!

Zara spends just 0.5 percent on advertising while other clothing retailers spend 4-5 percent of sales. The little it does spend goes to reinforcing its identity as a clothing retailer whose goal is to 'democratize fashion'. While competitors will use high-profile celebrities to endorse their product and generate sales, Zara relies only on its stores to communicate its brand image. Consequently Zara locates its store in busy, prestigious, and city centre shopping streets.

More specifically, the first store in a new country acts as a flagship for the future stores to be opened. So Zara looks for upscale locations in the world's largest cities such as the Champs Elysée, in Paris, France, the most expensive commercial location in Europe in 2011, which sees 500,000 people per day during the week and up to 750,000 on the week-end.

With the globalization and the raise of the brand image of Zara, the inauguration of a new Zara store is now a wonderful event for public relations as huge crowds of aspirant shoppers are waiting the opening of the new shop and then grabbing what they can get before it is sold out. Recent inaugurations in Shanghai, Moscow, Sidney, and 5th Avenue in New York City have been incredibly popular and have generated –for free- a high exposure of the Zara brand name in all the media, the traditional ones as well as the digital ones.

Zara has a special organization in charge of scouting for prime real estate along established shopping corridors. Zara plans its arrival in various countries over a long period of time, and is patient in waiting for the right opportunities. Says Echevarria: "Wherever we plan to open a new Zara store, we will do research into the areas we feel are suitable for our brand, and choose locations that are prominent in each city. We are patient in this process and, if nothing comes up, we will not compromise, but, instead, wait until a good opportunity arises".

Meticulously Planned Shop Windows and Interior Architecture

Beside locations, shop windows–shop fronts in Zara terminology-are the second element that Zara uses to communicate its brand image. Zara communication strategy is based on the belief that an iconic physical store well located and a well-designed window front are very effective at attracting shoppers. Store windows are critical for Zara to remain visible and entice customers to visit, enter, and buy.

The displays are changed regularly, in synchronization with the arrival of the new collection. The goal is that all persons walking past a Zara store should be greeted by a beautiful window display where the latest designs are exposed so that they would instinctively want to enter the store, browse through the collections, and try on a few outfits.

All the store windows are designed centrally in La Coruña. Zara has a full team of window front designers who constantly travel around to our international locations to understand the culture and customers of each store. They then come back and create the window design that is unique to the store in an artistic and attention grabbing way. Next all the props and details are then shipped to each store managers and are put up under strict guidelines.

Though the shop front is centrally designed and managed, the store manager is allowed to change the displays on the shop mannequins which are at the entrance and within the store. On the average, those mannequins are change every two to three days; it gives the impression to the customers that something has changed within the Zara store and may lure them to enter.

The same kind organization is used for the design of the lay-out of each store. A centralized dedicated team mixing designers and merchandisers aggregate all the information from the inside and the outside in order to create the most truly attractive arrangement for the Zara customers so that they get a unique and rewarding experience. In the words of Liz Jones: "I find shopping in Zara exciting, but not overwhelming. There are fewer clothes crammed on rails, so everything can breathe. Trends are grouped well; it feels 'cool', and wearable: it's not scarily 'fashion'. Nothing is over decorated."

This centralized organization is made to save time to the store manager and employees which do not have to think about the lay out and the equipment of the store windows and can focus on more productive activity. This makes even more sense when one considers that a typical Zara shop will change its shop windows and the store lay-out between 18 to 26 times in a year, in line with the arrival of new collections. Furthermore, the centralization is a good way to ensure the same level of quality in all the shops all over the world. It also reduces costs in sourcing and production of all the accessories as the centralization allows economies of scale. The central designers' team can also build knowledge as it consolidates all the feed backs coming from the stores about the commercial impact of a new concept of window. The errors are quickly acknowledged and not repeated while the successful concepts are extended to other shops in other markets.

Precise Product Coordination and Customer Feed Back

Being customer centric, Zara has managed to become an expert in figuring out the kind of products that fashion-enthusiast customers are looking for. And it all starts at the store with the collection of information through a mix of quantitative and qualitative methods.

Zara has equipped all the store managers with handheld PDA devices that are linked to the store's Point-Of-Sale (POS) system and show how garments rank by sales. The PDAs are also used to gather clients input as staff regularly chats with customers to gain feedback on what they'd like to see more, asking about the preferred length of a shirt or the desired color for a trouser, or the most desired neck for a kind of shirt. They also casually check which outfit on the catwalk do they like, or which celebrity's get-up are they coveting.

At the end of the day, when doors are closed, the staff finds other customer information in analyzing the piles of unsold items that customers tried on but didn't buy. They often reveal if there are any preferences or disappointment in cloth, color, or styles offered.

Then, in less than an hour, managers can send updates that combine the hard data captured at the cash register combined with insights on what customers would like to see. The data are compiled at a central analytics facility using a sophisticated but robust proprietary software program, designed especially by and for the company. Analysts look for patterns in customers' shopping trends and use their findings to advise store managers on how to adjust merchandise layouts to maximize sales and product turnaround.

The PDAs are also used for the ordering by each store, both for replenishment items as well as new products. This is critical for the company as the goal is to deliver just what the customers want and to have the lowest stock possible. It is also important for the store managers, as a part of their remuneration depends on the accuracy of their sales forecasts and sales growth.

Each evening the newest designs which are available for order are sent digitally by headquarters. Order deadlines are twice weekly, and are issued via the PDAs. Store managers who fail to order by the deadline receive replenishment items only. Deliveries arrive at stores twice per week from Zara headquarters a few days after the order is made.

Zara store operations are designed so that the store staff is completely dedicated to sell and to help customers find what they want. All store logistical operations are centralized to save time. Similarly, all garments are ironed in advanced, packed on hangers, with security attached directly at the central logistical centers in Spain. Thus employees in Zara stores have only to move items from shipping box to store racks and spend the rest of the time catering the customers. Efforts like this help store staff regain as much as three hours in prime selling time.

Zara knows that retailers are only as successful as their sales staff and is not thrifty in terms of resources. In 2011, 9,374 new jobs were created by the group meaning about 2000 new jobs for Zara. The company invests also significantly in training: 87% of the Company work in stores and more than 80% of the Group's training investment targets store staff.

Store training plans have an extremely practical focus on subjects such as customer service, product, and recent fashion trends. The training concentrates also on the capacity to capture and formalize the information received from clients each day. In order to have standard quality training of store personnel, Zara has specific instruction materials with guidelines, advice, and periodic evaluations in addition to other content that helps both trainers and apprentices. Among these materials, the Zara´s store organization manuals are particularly important and are constantly updated. They include detailed information on all aspects of the in-store work and detailed information on Zara and Inditex.

All the store managers have the manuals available for use by the employees in any concrete situation. For example, in the case of Zara in 2010 there was special emphasis placed on new procedures required in the stores as a result of introduction of online sales via Zara.com in some European countries.

Zara employees are also self motivated with a strong commercial culture which was set up by the founder. Luis Lara says, "Zara has a very powerful customer oriented culture: everything is made for the customer. The stores are there to welcome the customers and the central operations are there to support the store. I have never seen at Zara the kind of conflict which is so typical in retail, between the shops and the central, them vs. us. The commercial corporate culture is very strong and those who cannot fit in do not stay very long". Another important element of the Zara culture is autonomy and common sense. Zara employees like to try things, they're not afraid to make a mistake, and they react fast in order to try to improve.

Excellent Customer Service

Attention to the customer is another area to which Zara pays most attention, mainly as the content of periodical training for the teams in the stores. Zara sees customer service as the key enabling chains to attend to customer desires as swiftly as possible. More than 80% of the company training budget targets store personnel and customer services is one of the areas that is most emphasized on training days.

In addition, customers have other communication channels with Zara for resolving any questions regarding products or the organization that could not be dealt with in the store. A specialist professional team offers personalized service to all customers who require it, by phone, e-mail, or post and in several languages so as to make the query easier.

During 2010, Zara's customer services have been reinforced with the launch of the chain's online store in European countries. The online store has a team of over twenty people for attention by phone or e-mail in eleven languages in working hours.

Furthermore, all the Zara store teams and the regional management teams of stores or offices in the countries in which the online store is operative have received specific training in online customer services, as the customer who shops at Zara. com can pick up his or her order at any store in the chain in these countries.

The limited number of complaints received by the chain indicates that the service is efficient. Overall in 2010, 117,421 queries were attended by the company customer service channel, a figure which has to be compared with the roughly 850 millions of item sold. This same year, using official figures from Consumer Authorities, the company reported a complaining ratio of 0.002% per garment from Spanish customers.

The unique approach of "fashion for customers" combined with the pivotal role of the store allows Zara to built a very high level of trust with its customers. Various authors have underlined the importance of trust to successful relationship marketing (Morgan and Hunt, 1994; Berry, 2000; Palmatier et al., 2006). While various studies have proposed different characteristics of trust, the most commonly used characteristics are honesty, reliability, fulfillment, competence, quality, credibility, and benevolence (Kantsperger & Kunz, 2010). The customer centric marketing stategy of Zara address perfectly those various dimensions. Most specifically Zara has developed a strong ability to demonstrate its benevolence to the customers when they are in the store. Benevolence is based on the degree to wich customers believe that the company is motivated to act favorably and positively in the interest of the customers ´welfare (Kumar et alii, 1995), and that is reflected in an emotionally secure feeling of the customer (Delgado-Ballester & Munuera-Alemn, 2001).

A DISTINCTIVE BRANDING STRATEGY

In another striking difference with the rest of the fashion industry, Zara spend very few money in advertising. Its budget is about 0,5% of annual sales while the average advertising budget for its competitors is between 4 to 5%. "Advertising is about building up expectations, and telling customers what they can expect and what we can deliver. At Zara, we want expectations to come from the in-store experience and to come from the customer's personal journey and satisfaction from shopping at Zara" says Echevarria.

With such a customer centric branding strategy, there is no opportunity for disappointment and there is no way for Zara to give false promises. The brand name is built essentially with the word of mouth of satisfied customers telling, and showing, their family, friends and social relation how pleased they are to shop at Zara. And it works! Indeed, in the 2012 ranking of the 100 top brands in the world by MillwardBrown, Zara is ranked 66 and it stands out as the third most valuable brand in the apparel category, behind Nike ranked 44, and H&M, ranked 58. Even more interestingly, the brand value of Zara is evaluated at $M 12,616 while H&M´s is only 7% superior at $M 13,485 as shown in Table 1.

The Zara strong brand recognition is confirmed with its position as being in the 82th position in the Reputation Institute evaluation of the world's most reputable companies. In this survey, H&M shows slightly ahead at the 76th spot while Nike is number 15.

Thus, Zara has managed to enlarge the trust related to individual shop or employees to the trust towards the entire company through positive word of mouth and smart public relation communication. This trust in the entire company is particularly relevant in service chains where the service is performed by changing personnel (Kandampully, 2002). Then consumer trust can be converted into value and loyalty in relational exchanges (Sirdeshmukh et al., 2002; Grayson et al., 2006; Brodie et al., 2009).

Table 1. Value of the leading worldwide apparel brand

#	Brand Name	Brand Value $M	#	Brand Name	Brand Value $M
1	Nike	16,255	6	Uniqlo	3, 689
2	H&M	13,485	7	Hugo Boss	3,257
3	Zara	12,616	8	Next	2,973
4	Ralph Lauren	5,086	9	Metersbonwe	1,395
5	Adidas	3,863	10	Calvin Klein	1,183

Source: http://www.millwardbrown.com/BrandZ/Top_100_Global_Brands/Categories/Apparel.aspx

The powerful brand image of Zara is an important asset as the trust generated between a customer and a brand is central to mutually beneficial relationship (Lymperopoulos et al., 2010) that leads to customer satisfaction and loyalty (Ball et al., 2004; Kenning, 2008). For instance, the Reputation Institute estimates that if a company improves its reputation by 5 points, the number of people who would definitely recommend the company goes up by 7,1%. It contributes also to a steady price policy as it was shown in 2011: in time of economic recession and pressure to discount, Zara–and H&M-were the two companies which managed to get most of the full mark up for their products because consumers, perceiving value, switched to these brands.

A CUSTOMER CENTRIC PRICING STRATEGY

In order to reinforce its image of leader in the democratization of fashion, Zara offers affordable prices in order to encourage purchases. But its pricing policy differs by country markets. For instance, Zara products are low-priced in Spain, while in China, Australia, and Japan, they are priced as a luxury fashion items, as illustrated in Table 2 which indicates the price of a Zara Summer dress in various locations. Figure 2 provides another price comparison of 12 different items in 7 countries.

Similarly, the price will vary from one location to another. Fashionista.com, a famous fashion news site, reports that the average spending at Zara is $92.03 in New York and $68.05 in Miami on the basis of data collected from customer credit card transactions.

Being a customer centric company with an intimate knowledge of the clients reaction, Zara sets prices according to individual market conditions, rather than using the "cost plus margin" like most of its competitors. When it comes to competition, Zara generally prices its products somewhat higher than C&A and H&M, but below Gap, Next, and Kookai.

Prices are managed centrally: they are marked in the stores with a device that reads the bar code, gets the correct local price from the headquarter information system, and prints the label before it is put on the item.

Table 2. Price of one summer dress in a Zara chain store

Barcelone	26	euro
Madrid	29	euros
Paris	35	euro
London	43	euro
Los Angeles	37	$
Seoul	40	$
New York City	43	$
Milan	45	$
Shanghai	51	$
Mexico city	51	$
Beijing	58	$
Sydney	72	$
Tokyo	74	$

Source: www.numbeo.com

Figure 2. Price differences of 12 Zara products in different countries

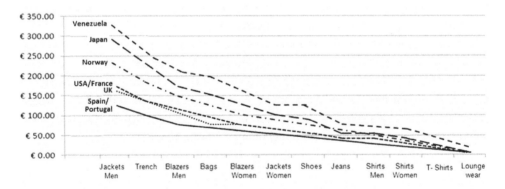

Source : https://gupea.ub.gu.se/bitstream/2077/25661/1/gupea_2077_25661_1.pdf

THE ROUTES TO EXPANSION

Table 3 shows clearly the avenues for Zara future expansion. While Zara home market relative importance is declining, the rest of Europe and America stay unchanged and Asia keeps on growing. Consequently, Zara has recently increased its focus on two markets: China and the Internet: China is identified as one of the key market for the future and as the leading territory for Zara expansion in Asia. On the other hand, Zara sees the development of the digital market as a way to revitalize the mature European market and a solution to accelerate its penetration of the US market, its online offer is also a diversification in order to reach digital fashionistas who are living outside of the affluent cities that Zara is targeting. Thus Zara will also launch its Zara on-line in China in September 2012, ahead of other Asian countries.

Zara in China

Zara was the first brand with which Inditex entered the Chinese market in 2006. Since that date, it has been increasing its number of stores at a steady pace and five years later it had 275 stores in China, with 120 Zara stores representing about 43% of the total. Inditex had a goal of opening 150 new shops in 2012 including about 60 new Zara stores. Table 4 shows the evolution of the Zara stores opening in China.

Zara was one of the first apparel makers to go to China, following the Uniqlo which first came to the Chinese market in 2002; H&M followed in 2007 and Gap in 2010. All of them have just begun to tap the market and have still room for growth. As indicated in Table 5, Zara has 120 stores in China, while Uniqlo has 64, H&M has 33, Benetton has 25 and Gap has five. By contrast, Nike and Adidas, which entered in the early 1980s for the former and in the early 1990s for the later have about 6,000 stores each in the country, many of them franchises.

Table 3. Relative evolution of revenues 2010-2011 by geographical area and perspectives

Area	2010	2011	Trend
Spain	28%	25%	↘
Rest of Europe	45%	45%	→
America	12%	12%	→
Asia and RoW	15%	18%	↗
Total	100%	100%	

Source: Inditex Annual report, compiled by the author

Table 4. Evolution of Zara stores opening in China

Year	Number of Openings	Total Stores
2006	1	1
2007	12	13
2008	10	23
2009	21	44
2010	21	65
2011	55	120
2012*	60	180

*·Forecasts.

Source: Inditex Annual Reports compiled by the author

When Zara came into China, it had to adapt to the specificities of this appealing but sometime difficult market for western companies. There was a strong potential as the growth of the Chinese economy had been fueled by a burgeoning demography combined with the political stability of its one-party system and the deregulation of most sectors including a new textile policy. The country is gigantic, with a clear difference between rural and urban culture. There are also differences at the urban level between people living in the 6 large megacities of more than 10 million people (Beijing, Shanghai, Chongqing, Guangzhou, Shenzhen and Tianjin), those living in the 120 cities that have more than 1 million people and the 440 other cities. The cultural Confucian conflict between status projection and self protection, between upward mobility and fear-based conformism is also typical of the Chinese society, especially since the late nineties where increasing wealth and the opening society has allowed the Chinese to express their individuality through fashion.

But Zara is doing well in China. It has found that urban Chinese fashionistas are not that different from the European Zara girl. Chinese office ladies like Zara's slim fits more and Chinese women choose pastels to flatter their pale skin rather than the stronger colors Europeans prefer; but otherwise they have surprisingly similar tastes, says Iria Campos a Zara designer. The Zara brand appears also to be one those brands which help customers to resolve their Confucian inner conflict by allowing them to simultaneously stand out and fit in.

Table 5. Relative stores presence of foreign apparel retailers in China in 2011

	GAP	Benetton	H&M	Zara	Uniqlo
China	5	25	33	120	64
Total	3095	6500	1988	1830	930
%	0,13%	0,38%	1,66%	6,55%	6,88%

Source. www.slideshare.net/empan/zara-in-china

The apparel market perspective in China looks very promising as Chinese consumers are expected to continue to grow in strength and sophistication according to a recent report from the Boston Consulting Group. Fashion shoppers in their 20s and 30s, who were born after the Cultural Revolution, already, outspend the urban average by 18 percent. They are ignorant of the rough conditions that their parents had lived when they were their age and many of them have a good job at a foreign or local company; accordingly they are much more optimistic and prone to spend for themselves. In addition, women living inland or in "low-tier" cities are also expected to spend more on fashion over the coming decade. Consequently, annual fashion expenditures should triple from $67 billion in 2011 to 200.7 billion in 2020.

Zara is ready to grab a good piece of this market with its customer centric approach. It will keep up to open new stores but it will also adapt its offer. Says Echevarria: "Zara is a constantly evolving brand and with our designers travelling to Asia and learning the trends and fashion preferences of our new consumers, this will definitely influence our future collections".

Internet

Using the store has its primary point of interface with the customer, Zara has been deliberately slow in embracing the Internet. Its first online experience came with after-sales services. It proved to be extremely successful: in 2009 more than 85% of the total customer queries were made on-line.

Zara online was officially launched in September 2010 and was made available in eleven countries and 14 languages. In 2011, Zara online was rolled out in the US, Japan, Switzerland, Monaco, Sweden, Denmark, and Norway. In 2012, it should be launched in China for the Autumn-Winter season.

Zara online has been designed as a support to the physical store, and not as a replacement. The goal is to provide a new service to Zara customers and with a purchasing experience that is as close as possible to the physical store. It has been conceived as a showcase for Zara to demonstrate its fashion options and maintain a close and direct relationship with its customers.

The www.zara.com website has been designed to make online shopping as consumer friendly as possible. The garment search function has been enhanced by a number of filter options (by garment characteristics, colors, sizes, prices, etc.). Shoppers can also find specific items by reference number, garment description, category, and so forth. Garment prices are identical online and in-store. Customers can view their shopping baskets at any time while browsing, editing their product selections right away. Clients can either have the products deliver at home or pick up their orders at a conveniently located store choice within a period of three to five days. In that latter case, the website provides a store search and mapping tool in order to to help them to automatically locate the nearest Zara store. For home delivery, clients can choose between three options: Standard, Express, and Defined Date Delivery. Shoppers opting for standard delivery receive their orders at home within two to four days. With the express delivery, the orders are delivered within 24-48 hours, except specific areas. The Defined Date Delivery is a special option in which shoppers can choose the date and time of delivery at no extra charge. All product orders are wrapped in purpose-designed eco-friendly packaging which keeps purchased garments in an optimal state until delivery. Payments can be made using major credit cards.

The exchange and return policy is identical to that offered in-store: during a 30-day period any unwanted items can be picked up at home or returned to Zara stores. In each country were the online store is available, Zara has hired a logistics operator with a proven track record in the field to handle nationwide distribution. Site users can also call toll-free customer service or write to a dedicated e-mail address for help with order-related queries or problems.

Additionally, Zara online website displays visual content of the collections with photos, lookbooks, videos, and a fashion collaboration section called "People!" so that shoppers can get an overall impression of the current range. Moreover, this content can be shared on the various social networks. Users can also sign up for a newsletter to stay abreast of the latest fashion trends.

Zara.com had more than three hundred people (graphic designers, retouchers, sales people, models, stylists, IT people, customer service, and logistics people, among others). It has also the unconditional and permanent support of all Zara teams, especially the stores team, which have had specific training regarding the new channel in order to give better customer service at the point of sale.

The online store team work closely with the Zara design and sales teams, as well as with the chain coordination and show window teams. This is essential given that it has become one of the prime fashion show windows.

Indeed, the popularity of the online "store", as it is called in the group about Zara online, has been growing fast: the Zara website had 33,5 million visitors in 2010 and ten time more at the end of 2011. In March 2012, the CEO was mentioning in an interview that the site was receiving more than one million visitors a day! This does not include the millions of Zara followers in social networks. For instance, in March 2012 Zara had 13.070.961 fans on Facebook and was ranked as the 24th most popular worldwide brand pages; the other apparel brands in the ranking are Victoria´s secret, number 15, and Adidas Original, number 22.

With Zara online, the company wanted first to rejuvenate its customer base in its European mature markets. In Spain for instance, where Zara has a leading market share of 9,8%, studies showed that only 2.7% of women between 30 and 50 years old –the fashion's biggest customer segment in Spain–go online to shop for clothes.

The main reason is the absence of physical contact with the merchandise which is making those fashionistas uncomfortable. But teens and young women do not have those inhibitions: they go shopping online or offline at their whim. With the introduction of Zara Online, the company had a 34,5% market share in the Apparel category in 2011 with revenues of € 35,2M representing 1, 6% of its total sales in Spain. Recent figures from Euromonitor international forecast a steady growth of the sales of apparels over the internet in Spain with a 87.7% CAGR over the period 2012-2016, as illustrated in Table 6.

Spain has been lagging behind the rest of Europe in terms online sales, both in term of buyers and amount, and is now catching up (see Table 7). But overall, digital sales have a good future in all Europe, where consumers are increasingly getting used to shop over the Internet. According to Forrester, Europeans online sales will increase 10% year-over-year from now until 2015, matching the growth rate of online retail in the U.S. The consumer electronics category will lead the expansion, increasing its share of the e-commerce market from 25% to 28% by 2015; shoes will grow 13% year-over-year and clothing, the second-largest category, will generate €21 billion in online sales in 2015.

In the US, Zara online should allow the company to expand faster in order to reach its target market of fashion conscious young women aged 18 to 25 who have the Zara brand in high regard, are digitally agile and do not have any kind of reluctance to shop over the net. As Zara is nationally recognized, it is much cheaper to launch a Web store than to invest in real estate in 50 more malls in the U.S.

The competition is severe as some apparel retailers such as Gap for instance have been selling items online for more than a decade. But the Zara logistic model is better tuned to its online strategy than its competitors and is likely to be more profitable than rival H&M´s. Zara can deliver products from its distribution centers in Spain to the U.S. within 48 hours while H&M has to invest in distribution in the U.S., since it doesn't make its own clothing and relies exclusively on suppliers. It is estimated that Zara yearly online sales could reach €1, 4 billion by January 2014, just three years after the inauguration of the website representing 7% of the total sales in the U.S.

Table 6. Internet retailing forecasts for apparels category: value 2011-2011

Year	2010	2011	2012	2013	2014	2015	2016
Total Apparels M€	85,1	101,9	116,7	134,4	156	175,1	191,1

Source: Euromonitor International, International Retailing in Spain, May 2012

Table 7. Online commerce penetration and average online spend

	France	Germany	Italy	Netherlands	Spain	Sweden	UK	EU-17
Online buyers as % of online population	59	66	34	70	34	70	72	57
Average Spend per buyer online (€)	445	495	270	386	255	344	871	517

Source: Forrester Research Online Retail Forecast, 2012 to 2015 (Western Europe)

CONCLUSION: THE CHALLENGES AHEAD

Looking forward, Zara has some clear challenges to meet in order to keep its number one position in the apparel industry and to keep on growing. First, the Zara formula has not worked everywhere, like in America, for instance, where Zara has struggled; the company has reacted with the launching of its online store in 2011 and the inauguration in March 2012 on New York City's Fifth of the New Zara Global Concept Store which is going to become the global standard for all the Zara stores in the world.

Zara is also susceptible to conditions to the Spanish market which is still making 25% of its revenues. As Spain has been entering a severe recession since the beginning of 2012 that could have an impact on Zara sales for the next coming years.

In addition, being a worldwide leader generates also political issues. In 2011, China's consumer watchdog attacked Zara for poor quality. The firm denies that it was singled out for political reasons but the Chinese government routinely targets large foreign firms for minor lapses, as in other cases like Google, McDonald's, Danone, or Carrefour. Also in 2011, Zara was accused in Brazil of using suppliers who were running sweatshops with Bolivian workers brought illegally to Brazil for their outsourced production. Since that date, Inditex has strengthened the supervision of all its outsourced production operations and had produced a code of ethics with strict conditions mandatory for all its suppliers.

Finally, competitors do not stay idle and are catching up. Though they cannot break their company and rebuild it from scratch in order to duplicate Zara, they have reduced the gulf between them and Zara. Gap has moved production away from Asia and closer to home. Adopting Zara commercial approach, H&M has increased the frequency of new items in stores; similarly, Benetton now frequently updates its collections and it replenishes its stores as fast as once a week. Other fast fashion rival like Renner rolls out mini-collections every two months while Forever 21 and Uniqlo stores get new looks within 6 weeks.

But Zara is confident: its customer centric model is the best way for continuing growth and profitability. Concludes Echevarria: "In the last 40-over years, Zara and Inditex have risen to where we are based on flexibility and understanding our consumers. This will continue to be our principle and, if changes are necessary, we will respond with what is best for the company and for our customers".

REFERENCES

Abernathy, F. H. (2000). Retailing and supply chains in the information age. *Technology in Society, 22*, 5–31. doi:10.1016/S0160-791X(99)00039-1.

Ball, D., Coelho, P. S., & Machas, A. (2004). The role of communication and trust in explaining customer loyalty. *European Journal of Marketing, 38*(9/10), 1272–1293. doi:10.1108/03090560410548979.

Berry, L. L. (2000). Relationship marketing of services–Growing interest, emerging perspectives. In Sheth & Parvatiyar (Eds.), Handbook of Relationship Marketing (149-170). Thousand Oaks, CA: Sage.

Birtwistle, G., Siddiqui, N., & Fiorito, S. (2003). Quick response: Perceptions of UK fashion retailers. *International Journal of Retail & Distribution Management, 31*(2), 118–128. doi:10.1108/09590550310462010.

Brodie, R. J., Whittome, J. R. M., & Brush, G. J. (2009). Investigating the service brand: A customer value perspective. *Journal of Business Research, 62*(3), 345–355. doi:10.1016/j.jbusres.2008.06.008.

Bruce, M., & Daly, L. (2006). Buyer behaviour for fast fashion. *Journal of Fashion Marketing and Management, 10*(3), 329–344. doi:10.1108/13612020610679303.

Bruce, M., Moore, C., & Birtwistle, G. (Eds.). (2004). *International retail marketing: A case study approach*. Oxford, UK: Butterworth-Heinemann.

Delgado-Ballester, E., Munuera-Alemn, J. L., & Yague-Guillen, M. J. (2003). Development and validation of a brand trust scale. *International Journal of Market Research, 45*(1), 35–52.

Grayson, K., Johnson, D., & Chen, D.-F. R. (2008). Is firm trust essential in a trusted environment? How trust in the business context influences customers. *JMR, Journal of Marketing Research, 45*(2), 241–256. doi:10.1509/jmkr.45.2.241.

Hines, T. (2001). From analogue to digital supply chains: Implications for fashion marketing. In Hines & Bruce (Eds), Fashion Marketing, Contemporary Issues (34-36). Oxford, UK: Butterworth-Heinemann.

Jones, L. (2012). *Fashion therapy, Daily mail.* Retrieved from http://www.dailymail. co.uk/femail/article-2160686/LIZ-JONES-FASHION-THERAPY--Why-Zaras-step-ahead.html#ixzz1z5C003rV.

Kandampully, J. (2002), *Services management: The new paradigm in hospitality.* Melbourne, Austrailia: Pearson Education.

Kantsperger, R., & Kunz, W. H. (2010). Consumer trust in service companies: A multiple mediating analysis. *Managing Service Quality, 20*(1), 4–25. doi:10.1108/09604521011011603.

Kenning, P. (2008). The influence of general trust and specific trust on buying behavior. *International Journal of Retail & Distribution Management, 36*(6), 461–476. doi:10.1108/09590550810873938.

Kumar, N., & Linguri, S. (2006). Zara fashion sense. *Business Strategy Review, 17*(2), 81–84. doi:10.1111/j.0955-6419.2006.00409.x.

Kumar, N., Scheer, L. K., & Steenkamp, J.-B. E. M. (1995). The effects of perceived interdependence on dealer attitudes. *JMR, Journal of Marketing Research, 32*(3), 348–356. doi:10.2307/3151986.

Lymperopoulos, C., Chaniotakis, I. E., & Rigopoulou, I. D. (2010). Acceptance of detergent-retail brands: The role of consumer confidence and trust. *International Journal of Retail & Distribution Management, 38*(9), 719–736. doi:10.1108/09590551011062457.

Mattila, H., King, R., & Ojala, N. (2002). Retail performance measures for seasonal fashion. *Journal of Fashion Marketing and Management, 6*(4), 340–351. doi:10.1108/13612020210448637.

Morgan, R. M., & Hunt, S. D. (1994). The commitment-trust theory of relationship marketing. *Journal of Marketing, 58*(3), 20–38. doi:10.2307/1252308.

Naylor, J. B., Naim, M. M., & Berry, D. (1999). Leagility: Integrating the lean and agile manufacturing paradigms in the total supply chain. *International Journal of Production Economics, 62*, 107–118. doi:10.1016/S0925-5273(98)00223-0.

Palmatier, R. W., Dant, R. P., Grewal, D., & Evans, K. R. (2006). Factors influencing the effectiveness of relationship marketing: a meta-analysis. *Journal of Marketing, 70*(4), 136–153. doi:10.1509/jmkg.70.4.136.

Popp, A. (2000). Swamped in information but starved of data: Information and intermediaries in clothing supply chains. *Supply Chain Management: An International Journal, 5*(3), 151–161. doi:10.1108/13598540010338910.

Sirdeshmukh, D., Singh, J., & Sabol, B. (2002). Consumer trust, value, and loyalty in relational exchanges. *Journal of Marketing, 66*(1), 15–37. doi:10.1509/jmkg.66.1.15.18449.

Sull, D., & Turconi, S. (2008). Fast Fashion Lessons. *Business Strategy Review, 19*(2), 4–11. doi:10.1111/j.1467-8616.2008.00527.x.

Van Hoek, R. (2000). The thesis of legality revisited. *International Journal of Agile Management Systems, 2*(3), 196-201.

Chapter 8
Consumer Behavior Perspective for Fairness Creams:
A Case of 'Fair & Lovely'

Yasser Mahfooz
King Saud University, KSA

Faisal Mahfooz
Ogilvy & Mather, India

EXECUTIVE SUMMARY

The market for fairness creams around the globe was an untouched territory till mid-1970s. No cream was available which could claim an effect on the fairness of skin. The first product for this market was Fair & Lovely (Fair & Lovely) by Hindustan Unilever Ltd (Hindustan Unilever Ltd.:HUL) which was launched in India in 1975. It was a turning point for the fairness cream business and several companies followed soon. Fair & Lovely didn't take much time to become a household name with more and more women putting their trust in the product for giving them the much needed fair skin they always desired. A product which started as another addition to the product line, acquired the status of a super brand by 2004. It became a part of the customer's persona. In a society where the general population is genetically brown in skin color, yet has resentment to it; fair color of skin is an obsession and is equated with beauty, happiness and success. This craze for fair skin is marketed aggressively and a range of products are available in the market, which gratify the likes of teenagers as well as grown women. The following case on the product Fair & Lovely gives a background of the market for fairness creams in India and focuses on different aspects of behavior of women as consumers of this product.

DOI: 10.4018/978-1-4666-4357-4.ch008

Copyright ©2014, IGI Global. Copying or distributing in print or electronic forms without written permission of IGI Global is prohibited.

ORGANIZATION BACKGROUND: HINDUSTAN UNILEVER LIMITED

Hindustan Unilever Limited (HUL) is India's largest fast moving consumer goods company, with leadership in home and personal care products, as well as foods and beverages. HUL brands vary from soaps to soups, which meet the need of consumers from the morning cup of tea to the brushing routine at bedtime. With over 35 brands spanning 20 distinct categories such as soaps, detergents, shampoos, skin care, toothpastes, deodorants, cosmetics, tea, coffee, packaged foods, ice cream, and water purifiers, the products are used by around 700 million consumers across India (HUL Magazine, 2012). Brands like Axe, Lux, Liril, Lifebuoy, Pears, Vim, Surf, Cif, Rin, Wheel, Closeup, Brooke Bond, Bru, Clinic Plus, Fair & Lovely, Pond's, Lakmé, Vaseline, Sunsilk, Kwality Wall's, Kissan, Knorr, and many others have become household names. HUL shares the mission of its parent company which is working to create a better future every day.

The company has over 16,000 employees and has an annual turnover of around Rs.19, 401 crores (Financial year 2010-2011). HUL is a subsidiary of Unilever, one of the world's leading suppliers of fast moving consumer goods with strong local roots in more than 100 countries across the globe with annual sales of about €44 billion in 2011. Unilever has about 52 percent shareholding in HUL (HUL, 2012).

For the financial year 2010-11, a major share of revenue was from soaps and detergents (44.6%), personal products (29.7%), and beverages (11.9%). Whereas the total expenditure of the company segment wise shows a different trend. The highest investment was for personal products (54.6%); followed by soaps/detergents (30.5%), and beverages (13.1%) (HUL Annual Report, 2012).

One big reason for the focus on personal care products is the targeted growth rate of 15% year-on-year for the next five years; which is due to the continuous growth seen by domestic players, and the entry of multinational companies through innovative products. The industry has recorded eight per cent growth in the last few years (Jha, 2011).

The personal product portfolio of HUL comprises of soaps (Dove, Lux, Lifebuoy, Pears, Hamam), shampoos (Clinic Plus, Sunsilk), Toothpaste (Closeup, Pepsodent), and face cream (Ponds, Lakme, Fair and Lovely). Out of all the products of HUL, Fair & Lovely is playing a decisive role in the companies' personal care business with a presence in more than 30 countries and over 250 million consumers. HUL continues to dominate the Rs. 1,800-crore women's fairness cream market in India with an over 70 per cent share (Pinto, 2011).

PRODUCT BACKGROUND: FAIR & LOVELY

People across Asia have demonstrated a marked preference for skin lightening and glow. Over 90 percent of women in India cite skin lightening as a high-need area (Challapalli, 2002).

So, keeping in mind that a woman's passion for beauty is universal and there was a strong need to cater to it, this product was developed in 1975 (HUL, 2011a). This was based on a revolutionary breakthrough in skin lightening technology. Scientists at the Unilever Research Laboratories in India were the first to discover the skin lightening action of Niacinamide (Vitamin B3) that led to the development of a unique and patented formulation for Fair & Lovely in 1972 (HUL, 2011b).

The Fair & Lovely brand today offers a substantive range of products for women and men. For women they include Winter Fairness, Anti-marks, Forever Glow, Ayurvedic Balance, Multi-vitamin (Cream and Facewash), and Spot Erase Pen.

CASE OF FAIR & LOVELY

Lata Sharma bought a tube of skin whitening cream from a pharmacist in New Delhi, India, with the hope it will improve her daughter's chances of finding a handsome groom. "Let's face the truth. Fair skin is a ticket to a happy matrimony," Lata, 42, said while making payment for HUL's Fair & Lovely Fairness Cream.

Hindustan Unilever, L'Oreal SA, Beiersdorf AG, and several others target Indians with similar products pledging to make them more attractive and more successful by lightening their skin.

The fascination for fair skin has several reasons. One, dark skin is associated with labor and field work in the sun and fair skin with wealth and higher education. Another theory is that light-skinned conquerors from the Aryans to the Moghuls and European colonizers set the standard for attractiveness in the poorer colonies with their dark-skinned majority (Islam et al., 2006). The physical appearance of an individual plays an important role in contemporary society (Gill et al., 2005). Skin lightness affects perceptions of a woman's beauty and also her marital prospects (Li, et. al., 2008; Sarpila & Rasanen, 2010). It has further impact on success in the labor market, and especially on women's career, earning potential, and social status (Harkonen, 2008; Hamermesh & Biddle, 1994). People also have a preference for a person who is physically attractive (Andreoni & Petrie, 2008).

In India, a person with fair skin was considered to be a part of a higher class or caste and this complexion was an asset for them (Leistikow, 2003). Women in most parts, especially South India used to bathe with turmeric because of its properties related to skin lightening (Li, et al., 2008). India has a tropical climate with the maximum number of months having the sun shining. Moreover, the temperatures are rising day by day. These factors create a need for the otherwise darkened skin, due to over-exposure to the shining sun, to be lightened. Companies are reaching out to customers through wide range of fairness creams. Aloe vera extract, turmeric, vitamin-E, and lemon extract are some of the ingredients which form major formulations (ArticlesBase, 2009). Described as a 'dark skin product,' fairness creams are as popular in India as sun blocks or anti-ageing creams are in the West. The largest markets are in the states of Andhra Pradesh and Tamil Nadu, though skin color consciousness is highest among North Indian women (Bhatia, 2002).

An article in The New York Times noted, "Skin-lightening products are by far the most popular product in India's fast-growing skin care market, so manufacturers say they ignore them at their peril." Euromonitor International, a research firm, estimates the $318 million India market for skin care has grown by 43 percent since 2001. Half of this market is fairness creams with 60-65 percent of Indian women using these products daily (Melwani, 2007).

Similar products available in Indian market include CavinKare Fairever, Godrej Fair Glow, Pond White Beauty, Lakme Perfect Radiance, Shahnaz Husain Fair One, Nivea Visage Sparkling Glow, Avon VIP Fairness, Oriflame Natural Northern Lights, Olay Natural White, Garnier Light, L'Oreal White Perfect, Neutrogena Fine Fairness, and Elizabeth Arden Visible Whitening Pure Intensive.

CONSUMER BEHAVIOR ASPECTS

Motivation and Values

Motivation occurs when a need is aroused that the consumer wishes to satisfy (Solomon, 2011). Once a need has been activated, a state of mind exists that drives the consumer to attempt to eliminate or reduce the need. It is the process of influencing behavior of a person. Abraham Maslow proposed the hierarchy of needs theory with second last stage related to 'Esteem' with respect to self respect, autonomy, achievement, status, attention, and recognition (Robbins, 2000).

In an affluent society, individuals turn to goods and services to satisfy needs. Many products directly address the requirements of one or more of these need states (O'Guinn et al., 2009). Personal care products like fairness cream promote feelings of self esteem, confidence, attention, and recognition. According to McNeal and McDaniel (1984), esteem is the main need-appeal in personal product advertising. One way advertising works is to activate needs that will motivate consumers to buy a product or service.

Values represent basic convictions that a specific mode of conduct or end-state of existence is personally or socially preferable to an opposite mode of conduct or end-state of existence. Values help in the understanding of motivation in an individual, and influence his behavior (Robbins, 2000). It is a belief that some condition is preferable to its opposite. Values play an important role in the consumption activities, since many products and services are purchased because it is believed that they will help attain a certain goal (Presi, 2009; Solomon, 2011).

A research study (Kumar et. al., 2007) identified several cultural values for marketing in India. These values were categorized according to culturally-specific needs: allegiance to traditionalism, a need for belonging and contemporary values that are more likely to embrace western culture, and the forces of globalization. Contemporary values are focused on achievement and prosperity seekers, celebrity orientation and neo-mindset orientation of breaking conventions. This is why fairness creams find their place instead of conventional creams and moisturizers.

Advertising should appeal to consumer needs. An unsatisfied need is the motivation for a consumer to take action that attempts to satisfy that need, advertisers should and do attempt to depict how their products can satisfy a particular unsatisfied need (McNeal & McDaniel, 1984).

The advertisements and marketing strategies of HUL are specifically focused on the Motivation and Value aspects of individuals with interest in fairness products. Cultural values are important brand differentiators in emerging markets like India with heterogeneous consumer groups. The artful combination of cultural values and marketing communication strategies delivers a pioneering marketing exercise for any brand entering an emerging market (Kumar, 2009).

One advertisement from HUL portrays the desire of a middle-class girl to become a cricket commentator. The girl eventually succeeds, making her family happy. Success is made possible through use of Fair & Lovely which contributes to her self-confidence. The girl becomes a leading cricket commentator, winning the admiration of a well-known cricket celebrity. Incidentally, cricket commentary, until recently, has been an exclusively male activity. The values identified are individualism, self esteem, and recognition. The association of achievement by lightening one's skin is a message conveyed in the TeleVision Commercial (TVC).

In another TVC, a girl named Rupa has just finished college, and is on the lookout for a job and a husband. She has 'dusky' looks but to those who matter, she is plain dark. And they 'know' she doesn't stand too many chances of getting a good match. Rupa, a 21st century lass, though disheartened by her failure to find a guy or job, deals with it in a typically 21st century way. She is shown using a fairness cream with a result of jobs as well as eligible bachelors queuing up to win her hand (Challapalli, 2002).

Attitude

Attitudes are beliefs, emotional attachments and behaviour tendencies towards an object and have a strong impact on consumer behavior (Mason, 2005). It is considered to be a lasting, general evaluation of people, objects, advertisements, or issues (Solomon, 2011). Emotions are one of the sources for the formation of consumer attitude and behavior at the same time (Banyte et. al., 2007). Solomon (2011) argues that attitudes exist simply because they perform a particular function to a person.

According to the Cognitive Learning Theory of attitude formation, situations where consumers seek to solve a problem or satisfy a need, they are likely to form attitudes (either positive or negative) about products on the basis of information exposure and their own knowledge and beliefs (Schiffman & Kanuk, 2000). Attitudes make our lives easier because they simplify decision making; that is, when faced with a choice among several alternatives, we merely select the alternative we think is the most favourable (O'Guinn et al., 2009). The formation of consumer attitude is influenced by direct marketing and mass media. Mass media tools provide consumers with the information needed that helps building attitudes (Banyte et al., 2007).

According to Schiffman et al. (2010), consumers, who form their attitude towards a good and do not have a direct contact with the product, are more influenced by the message of advertisement in comparison with those consumers who have the experience of using the same product. So, it can be concluded that it is easier to affect consumers with no direct experience about the product by applying the means of mass media.

The advertising in HUL ranges from huge billboards splashed across strategic locations in the major Indian metropolitan hubs to radio, TV, and print media in leading magazines and newspapers. It is almost impossible to escape the widespread influence of the brand's advertising campaign. A typical print advertisement involves a montage of images of the 'Fair & Lovely woman' as she progresses through the various stages of the skin-whitening process. The Fair & Lovely model has come to be emulated as a brand character by millions of women across the nation who wish to be as successful as she is, with the promise of paler and more beautiful skin. Additional visual imagery, such as pastel-colored flowers (lotuses and roses), has been attached to fairness creams and has therefore become accepted as appropriate motifs for them.

Television advertisements for this product are more blatant in employing the promise of social and cultural benefits. One such advertisement depicts the dejection of a young girl upon being tormented by her father for not being born male, followed by him dismissing the limited job prospects she had as a woman due to her dark complexion. Subsequently, she uses the Fair & Lovely cream and impresses the interviewers with her newfound beauty, thereby securing the job and winning the approval of her father. Another popular advertisement on television shows a dark-skinned woman using the Fair & Lovely skin-whitening routine before the arrival of a prospective groom, who instantly falls in love with her due to the radiant glow on her newly beautified face. Some advertisements depict the benefits of having lighter skin in the professional beauty industry, as in another spot where the dusky woman aspires to be a model but does not qualify for the role till she discovers the benefits of Fair & Lovely moisturizer.

There have been several television commercials from HUL which highlight the belief, emotional attachments and behavior tendencies towards a fairness cream like Fair & Lovely. One such commercial is where a girl's father receives a call stating that the eligible groom's family will be visiting them next month for the engagement and to plan for the wedding. The girl overhears the conversation and states, "Let them come". This indicates her confidence as she is a regular user of Fair & Lovely. Further we are shown a party going on, where the prospective bride and groom are supposed to be introduced. The fiancé on seeing her is totally mesmerized by the beauty of his bride to be.

So, it was the belief and attachment of the female with Fair & Lovely which helped her through. She is portrayed as a regular user of the product and the effects of continuous use have been depicted.

Consumer Identity

A consumer's age exerts a significant influence on his identity. All things being equal, we are more likely to have things in common with others of our own age than with those younger or older (Solomon, 2011).

The four important age cohorts are teens, college students, baby boomers, and older adults. Teenagers are making a transition from childhood to adulthood and their self-concepts tend to be unstable. College students are an important, but hard to teach market. Baby boomers are the most important segment because of their size and economic clout. As the population ages, the needs of older customers become increasingly influential (Solomon, 2011). Even if they are not buying a product for themselves, they may influence the purchase decision of their younger ones. The reason for the purchase of a fairness cream might differ among all four listed cohorts. The advertisements and all other form of promotions have to be perfectly targeted for maximum results.

One of the estimations of the Indian personal care ingredients market was approximately $300-350 million, of which 16 percent was the skin care segment (Kadakia, 2009). The brand is marketed primarily to young women. The price of a standard tube of Fair & Lovely best suits the middle class and above, but it is sold in many convenience shops and drug stores in cities across India (Shevde, 2008).

According to the 4th Brandz 100 most valuable global brands report (Seddon, 2009), personal care brands are particularly vulnerable in the current environment, and several are attempting to improve their appeal to younger clientele. According to another report by Pilgrim Research and Consultancy on premium skin care products (Kaya, 2005), teen income through pocket money or call centre jobs is ensuring sufficient cash to spend on personal products. The target consumer profile for Fair & Lovely is in the age group of 18 and above. The bulk of the users are in the age group of 21-35 and the brand communication has always been targeted at this age group. Marketers are not yet targeting the 12-15 year olds because they do not want to dilute the image of their brands.

The age groups which house the bulk of fairness cream users are 20-29 years (35 percent), 15-19 years (22 percent), and 30-39 years (20 percent). The growing usage has made the fairness cream market of the order of Rs 1,500 crore in size, making it the largest segment in the skin cream market in India (Singh, 2009).

At the rural level, Fair & Lovely is being made available to poor villagers in the form of inexpensive sachets. South India (where the population is dominated by people with darker complexions) is the largest market, while the relatively fairer populations in Northern and Western India each have a smaller yet significant market share (Shevde, 2008).

The brand's positioning evolved based on the understanding of the evolving consumer. When the dreams and aspirations of the consumer were about getting the 'right partner in life,' the brand reflected that. Subsequently, the consumer evolved and even though getting the right man still remained important, it became more important to have a status change in life and to be more empowered. It is with this consumer understanding the central philosophy of Fair & Lovely has changed to women empowerment and allowing women to make their dreams their destiny and live life on their terms (Anand, 2009).

CONCLUDING THOUGHTS

Today, Fair & Lovely is marketed in more than 30 countries and has become the largest selling skin lightening cream in the world. Skin whitening and fairness creams have spread to other regions with dark skinned people like Malaysia, Egypt, Nigeria, and other African countries (Shankar & Subish, 2007).

In the beginning, Fair & Lovely was specifically designed to meet the needs of the middle-class Indian customer. The growing Indian middle class had become increasingly fashion conscious and was enjoying higher levels of disposable income and so it was launched with that specific target audience in mind. Unilever distributed the product widely in urban areas both at a micro level via corner shops, local retailers, drug stores, and chemists and a macro level via the cosmetic sections of larger departmental stores in malls and shopping plazas.

The role played by Indian Film Industry (Bollywood) in propagating the Indian obsession with fairness also deserves mention, given its social power as the largest film industry in the world. Famous light skinned celebrities in India, such as Sushmita Sen, John Abraham, Salman Khan are examples of this trend.

In the last decade, Indian women have won several International beauty pageants like Ms Universe, Ms World, and Ms Asia Pacific. Most of these beauty queens have joined the Indian film industry as actresses or have turned to modeling as a career. Advertisements tend to use these beauty queens and actresses to endorse beauty products.

Needless to say, Fair & Lovely has created a bone of contention between supporters and active users of the product and feminist groups, both of which adopt a very different approach to the issue of using fairness creams. While the former have no qualms in leveraging the product as a way to springboard out of social or economic constraints, the latter consider the very concept of make-up and grooming practices, such as skin-whitening, as pretentious lies (Shevde, 2008).

C.K. Prahalad, late professor at the University of Michigan, argued that the use of the fairness cream is 'aspirational'. The option, he said, makes them better off by providing real value in dignity and choice (Melwani, 2007). According to Karnani (2007), associate professor at the University of Michigan, the way to truly empower a woman is to make her less poor, financially independent, and better educated.

Consumers should be aware that a regular fairness cream will not give a complete solution. To address this condition, they are opting for products to get to a fair skin color. Fairness cream manufacturers have always been big advertising spenders and the message dished out has always nurtured the Indian beauty myth. Today the advertisements project fairness as a quality that is competitive, not just for the marriage market but also for the job market, but they still use prejudice of color. The advertisements put pressure on the woman and make her feel insecure for being dark. Fairness creams need to be positioned as any other beauty product.

Indian females are made to believe that fair skin is their key to success in their professional and personal lives and so the high demand of fairness products. The proposition that advertising was influencing women to use fairness creams was much debated. The majority of women have condemned the advertising of fairness products. Some are skeptical about the content of the product claims and some state their disbelief in the advertisements and did not use the fairness products. Marketers have exploited the notion of fair is beautiful to their advantage in promoting fairness creams. The notion whether fairness can be attained with a fairness cream is still debatable because no data is available on how they work and how effective they are. Still the market is open to new competitors as people do believe in advertisements and buy these products.

The current market has witnessed launches from many local and international brands. What remains to be seen is whether Fair & Lovely will maintain its superiority and leadership even in this high competitive market scenario.

REFERENCES

Anand, T. (2009). *Brand yatra: Fair & lovely-From getting a life partner to getting a life.* Retrieved from http://www.exchange4media.com/brandspeak/brandspeak_FS.asp?Section_id=42&News_id=35377&Tag=31042.

Andreoni, J., & Petrie, R. (2008). Beauty, gender, and stereotypes: Evidence from laboratory experiments. *Journal of Economic Psychology*, *29*(1), 73–93. doi:10.1016/j.joep.2007.07.008.

Annual Report, H. U. L. (2012). Growing sustainably. *Annual Report (2010-11)*. Retrieved from http://www.hul.co.in/Images/HULAnnualReport201011tc-m114268010tcm114268010.pdf.

ArticlesBase Online. (2009). Fairness creams-For the glowing skin. Retrieved from http://www.articlesbase.com/health-articles/fairness-creams-for-the-glowing-skin-930916.html.

Banyte, J., Joksaite, E., & Virvilaite, R. (2007). Relationship of consumer attitude and brand: Emotional aspect. *The Engineering Economist*, *52*(2), 65–77.

Bhatia, G. (2002). Cream and added color. Retrieved from http://www.outlookindia.com/article.aspx?214596>.

Challapalli, S. (2002). All's fair in this market. *Business line: The hindu.*

Gill, R., Henwood, K., & McLean, C. (2005). Body projects and regulation of normative masculinity. *Body & Society*, *11*(1), 37–56. doi:10.1177/1357034X05049849.

Hamermesh, D. S., & Biddle, J. E. (1994). Beauty and the labor market. *The American Economic Review*, *84*(5), 1174–1194.

Harkonen, J. (2008). Labor force dynamics and the obesity gap in female unemployment in finland. *Research on Finnish Society, 1*, 3–15.

HUL. (2011a). *Hindustan unilever limited-Our brands*. Retrieved from http://www.hul.co.in/brands/personalcarebrands/FairAndLovely.aspx.

HUL. (2011b). *Hindustan unilever limited-Know us*. Retrieved from http://www.fairandlovely.in/knowledge_center/about_fairandlovely.aspx.

HUL. (2012). *Hindustan unilever limited-Introduction to HUL*. Retrieved from http://www.hul.co.in/aboutus/introductiontohul/.

Islam, K. S., Ahmed, H. S., Karim, E., & Amin, A. M. (2006). *The whiter the better, 5*(94). Retrieved from http://www.thedailystar.net/magazine/2006/05/02/cover.htm.

Jha, D. K. (2011). Personal care industry set to grow 15% in 5 years. *Business Standard*. Retrieved from http://www.business-standard.com/india/news/personal-care-industry-set-to-grow-15-in-five-yrs/457480/.

Kadakia, P.; Nigam, A. & Rao, A. (2009). Outlook for personal care industry: An indian perspective. *Chemical Weekly*, 208-210.

Karnani, A. (2007). Doing well by doing good-Case study: 'Fair & lovely' whitening cream. Michigan Ross School of Business, 28(13), 1351-1357.

Kaya. (2005). *Consumer trends report*. Retrieved from www.pilgrim.co.in/images/kaya_report.pdf.

Kumar, S. R. (2009). Adapting IMC to emerging markets: Importance of Cultural values in the indian context. *Journal of Integrated Marketing Communication*, 38-42.

Kumar, S. R., Guruvayurappan, N., & Banerjee, M. (2007). Cultural values and branding in an emerging market: The Indian context. *The Marketing Review, 7*(3), 247–272. doi:10.1362/146934707X230086.

Leistikow, N. (2003). Indian women criticize 'fair and lovely' ideal. *Women's ENews*. Retrieved from http://oldsite.womensenews.org/article.cfm/dyn/aid/1308/context/archive>.

Li, E. P. H., Min, H. J., Belk, R. W., Kimura, J., & Bahl, S. (2008). Skin lightening and beauty in four Asian cultures. *Advances in Consumer Research. Association for Consumer Research (U. S.), 35*, 444–449.

Magazine, H. U. L. (2012). Doing well by doing good. *Hamara-The Hindustan Unilever Employee Magazine, 8*. Retrieved from http://www.hul.co.in/Images/HUL_75Years_Special_Issue_tcm114-194253.pdf.

Mason, K. (2005). How corporate sport sponsorship impacts consumer behavior. *The Journal of American Academy of Business-Cambridge, 7*(1), 32–35.

McNeal, J. U., & McDaniel, S. W. (1984). An analysis of need-appeals in television advertising. *Journal of the Academy of Marketing Science, 12*(2), 176–190. doi:10.1007/BF02729495.

Melwani, L. (2007). The white complex. Retrieved from http://www.littleindia.com/news/134/ARTICLE/1828/2007-08-18.html.

O'Guinn, T., Allen, C., & Semenik, R. J. (2009). *Advertising and integrated brand promotion* (5th ed.). Independence, KY: Cengage.

Pinto, V. S. (2011). Garnier steps on the gas. *Business Standard.* Retrieved from http://business-standard.com/india/news/garnier-stepsthe-gas/430274/.

Presi, C. (2009). Motivation and values. *LUBS5402 Consumer Behavior. Week Three Lecture,* 5.

Sarpila, O., & Rasanen, P. (2010). Personal care consumption in finland: Trends in the early 2000s. *The International Journal of Sociology and Social Policy, 31*(7/8), 441–455. doi:10.1108/01443331111149879.

Schiffman, L. G., Kanuk, L. L., & Kumar, S. R. (2010). *Consumer behavior* (10th ed.). Delhi, India: Pearson Education.

Seddon, J. (2009). *BrandZ top 100 most valuable global brands.* Retrieved from http://www.brandz.com/upload/brandz-report-2009-complete-report(1).pdf.

Shankar, P. R., & Subish, P. (2007). Fair skin in south asia: An obsession? *Journal of Pakistan Association of Dermatologists, 17,* 100–104.

Shevde, N. (2008). All's fair in love and cream: A cultural case study of fair & lovely in india. *Advertising and Society Review, 9*(2). Retrieved from http://muse.jhu.edu/login?uri=/journals/advertising_and_society_review/v009/9.2.shevde.pdf.

Singh, N. (2009). *Youngest user of fairness creams is just 12.* Retrieved from http://timesofindia.indiatimes.com/Business/India-Business/Youngest-ser-of-fairness-creams-is-just-12/articleshow/4371786.cms.

Solomon, M. R. (2011). *Consumer behavior: Buying, having, and being* (9th ed.). Upper Saddle River, NJ: Pearson.

Chapter 9

International Branding at Mirza International:
Dilemma Unsolved

Gautam Dutta
Indian Institute of Foreign Trade, India

EXECUTIVE SUMMARY

Today, due to globalization, enterprises are increasingly looking towards the global marketplace to market their products. The business opportunities in the foreign markets are no longer considered as only available to large multinational enterprises with long term foreign market presence. Enterprises today, regardless size, take part in a global competitive market which is supported by great advances in information technologies, communication, and transportation. This trend solves one of the main weaknesses found in comparatively smaller enterprises of traditional focus: home country market dependency. The case focuses on Mirza International Limited which originated from a small Indian Tannery business. The company is led by an ambitious, aggressive management team which has helped in achieving phenomenal growth. The company has emerged as a frontrunner in the manufacturing and marketing of footwear. Headquartered in New Delhi, the company markets its leather and leather footwear products, across the globe the UK, Europe, South Africa, the Middle East, and so forth. However, company management is now at a crossroads in regards to a more aggressive approach to international brand building for its product and strategic decisions. This case aims to address these issues regarding smaller company's internationalization and marketing. The case focuses on the dilemma often faced by medium sized firms from Asia in entering developed country markets in terms of branding or generic product development strategy. The case illustrates the differences in brand building that exist in a big multinational company and in smaller companies during internationalization.

DOI: 10.4018/978-1-4666-4357-4.ch009

Copyright ©2014, IGI Global. Copying or distributing in print or electronic forms without written permission of IGI Global is prohibited.

INTRODUCTION

It was mid-winter morning in Kanpur, an upcoming industrial town of northern India, and Mr. Irshad Mirza was standing in his sprawling office room pensively thinking how the globe was possibly shrinking for the Mirza International. It's something that the 1970's born, Mirza Tanners of Kanpur always dreamt of. Irshad, now the CEO of Mirza International, was struggling at that time with a small start up tannery business, but with a big dream of internationalisation. It was known in the tannery circuit of Kanpur that Irshad of Mirza Tanners always fought against the odds and strived hard to improve performance. Now, almost after four decade it is the time to celebrate the accomplishment. Red Tape, the flagship brand of Mirza International has not only helped the Mirzas in getting a foothold in the international market, it also assisted them in transforming a fledgling tannery business into one of the country's largest leather exporting companies. For a company that started as a small tannery and with occasional exports of handbags from Kanpur to countries in Western Europe owning an international brand of its own was a dream at that time only. Now, after four decades of ups and down the dream has become reality. It now owns the internationally popular 'Red Tape' shoe brand. Irshad knew that his initial zeal of capturing the world market helped Mirza International to cross this long way. The company has grown up as an export oriented company which now gets 80% of its business from abroad. Mirza International now sells products across 24 countries including the UK, Europe, South Africa, the US, Canada, New Zealand, and the Middle East. The success was such that Mirzas continue to supply shoes to some of the biggest retailers in the western countries including Next, River Island, Monsoon Dune, Oasis, and Harrods (Flourishing on Red Tape, 2009).

Irshad was remembering the bold decision made years ago to go all out for international branding and how he supported the move. In fact, it was the success of flagship brand 'Red Tape' in the UK in 1996 that gave Mirzas a foothold in the overseas market. "We realized that the trade margins were much higher when we sold shoes under our own brand. That was the trigger for starting Red Tape," remarked Tauseef Mirza, Irshad Mirza's younger son and director of Mirza International. Mirza's Red Tape branded shoes are sold through more than 350 outlets in the western markets. Britain itself has about 300 outlets Irshad recalled that his marketing strategy for projecting 'Red Tape' in foreign market as a premium brand really paid off. Because of his vast experience, Irshad knew that the branding decision, faced at that time by the company could be the most critical, but important yet. Irshad realized that his company must come out from behind the screen and should not end up as the supplier of the private label retailers only. Irshad knew that many small businesses like his continued in this way and remained unknown to the world due want of own brand internationally. It is not that all of them were not interested in creating their own brand. In fact, many thought about it, but made a retreat subsequently primarily because of substantial investments required in brand building and nurturing it in the distant markets. Even in case of Mirzas it is almost 85% of the shoes manufactured by them are sold through the retailers of the west under their own labels. It is only 15% of the company's total export that comes from from Red Tape branded shoes. Irshad, in fact, was confident that this pattern will be reversed in the days to come when Mirzas would be selling 85% of its production through their own brand internationally.

Though Mirza's Red Tape brand was more internationally known than nationally in the initial years, soon the company realized the importance of branding in the domestic market. Similar attempts were made to popularize Red Tape brand in its home country (i.e. India) and as a result about 40 exclusive stores are now operating across the country. The shoes of the company are sold under the brand name only through exclusive company owned stores as well as the retailers. This effort needs to be replicated in the international market as well. The old members of the company, who had been with the company from day one, feel that the success achieved, particularly in the international market, has been phenomenal. The newer, internationally educated team members, however, have been pointing towards a change of strategy and advocating the creation of a stronger globally accepted "Red Tape" brand. The arguments for and against were finely balanced. On the one hand, the current strategy "bulk sells through the retailers under their own labels" is allowing lower marketing and legal costs and more flexible quality control. On the other hand, there would certainly be increased costs in building a Red Tape global brand although there were clear advantages in the longer term of price protection, better profitability, customer loyalty, trust and a clearer company, and product identity (Wong, 2008). Irshad also knew that the efforts to build a global brand would be challenging and something that many Indian shoe manufacturers had not done so far. But his understanding and conviction in this direction came from other successful Asian companies. Companies such as Samsung and Goldstar started out as generic suppliers and subsequently developed themselves as highly successful consumer global brands. Irshad wondered whether the company might already be too late in the effort in spite of high acceptance of Red Tape brand in certain markets like UK.

THE ORIGIN

Mr. Irshad Mirza was born in 1935 at Kanpur and got an early education from Aligarh Muslim University. He started his career with 'Bata India Limited' as a manager in a Bata factory at Mokama (Bihar). However, Mr. Mirza was not satisfied with his salaried job and after 5 years of a service career, he started his own small scale tannery in the name Mirza Tanners at Kanpur with the full support of his father who was a renowned leather technologist at that time. He started with a meagre capital of Rs. 25,000 and 40 employees but with unlimited enthusiasm and energy. Mirza started exporting of leather goods (saddlery products) in the year 1973 in a modest way. Irshad's entrepreneurial mind never knew to stop in the mid way. Mirza Tanners Pvt. Ltd. was finally grown enough to be incorporated on 5th September 1979 as a private limited company. Another tannery unit of the Mirza Tanners was set up at Magarwara in Unnao district of Uttar Pradesh during 1981. The company became a deemed public limited company from 1st July, 1993. All along, Irshad carefully guided the company to retain the export focus intact. As a result, today, the Mirza International Limited is a grown up company with focus on export and providing direct and indirect employment of 11,000 people in India.

The thrust for more intense internationalization started after the entry of new generation in the business. Rashid Mirza, son of Mr. Irshad Mirza, obtained a Diploma in Leather Technology from the UK and was soon inducted in the business as the Managing Director of the company. Mr. Tauseef Mirza, younger brother of Rashid Mirza, was also inducted as a whole-time Director of Mirza International Ltd during 1989 on completion of his education in shoe technology from London. The company tapped the capital market in September 1994 and became a public limited company incorporated in India with management having more than 75% of the equity; 11% is held by financial institutions and rest is with public. During 2001-02 the company issued, on private placement basis, secured redeemable non-convertible debenture with a face value of Rs. 5 crores. Along with arrangement of financial resource the company paid attention to improve its management efficiency and appointed Price Waterhouse Coopers (P) Ltd as a consultant to examine various restructuring options. Soon the result of hard work started paying in terms of increased sales abroad. The Council for Indian Leather Exports, conferred the recognition to Mirza international as 'best exporter of the year' during 1998 and thereafter consecutively for the last eight years the crown remained with the company because of the sustained outstanding performance in the field of export.

THE GROWTH

Mirza International Limited has emerged as a frontrunner in the manufacturing and marketing of leather and leather footwear. Presently headquartered in the Indian capital of New Delhi, the company markets its products across the globe to countries like the UK, Europe, South Africa, and the Middle East, to name a few. The company is listed on the NSE, BSE, and UP Stock exchanges and is ISO 9001,

9002, and 14000 certified. Manufacturing is a key strength at Mirza. The company has a fully integrated in-house shoe production facility backed by a state-of-the-art double density direct injection polyurethane plant, a tannery with its own pollution treatment plant, and a dedicated design studio in London. The manufacturing plants are located at Magarwara and Sahjani in Unnao and in Noida districts. The tannery is located at Magarwara in Unnao. These plants are backed by more than 25 dedicated ancillary units. The company has capacity to manufacture 0.6 million pairs of shoe uppers and 0.45 million pairs of shoes per annum at Shahjani-Unnao, UP. The tannery at Magarwara-Unnao, UP can produce about 6 million square feett of finished leather per annum. Subsequently, the company established a complete shoe factory in the year 1990 at Magarwara, Unnao district for manufacture of 0.23 million pairs of shoes per annum which was increased to 0.45 million pairs of shoes during 1992-1993. The objective of the Company behind setting up these factories was mainly for catering to the quality conscious export markets of United Kingdom, Germany, Italy, Portugal, and Australia. After the successful launching of double density PU shoes, the company added a second plant at its Noida Factory for doubling the capacity (Production start at new unit of the company, 2011). About 9 million pairs of shoes per annum by the year 2010 was the production target fixed for the company.

The company also sources its cowhides from Europe and manufactures leather in stringent adherence to international norms, ensuring that no banned chemicals are used in the production process. In addition, to direct sales to leading global footwear retailers, the company also started building its own brand port folio: Red Tape, Oak Tape, and Red Tape Gal. The Red Tape brand was introduced in the UK in the mid 1990s as a fashion brand in some of the boutiques—and it became an instant hit. Since the spadework for the brand coincided with the collapse of the Soviet Union, which signalled the end of red tapism and the start of a new era, company officials decided to christen it as 'Red Tape'. Their first advertising campaign in the UK titled 'Cut Red Tape' had shown a pair of scissors cutting red tape. Like in the UK, the brand positioned itself as a lifestyle product, targeting young and fashion conscious consumers elsewhere including in India and was backed by heavy advertising since its launch. In order to put the company as "category supplier" it launched adult apparel products under Red Tape brand to seduce its targeted teen agers customers more intensely. The company was thinking of the achieving more in times to come. "We will have 200 exclusive Red Tape stores in India by 2011 and will also expand internationally by getting in to countries like France, Poland and Eastern European countries," says Rashid Mirza. (Mirza International targets Rs 480-500cr, 2010). In spite of early success in overseas market, the company had always kept attention to its home turf, India. The company always believed in having a solid home country foundation to ensure sustained internationalization. Lack of a true-blue fashionable shoe brand in India provided an ideal launch pad for Red Tape (Indian footwear market,2009). Mirzas introduced Red Tape it in India in 1997 with the launch of RTS-8 model, which instantly caught the fancy of the Indian consumers. In fact, it was so successful that the company had to work overnight to meet demand. "It was India's first square-toed shoe. Even our competitors aped the design. And after that, there was no looking back," remembers Mr.Tauseef Mirza. Today, Indian teenagers regard the Red Tape brand as style statement. The company, which spends 10-15% of sales on advertising, roped in Salman Khan in 2004 to endorse Red Tape. Although Salman's engagement with the brand was for a short time but it served the purpose i.e. of raising awareness of the brand. (Red Tape plans, 2007).

In order to craft products as per the latest fashion in the foreign market, Mirza International set up its design units at global fashion centers such as Milan, London, New York, Paris, Tokyo. The company, which claimed to churn out a thousand designs a day, employed 40 people in its design and development wing in India also. The grand success of Mirza International also meant that it was on the buyout radar of private equities and other companies. Over the years, while Mirzas had attracted offers from private equity firms and competitors, it thwarted them away successfully.

EXPORT FROM MIRZA INTERNATIONAL

The company performance of Mirzas has always been of an encouraging nature. The gross income of the company increased from 70.03 million USD during 2007-08 to 84.40 million USD during 2009-2010. The company depended a lot on export earnings as it constituted a major part of the company income. Export market dependency of the company, in terms of yearly revenue earned from export out of gross income in percentage terms, increased from 79.69 percent during 2007-08 to 80.05 percent during 2008-09. It only reduced marginally to 77.77 percent during 2009-10 possibly because of the recession which the entire European countries had to face during the year (see Table 1). (Mirza International., 2010 and 2011)

FOOTWEAR INDUSTRY IN INDIA

The Indian footwear market has seen very strong growth in recent years and the forecast is for this to continue at a steady rate. The Indian footwear market had total revenue of $4.10 billion in 2009, representing a Compound Annual Growth Rate (CAGR) of 9.3% for the period spanning 2005-2009 (Datamonitor, 2010). In comparison, the Chinese market increased with a CAGR of 9.6%, and the Japanese market declined with a CAGR of 0.7%, over the same period, to reach respective

Table 1. Export from Mirza International

	2007-08	**2008-09**	**2009-10**
Gross Income	70.03	80.26	84.40
Profit after tax	0.80	1.19	4.19
Export revenue	55.81	64.25	65.64
Export as % of total income	79.69	80.05	77.77

Source: Annual reports of the company.

values of $11.56 billion and $10.68 billion in 2009. India is the second largest global producer of footwear after China, accounting for 13% of global footwear production of 16 billion pairs. India produces 2,065 million pairs of different categories of footwear (leather footwear-909 million pairs, leather shoe uppers-100 million pairs, and non-leather footwear-1056 million pairs). India exports about 115 million pairs. Thus, nearly 95% of its production goes to meet its own domestic demand. Footwear exported from India are Dress Shoes, Casuals, Moccasins, Sport Shoes, Horrachies, Sandals, Ballerinas, Boots, Sandals and Chappals made of rubber, plastic, P.V.C., and other materials. Table 2 shows that a number of reputed foreign brands are sourcing their products from India. However, Indian company's internationalization efforts in popularizing Indian brands abroad have been pretty low or insignificant. Only a handful of companies like Liberty, Khadims, Lakhani, Metro, and Action are present in the international market with their own brand and still to make their presence felt in a big way.

US Retail giant Wal-Mart has also begun sourcing footwear from India within the last two years. The Footwear sector is now de-licensed and de-reserved, paving the way for expansion of capacities on modern lines with state-of-the-art machinery. To further assist this process, the Government has permitted 100% Foreign Direct Investment through the automatic route for the footwear sector (Council of leather exports, 2011).

Table 2. Sourcing status from India in footwear

MNC Brands Sourced from India	**MNC Brands Sold in India**	**Indian Brands Sold in India**
Acme, Clarks, ColeHann, Deichmann, Ecco, Elefanten, Florsheim, Gabor, Hasley, Hush Puppies, Double H, Justin, Marks & Spencer, Nautica, Nike, Nunn Bush, Reebok, Salamander, Stacy Adams, Tony, Lama, Next, Bally	Aldo, Bally, Clarks, Ecco, Florshiem, Ferragammo, Hush Puppies, Lee cooper, Lloyd, Marks & Spencer, Nike, Nine West, New Balance, Reebok, Rockport, Stacy Adams	Red Tape, Bata, Liberty, Khadims, Lakhani, Metro, Action

Source: Council of leather exports, India

Attempts are being made to retain investment climate favorable through increasing cost competitiveness so as to attract overseas more investments. The Government of India has also set up some dedicated 'Footwear Complex' in the recent times where the footwear components manufacturers are located in the form of footwear clusters to take advantage of agglomeration benefits. In fact, this has increased the interest of European companies from countries like Italy, Spain, and Portugal in collaborating with Indian footwear companies.

FOOTWEAR: GLOBAL SCENARIO AND INDIA'S SHARE

The global import of Footwear (both made of leather as well as non-leather) increased from US$ 59.77 billion in 2004 to US$ 87.23 billion in 2008, growing at a CAGR of 9.91%. During 2008, the India's share in the global import was just 1.76%. In fact, since 2004 India's share in the global imports hovered around 1.5 to 1.8 percent only (see Table 3) (Datamonitor, 2010).

Footwear is the engine of growth of the leather industry in India. India's export of footwear touched US$ 1507.51 million in 2009-10, with a share of 44.33% in India's total export from the leather sector. No doubt export of footwear from India increased manifold over the last four decades but lack of branding efforts from the Indian companies while marketing in the international markets has not allowed a corresponding jump in the revenue.

MAJOR MARKETS

During 2009-10, the main markets for Indian footwear were UK with a share of 19.66%, Germany 14.88%, Italy 13.93%, USA 8.20%, France 9.58%, Spain 6.37%, Netherlands 4.32%, Portugal 1.50%, U.A.E 2.63% and Denmark 1.13.%. These 10 countries together accounts for 82.20% share in India's total footwear export. Nearly

Table 3. Export/import of footwear from India in million USD

	2004	2005	2006	2007	2008
Global import of Footwear	59779.52	67066.21	72747.35	80722.29	87234.28
India's export of Footwear & Footwear Components	910.77	1045.24	1236.91	1489.35	1534.32
% Share of India	1.52%	1.56%	1.70%	1.85%	1.76%

Source: ITC, Geneva & Director General of Commercial Intelligence &Statistics, Kolkata

90% of India's export of footwear went to European Countries and the USA. It is expected that future growth of Indian footwear exports would be depending on European countries and the US (see Table 4).

MAJOR PLAYERS

The footwear industry in India is largely in the hands of small, disorganized players. The industry size is estimated at Rs 70 billion in value terms and 620 million in volume terms. The industry has been growing at 10-12% per annum. Bata is the largest player with around 10% volume share and around 60% market-share in the organized segment. The company has a market share of 70% in canvas shoes segment while it has a share of 60% in leather shoes. The company competes with Liberty Shoes in the popular segment of the organized market and with regional/local players in unorganized market. Other leading organized sector players are Phoenix International, Action Shoes, and Lakhani Shoes. The smaller players con-

Table 4. India's export of footwear to different countries: (value in million US $)

Country	2005-06	2006-07	2007-08	2008-09	2009-10	% Share
Germany	170.97	217.23	246.84	229.65	224.27	14.88%
UK	195.78	208.2	241.37	247.06	296.45	19.66%
Italy	134.35	186.11	229.81	221.09	209.95	13.93%
USA	131.07	127.15	136.92	163.03	123.6	8.20%
France	74.48	99.81	116.03	119.2	144.45	9.58%
Spain	63.7	64.57	76.69	91.86	95.99	6.37%
Netherlands	32.96	48.57	72.91	76.2	65.13	4.32%
Portugal	22.15	35.03	37.34	28.21	22.63	1.50%
UAE	25.78	34.64	39.23	39.4	39.61	2.63%
Denmark	18.37	14.65	17.48	14.78	17.02	1.13%
Australia	11.58	10.11	12.52	13.34	15.49	1.03%
Sweden	6.77	7.99	12.04	12.64	12.2	0.81%
Canada	11.95	10.91	10.41	8.96	9.3	0.62%
South Africa	8.26	12.11	8.52	8.49	9.87	0.65%
Japan	3.17	3.07	4.63	8.23	5.45	0.36%
Others	133.9	156.76	226.61	252.18	216.37	14.35%
Total	1045.24	1236.91	1489.35	1534.32	1507.51	100.00%

Source: Director General of Commercial Intelligence &Statistics, Kolkata

sider international branding as an exclusive domain for the larger companies hence deficiencies in commitments. In order to play a dominant role in the global footwear sector, it is important that the smaller ventures understand the overseas market situation and employ appropriate international marketing practices. In developing such a capability, international commitment to international business is important.

INTERNATIONAL BRANDING EFFORTS AT MIRZA

Shuja Mirza, Vice President–Marketing, Red Tape of Mirza International was talking at a team meeting for deciding about his desire for promoting company's own brands like Red Tape more aggressively in international markets. At the outset he narrated the objective of the meeting. "The company has been selling products in international markets like UK, USA, and UAE with own brand name–Red Tape. For other countries the products are exported out to established brands who in turn market the products. So far in many countries, the company acted as a supplier to the leading brands. In fact, though 80% of our business comes from abroad, revenue earned through marketing of our own brand is low. However, if the company sells through its own brands more, this would progressively provide the required leverage in enhancing revenue from foreign operation." He also did not forget to mention that personally he favored aggressive international branding. Then he placed the following issues for discussion in the meeting:

- There are many pros and cons of more intensive branding abroad particularly for a medium size company like Mirza International. Issues like country of importance need to be sorted out like UK first followed by USA or simultaneously?
- There are various countries which may be reached in both ways; selling similar shoes under own brand as well as supplying them directly to other brands. Looks interesting, but it involves cannibalization of own brand building exercise. How to resolve this conflict?
- Positioning of the products in different foreign markets differently based on their taste preferences etc? Or, continuing with standardized "fashion and lifestyle" positioning for all the countries? How much market share it should target? Market leadership can only come if the company is able to differentiate its product offerings from competitors (Successful product, 2010).
- The company is travelling back to home country market which may be quite unusual for a traditional company. That is, being a known brand in foreign market first and then put efforts to popularize the brand in home country market. Is this going to provide any leverage in international market?

- About the recent diversification plan i.e. to establish Red Tape as a fashion brand and for which the company is willing to enter all segments of dressing, including accessories. Is that strategically correct to international markets also? Weather it will pay off in brand building internationally?

The meeting saw a detailed discussion on the issues raised by the Vice President– Marketing of the company. As the team was leaving the room after long deliberations on the above issues at 10 pm in that night, Mr. Shuja, reflected that a majority of the team members nurture a dream of making "Red tape" a true global player and consider the desire of Mr Shuja justified and a step in the right direction. But Mr. Shuja was thinking on the lavish spending required for brand building in foreign markets because of risk as style symbol change frequently. Mr Shuja knew from his past marketing experience that taking a brand to a new height in international markets has always been full of challenges. The challenges are on many counts; required spending commitments, competition from reputed brands, convincing a traditional company in this risky effort, and so on. He kept on asking himself, "should I continue to push for efforts in this direction?" At the end, Mr Shuja, decided to remain neutral and allowing everyone's views in the company to be heard. But, in heart, he was convinced that it would not be a good idea for the company to delay the decision any further. A decision in the direction of international branding would require the company to allocate resources and plan accordingly for the future. This required an early decision making with full commitment of the company. Should they play safe and focus on domestic market or follow a riskier but potentially more profitable route? It was, indeed, a dilemma.

CASE USE AND LEANING OBJECTIVES

The case has been created for the students and the practitioners of international marketing delving into the subject of developing the brand at the international level. In addition, the case provides readers with ample scope to explore the problem associated with a small company for sustaining the international sales through developing its own brand in conjunction with the dilemma associated with profound brand building involvement or submitting to the mercy of private label brands of the big retailers in the international market. Among the learning objectives, the following are important:

- To introduce Mirza International, an Indian SME in the leather sector, as an emerging international player in the trendy and stylish footwear business;
- To introduce the requirements and threshold for international branding particularly for SMEs;
- To introduce a practical ground for understanding the pros and cons of more intensive branding abroad for a small size domestic company;
- To discuss requirements of domestic presence for a company to be successful in an attempt to launch its international brand in the target foreign markets.

The fundamental lesson of the case, however, is that international branding attempt is a very crucial decision for a small and medium size company. It offers opportunities of increasing marketing presence through own brand in the foreign markets but at the same time ground requirements pulls the company towards consolidation in the domestic market before embarking on huge pricey task of international brand building.

Discussion Questions

1. How accomplished is Mirza International in the domestic market, particularly in trendy and stylish footwear Segment?
2. How Mirza International attained a respectable position in the target foreign market? Were the foreign sales testified the respectability?
3. What was the marketing strategy of Mirza International in the target country markets? Do you think that Mirza International was more than a normal exporter of finished products to the foreign markets?
4. What were the problems for Mirza International to go all out for creating and nurturing its brands in the foreign markets? What are the primary issues the company should take in to account before embarking on a task of international brand building?
5. What was the presence of Mirza International's in the domestic market? What was the status of 'Red Tape' brand in Indian market? What is the relationship between company's domestic brand image and that international brand image?
6. What are the factors a domestic company like Mirza International should consider while taking a decision of extending domestic brand to the international level?
7. Do you think that Mirza International should strive for building brand in the target market? Suggest a framework to assess the brand building eligibility of the company.

REFERENCES

Council of Leather Exports. (2011). *Indian footwear industry–A status note.* Retrieved from http://www.leatherindia.org/products/footwear.asp.

Datamonitor. (2010). *Industry profile, footwear in india.* Retrieved from Business Source Complete database.

Datamonitor. (2010). *Industry profile, global footwear.* Retrieved from Business Source Complete database.

Flourishing on Red Tape, Mirza International leaves global footprint. (2009). *The Economic Times.* Retrieved from Newspaper archive.

Indian footwear market has large potential. (2009). *One India News.* Retrieved from http://news.oneindia.in/2009/07/13/indianfootwear-market.

Mirza International. (2009). *Annual report.* Retrieved from http://www.mirza.co.in/annual_report_currentyear.html.

Mirza international reports Rs 95.09 crore turnover for quarter ended June, 2010. (2010). Retrieved from www.moneycontrol.com.

Mirza International targets Rs 480-500cr top line this year. (2010). Retrieved from www.moneycontrol.com.

Production starts at new unit of the company. (2011). *Press releases of mirza international.* Retrieved from www.mirza.co.in/announcements.html.

Red tape plans 16 more exclusive outlets. (2007). *The business line.* Retrieved from www.thehindubusinessline.com/todays-paper/tp-marketing/.

Successful Product Differentiation Strategies. (2010). *Strategic direction.* Bingley, UK: Emerald Group Publishing Limited.

Wong & Bill. (2008). Determinants of SME international marketing communications. *Journal of Global Marketing, 21*(4).

ADDITIONAL READING

Barwise, P., & Robertson, T. (1992). Brand portfolios. *European Management Journal, 10*(3), 277–285. doi:10.1016/0263-2373(92)90021-U.

De Chematony, L., Halliburton, C., & Bemath, R. (1995). International branding: Demand or supply driven opportunity? *International Marketing Review, 12*(2), 9–21. doi:10.1108/02651339510089765.

Douglas, S. P., Craig, C. S., & Nijssen, E. J. (2001). Integrating branding strategy across markets: Building international brand architecture. *Journal of International Marketing, 9*(2), 97–114. doi:10.1509/jimk.9.2.97.19882.

Hsieh, M. H. (2002). Identifying brand image dimensionality and measuring the degree of brand globalization: A cross-national study. *Journal of International Marketing, 10*(2), 46–67. doi:10.1509/jimk.10.2.46.19538.

Kuvykaite, R., & Mascinskiene, J. (2010). Transformation of a national brand into an international brand. *The Engineering Economist, 21*(4), 446–455.

Schuiling, I., & Kapferer, J. N. (2004). Real differences between local and international brands: Strategic implications for international marketers. *Journal of International Marketing, 12*(4), 97–112. doi:10.1509/jimk.12.4.97.53217.

Chapter 10

Delhi Bank of India:
Dilemma of a New Bank Manager

Sandeep Puri
Institute of Management Technology, India

Jayanthi Ranjan
Institute of Management Technology, India

EXECUTIVE SUMMARY

Delhi Bank of India (DBI) is a leading private banking and financial services organization in India. DBI Bank offers a wide range of banking products and financial services to corporate and retail customers through a variety of delivery channels in the areas of investment banking, life and non-life insurance, venture capital, and asset management. It has entered the banking consortia of over 30 corporations for providing working capital finance, trade services, corporate finance, and merchant banking. DBI is also providing sophisticated product structures in areas of foreign exchange and derivatives, money markets and debt trading, and equity research. Dwarka Branch of DBI has not been doing well since its inception in March 2008. It is having a very low customer base and many customers have shifted their accounts to other banks because of dissatisfaction with the bank. In the last 6 months, the number of customers has reduced to 2875 from 2900. This branch is having allocation of ₹1.50 Crores only for loan disbursements during Jan-March, 2011 period but the loan applications are for ₹2.20 crore. There are six applicants with different backgrounds and this amount cannot be increased. Bank manager Siddhant, needed to take the call for final disbursements.

DOI: 10.4018/978-1-4666-4357-4.ch010

Copyright ©2014, IGI Global. Copying or distributing in print or electronic forms without written permission of IGI Global is prohibited.

INTRODUCTION

It's a bright January day and sun rays filter in through the window pane of the office of Siddhant Gabriel, Branch Manager at Dwarka Branch of Delhi Bank of India (DBI) at New Delhi. Siddhant moves over to the tea machine for his second cup and turns it on. His door opens and Aarti, Assistant branch manager enters in with a grim look on her face. Siddhant looks at Aarti and asks, "What happened, what's bothering you?" "These loan applicants," replies Aarti. "Why, what happened?" enquires Siddhant with inquisitiveness. "The six loan applicants are visiting me almost daily and we need to decide about their loans as early as possible otherwise they may shift to some other bank. Problem is we are having allocation of ₹1.50 crores only for loan disbursements for the first quarter of 2011 whereas the loan applications are for ₹2.20 crores," replies Aarti. "All right Aarti, let me pour you a cup of tea and let's discuss this matter," quips Siddhant.

Siddhant joined DBI as a Relationship manager after doing his MBA from IMT, Ghaziabad, the premier B-school in India. He has performed well in the last 3 years at CP branch of the bank at Delhi. He consistently achieved his targets during this period and opened accounts for many High Net Individuals (HNI). He was appreciated many times for developing good relations with HNIs. He was the key figure to enroll 9 corporations for providing working capital finance, trade services, corporate finance and merchant banking. He is the winner of the Chairman's Excellence Award for 2008 and 2009. Senior Management at DBI is quite confident that he will do well in his new role.

Siddhant's Key Performance Indicators (KPIs) as a Branch Manager are:

1.   CASA (current and savings account) ratio of 20% in 2013;
2.   Increase in the customer base to 7500 by Decemeber 2013;
3.   Reduction in the high churn rate;
4.   To enhance the image of DBI bank among the local residents.

DELHI BANK OF INDIA (DBI)

Delhi Bank of India (DBI) is a leading private banking and financial services organization in India. The bank has a network of more than 6,000 branches (as of Dec, 2010) and over 1,200 ATMs in 250 cities in India, and all branches of the bank are linked to an online real-time basis. It has more than 5 million customers (at the end of Oct, 2010). DBI Bank offers a wide range of banking products and financial services to corporate and retail customers through a variety of delivery channels in the areas of investment banking, life and non-life insurance, venture capital and

122

asset management. It has entered the banking consortia of over 30 corporate for providing working capital finance, trade services, corporate finance and merchant banking. DBI is also providing sophisticated product structures in areas of foreign exchange and derivatives, money markets and debt trading and equity research.

DBI reported a 2% rise in net profit to ₹3, 00.21 crores on a 3.5% increase in total income to ₹1,817.26 crores in Q2 September 2010 over Q2 September 2009. The bank's CASA ratio increased to 18% in 2010 from 15% in 2009.

DWARKA BRANCH OF DBI

Dwarka Branch of DBI is not doing well since its inception in March 2008. It has a very low customer base and many customers have shifted their accounts to other banks because of dissatisfaction with the bank and in the last 6 months number of customers are reduced to 2875 from 2900. The detail of number of customers is shown in Table 1.

CASA ratio for this branch is 11% in 2010 which is much below the overall CASA of 18% for the bank. The bank is also facing a high churn rate and this has resulted in huge losses as many customers closed their accounts after tenure of 7-8 months. The bank conducted a customer satisfaction survey with 500 customers and the major factors for high churn rate in DBI bank, Dwarka are shown in Table 2.

Table 1. Number of customers

Year 2010	Total Number of Customers	Year 2011	Total Number of Customers	Year 2012	Total Number of Customers
January		January	1120	January	2830
February		February	1245	February	2950
March	180	March	1460	March	2835
April	210	April	1550	April	2950
May	340	May	1675	May	3070
June	400	June	1805	June	2900
July	525	July	1940	July	2910
August	660	August	2070	August	2900
September	775	September	2115	September	2870
October	810	October	2250	October	2865
November	930	November	2375	November	2870
December	1070	December	2450	December	2875

DWARKA

Dwarka is a sub city, located in the South West of Delhi. It is developed by Delhi Development Authority. It is frequently referred to as the "Model Township"-The largest residential Area in Asia. It is located in the vicinity of International and Domestic airports. Population of Dwarka is around 1,100,000 and it is well connected by the Metro train service to the other parts of Delhi. Dwarka is also very near to Gurgaon (High growth city). Dwarka has witnessed a massive retail boom in the past couple of years with most of the major brands setting their retail stores in this sub city. The price of commercial space has skyrocketed in recent times and is expected to rise further as more middle and upper class residents begin to move in. Commercial zone in Dwarka consists of two major markets in sector 6 and 10. Newer markets like Ashirwad Square- which is the juncture of sectors 4, 5, 11 and 12, have recently come up. Head office of Exattosoft, the famous software company is also in Dwarka. There are 2 Five star hotels,3 universities, 5 Business Schools, 3 Sports Complexes, 3 Engineering colleges, 2 science colleges, and many schools in Dwarka.

THE DILEMMA

Branch is having allocation of ₹1.50 Crores only for loan disbursements during Jan-March, 2011 period but the loan applications are for ₹2.20 crore. This amount can not be increased. There are 6 applications and the details of applications are:

1. Anoop, handicapped since birth wants to start his STD, PCO, Computer, and Photostat shop in Sector-11 of Dwarka. He has worked as assistant at BSK,

Table 2. Reasons for high churn rate

S. No	Factors
1	Poor Customer service
2	Complex features of website
3	Less number of ATMs
4	Low Interest rates for deposits
5	Quality of customers
6	Less Branches
7	Crowded
8	Long waiting time

renowned business support centre in Dwarka. He is having experience to manage a Computer and Photostat shop. He wanted to start this business with a rented space. Monthly rent for a shop in this area is around ₹10-15,000. He is expecting a business of ₹40-50,000 per month. He has requested for a loan of ₹15 lakh. Interest rate for loan is 12.5%. He can start the repayment from the next month. See Table 3 for an interest rate chart.

2. Education Student loan of ₹15 lakh as Shraddha wants to do her MBA from IIMA. IIMA is the Best Business school of India with an average salary of ₹ 14.94 lakh during placements in 2010. Most of the top managers in India are alumnus of IIMA. She is from a poor family and cannot give a bank guarantee. She will start repaying her loan 6 months after her placements in 2013. Current rate for education loan is 11.5%.

3. IT Guy, Murli wants to start his own Business process outsourcing (BPO) Company in Dwarka. He had worked as a team leader for Bitro BPO for 7 years. He wants a loan of ₹75 lakh. BPO is one of the fastest growing segments of the Information Technology Enabled Services (ITES) industry in India. He is expecting high returns from this venture. His expected turnover is around ₹10 lakh per month. He is an old customer and can give his flat in Dwarka as a bank guarantee. Current value of his flat is ₹90 lakh. He will start repaying within 2 months. Interest rate for his loan is 12.5%.

4. Shreya Sarabhai is a war widow. She is a renowned social worker in Delhi. She wants to start a vocational training school for poor girls of Dwarka. She is planning to offer 6 month diploma courses in knitting, teacher training, home science, garment designing, jewellery designing and computer applications. She is expecting enrollment of around 300 students for these courses. Planned fees are ₹7500 per course. She is also expecting sponsorships from some big corporate houses. She has requested for a loan of ₹30 lakh and has also requested for repayment after 6 months. Interest rate for loan is 12.0%.

5. Jatin Banani, an old customer is having his retail store in Sector 11 of Dwarka. Currently he is having one shop. He wants to expand his retail business by buying the adjacent shop. He has requested for a loan of ₹75 lakh. His annual turnover is Rs 50 lakh. He is expecting good growth in his business because

Table 3. Interest rate chart

Category	PNB	SBI	HDFC	BOI	DBI	OBC	ICICI	Citi Bank
Education Loan	12	12	12.5	11.5	11.5	11.5	NA	NA
Personal Loan	13	12.5	13	12.5	13	12.5	13	13
Home Loan	9	9	9.5	9.25	9.5	9	9.5	9.5

of booming retail business in Dwarka. He is ready to pay interest of 12.5% on this loan and he will start repaying from the next month.

6.   Janvi who recently completed her course from VLCC wants to start her Beauty Parlor in Sector 6. VLCC Institute of Beauty & Nutrition offers specialized professional courses in beauty, hair, cosmetology, make-up, spa therapies and nutrition. It is considered to be one of the best in its category. Many of its students are doing well professionally. Janvi has requested for a loan of ₹15 lakh at interest rate of 12.5%.

Siddhant is in a dilemma. He wants to acquire new customers and also want to retain his old customers. Top management is unable to support him with a higher amount because of low CASA ratio and higher default rates at this branch. Time is running fast and he has to take decision. Clock is ticking.

Chapter 11
Facebook:
An Application of Cloud Computing

Lokesh Sharma
Jaypee University of Information Technology, India

EXECUTIVE SUMMARY

This case study is prepared for the informative purpose, as it will provide the Literature over Facebook and the technologies it is using. We also include the technology change and the shortcomings that Facebook was facing and how developers resolve them. There are detailed explanations of each and every topic which is included in this chapter.

INTRODUCTION

Facebook is a name which is well known to all of us. There is lot of mystery in finding the secrets of Facebook. They never disclose the strategy they adapt and their work ethics. In August 2012 it will reach 1 billion user accounts (14% of world population), 3 billion photos uploaded every month, 14 billion videos uploaded every month, 3.5 million events created every month,70 translation are available, and 350,000 active applications (. It's a mammoth of facts and figures. Facebook currently accounts for about 9 percent of all Internet traffic, slightly more than Google, according to Hit wise (Data Center Knowledge, 2010). Mark Zuckerberg, the owner of Facebook, is recently the youngest billionaire on the Forbes list. He is the 35th wealthiest individual on the globe. To know how this giant elephant works is a great desire. Well there is a concept called Cloud Computing which is efficiently working even the best application that has been used over this globe.

DOI: 10.4018/978-1-4666-4357-4.ch011

Copyright ©2014, IGI Global. Copying or distributing in print or electronic forms without written permission of IGI Global is prohibited.

Mark Elliot Zuckerberg (born May 14, 1984) is an American computer programmer and internet entrepreneur. He is one of the co-founders of Facebook, as well as the chairman and chief-executive.

Zuckerberg was born and raised in a Jewish family. He had a great interest in programming and it soon became a hobby of his. His father helped him in his hobby by teaching him BASIC, the first programming language he learned. After that he gained an even greater interest in programming so his father hired a tutor to help Zuckerberg develop his programming skills. Zuckerberg started developing small computer programs like music players and even installed a primitive home network called "zucknet." His father used his program in his dental shop so that the reception attendee will send another patient without calling to her. His tutor called him a prodigy. Once he completed high school, he enrolled in the Computer Science and Sociology fields at Harvard University. At Harvard he designed a project called "Facemash," in which students vote on other student's photo attractiveness. This later became the first template for Facebook.

Facebook began on the campus of Harvard and soon became global. In 2005, Zuckerberg's enterprise received a huge venture capital from Accel partners. Accel invested 12.7 million dollars into his network. After that Facebook became accessible to other colleges. By December 2005, 5.5 million users were on Facebook. Then the controversy began. Facebook was receiving a great deal of positive attention when the creators of Harvard Connection claimed that Zuckerberg had stolen their idea. They drug Zuckerberg to court and claimed the idea behind Facebook was their intellectual property. Later a settlement of $65 million was reached between the two parties. In 2009, Ben Mezrich's book, *The Accidental Billionaire,* hit stores as a narrative of Zuckerberg's life. Later on Sorkin and Fincher's acclaimed film, "The Social Network" received eight Academy Award nominations.

Zuckerberg has used his billions of funds in philanthropic causes, such as he donating $100 million to save the failing Newark Public School system in New Jersey. He promised to donate 50 percent of his wealth to charity over the course of his lifetime with the "Giving pledge."

RECENT NEWS OF FACEBOOK

Facebook Camera

Now you can surf with your friends and also watch their visuals. Facebook shares photos and videos with people you care about. You can also share multiple photos at once instead of individually selecting a photo. There is lot of customization available to share a picture simply by tapping the checkmark on the image and share it (Facebook, 2013).

Donation

As Facebook is the largest and the biggest social networking site you can connect and share with your friends about you and your life. Today millions of people waiting for heart, kidney, or liver transplantation. Facebook is providing a common channel where donor and receiver both are available at the same place. You can keep in contact with the donors that saved your life (Facebook, 2013).

Timeline Application

Today Facebook has adopted a new way to look completely innovative and creative in which users can make their timeline view in which monthly developments will be seen. This application was launched in February 2012 and is gaining pace among the users. It increases 300% traffic over Facebook and also attracts new users by 200,000 per week (Facebook, 2013).

Facebook IPO

It is expected to be one of the largest technology based deals ever. Rumored evaluations stand at $100 billion. According to statistics Facebook has introduced 421,233,615 shares in common stock at a price of $38 per share. The shares started trading from May 18, 2012, in the market of NASDAQ Global Select Market (Facebook, 2013). The number of transactions done in stock trading under the symbol "FB" is computed to be the average daily total on the New York Stock Exchange, on its very first day of sale (*India Times*).

FACEBOOK DATACENTER

Initially Facebook had one server which was located in Mark Zuckerberg's dormitory room at Harvard University. Now servers will soon number over 60,000. The company's web servers and storage units are in data units around the globe. By the help of fiber optic cables the computer servers are networked and data centers can send and receive information to other servers. According to Facebook Statistics everyday 300 millions new photos are uploaded. Facebook has four huge datacenters. Of those, two are in the United States and the other two are under-construction. Facebook has announced its first non-U.S. data center in Lulea, Sweden (October, 2011). Whenever a user is accessing his homepage it requires hundreds of servers, processing tens of thousands of individual pieces of data, and delivering them in seconds. Most of the Facebook datacenter is leased by "Wholesale" providing him datacenter space for 5 months rather than of 12 months it make them to scale rapidly (Facebook Datacenter, 2010).

Facebook Servers are powered by chips from Intel and AMD with custom modified motherboards. The servers use a 1.5U (2.65 inches) chassis use larger heat sinks and fans to improve cooling efficiency. They include power supplies of 277-volt AC power, bypassing the step-downs in most data centers.

HOW FACEBOOK WORKS

This is the most fascinating question that makes most of the software developers to hype the curiosity of knowing. Facebook is a social networking site and its main objective is to connect those peoples which having the same interest. In this we can make communities of our specific interest and the people which also have the interest and are globally apart can be the part of our community. From the last 6 years we are Face booking and time to time the developers are changing and enhancing their technologies to provide better efficiency and accessing. Facebook having its own architecture, frontend, backend that makes it more reliable in real world.

There are variety of technologies that are used by Facebook in developing its infrastructure, at front end Facebook is using LAMP (Linux, Apache, Mysql, and PHP) stack with memcache. We are exploring each of the technologies in details (MakeUseOf, 2010).

Linux

Linux is a Unix like operating system that was designed to provide personnel computer a very low cost operating system comparable to the expensive high cost Unix operating system. It was developed by the members of Free software Foundation for GNU project. Linux is efficient and fast performing system. It's a graphical user interface, X Window system, TCP/IP, The Emacs editor and lot of components found in Unix system. Linux is distributed using free software foundation's and is freely available (Search Enterprise Linux, 2008).

Apache

It is Apache Web Server which is in short called to be Apache, it is public-domain open source web server developed by Knit group of programmers. The Apache web server code is freely available anyone can access it for their specific needs. It also having lot of versions such as in OS/2, windows and other platforms. Apache web server was designed by 20 volunteer programmers, called the apache group. [6]It is a HTTP Server established standard in the online distribution of website services, which gave the initial boost for the expansion of the World Wide Web. Apache provides lots of modules for apache server which supports various scripts and allow dynamic scripts to be run on the server, it support CGI (Common Gateway Interface) provide communication between external application software and the web server and also SSI (Server Side Includes) it's a simple server side scripting language. other apache modules such as CGI scripts execution, user authentication, URL redirection, anonymous user access, automatic directory listings, support for HTTP header metafiles, support for loading modules, content negotiation, caching proxy abilities, server status display, user home directories, and so forth (Module Hosting, 2008).

Mysql

It is also called "My Sequel" open source relational database management system based on structure query language having functions like adding, removing and modifying information in database, commonly found on web servers. Websites that use dynamic Web pages are often referred to as database-driven websites.PHP is the scripting language that is used by MySql to access information's from the database. There is good compatibility among PHP and Mysql, commands of Mysql can be incorporated on PHP. The combination of PHP/MYSQL is the popular choice for database driven websites (Teach Terms, 2013).

PHP

Php:Hypertext Preprocessor is a widely-used open source general-purpose scripting language that is especially suited for web development and can be embedded into HTML. PHP is server side scripting language, it also provide configuration with your web server to process all your HTML files with PHP (2013).

WHAT IS MEMCACHED?

Free and open source, high-performance, distributed memory object caching system, generic in nature, but intended for use in speeding up dynamic web applications by alleviating database load.

Memcached is an in-memory key-value store for small chunks of arbitrary data (strings, objects) from results of database calls, API calls, or page rendering.

Memcached is simple yet powerful. Its simple design promotes quick deployment, ease of development, and solves many problems facing large data caches. Its API is available for most popular languages (Memcached, 2011).

WHY FACEBOOK IS USING THESE TECHNOLOGIES

Mike Schroepfer, Facebook's Vice President of Engineering says that scaling any website is the biggest challenge whereas scaling any social networking site has unique challenges. As Facebook has huge interconnected dataset, new connections are created all the time due to user activity. As Facebook is huge and complex there are lot of issues regarding database queries, caching, and storage of data. In order to reduce this set of problems we used open source projects and backend services (MakeUseOf, 2010).

How Scalability is Improved

The Apache Thrift is a software framework for scalable cross-language service development, combines a software stack with a code generation engine to build services that work efficiently and seamlessly between C++, Java, Python, PHP, Ruby, Erlang, Perl, Haskell, C#, Cocoa, JavaScript, Node.js, Smalltalk, OCaml, Delphi, and other languages (ApacheThrift, 2013).

Scribe is a server for aggregating log data streamed in real-time from a large number of servers. It is designed to be scalable, extensible without client-side modification, and robust to failure of the network or any specific machine (Wikipedia, 2013a).

What is Cassandra?

Cassandra is a Database management system designed to handle large amount of database which is spreaded over the distributed servers. Cassandra was designed by Apache group it having high scalability and availability without compromising performance. It is designed to accomplish its objective over cloud infrastructure computer's. It support for replicating across multiple datacenters is best-in-class, lower latency for users.

Cassandra's ColumnFamily data model offers the convenience of column indexes with the performance of log-structured updates, strong support for materialized views, and powerful built-in caching.

Advantages of Cassandra with Facebook

Proven

Cassandra is in use with many social networking websites as well as companies having large active datasets such as Twitter, Cisco, OpenX, and CloudKick. The largest known Cassandra cluster has over 300 TB of data in over 400 machines.

Fault Tolerant

Data is automatically replicated to multiple nodes for fault-tolerance. Replication across multiple data centers is supported. Failed nodes can be replaced with no downtime.

Decentralized

There are no single points of failure. There are no network bottlenecks. Every node in the cluster is identical.

You're in Control

Choose between synchronous or asynchronous replication for each update. Highly available asynchronous operations are optimized with features like hinted handoff and read repair.

(Hinted Handoff is an optional part of writes whose primary purpose is to provide extreme write availability when consistency is not required. Read repair means that when a query is made against a given key, we perform a digest query against all the replicas of the key and push the most recent version to any out-of-date replicas.)

Rich Data Model

Allows efficient use for many applications beyond simple key/value.

Elastic

Read and write throughput both increase linearly as new machines are added, with no downtime or interruption to applications.

Durable

Cassandra is suitable for applications that can't afford to lose data, even when an entire data center goes down (Cassandra, 2009).

What is Cloud Computing?

Cloud computing is an emerging technology that allows anyone to be connected with rest of the world, in order to use the hardware and software which are distantly apart. It provides scalability, built in elasticity, remote accessibility, and better utilization of resources. Cloud computing is TCP/IP based high development and integration of computer technologies such as fast microprocessor, huge memory, high speed networks, and reliable system architecture. There are so many service oriented characteristics that make cloud computing more attractive such as loose coupling. Strong fault tolerance makes it a more widely adopted network and the economical pattern is the wide pattern of adopted network structure. IBM had classified cloud computing in three types according to their usage. They are Private Cloud, Public Cloud and Hybrid Cloud. The private Cloud is owned by single organization and public Cloud are shared on larger scale whereas Hybrid Cloud is a combination of both Private as well as Public and its utilization is mostly in Industries (Gong, 2010; Zhang, 2010; Begum, S. & Khan, 2011).

The US National Institute of Standards and Technology (NIST) define cloud characteristics as following:

1. On demand Self Service,
2. Ubiquitious Network Services,
3. Resource Pooling,
4. Rapid Elasticity (Resources can be Scaled),
5. Metered Services,
6. Pay as you consume model.

There was a traditional method of purchasing the resources for usage but now days they are hired by such type of technologies, so that companies manufacturing cost reduced. Cloud computing technology hands on with Virtualization, grid computing, Distributed computing and parallel computing.

Virtualization: For better Transparency Cloud computing has features of Virtualization which define images of Operating System, Middleware and Applications (Begum, S. & Khan, 2011).

Grid Computing: It is a Collection of computer resources from multiple administrative domains having the common goal. Grid computing from conventional high performance computing systems such as cluster computing is that grids tend to be more loosely coupled, heterogeneous, and geographically dispersed (Alabbadi, 2011). Grids are also constructed for software's which are known as middleware's. The goal of grid computing is to provide user's the access of resources which are geographically distant apart and aggregating processing power. Grid also encompasses the sensors, data storage systems. As now days Grid provide virtual implementation over Super computers by using resources over LAN and WAN. Grid computing always require a piece of software that divides a task into large number of computers, in Grid if one node fails the whole software will have the impact of it.

Distributed Computing: A Distributed System is one in which components located at networked computers communicate and coordinate their actions only by passing messages. The characteristics of Distributed Systems are: Concurrency of Components, lack of global clock and independent failures of components.

Parallel Computing: Parallel Computing is a computation in which operation done parallely, and the principle behind is to divide the larger modules into smaller modules. In this way the resources of memory and ability to do calculation enhanced.

The major challenges faced by Cloud computing are following:

Security

As Security is concerned about the privacy, confidentiality and the network traffic. These are the issues which need to be authenticating while communication is established among users. Cloud Architecture don't automatically grant security to end user's so it's the user's responsibility to be secure on their own terms (Kalagiakos & Karampelas, 2011).

1. **Data Integrity:** As cloud doesn't differentiate between a sensitive data and common data so that anyone can access the data freely. There is lack of data integrity in cloud computing.
2. **Data Theft:** As the cloud vendors instead of acquiring a server tries to lease a server which is more cost effective and flexible for operations. There is high possibility of data can be stolen to any other external server for its use.
3. **Infected Application:** Vendors have rights to freely access the server for monitoring and maintenance purposes. If any malicious user try to upload an

infected program over cloud network it will cause serious effects to the cloud users and network.

4. **Data Loss:** If the Vendor closes due to financial or legal problems there will be loss of data for the customers. In future that data will not accessible.

Interoperability

It provides Customer choices that make to adopt from various ways.

Incomprehension

The problem of data migration and adaptation of data structure from different clouds is the biggest challenges among all. There are so many misunderstandings about how easy it is to move from one kind of infrastructure to another, misunderstanding of public and private clouds.

Overutilization of Capacity

For Cloud providers capacity was forced to sell more so that they can actually be in the competition and provide better services to cloud users.

Network Limitation

When you are deploying a system using infrastructure that isn't aware of IPv6 it will generate dangerous results. As IPv4 are more numbered so one has to keep in mind about the technical flexibility provided to cloud computing. As the conversion would take time to decode the headers.

Future of Cloud Computing

1. Cloud Computing is widening, as the servers are increasing everyday.
2. The number of firms are increasing and adapting the functionality of Cloud computing in full flash way (Zhang et al., 2010).
3. Today the social networking is adapting this technologies and make it more popular in this era (Hinchcliffe & Kim, 2010).
4. Cloud Computing is quickly beginning to shape up major changes and the thousands of customers adapting the cloud offering from Amazon,Salesforce and google.It shows the momentum in space.
5. Provide more tolerance for innovations and give freedom to do experiments. It reduces the technical and economical barriers.

6.	It generates new Lightweight partnerships and outsourcing with IT Industries which are geographically apart (Zhang et al., 2010).

Cloud Computing in Social Network

As today Social networking sites are part of many people's providing user community and facilitate communication and sharing between users(for example Calgary Airport authority in Canada use Facebook connect to grant access).The infrastructure of a Social network is essentially a dynamic virtual organization, Cloud environment provide low level abstractions of computation and storage. There are large number of commercial cloud service provider such as Amazon EC2/S3,Google App Engine, Microsoft Azure, and so forth. A social cloud provides virtualized resources and hence make it Scalable computing model.

Social Cloud Architecture: In Social cloud services can be mapped through the Facebook identification, under which interaction, limit trading with all friends or even friends of friends, transfer of credits between users and also storing information. A high level architecture of Social Cloud is shown in Figure 1.

FaceBook Markup Language (FBML) is a subset of HTML enables creation of application and integrate with Facebook completely. Facebook Java Script is Facebook version of Java Script to create virtual application scope. Whenever a page is requested by user through Facebook URL, then the server forward the request for that web page. Facebook parsed that page and then returned to the user, this routing structure would be expensive if it gone through Facebook Server. In order to reduce

Figure 1. Social cloud architecture

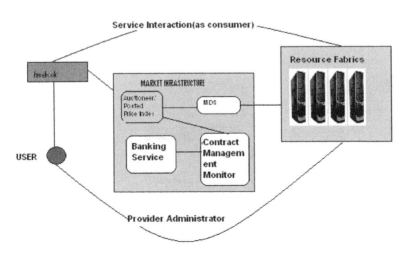

the expensiveness FBJS is used which asynchronously request data from the specified service in a transparent manner as shown in Figure 2.

Cloud computing provides virtualized resources as one of the services to its users such as photo sharing. Basically there are two generic requirements for such services. The interface need mechanism to create state full instance for reservation. Discovered the services to advertise capacity based on XML metadata.

All Services use Web Service Resource Framework (WSRF) and run on Globus WS-core/Tomcat. Grid Remote Application Virtualization Interface (GRAVI) was used to create a base storage service,SORMA (Build open grid market for grid resource allocation) do WS-Agreement and DRIVE (Distributed Resource Infrastructure for a Virtual Economy) provides the auction framework (Chard, 2010).

CONCLUSION

As cloud computing is one of the major research topics it provides more functionality and reduces economical and technical barriers. It also reduces the cost which is of major concern for many corporate sector by which research and utilization of resources will be availed with ease. In the globalization environment there are so many servers which are spread over the globe that need to be synchronized. Social networking sites have the major application of cloud computing. As this topic is

Figure 2. Facebook application hosting environment

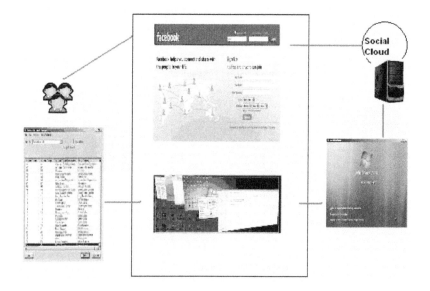

so vast and so much new research is always in queue, because of this it is quite difficult to cover all the topic of cloud computing, but we try to cover all the major topics in this case study.

REFERENCES

Alabbadi, M. M. (2011). Cloud computing for education and learning: Education and learning as a service. In *Proceedings of 14th IEEE International Conference on Interactive Collaborative Learning*. Washington, DC: IEEE Press.

Begum, S. & Khan. (2011). Potential of cloud computing architecture. In *Proceedings of IEEE International Conference on Information and Communication Technologies*. Washington, DC: IEEE Press.

Cassandra. (2009). *Welcome to apache Cassandra*. Retrieved from http://cassandra. apache.org/.

Chard, K. (2010). Social cloud: Cloud computing in social networks. In *Proceedings of 3rd IEEE International Conference on Cloud Computing*. Washington, DC: IEEE Press.

Data Center Knowledge. (2010). *The facebook data center FAQ*. Retrieved from http://www.datacenterknowledge.com/the-facebook-data-center-faq/.

Facebook. (2013). *Facebook newsroom*. Retrieved from http://newsroom.fb.com/News/The-Next-Web-Conference-New-Timeline-Apps-14f.aspx.

Gong, C. (2010). The characteristics of cloud computing. In *Proceedings of 39th IEEE International Conference on Parallel Processing Workshops* (ICPPW). Washington, DC: IEEE Press.

Hinchcliffe, D., & Kim, P. (2012). *Social business by design: Transformative social media strategies for the connected company*. Hoboken, NJ: Jossey-Bass.

India Times. (n.d.). Retrieved from http://economictimes.indiatimes.com/tech/software/mobile-internet-startups-to-shine-despite-dim-facebook-ipo/articleshow/13683334.cms.

Kalagiakos, P., & Karampelas, P. (2011). Cloud computing learning. In *Proceedings of 5th IEEE International Conference on Application of Information and Communication Technologies*. Washington, DC: IEEE Press.

Mail, D. (2012). *Valued at $100bn, Facebook expected to hold record-breaking IPO launch in third week of May.* Retrieved from http://www.dailymail.co.uk/news/article-2087557/Facebook-IPO-date-Launch-expected-week-May.html.

MakeUseOf. (2010). *How does facebook work? The nuts and bolts.* Retrieved from http://www.makeuseof.com/tag/facebook-work-nuts-bolts-technology-explained/.

Memcached. (2009). *What is memcached?* Retrieved from http://memcached.org/.

Module for Hosting. (2013). What is apache HTTP server? Retrieved from.http://www.modulehosting.com/apache.html

PHP. (2013). What is PHP? Retrieved from http://php.net/manual/en/intro-whatis.php.

Search Enterprise Linux. (2008). *Definition: Linux.* Retrieved from http://search-enterpriselinux.techtarget.com/definition/Linux.

TeachTerms. (2013). *MySQL.* Retrieved from http://www.techterms.com/definition/mysql.

Thrift, A. (2012). *Getting started.* Retrieved from http://thrift.apache.org/.

Webopedia. (2013). *Apache web server.* Retrieved from http://www.webopedia.com/TERM/A/Apache_Web_server.html.

Wikipedia. (2013a). *Scribe (log server).* Retrieved from http://en.wikipedia.org/wiki/Scribe_(log_server).

Wikipedia. (2013b). *Mark zuckerberg.* Retrieved from http://en.wikipedia.org/wiki/Mark_Zuckerberg.

Zhang, Z. Chen, & Huo. (2010). Cloud computing research and development trend. In *Proceedings of IEEE International Conference on Future Networks.* Washington, DC: IEEE Press.

KEY TERMS AND DEFINITIONS

Cassandra: It is Database management system to handle large amount of database which is spreaded over the distributed network.

Cloud Computing: It is a computing model over network for remote servers hosted on Internet to store, manage and process data.

Distributed Computing: In this various network components are located at different places and they communicate and coordinate by message passing.

Grid Computing: In this various interconnected computers use the same resources collectively.

Memcached: It is general purpose distributed memory caching system.

Parallel Computing: It is a computation in which operation done parallel provide better results in less time.

Virtualization: It is creation virtual version of hardware platforms, server or network resources.

Chapter 12
Price Effectiveness in Hotels:
Case Study Comparing Strategies Adopted by Mid-Size Hotels in New Delhi

Nidhi Chowdhry
Jaipur National University, India

EXECUTIVE SUMMARY

This case study focuses on the mid-size hotel industry in India. It will analyze the extent to which the pricing strategies are adopted in order to optimize revenues. The mid-size segment is comprised of three and four star hotels, which cater to the average foreign and domestic leisure travelers. Pricing is the single greatest challenge facing independent hotels today. It is studied how determining optimal rates based on the patterns of price sensitivity of demand still remains the biggest challenge for these hotels. Price sensitivity and its impact on revenue are examined. To determine and analyze this challenge faced by mid-size hotel industry, the case will focus on pricing strategies and challenges faced by a midscale chain hotel and a stand-alone economy hotel in New Delhi. The hotels have been taken from National Capital Region (New Delhi) which is the largest hotel market in the country both in terms of active assets under development and potential projects in planning.

DOI: 10.4018/978-1-4666-4357-4.ch012

Copyright ©2014, IGI Global. Copying or distributing in print or electronic forms without written permission of IGI Global is prohibited.

BACKGROUND

Breakfast time at the coffee shop of a High-rise hotel was always refreshing. The majority of the guests who stayed at the hotel in the last 11 years gave that feedback. For Prashant Agnihotri it was surely one of the 'wow' factors for his hotel. He has already served as General Manager of the hotel for the last 5 years. He had joined the group in 2002 and had been promoted from an Executive to GM level in the same chain with maximum years spent in this New Delhi property. Prashant always felt that interacting with the beaming guests at this time was the best way to start his day.

The High-rise Hotels, established in the year 2000, is one of India's largest chains of upscale hotels and resorts. It has been the perfect choice for today's discerning and value conscious traveler. Whether it's business or pleasure that brings you to India, this chain of hotels adds great value to your travel experience. The hotel chain is generally comprised of hotels with inventory from 50-100 rooms. Within a span of 10 years they have set up hotels in major cities of India. High-rise Hotels in Gurgaon, Delhi, Bengaluru, Chennai, Hyderabad, Indore, Chandigarh, Pune, Goa, and other cities are located within a convenient distance of key local attractions or business hubs. While 5 Star hotels in India are at par with global competitors, there is a near absence of internationally acceptable mid-market hotels. This gap is now being proficiently filled by this hotel chain which operates in the midscale segment in India.

This High-Rise Hotel, in New Delhi has 50 well furnished rooms. Guests can enjoy contemporary accommodation at reasonable rates, personal yet highly efficient service, and premium amenities, including fitness center, swimming pool, business center, on-site restaurants, and meeting rooms.

High-rise, New Delhi is rated in the top ten by trip advisor. It is highly rated in most Tourist/Traveller's Guides. It is in the heart of the downtown/suburban area, close to the business, entertainment, and shopping areas. Most rooms are deliberately maintained to cater to the needs of a business traveler.

The hotel gets 85% of its customers as foreign tourists. The occupancy rate in this hotel is 100% in busy months of February to April and September to mid-December. Rest of the year the occupancy is approx 75%. The rooms are occupied for the 365 days in this year. Most of the days, especially weekdays, demand is more than supply in this hotel. With a multi cuisine restaurant and 24 hour room service, the hotel does not practice differential pricing for its customers. It charges single price for all of its customers irrespective of different nationality. Tourists generally would like to stay in this hotel for the wonderful service provided by the hotel. Generally the hotel gets repeat customers and the customer loyalty is very excellent.

The daily morning meeting will start in some time. These meetings helped Prashant set agendas for the day and discuss and solve any last night issues, interact with his team, and understand daily problems. Though he knew, the real agenda was always the same: to ensure meeting budgeted revenue targets of the hotel. For the last five years he has managed to keep this property in the top three, not only in the city in this segment of the hotel, but always amongst the High-Rise Chain.

He knew that according to World Travel and Tourism Committee (WTTC) estimates that the Hotel Industry in India has witnessed a tremendous boom in recent years. The current count of hotel rooms is 130,000, and the country is expected to require an additional 50,000 rooms over the next two to three years.

The competition had really increased in the last two years. Not only chain hotels of various segments were mushrooming in the city, but various stand alone properties coming up as well. One such stand alone property in the same segment, though established in 2010, has been giving tough competition to High-Rise.

Prashant has had few occasional informal meetings with Vaibhav Singh, the GM of Rest Inn hotel. Vaibhav had also invited Prashant for breakfast and evening tea and snacks as a friendly gesture. Prashant understands that the Rest Inn Hotel, New Delhi is a modern midscale/economy hotel in Delhi. It was established in the year 2010 with a corporate motto to provide an excellent delight for the corporate and leisure travelers offering a 'home away from home' concept.

Strategically located close to major commercial and shopping complex of the city, this budget Delhi hotel is a pleasant place to stay, near the biggest commercial centre in Delhi. It boasts of modern architecture and exquisite interiors, offering its guests traditional warm Indian hospitality, to ensure a comfortable stay.

This hotel has 40 rooms and suites, well-equipped with an array of amenities. All the rooms are nicely styled and look cozy and inviting. All rooms are well maintained. Its homey atmosphere, along with friendly staff, makes it a haven of solace and comfort for your complete accommodation in Delhi. It has a 24-hour multi-cuisine restaurant that serves amazing food and beverages, offering good delightful dining in Delhi. Due to its location and proximity in the hub of some of Delhi's most happening restaurants, pubs and bars, eating out is always an option to experience Delhi.

The one three impressive conference room is ideal to hold any sort of business or corporate meetings in Delhi and a large banquet hall for large scale functions. The health centre and other amenities like Wi-Fi technology, round the clock security, friendly staff, pick and drop facilities, etc. are some of the advantages you can enjoy.

SETTING THE STAGE

Reema Gulati, sales manager is always present in the daily morning meeting. She and team have been the key factor apart from the background teams to ensure that all targets were always met. Prashant again questions her on the tough competition High-rise gets from their neighbor Rest Inn.

Reema elaborates, "The main features and marketing policies followed by us for years have been:

- We have been an established chain of hotels, and hence relies heavily on Global distribution system (GDS) for booking. We have had exclusive tie-ups with the known names and therefore get majority bookings through internet.
- Due to the above reason, guests generally book the rooms on their own, i.e. 40% reservation is done directly by the guests.
- Only 20% booking is done by travel agents who operate on contract basis.
- The rest 40% is helped the very efficient sales team who facilitate bookings by relationship building with corporate and direct the requirements to their hotels.
- We have a strong Revenue management department which helps is managing the day to day Best available rates (BAR rates) to earn maximum revenues on daily basis.
- Our Housekeeping staff has always been efficient. They are excellent in communication and they meet the customer demand promptly.
- Generally in this hotel, 80% of the customers are repeated which means there is customer loyalty to the maximum extent.
- Customers have been retained, because of the group effect. The guests have approved of the same chain hotel in Bangalore, prefers the same hotel in NCR.
- On 100% occupancy days, overbooking is done to maximize revenue in case of any last minute cancellations.
- Checkin and check out time has always been fixed at 12 noon.
- The hotel is strict in charging penalty amount for cancellations or retentions."

Prashant realizes that this seems like a perfect strategy, then how has a standalone property like Rest Inn snatched away so many guests and bookings.

Reema at this time mentions the various features and Marketing policies followed by the Rest Inn hotel:

- The average occupancy rate is 65%. Usually they get repeated customers.
- Most of the customers are tourists. Majority of guests are domestic in nature. Either tourists or business traveler.
- The length of stay is 1-2 days.
- They get the customers through travel agents.

- To get more customers they provide discounts in the off-season. They charge different tariff to different customers.
- They do overbook the rooms to maximize the revenues. But that is very rare.
- Check in and checkout time is not fixed. They may cater to half day (5 am-12 pm), post lunch (2 pm-7 pm) and night only (8 pm–12 pm) timings. Thereby even booking the same room 3 times in day if required.
- They are also not strict in cancellation policy and may charge anything from no charging to a day depending on the level of guest, his length of stay and bookings available on that day.
- They maximize revenue by ensuring good occupancy by giving discounts and through the banquet business.

With the above facts in knowledge Prashant and Reema brainstormed on various hotel industry facts they had learnt and experienced in their professional careers.

MARKET SEGMENTATION

Hotels in India are broadly classified into 7 categories (five star deluxe, five-star, four star, three star, two star, and one-star and heritage hotels) by the Ministry of Tourism, Government of India, based on the general features and facilities offered. The ratings are reviewed every five years. As shown in Table 1, 3 and 4 star hotels (Mid-market) are approx 50% of the total hotels in numbers as well as rooms.

The unorganized sector which is not listed accounts for 29 – 30% of the total hotel rooms in the country.

The mid-size hotel segment also caters to the middle level business travelers since it offers most of the essential services of luxury hotels without the high costs since the tax component of this segment is lower compared with the premium segment. The expansion plans especially are focused in metro and especially in tier II cities.

New Delhi and its surrounding areas, referred as NCR (National Capital Region) is the largest hotel market in the country both in terms of active assets under

Table 1.

Star Category	No. of Hotels	No. of Rooms
4-star	132	9401
3-star	704	31039
Total	1934	103973

146

development and potential projects in planning. NCR witnessed a growth of 15% in supply in 2010/11. There is an expectation of only 75% (13,906 rooms) of these projects to be built over the next five years.

Pricing: The Key Value Driver

The "core offering" of a hotel-price, room, and location-still account for about 70% of the choice criteria. Only 30% of the selection process is led by new value drivers such as technology (Internet reservations, high-speed in-room Internet access), loyalty points and customization options. One of the single greatest challenges facing independent hotels today is pricing. Pricing the inventory effectively can lead to profitability and helps lay the foundation for long term success. But, pricing the inventory ineffectively can lead to disaster. Various kinds of prices generally prevalent in the industry are as follows:

- **Rack Rates:** Without any affiliations to warrant discounts, the Rack Rated customer paid the published rate, which was the highest rate.
- **Consortia Rates:** This was the same customer who booked through a travel agent using the GDS and received a 5%-10% discount off Rack Rates.
- **Corporate Rates:** Having met the hotel's qualifying criteria, such as volume, businesses were guaranteed discounted rates.
- **Group Rates:** With a block of rooms, rates varied based on time of year and the nature of the group.
- **Weekend Rates:** Individual leisure travelers, usually within a drive distance to the hotel.
- **Promotional rates:** These rates were originally used sparingly and used as a means to stimulate business by using discounted rates to anyone, regardless of affiliation.

For many hotels developing effective pricing strategies remains a complex issue. Increasingly, savvy hoteliers turning to specialist revenue managers whose goal, ultimately, is to maximize companywide revenue and profits while building strong hotel partner relationships across the country. Some examples of historical data which are important in a rate optimization analysis include room types; competitor information; total occupancy and revenue; occupancy by date and available capacity.

Optimal rates are determined based on the patterns of price sensitivity of demand derived from historical data. As different markets may have diverse price sensitivities and ranges of acceptable rates, a careful analysis of the historical data is necessary to determine the best way to adjust these rates. Hotels should identify the type of customers and the price they are willing to pay for utilising the service.

'Price Sensitivity of Demand' is a measure of the change in demand relative to a change in price. If a small change in price is accompanied by a large change in demand, the product is said to be elastic (or responsive to price changes). However, a product is inelastic if a large change in price is accompanied by a small amount of change in demand.

Price sensitivity can have a dramatic impact on revenue. For example, if the price offered for a room in an hotel is too low, the demand for the product may be significant; however the revenues from the sale of the product will also be low. In turn, if a rate offered is too high, there is a risk that not enough demand will materialize, and both situations may result in a reduction of potential revenue.

Pricing and demand are inter-related and need to be coordinated. In the hospitality industry, demand for a room is cyclic in nature and follows a trend. Revenue management models help pinpoint demand by minimizing uncertainty and producing the best possible forecast.

This can be done on the basis of the general parameters shown in Table 2.

OPTIMAL PRICING AND ITS EFFECT ON REVENUE MANAGEMENT

Revenue Management is a technique to optimize the revenue earned from a fixed, perishable resource. The challenge is to sell the right resources to the right customer at the right time. Revenue Management is of especially high relevance in cases where

Table 2.

Physical Characteristics	High Price	Low Price
View	Pool view, ocean view, hill view	Non-scenic view
size	Bigger rooms with more facilities	Small rooms with few facilities
Temporal	Week day bookings	Week end bookings
Logical fences		
Length of stay	Short stay (1-2 days)	Longer stay
Flexibility	Cancellations and re-scheduling are allowed at a low penalty	High penalty for cancellation and schedule change
Time of purchase	Bookings are made very close to date	Bookings are made quite early
Privileges	Are rewarded loyalty privileges	No privileges
Size of business provided	Corporate business, Customer booking frequently	Self funding vacationers booking rarely
Point of sale	Physical delivery and confirmation	By email or phone

the constant costs are relatively high compared to the variable costs. The less variable costs there are, the more the additional revenue earned will contribute to the overall profit. Revenue Management in other words tries to maximize revenues by managing the tradeoff between a low occupancy and higher room rate scenario (business customers) versus a high occupancy and lower room rate (vacation customers).

Room Allocation: Revenue management also puts light on the allocation of inventory (hotel rooms) among different segments if, for instance, a hotel has two price categories of rooms, say Rs.4500 and Rs. 6000. Since the pricing is different for the two rooms, these rooms are each targeted at a different customer set. Based on the historical preference pattern of customers in each segment, it would be possible to estimate the number of customers who would be willing to buy these rooms at a given price with a reasonable variance.

From Table 3, it can be analyzed that the hotels maximize their revenues through differential pricing strategies and by targeting different customers. Hotels target at the right customers by charging the fixed prices.

Hotels also resort to the practice of overbooking to increase revenue. This is a practice of intentionally selling more rooms than available in order to offset the effect of cancellations. For example, if a hotel has 100 rooms. If 90 rooms are booked in advance in season there is no certainty that all the rooms would be occupied by end of the day. There can be cancellations and no further booking as well. That is a hotel might end up with just 85 rooms occupied on a season day when it could have had 100 percent occupancy. To avoid this, the hotel takes booking of 110 rooms and manages 100 percent with all adversity prevailing and maximizing revenue.

Table 3. Analysis of various hotels on the basis of tariff plans, available on their respective websites/booking portals

Name and Location	Type of room (Base category)	Single Occupancy	Double/twin occupancy	Facilities
Park Land, Green Park, New Delhi	Executive room	6000	6500	Buffet breakfast, tax and basic room facilities
Lemon Tree Hotel, City Center, Gurgaon	Deluxe/Executive room	6599 + tax	7299 + tax	Buffet breakfast, complimentary internet {at business center}, comp wifi internet for 30 mins. daily, modern in-room amenities
Clarks Inn, Nehru Place, New Delhi	Superior room	4500 + tax	5000 + tax	Superior Room includes buffet breakfast, mineral water and newspaper.
Rockland Inn	Deluxe room	5000	6000	Rate are inclusive of Breakfast and all taxes

* rates as on 12th Feb 2012 available on their respective websites

With recall of all the above facts and knowledge, Prashant asked Reema to compile a list of comparisons between the High-Rise hotel and Rest Inn Hotel in Tables 4 and 5.

PRICING STRATEGIES ADOPTED BY EACH HOTEL

- It is believed that the hotels, which are functioning at the large scale, are good in revenue management and they apply most advanced techniques to manage their revenues. High-rise also has an upper edge as they provide the state of the art facilities and services to the customers.

Table 4. Rate charged by high-rise hotel for 3 room bookings done on a high demand day

Check in -Checkout	Occupancy	Rack Rate (Rs)	Rate Charged (Rs) *	Facilities
12 noon	single	6000	5500	Incl of Breakfast + tax
12 noon	Twin	7000	6500	Incl of Breakfast + tax, airport drop
12 noon	double	7000	6500	Incl of Breakfast + tax + office drop
Total Revenue per day			18500	

Table 5. Rate charged by Rest Inn hotel for 3 room bookings done on a high demand day

Check in -Checkout	Occupancy	Rack Rate (Rs)	Rate Charged (Rs)	Facilities
5 am -12 pm	single	5500	3500	Incl of lunch + tax
2pm -7pm	single	5500	4000	Incl of evening snacks + tax
8 pm – 12 noon	single	5500	4500	Incl of Breakfast + tax
12 noon	double	6000	5500	Incl of Breakfast + tax, airport drop
12 noon	twin	6000	5000	Incl of Breakfast + tax
Total Revenue per day			22500	

*rate charged is the best available rate for the day formulated by revenue dept.

- In case of the occupancy rates measure in terms of foreign tourists, High-rise hotel does exceedingly well. But the general domestic traveler is picked by Rest Inn hotel as well. A general traveler from airport and railway stations is picked by travel agents where a hotel sales person and GDS may not always help.
- High-rise hotel attract more business class customers by providing good and efficient services to them. And by being inter connected. The supply is more than demand in our case.
- Rest Inn gives importance to the cultural values of the city.
- The concept of overbooking is followed in both kinds of hotels.
- The market segmentation is not there in case of Rest Inn. But it is practiced in our chain hotels.
- In both type of hotels the maximum number of customers are tourists.
- Stand alone hotels do not practice revenue management techniques neither through its differential pricing nor through market segmentation. They just manage their revenues by applying the concept of logical booking.

PRICING STRATEGY

The objective of a revenue maximizing can be achieved by capturing the optimal price for the room in a particular season. Apart from various factors such as location, service quality and technology, the assessment of competition in the market and achieving flexibility in deciding price when required can be produce maximum revenue from the projected demand. Interdepartmental Integration eg conference room and banquet bookings help in achieving the revenue strategies.

With this revelations, Prashant and Reema both agreed and listed the various Challenges and the route forward to best pricing strategy.

CHALLENGES AND THE ROUTE FORWARD TO BEST PRICING STRATEGY

- While the emergence of revenue management and rate optimization is helping to demystify pricing practices, it is important that hoteliers across the region understand the demand characteristics of the various grades of rooms in their facility, along with how price affects demand and design a rate spectrum that is tuned to all of these. This allows hoteliers to take full advantage of their business opportunities, ensuring that they are capturing the maximum revenue at all levels.

- Beyond the scope of regular revenue management practices - such as selecting the correct overbooking, rate restrictions and best available rate, lies the challenge of selecting the correct rates to choose from in the first place. Rate Optimization is the practice of selecting the room rates offered in a rate (or price) range based on the historical price sensitivity of demand. The goal of rate optimization is to understand the demand characteristics of rooms and the price sensitivity of demand and utilise the data to define room prices that will capture the maximum revenue over time.

- Between these two extremes of over discounting and overpricing, is a rate offering that will capture the demand to maximize the overall revenue. It is crucial to determine, in advance, the correct rates to be used when there is excess capacity or excess demand. An incorrect determination of the rate, or price, range is likely to affect the overall revenue for a variety of rooms.

- Price elasticity analysis must be augmented by accounting for real world factors. Hotels need to be able to adapt and learn to deal with non-quantifiable events such as major sporting events and random effects on demand.

- Once the refined price range is introduced, an increase in hotel revenues across defined rate periods can be expected. After the refined rate spectrum has been in effect for 120 days, a comparison should be made by the hotel to determine the improved revenue performance.

- Price will always be a major determinant of a success of the hotel and the deciding factor for guest to check-in.

- In-depth forecasting of price on quarterly, half-yearly and annual basis will help in formulating a model of revenue management which will not only impart flexibility to the system but higher profits.

- Sophisticated hotels will evolve to one-to-one revenue management; each individual will be a market segment in themselves.

- Forecasting and yielding of function space will be a focus in the future for hotels.

- Many large hotel companies and revenue management systems are working to develop effective models in this area.

- The goals of the entire hotel team, from property level to corporate, will need to be aligned in order for revenue management to reach its fullest potential.

- There is a gap between the sophistication of the revenue management practice and the technology available to support it. We need to adopt the new technologies as they are available and use our minds to manipulate them expertly to achieve ultimate success.

- In the future, technology will support calculating the total customer value and the potential total customer spend, based on history and future potential from demographics, to determine what rate and what availability to offer to a potential guest.

Chapter 13
Indian Luxury Car Market Changing Lanes:
A Case of BMW India

Pardeep Bawa
Lovely Professional University, India

EXECUTIVE SUMMARY

Aston Martin has recently introduced itself to India. Many perceive it as a routine entry of another car maker. However, this specific entry isn't coincidence, but a calculated move. It has to do with the recent unexpected growth in the Indian luxury car market which is more than just market dynamics. It is something which reflects a changing lifestyle pattern of a class which is called affluent. The growth rate for these cars with a price tag which is above Rs. 25 lacs has been 20% on average for the some years. When the whole world was facing recession the Indian luxury car market grew by 23% to 6671 units as per the Society of Indian Automobile Manufacturers (SIAM) despite half a percent decline in passenger car sales, to 11.04 lakh vehicles (Dovel, 2011). 2010 has shown growth in the automobile sector which was up by 25%. Indian luxury car market had been dominated by Mercedes Benz (entered in India in mid 1994) until 2009 where it was outscored by BMW which entered India in 2006. Mercedes Benz's market share of 90% shrank to 38% and its market share largely fell to BMW which has 42%. This case will study the factors responsible for the growth of the Indian luxury car market with reference to BMW's quick growth to the top with the help of cars customized for Indian infrastructure conditions, an aggressive distribution strategy, pricing designed in lieu of competition, and comprehensively smart promotional efforts.

DOI: 10.4018/978-1-4666-4357-4.ch013

Copyright ©2014, IGI Global. Copying or distributing in print or electronic forms without written permission of IGI Global is prohibited.

INTRODUCTION

A recent study conducted by Booz & Co. reveals that the widespread paradigm shift of the global economy in Asia towards the automotive industry will drive India to bag 4th position in the global market by 2015 and surpass the European Nations. The automotive industry is one of the leading industries in India for FDI, and the U.S. automakers have made considerable investments since the early-1990s. With a large and growing middle class population, the smaller car segment has seen a fair upswing in recent years as per the report. As income levels go up, the share of larger cars will also increase in the times to come. There is a potential for Indian market to touch revenues of $150-$200 billion by 2030, projecting that India will soon be bigger than most other markets as per the same report. Report further shown that the FDI in the auto sector is expected to exceed that in most other sectors. India is likely to attract $ 25-35 billion in FDI over the course of the next 10 years for the automotive industry. Over the next 20 years, India will be part of global automotive triumvirate the global BIG 3 in light passenger vehicle segment.

GROWTH DRIVERS OF INDIAN LUXURY CAR MARKET

Youngest Population

India has the youngest population in the world. India has world's 17% (765 million) of working population (17-64 years) as per a Morgan Stanley report. The philosophy of this younger population is quiet different than others. Demand for young engineers, MBAs, CAs, and doctors is greater than ever as Indian, as well as MNCs, are expanding like never before. They want to work & enjoy. A substantial part of their income goes into leisure activities like dining out, travelling, owning latest gadgets, cars, and so forth. This has caused the demand for these kind of products & services to soar. Average age of luxury car buyers has constantly been decreasing. In case of BMW it has come down to just 40 years. Figure 1 gives a clear picture of this phenomenon.

Easy Financing

Getting a car financed in India is very easy if one has got positive credentials in terms of income. Interest rates are very competitive due to a large number of private & public sector banks. Banks are ready, more than they ever to fund. As much as 95% of the showroom price of the vehicle is being funded by many banks. Manu-

Figure 1. Indian demographic profile

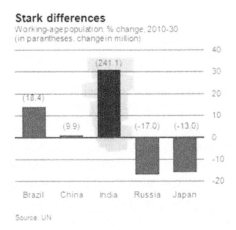

Stark differences
Working-age population, % change, 2010-30
(in parantheses, change in million)

Brazil　China　India　Russia　Japan

Source: UN

facturers have corporate tie-ups with banks for smooth & easy financing. This has positively contributed to the growth of Indian automobile industry & luxury car market for that matter.

High Disposable Income

Now days Indians are saving less & spending more. Their disposable income has increased as a result of their changed life style which demands a living which is high class. An EMI of Rs. 40000 for a family of two, with both of them working & earning Rs. 70,000, is an easy task. People are keener now a days to experience life style commodities and their rising income levels are helping them in it.

Rising Number of Millionaires

Growth of Indian economy has been faster than other emerging economies during recent times. Globally, India had the highest growth-rate (22.7%) of millionaire population during the year 2007 (see Figure 2). India added 23,000 millionaires from 2006 to 2007, taking total figure to around 123,000 millionaires; wealth as measured in US Dollars (Merrill Lynch Cap Gemini Report). However, during recession, the country noticed a decline of 31.6% in number of millionaires. But post-recession recovery was much faster compared to other economies. These numbers are expected to grow up to 140,000 by the year 2010. This robust growth in the number of millionaires in the country, being one of the highest globally, paves the way for further growth of the luxury car market.

Rising Middle Class

The Indian middle class, who are target consumers for many global companies, is expected to swell up to 267 million people in the next five years, up 67 percent from the current levels, thus providing a great market opportunity for firms, according to NCAER. A report by National Council for Applied Economic Research's (NCAER) Center for Macro Consumer Research shown that by 2015-16, India would be a country of 53.3 million middle class households, translating into 267 million people falling in the category. As per the study, which uses "household income" as the criterion, a family with an annual income between Rs. 3.4 lakh to Rs. 17 lakh (at 2009-10 price levels) falls in the middle class category? Interestingly, as per NCAER findings, the middle class that represents only 13.1 percent of India's population currently owns 49 percent of total number of cars.

Standard of Living

As India begins to build more and more infrastructure, export more; the level of money for each individual then goes up. This means that people are able to purchase more, which raises their standard of living and the standard of living for the people they buy from. Current estimates by Capgemini and Merrill Lynch World Wealth Report 2011, Indian middle class would be increased by 100 million in the next decade given how fast the economy is going. The current purchasing price parity adjusted gross domestic product in India is $3,176, which is still quite low. However, India has a growth rate of roughly eight percent per year, which means that it is growing quite fast and it has what may be the largest middle class in the world.

Figure 2. Growth of millionaires in India

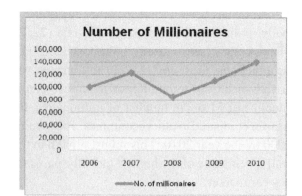

Source: Raygain Technologies: Indian Luxury Car Market-An Insight, 2011

The current number of citizens in the Indian middle class stands at 300 million; which is lower than the standards set in Europe and the United States. However, the growing middle class means that by 2015, the PPP-Adjusted GDP will be six percent higher than it is now. The level of poverty has also gone down in India over the past few years, currently sitting at 22 percent of Indians living under the poverty line. This number used to be much higher and India is hoping to eradicate poverty by the year 2020 as per the same report. High standards of living helps different consumption & lifestyle related commodities' market to grow & same is the case with luxury car market.

CASE OF BMW

About BMW

BMW (Bavarian Motor Works) is a German automobile, motorcycle and engine manufacturing company founded in 1917. BMW is headquartered in Munich, Bavaria, Germany. It also owns and produces the Mini marque, and is the parent company of Rolls-Royce Motor Cars. In 2010, the BMW group produced 1,481,253 automobiles and 112,271 motorcycles across all its brands. For BMW 2011 had been proved a bumper year, with new records in unit sales, revenues and profits. BMW booked net profit of 4.907 billion euros ($6.5 billion) in 2011, an increase of 51.3 percent year-on-year, and pre-tax profit rose by 52.1 percent to 7.383 billion euros. Unit sales were up 14.2 percent at 1.669 million vehicles, pushing up revenues by 13.8 percent to 68.821 billion euros in the same period. Unit sales of the main BMW brand were up 12.8 percent, Mini sales raced ahead by 21.7 percent and Rolls-Royce were up as much as 30.5 percent. The financial services division reported a 47.4-percent increase in pre-tax earnings to 1.79 billion euros. Shareholders were equally benefitted with the dividend payout being increased by 1.0 euro to 2.30 euros per share in year 2011. BMW's financial figures are shown in Figures 3 and 4.

BMW INNOVATION NETWORK

Maximum Freedom for Visionary Concepts

Based in Munich, BMW Group Research and Technology is a wholly-owned subsidiary of BMW AG and has been responsible for BMW Group research activities since 2003. The roughly 250 specialists working for the company have the clear mission to develop new technologies for use in the automobile. To reach this goal,

Figure 3. BMW group sales, production, and financial figures over the years

BMW Group in figures	2006	2007	2008	2009	**2010**	Change in %
Sales volume – Automobiles						
BMW	1,185,088	1,276,793	1,202,239	1,068,770	**1,224,280**	14.6
MINI	188,077	222,875	232,425	216,538	**234,175**	8.1
Rolls-Royce	805	1,010	1,212	1,002	**2,711**	. .
Total	**1,373,970**	**1,500,678**	**1,435,876**	**1,286,310**	**1,461,166**	**13.6**
Production – Automobiles						
BMW	1,179,317	1,302,774	1,203,482	1,043,829	**1,236,989**	18.5
MINI	186,674	237,700	235,019	213,670	**241,043**	12.8
Rolls-Royce	847	1,029	1,417	918	**3,221**	. .
Total	**1,366,838**	**1,541,503**	**1,439,918**	**1,258,417**	**1,481,253**	**17.7**
Financial figures *in euro million*						
Revenues	48,999	56,018	53,197	50,681	**60,477**	19.3
Capital expenditure	4,313	4,267	4,204	3,471	**3,263**	-6.0
Depreciation and amortisation	3,272	3,683	3,670	3,600	**3,682**	2.3
Operating cash flow	5,373	6,246	4,471	4,921	**8,150**	65.6
Profit before financial result	4,050	4,212	921	289	**5,094**	. .
Profit before tax	4,124	3,873	351	413	**4,836**	. .
Net profit	2,874	3,134	330	210	**3,234**	. .

Source: BMW Group Annual Report, 2011

Figure 4. Sales, revenue, and financial figures till Q3, 2011

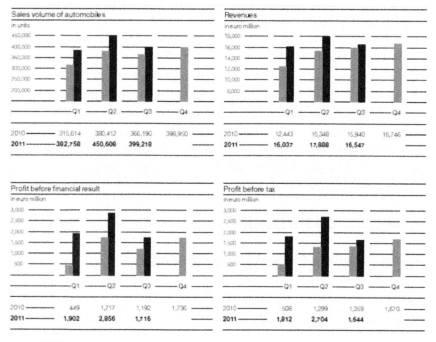

Source: BMW Group Annual Report, 2011

the project teams work on five research highlights crucial to the future of the automobile in our modern world: VehicleTechnology, CleanEnergy, EfficientDynamics, ConnectedDrive, and ITDrive. The legal independence of BMW Group Research and Technology and flat hierarchies with short decision-making routes give the specialists creative freedom and maximum flexibility – essential prerequisites for a climate suited ideally for innovation. Integrated labs and workshops, in turn, ensures rapid practical implementation of the technologies developed in the car. Precisely this provided the possibility to complete the overall concept for the BMW H2R Hydrogen Car in just ten months in 2004, the car subsequently setting up nine international, officially acknowledged records.

Worldwide Network

Through a comprehensive, in-house and external network, BMW Group Research and Technology has access to new trends and technologies. This includes the BMW Group's worldwide innovation network with centres in the USA, Japan, and Germany as well as joint ventures with companies, universities, colleges and research institutes such as the German Research Centre for Artificial Intelligence (GRAI) in Saarbrücken. BMW Group Research and Technology cooperates closely with the Eurécom Institute in the area of information and telecommunication technology. Together with nine international partners in industry and four universities, this Inter-European Institute is based in the Sophia Antipolis Science Part near Nice. The main areas of cooperation are Network Technologies, Broadband Wireless Networks as well as Mobility and Security.

BMW India

This European major BMW entered India in 2006. The company with headquarters in Gurgaon and production unit in Chennai had initial investment of 1.1 billion rupees. It has swiftly developed both infrastructure and dealership network. The production plant at Chennai, established in 2007, has an annual capacity of 3000 units in a single shift and it produces BMW 3 series and BMW 5 series sedans. The rest of models- BMW 7 series, X3 and X5 are imported as CBUs. BMW 3 and 5 series account for 80% of the total sales of company in India, of which BMW 5 series has highest sales. In just four years i.e. from 2006 to 2010 BMW has reached at top spot in Indian luxury car market. Most striking was the fact that it displaced none other than Mercedes Benz which was the only player till 2006. For recent sales data on the luxury car market, and BMW in particular, see Figures 5 through 7.

MARKETING STRATEGIES OF BMW IN INDIA

Aggressive Pricing

In an effort to bring a new set of consumers on board, luxury car maker BMW launched its least expensive name-plate-the BMW X1 (Menon, 2011). The Sports Utility Vehicle (SUV), available in both diesel and petrol variants, are made available in the price range of Rs 22 to Rs 29.9 lakh (Rs 2.2-2.9 million). BMW strategically priced BMW X1 so as to put it as the least expensive entry level luxury sedan & a product for consumers who are looking to upgrade from a Toyota Fortuner, Ford Endeavour or a Hyundai Santa Fe, which are available at slightly lower price tags. In

Figure 5. Segment wise break up and month wise sales fluctuation of top 3 luxury players in India

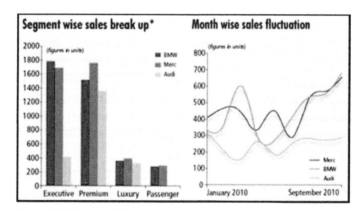

Source: SIAM Jan-Sep 2010

Figure 6. BMW India 2011 sales volume

Mon	3 Series	5 Series	6 Series	7 Series	Gran Turismo	X1	X3	X5	X6	Z4	Total
Jan	164	271	1	17	7	15	2	9	9	5	500
Feb	176	264	1	38	8	110	0	10	12	1	620
Mar	315	380	1	60	11	203	0	30	17	10	1027
Apr	240	255	1	32	5	215	0	18	13	1	780
May	195	264	3	23	4	190	0	8	18	2	707
Jun	163	246	3	30	9	403	2	17	14	3	890
Total	1253	1680	10	200	44	1136	4	92	83	22	4524

Source: BMW Group Annual Report, 2011

Figure 7. Sales trend of top three luxury car sellers in India

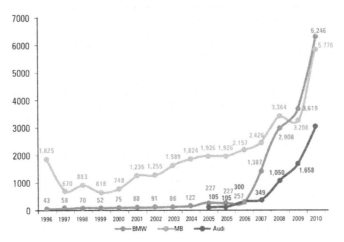

Source: Raygain Technologies: Indian Luxury Car Market-An Insight, 2011

this way BMW has managed to tap consumers early in their buying cycle, who can later upgrade to premium models of the company like X3 and X5. (Tiwari, 2011) Prior to the launch, the company had showcased the car at the 20-odd dealerships across the country to gauge the demand. "During the exclusive previews, the consumer interest generated was extremely high. Since launch, production for the next four months of BMW X1 had already been sold. BMW also priced their products very aggressively against parallel Mercedes Benz models as shown in Figure 8.

Just About Right Product Mix for an Indian Audience

So as not to lose tempo & in response to Mercedes Benz's plan to get its smaller cars, the A & B to launch in India, BMW India is trying to get even more aggressive by introducing smaller (and less expensive) cars which would be 'A' segment below the 3 series which will be a hatchback–the 1 series and the Mini range of cars (Krishnan, 2010). BMW India is planning its compact cars to hit the Indian shores in as less as 2 years. In this way BMW is trying to fill a gap which was tried unsuccessfully to fill by cars like VW Beetle & Fiat 500 if we will look at the meek sale figures of the rather looks-oriented Fiat 500 and VW Bettle. The BMW compacts may not only look good but perform and may hit great success as an executive city driving enthusiast's car. These compacts may force customer who are planning a buy a higher variant of a sedan of companies like Honda, Toyota, Ford or may be

Figure 8. Category wise pricing of BMW India and Mercedes Benz India

Model	Price	Model	Price
BMW 3 series	25-30 Lacs	MB C & CL Class	28-32 Lacs
BMW 5 Series	37.5-48 Lacs	MB E Class	40-49 Lacs
BMW 6 series	79-87 Lacs	MB CLS-SL Class	85-99 Lacs
BMW 7 Series	78.6-92 Lacs	MB S Class	85-99 Lacs
BMW Grand Tourismo	63-66 Lacs	XXX	XXX
BMW X1	22-28 Lacs	XXX	XXX
BMW X3	27-42 Lacs	MB M Class	48-53 Lacs
BMW X5	53-70 Lacs	MB GL	67-72 Lacs
BMW X6 & X6M	67- 100 Lacs	MB G55 AMG	100-115 Lacs
BMW Z4 Roadster	59-65 Lacs	MB SLK Class Roadster	65-62 Lacs
BMW M3 Coupe	74-80 Lacs	MB GL 500	80-84 Lacs

XXX= Don't have a product in that category

Source: BMW India Website

Hundai as well to change their mind & buy a BMW hatchback car. BMW's product mix is something which other players can't match as it has got cars in almost each category (see Figures 9 and 10).

Market Penetration

Luxury car-maker BMW has prepared a blueprint for the third wave of its India strategy, and plans to treble its dealership network to 60 across the country by 2015, including touch points in Tier II, III and IV cities (Sahota, n.d.). Observing that the key to success in India lay in the choice of retail partner who helps build a network, Dr Andreas Schaaf, President, BMW India, said that going forward the company expects nearly 60 per cent of its sales to come from smaller towns. "At present, around 80 per cent of our sales are from the NCR and Mumbai regions, but we expect that to change," he said. At present BMW has embarked upon the second wave of its India strategy under which it will expand its 24-strong dealer network to 40 by the end of 2012. In next phase BMW is planning to target emerging tier 1 and 2 cities like Jaipur, Aurangabad Kolhapur & Lucknow to compete with Mercedes whose 25-30% sales revenue comes from tier 2 cities. Reason may be the an increasing number of young entrepreneurs and professionals from various fields in tier II & Tier III cities are buying luxury cars and this affluent segment in these cities has been boosting sales volumes. If we look into city-wise wealth distribution, the Northern region in India (comprising of cities like Delhi, Chandigarh, Ludhiana, Shimla, and Jaland-har) comprises higher density of millionaire population than rest of the parts. This region therefore has the highest luxury car sales. After this come, Greater Mumbai, Ahmedabad, Pune, and Chennai. These cities have a luxury car sales pattern which is still higher compare to rest of the country. Anticipating higher sales, BMW India

Figure 9. Product mix of top 3 luxury car sellers in India

BMW	Mercedes-Benz	Audi	Jaguar	LandRover	Porsche
BMW 3 Series	MB C Class, CL Class	Audi A4			Porsche Cajun
BMW 5 Series	MB E Class	Audi A6	Jaguar XF		Porsche Cayman
BMW 6 Series	MB CLS · SL Class		Jaguar XK		Porsche Panamera
BMW 7 Series	MB S Class	Audi A8, R8	Jaguar XJ		Porsche 911 Turbo
BMW Grand Turismo		Audi A7			
BMW X1		Audi Q3		Evoque	
BMW X3		Audi Q5		Freelander 2	
BMW X5	MB GL · ML Class	Audi Q7		Range Rover Sport, Discover 4	Porsche Cayenne
BMW X6				Range Rover Evoque	Porsche Cayenne S
BMW X6 M					Porsche Cayenne S Turbo
BMW M3 Coupe		Audi RS 5			
BMW M3 Convertible					
BMW Z4 Roadster	MB SLK Class Roadster	Audi TT Roadster			Porsche Boxster, Boxster Spyder

Source: BMW India, Mercedez Benz, Audi India, Jaguar Land Rover India, Porche India websites

Figure 10. Product portfolio of BMW India

Model	Variants
BMW 3 Series	BMW 320i, BMW 320d, BMW 320i, BMW 320d Dynamic, BMW 320i, BMW 320d Exclusive
BMW 5 Series	BMW 523i, BMW 520d, BMW 525d, BMW 530d
BMW X1	BMW X1 sDrive 18i, BMW X1 sDrive 20d, BMW X1 sDrive 20d Exclusive
BMW X3	BMW X3 xDrive 20d, BMW X1 xDrive 30d
BMW 5 Series	BMW 535i
BMW 6 Series	BMW 650i
BMW 7 Series	BMW 730 Ld, BMW 740Li, BMW 750Li, BMW 760Li
BMW Grand Tourismo	BMW GT 3.0L Diesel
BMW Z4 Roadster	BMW Z4 sDrive 35i
BMW X5	BMW xDrive 30d, BMW xDrive 50i
BMW X6	BMW xDrive 30d, BMW xDrive 50i
BMW X6 M	BMW X6 M
BMW M3 Coupe	BMW M3
BMW M3 Convertible	BMW M3

Source: BMW India Website

has already hiked its production capacity at Chennai assembly plant to 10,000 units from 8,000 vehicles (single-shift) earlier. In total, it has invested 1.8 billion (Rs. 180 crore) in the Chennai plant. It has adopted a strategy where it invests in bringing a greater degree of flexibility in the production processes - flexibility in terms of how customers can change between the different model lines that it produces.

Research Focused Product Development and Customer Focus

BMW had gained significant volumes by bringing in a 'corporate edition' version of its 3-Series sedan into the retail market, which was priced relatively lower than competitors (Anand, 2011). Certain features like sunroof and its trademark on-board interface 'i-drive' were smartly stripped down to position it cheapest entry level sedan as these features company thought are not for Indians buying a entry level luxury car starting from 25 lacs. Top brass of the company claimed that they aren't stripping down the model in any way but rather tuning them to what a section of customers wanted. Also company managed to lower TCO* (Total cost of ownership) of BMW is lower than Mercedes Benz which helped them a lot in this journey from an entrant to the top position. BMW is perceived as a dynamic, sporty, innovative and aesthetic brand, and hence the company has done well with a younger target group. The average age of the BMW buyer in India has come down to 40 years due to its positioning as young & dynamic brand. It conducts innovative marketing activities - professional golf tournaments, wine tasting sessions, events with fashion designers & that has helped it to get closer to the customers. Company has also made minor adaptations for the Indian road and weather conditions. This includes a higher suspension as ground clearance in India is low, and different intake filters as the air in the country is more polluted.

Diversification and Value Addition

BMW is entering the lucrative second hand car sales business in India by the end of this year (Mishra, 2009). According to BMW's India head "We are almost ready to launch the used car business (pre-owned cars) for the BMW fleet of cars in India. We've been working on setting the parameters of certification, guarantee, age of the cars, and the pricing," he added. German rival Mercedes-Benz had launched its pre-owned cars business under the 'Proven Exclusivity' brand in mid-May 2010. Within six months, sales of second hand Mercedes had crossed 600 units, doing well in tier II and III cities. The starting price of pre-owned Mercedes is Rs 15-16 lakh, depending on the class of the vehicle and its age. According to Mercedes-Benz the pre-owned luxury car market in India is estimated to be around 10-15 per cent of the total number of luxury car sales. BMW, the leader in luxury cars in India with 41 per cent market share, has a total of 17,794 cars on road as of now. Aligning itself to customer demand in India, BMW India started offering its Secure Advanced service which is an additional service over the warranty and insurance policy. "The BMW Secure Advanced offers coverage for a year from the date of purchase and covers specific services including roadside assist, which comes free for two years. Till now, Secure Advanced was a paid service, as is its global practice but as Indian customers want the service but do not want to pay for it hence it is being bundled with the car. Company also learnt that India is a strong financing market and 80 per cent of the cars that it sells are financed. The financing option plays a very crucial part in the buying process so company has set up the BMW Finance Service. Company is also planning to introduce its leasing finance product for car owners, following owners to own the cars for two-three years, turn it in for a new BMW through their this Financial Service.

Road Ahead

"Been there & done that" is something which can be easily associated with what BMW has been doing in India but the actual story begins from here. In today's market conditions one has to run consistently to stay at the same place. Once competitors' are aware of your strategy it becomes difficult for you to sustain the same position (Raj, 2011). BMW India has reached where it intended to & now the question is how to stay there in the times to come? In a market like India where domestic players are globalising themselves by strategic tie ups with technology driven foreign automobile players & acquiring some big players giving themselves a modern look & raising the bar for competition. Tata acquired JLR (Jaguar Land Rover), M&M (Mahindra & Mahindra) bought Korean sports utility vehicle manufacturer Ssangyong in 2010 as well the Italian designer brand Engines Engineering & now it is in the race for acquiring Swedish automaker Saab. Challenge would be how to look different in a potential crowded luxury car market in India which is in sight of all which manufacture these kind of machines. (Lane, 2011) Another challenge might be at price front as these companies aren't manufacturing fully in India which give them a disadvantageous position than those which are manufacturing in India. At the same time it is forcing them to lower down prices by stripping their cars as BMW did which isn't always a good option as it may sometimes dilute the equity & integrity of the brand. Most challenging task would be to change the mental set up of Indian consumers who concentrate more on value for money & to develop the Indian Tier & 2 Tier 3 cities market which has a huge potential for these amazing machines.

REFERENCES

Anand, M. (2011). *Indian luxury car space leadership war persists.* Retrieved from http://newstonight.net/content/indian-luxury-car-space-leadership-war-persists

Booz & Company. (2011). Indian automotive market 2020. New Delhi.

Capgemini and Merrill Lynch Global Wealth Management. (2011). *2011 world wealth report.* Paris: Merrill Lynch.

Center for Macro Consumer Research. (2011). *2011 report: National council for applied economic research (NCAER)*. New Delhi: Center for Macro Consumer Research.

Doval, P. (2011). *Mercedes to step up price war with A and B Class*. Retrieved from http://timesofindia.indiatimes.com/business/india-business/Mercedes-to-step-up-price-war-with-A-and-B-Class/articleshow/7776778.cms.

Krishnan, S. (2010). BMW vs mercedes-Clash of the teutons. *The Business Standard*. Retrieved from http://bsmotoring.com/news/bmw-vs-mercedes-clashthe-teutons/2102/1.

Lane, R. (2011). *Mercedes benz, audi, and BMW: India war of the German triad*. Retrieved from http://www.bmwownersclub.com/forums/index.php/topic/5645-mercedes-benz-audi-and-bmw-india-war-of-the-german-triad-rush-lane.

Menon, J. (2011). *Mercedes, BMW continue the war of supremacy in india*. Retrieved from http://automotivehorizon.sulekha.com/mercedes-well-set-to-regain-top-slot-from-bmw-in-india_newsitem_2936.

Mishra, A. (2009). *Forbes india: The BMW-mercedes war in india*. Retrieved from http://ibnlive.in.com/news/forbes-india-the-bmwmercedes-war-in-india/100486-25.html.

Raj, A. (2011). *Mercedes, BMW may miss their yearly targets in india*. Retrieved from http://www.livemint.com/2011/11/09213328/Mercedes-BMW-may-miss-their-y.html.

Sahota, P. (n.d.). *Germany vs germany in india: BMW & mercedes benz*. Retrieved from http://www.indiancarsbikes.in/auto-news/mercedes-benz-vs-bmw-india-sales-4782/.

Tiwari, V. (2011). *The write handed drive: BMW merc audi faceoff*. Retrieved from http://www.themarketers.in/the-write-handed-drive/.

Chapter 14
Niche Marketing Strategies for Business Growth:
An Experiential Journey

Pradeep Kautish
Jaipuria Institute of Management, India

EXECUTIVE SUMMARY

The consumer behavior is the dynamic sum total of the range of political, economic, technological, demographical, and socio-environmental influences. The art of adapting to the changing environment may sound easy to accommodate to in marketing practice, but these changes are not visible to the insensitive myopic eyes. The essential condition for a professionally managed company to grow and keep growing is not taking pride in the high level of corporate marketing management. The strategy for seizing a market niche requires an understanding of important marketing concepts and strategies based on segmentation and targeting widely propounded marketing phenomenon. Considering the market as segmented into a host of individual homogenous elements implies a clear identification of the customers of each company to survive. It is thus necessary to determine, with absolute clarity, who the customers or target audience are for the company and to then offer products and services that match their needs effectively. This may also require the development of an optimal distribution mechanism framework to ensure quality of company offerings. The present case deals with the decision dilemma of a management professional who is in the process of deciding about acquiring a niche marketing company and the

DOI: 10.4018/978-1-4666-4357-4.ch014

Copyright ©2014, IGI Global. Copying or distributing in print or electronic forms without written permission of IGI Global is prohibited.

case elucidates four companies with respective marketing strategies employed for business operations by them. The case provides an opportunity to compare and contrast different marketing strategies with the protagonist's decision dilemma in light of market trends.

INTRODUCTION

Mr. Virendra Sahni had an uneasy feeling as he reads the newspaper headline. "Sahni Sold without a Qualm," it said ominously. All of a sudden a vibrant kaleidoscope of vehement memories of his childhood came back to him. Mr. Virendra Sahni, who travailed of the family business since childhood, always imbued the family business as his bequest and he was keen on joining his deep routed family business immediate after graduation for the simple reason that he was well versed with the idiosyncrasies of business. Mr. Sahni was born with a silver spoon so financially he was secured, but his aspiration was to take his legacy to the zenith. He was taken aback when he got to know that his father had sold the business which he was planning to join with a big bang. Now Mr. Virendra Sahni groaned as he had no other option but initially to start with a job in a company. After becoming a successful corporate lawyer with a multinational firm for many years, he honed analytical skills in the domain of management. Mr. Virendra Sahni spoke of his corporate lawyer job ad nauseam to his long time best friend Mr. Awadhesh Singh whenever and wherever they would meet. It was a piquant evening in April 2008, Mr. Virendra Sahni and his good friend Mr. Awadhesh Singh, were tête-à-tête at a local coffee shop. Mr. Awadhesh Singh shared information about New India Confectionery that was for sale to Mr. Sahni because he was aware of his best friend's business dream. That same day, Mr. Virendra Sahni stunned his friend by recapitulating pieces of information with Mr. Awadhesh Singh which he gathered about successful confectionary business companies. Now next Monday morning, the business proposal of New India Confectionary which they received from Mr. Sanjeev Baweja, an astute businessman, was on their table for discussion. Both of the friends knew Mr. Sanjeev Baweja for long time as a veteran businessman in his late seventies, before he left for the US with his daughter, putting his business up for sale. Finally Mr. Virendra Sahni patiently took this long awaited entrepreneurial call. He went out to look into it and spruce up the business proposal thoroughly along with castigated points of views of his best friend. The company was decrepit but perfectly operational for business purposes, Mr. Sanjeev Baweja was asking INR 50 Lakhs for the tangible physical assets of the company. Mr. Virendra Sahni was of a frivolous nature, but he was not in the mood to jeopardize his business credibility at any cost within the family and in the outside world. Eventually, Mr. Virendra Sahni mustered mettle to engage himself in the nitty-gritty of business and strategic modus operandi to get success. Long term business decisions can't afford shilly-shally approach, so at the outset he decided to go for some ground work on the confectionery business and also made few calls to meet a number of local confectioners to get some industry know how and thirdly, to dovetail his exploration excerpts to his decision after proper scrutiny.

Initially not competing with big players, Mr. Virendra Sahni focused on talking to those firms that adopted a niche marketing strategy. The case enunciates the brief summaries of those companies with their product offerings, management decision styles, market structure, marketing strategies, and future growth prospects. Mr. Virendra Sahni chewed his lips as he mulled over the intense debate he had had with Mr. Awadhesh Singh on this issue. As Mr. Virendra Sahni explained, he wasn't interested in financial and economic nuances with them at this stage, but surely wanted to contemplate on the proposals with utmost sincerity and full concentration of mind and soul putting aside all other concerns. Other aspects will come later if he decides to move ahead with the project and look seriously at the acquisition. His idea was to understand the latest happenings of the marketplace and to discover how small firms compete with big players.

Taking stock of change in an environment where many changes are occurring simultaneously is daunting. One often searches for a way in which to capture all that has been going on and figure out what it actually meant by the way we think about and do things. The cold beverage sector in India has changed dramatically over the last 10 years as a result of changing socio-economic conditions, liberalization of market, entry of foreign companies, dismantling of quantitative restrictions on import, and increase in disposable income. There were approximately 2.8 million or 28 lakhs hotels and restaurants in India in the year 2006. As the number of lodging or hotel units in India would not be more than 25,000 or 30,000, we can presume that the entire figure of 28 lakhs can apply to restaurant sector and they consume products from bakers and confectionaries. For consumer products, the growth patterns are different for different cities with metro cities achieving about 15-20% growth and smaller cities 5-8% approximately. Consumer markets appear more diverse because there is an increased supply of trade brands giving consumers a chance to express their individuality. According to a recent survey report on what Indian consumers spent on eating, less than 20% went to the organized sector, which means there is huge room for market expansion for small players in the industry.

BACKGROUND

Mr. Virendra Sahni, born in November 1968 in Bhatinda, Punjab, was the youngest son of the two children of Mr. Babulal Sahni and Ms. Savitri Sahni who hailed from Pakistan after partition. He did schooling from Bhatinda High School and graduated from Punjab University, Chandigarh. However, at the end of second year, he was transferred to Amritsar University where he met Mr. Awadhesh Singh and soon they became friends. Upon the successful completion of his MBA in marketing he obtained a gold medal in the class. After a significant and successful stint in Kolkata with the Price Water House Coopers, he joined the law firm of Chhabaria's in Delhi as a partner in 2003. Still single, he enjoyed a very comfortable living in a big bungalow in Chandigarh. When he was in high school and for two years he was with parents, Mr. Virendra Sahni worked every holiday and weekend for his father who owned a confectionery business, which is how he knows the business so very well. Since childhood his elder brother wasn't interested in the family business. He went off to Mumbai and settled as a successful doctor in a big multispecialty hospital. So, we can assume that Mr. Virendra Sahni always expected that finally his father would hand over the business to him and he will expand it according to his business aspirations.

AADHAAR CORPORATION PRIVATE LIMITED

Aadhaar Corporation Private Limited was incorporated in 1995, at a time when beverage consumption was predominantly of cola drinks. In late 2000, it began the sales and marketing of the first all-natural, lightly flavored candies, toffees, and fruit juices called VitaLife in Indian market. In January 2003, the company introduced a line of all-natural, low calorie fruit supplements, formulated and packaged specifically for children. This line was called VitaDay. The founder Mr. Jagjit Thakkar decided to experiment with a concept company that would sell the finest natural, hygiene products. In the market, he was sensing a great need of such products and according to him it was a great business proposition for coming years. Aadhaar' geographical market expansion for business throughout the country was carefully planned by long experienced marketing professionals that were handpicked by the management for the purpose. The management team agreed that all products would be owned and manufactured by the company rather than as a franchise. In building a strong brand, Mr. Jagjit Thakkar knew that he and his executive management team needed complete control to cultivate an unparalleled image of product quality. In too many other companies, franchisees did business their own way. Franchisees could potentially sacrifice Aadhaar's commitment to excellence in order to turn higher profits which they were not ready to go for. Aadhaar did not want to allow the corner-cutting that had caused the original decline in Indian's consumption of healthy beverages.

AADHAAR'S MARKETING STRATEGY

According to various market research reports, Aadhaar's product line is based on the observation that today's children in India are becoming heavier than ever before and it is a dangerous trend. Overweight kids are at risk for cardiovascular disease, diabetes, and other diseases. While liquid substances like water are recognized as an aid in weight control, most of us don't drink enough of it. The reason is very simple plain water is boring for the majority of consumers and difficult to drink as well. But at the same time, high-calorie sodas and exotic beverages with artificial preservatives are dangerous and unhealthy substitutes. The company's product line consists of seven low-calories fitness juices and shakes (with names such as Thunder Ball Rage and Typhoon Tea) that are bacteria-free and contain no preservatives. The VitaDay product line taste sweet and contain less than 15 calories per serving. Aadhaar distributes through various groceries where the products are introduced within the store as all-natural theme stores. They also sell through supermarkets and all-natural stores to cater more than 2 million customers per week. Among the distributors for Aadhaar are Health Brands Inc. which is the largest marketer and distributor of all-natural fruit juices-with 16 distribution facilities-available in over 15,000 retail stores in India with the largest publicly traded wholesale distributor with over 7,000 customers in almost all states through its 11 distribution centers. In terms of pricing, the fitness waters are available from the company's web site at a cost of INR 500 for 25 bottles of half liter. At this time, the VitaPlay line is not available online. The company would not provide any information as to its advertising and promotional strategies. However, it does promote its product line at trade shows.

In a nutshell, here are a few of the key strategies that enabled Aadhaar to achieve such remarkable growth in the very competitive industry landscape.

1. Product Innovations,
2. Competitive Toughness,
3. Product Integration and Extension,
4. Designing Effective Communication and Promotion Roadmap,
5. Aadhaar also hired the services of Procycle, a leading market research firm to get update on consumption patterns of consumers.

PROSPECTS FOR FUTURE GROWTH

According to Aadhaar's president and chief executive officer Mr. Dinesh Kapoor, the company anticipates excellent market response among health conscious youths and parents who seek healthier lifestyles for their growing children. Although the most recent revenue figures suggest that Aadhaar has total sales of more than a million marginally, industry observers highlighted that looking forward, the company has secured valuable shelf space in major retail outlets in the cities, which is expected to generate sales revenue in excess of 7 million in the coming year with even better performance at distributor end as Aadhaar brands are getting favor for sales. The company is perfectly positioned to dominate the 'all-natural' segment of the industry. The segment is growing by double digit point and will probably continue to do so in future as well. The results of the market research that the CEO had commissioned indicated that consumers were not only interested in the concept, but also liked the flavors in which VitaDay and VitaPlay had been test-marketed and similar plan is for VitaLife product line too which is going to be soft drink. However, breaking into the soft drinks market would not be simple. While the concentrates segment was stagnant, the aerated drink segment was dominated by global players with huge ad spends. The product had two overriding advantages. It didn't have the inconvenience of mixing, sugaring and stirring and disposing of the package unlike tetra pack. Company had worked out a third-party contract distribution arrangement with one of the leading player, which was also distributing beauty soaps, biscuits and hair color creams.

STANDARD CONFECTIONERY PRIVATE LIMITED

Founded in 1891 originally by a European conglomerate, Standard Confectionery started selling beer and flavored sodas in Europe. At the end of 1980s they came to India with an opportunity to sell beer and alcoholic beverages, but didn't want to deal with beer. So in 1988, Standard Confectionery was acquired by Indian business house, but the name had not been changed to maintain equity. However, competition became extremely tough in the confectionery business and was discontinued. The grandson, Mr. Anup Desai, took over in the early 90s and started manufacturing fountain syrups for colas as well as some other products used in confectionery business by biggies. That business became very difficult when an international player started a division and started to dominate the market. So, he looked around for new opportunities and decided there was a market for gourmet sodas. By August 1993, their first confectionery product of Standard's original business hit the shelves. Marketing discontinued around the same time. Today, Standard Confectionery does a business of approximately 5 million annually with three states in India and is growing in other segments too. The company official claims that soon the company is going to have broader product line with an efficient and dependable distribution system in place.

STANDARD CONFECTIONERY'S MARKETING STRATEGY

In terms of the products, Standard Confectionery produces syrup for its 10 flavor of soda along with juices, squashes (including black cherry, orange, grape, and ginger ale), two fruit beers and a diet beer at its Jalandhar, Punjab plant. While retaining its brewing traditions, the company has adopted new technological traditions that improve its business and marketing effectiveness. All products are caffeine free. The syrup is then shipped to some other location where the bottles are filled, crowned, and then shipped (direct to distributors). According to Mr. Anup Desai, the company offers a quality product. It uses cane sugar in place of corn syrup. While it is more expensive, he feels it produces a better product. Likewise, they use top quality flavors to produce a superior product. All Standard products are sold in the company's own glass bottles with raised lettering and a painted label. While it is much less expensive to use cans or plastic bottles, the company thinks their bottle creates a better image, one that (hopefully) resonates with those who, as children, grew up in a city and remember the bottled drinks. It is designed to be a classy bottle that customers will associate with a classy product. 40-45% of the company's sales occur in the metropolitan which is economically and financially very rich. The company distributes the products itself within this area. Outside the area, it is in virtually every major market nationwide. However, outside Punjab a network of local distributors handles distribution. It sees Delight's Great Real Fruit Juices, KBC's Flavored Water, and Golden-Jack's Soda plus a large number of small regional firms as its major national competitors. Unlike big players, Standard Confectionery does not emphasize sales through supermarkets and vending machines. They feel they are not set up to service them. Specifically, they don't have the people or the volume of business to go into a supermarket and fill up the shelves on a daily basis. They do work with a few supermarkets, but only if they are willing to carry the inventory and handle the shelves. Most of the company's clients are pizzerias, delis, and gourmet shops. They tend to be the high end of the market and want to offer something special. They also work with some food chains like WBC (as an exclusive suppliers of a couple of flavors) and Apple Bee's where they have an exclusive arrangement with them as their flavors are sold in bottles whereas coke, diet coke, and so forth is dispensed from a pump. The company admits that, price-wise, their products are more expensive. However, while they are at the top of the price scale, they don't feel their prices are prohibitive as there are more expensive products on the market. According to Mr. Anup Desai, they price their products to appeal to those consumers who want a premium product and are willing to pay a premium for it. Standard Confectionery uses advertising, publicity and direct marketing to stimulate awareness and exploration by new customers. Standard Confectionery currently does relatively less advertising and sales promotion. They used to do some 30-second television spots that run on cable which were reasonably successful. They also did some radio spots but found this wasn't too effective as people couldn't recognize the product. In recent years, most of the company's promotions were at trade shows. Potential buyers come to these shows and sample our various products. The company also has a growing relationship with some agencies. We set up on Wednesday and Thursday and then have a three-day road show. It gives people a chance to try the product and to recognize the brand. The company does not have its own web site. However, it does have a relationship with a number of distributors with websites and its products can be purchased through these firms. Understanding consumers means more than just gathering data on your own product or on your competitor's product. Standard Confectionery also analyzes consumer data gathered by Data Information Resources Inc. (DIRI), to track consumer purchasing behavior across a full range of product categories to get insights about buying patterns for better managerial decision making. Standard Confectionery successfully launched some brands after seeing data on consumer shifts in dietary habits in other food groups. Standard Confectionery uses a variety of internal and external data sources- including consumer demographics, retailer insights, POS, and market data—to guide effective product assortment decisions.

PROSPECTS FOR FUTURE GROWTH

The company has recently negotiated an infusion of capital, which will enable it to expand its operations. The president feels they have the potential to become a 50 million company within five years or so. As per Mr. Anup Desai's point of view, the company's main weakness is that it doesn't have a cola or a diet cola. Like any other confectionery business entity, the past few months for Standard Confectionery have been about tradeoffs. On the one hand, it wanted to launch more product offerings and increase revenues for which it needed to advertise and promote with better value proposition for consumers. On the other hand, it wanted to cut costs and selling expenses-a significant cost at 10-20% of revenues for other players in the industry-would draw the axe. Standard Confectionery has fared well: it has increased sales by 17% in the 12-month period, while spending just 2.25% more on selling. The objective of the company is to make profits through satisfying customers. The variables termed as marketing mix is combination of all the ingredients in a recipe that is designed to prove most attractive to customers. These variables are individual elements that as a marketing manager we can manipulate into the most appropriate strategy. Mr. Anup Desai says, We are working on cost control, improving efficiencies in our operations as well as looking at getting funds to reduce debts by selling our non-core assets, In the spirit of doing something interesting for our customers is very important and that is the reason that almost in every quarter we arrange the theme based festival which in turn promotes an individual category of food items. A study made on the industry by the Confectionary Association highlighted that out of the total consumption of confectionary, almost 34% are consumed by children so we chose the theme as per the target market. With emergence of new players' everyday studies shows that, people still want to drink well which does not necessarily mean healthy and indulge in something that resembles a style statement. The current economic boom has allowed people to spend as much as they can so now they have best of both worlds – not only can they afford the convenience of going out more often, but they can do so in a food service environment where they more bang for the buck.

CRESSMAN CONFECTIONERY INDIA LIMITED

Cressman Confectionery India Limited entered the market in 1982 with a fruit beer and some non-cola drinks. Originally sold in barrels, the company soon expanded into bottles and cans to explore the market in a better way. The current owners, who also distribute a number of major fruit beer brands along with some juice brands, were a major distributor for Cressman and took over operations in the late 80s. Careful local brand marketing tells the success story of the company. The company's brand image also rests on its fresh, cool offerings—a freshness that's measured in quality. The company's marketing is grassroots local. Cressman does not have a very impressive traditional media advertising budget. Rather, local community marketing managers enlist the aid of local groups and charities. For example, the company helps charities raise money by selling them its products at half price which they can re-sell at full price on some occasions. Local bake sales become a promotional tool for Cressman Confectionery India Limited.

CRESSMAN'S MARKETING STRATEGY

Cressman currently offers seven fruit juices and soda flavors: sarsaparilla, orange cream, black cherry, cream soda, red beer, lemon cream, and root beer. All products are sold in bottles and root beer, red beer, and orange cream area sold in 1 liter glass bottles. According to the Executive Vice President, Mr. Rajbir Chaddha, all its sodas and juices are caffeine free and have very low sodium. Cressman uses multiple blends in its extracts, which is more expensive. While they use corn syrup in their bottles (which are pasteurized and thus contain no preservative), the one liter bottles contain cane sugar and a preservative. Cressman manufactures the syrup in Bangalore and then it goes to four bottling plants (one in Punjab, two in West Bengal and one in Bangalore) and then to its distributors across the country. The one liter dark brown bottle (or barrel) is the company's own design with an expensive label. The goal is to create a quality image. The company emphasizes old-fashioned traditional flavors to maintain 'proudly old fashioned' status among end users. It doesn't offer a cola or a diet cola and has no intention of doing so. As management of the company observed, "our goal is to 'keep under the radar' of the big players. We have a great cola and flavored shake formula but that is not where we want to go." Cressman sells through a network of distributors and also direct to large retailers. It is represented in most of the major markets across the country where the product goes to independent convenience stores. The company prides itself on offering a gourmet soda that provides higher margins for retailers. For example, a four pack of bottles costs INR 50. The company's major competitors were Sitara (which is owned by an Indian Group), Standard, and Golden-Jack Confectionery, although they feel that Golden-Jack is more of a Generation X marketer. The company's advertising and promotion is limited to print advertisement in trade journals and displays at trade shows. They do some in-store ad, but rely heavily on taste testing in stores. The company is organizing a road show in their locations. If we consider the point of view of Mr. Rajbir Chaddha, they want people to have the opportunity to try the product and say, "I like that. It tastes like the drinks I remember." Also, the company gets a lot of feedback from its press releases that always produce a lot of calls. The company has a very active web site and believes this is a great way to get to people. In addition to the listing of its products and the connection to www.indianetgrocer. com, it also has a "What's New" section and a "Cressman Confectionery Sighting" section where we post photographs of people with its products. Apparently, customers send the photos in and the company awards prizes (T-shirts, caps, goggles, etc.). People also use the site to give the company feedback and comments. Cressman Confectionery is one of the most skilled marketers of consumer packaged goods.

PROSPECTS FOR FUTURE GROWTH

Mr. Rajbir Chaddha stated that they are trying to grow but not so fast as to attract attention of big players. He explained that the industry leaders don't seem to be terribly successful at introducing new products so they are going the acquisition route and he suspects that many of the smaller confectioners are trying to grow in order to make themselves attractive acquisition targets. Cressman wants to grow through increasing its distribution. However, there is a problem with this marketing strategy as the company has a policy of not allowing distributors to sell competitive flavors. Some of the independent distributors may be interested, but they have forgotten how to sell. Mr. Chaddha commented, They just cater to the local market. We are hoping for the growth of a new way of distribution. In the mean time, we continue to build up our own. We believe that people want to be different. They want a unique product. We also believe that kids drink what you drink.. and, if they see their parents drinking Cressman's product, they will do so. Even as Cressman has mindful of the immediate challenges, Mr. Chaddha is clearly focused on the long term opportunities. With a lot of promotional efforts, the company introduced new range of offerings in metropolitan towns. The results for first six months are encouraging and Mr. Chaddha is positive about this opportunity. The buyer supplier relationship is one of the mutual economic interdependence, both relying on the other for their commercial wellbeing. Factors in supplier environment are subject to change, such as delivery, cost fluctuations etc. At Cressman where we are present at almost all metros, we prefer to have the national tie ups with most of suppliers and for the fact we also prefer to source the supplier who is present nationally. Competition is very important as it prevents a company from complacent. Now a day's focus of maximum people is shifting from food driven to experience driven food outlets and because of the reason competition is getting extreme in the industry.

SUDARSHAN BRANDS LIMITED

Sudarshan Brands Limited was founded by first generation entrepreneur Mr. Krishna Sudarshan in 1996. The genesis of the company (according to a popular business magazine article) arose because Mr. Krishna Sudarshan (a rock climber, outdoor enthusiast and fitness freak) began to pay more attention to his health. He started shopping at natural-food stores, buying organic fruits and vegetables, and taking vitamin supplements. According to the article, it all fitted together. The single most important thing you can do to improve the quality of life is to drink more water, liquid substance like juice etc. but Mr. Sudarshan didn't want it to be just any ordinary water. He wanted it to be better product. All of the innovation in beverages had come from entrepreneurs, Mr. Sudarshan commented, "After all, Snapple was started by three childhood friends who sold natural juices."

SUDARSHAN BRANDS MARKETING STRATEGY

According to an online newsletter, Sudarshan Brands is proud of its liquid assets. The company is making waves with its Crassile Water, a line of low-calorie flavored water and fruit juices enhanced with electrolytes and other nutrients. Sudarshan Brands products are available in three varieties under the Crassile name: Healthy Times (which has extra electrolytes, the minerals your body loses during perspiration) was introduced in 1996. Two years later, the company introduced FruitTime, which has no electrolytes, calories or preservatives but contain some added fruit flavoring essence. Then. In 2000, the company introduced VitaminTime, which has stronger flavor than the previous products, plus added vitamins and hard-to-miss candy colors. Company recently introduced some flavored vitamin candies as fortified supplements to regular diets. The company started selling its Healthy Times products through health-food specialists first in Delhi and then nationwide. It followed the same approach with the FruitTimes line. According to a business article, instead of targeting health nuts, the company went main stream with the VitaminTime line. As Mr. Krishna observed, Once they had tried it, people said they wanted it everywhere - in universities, health clubs, spas, hotels, delis, grocery stores, gas stations, bodegas, etc. The company puts a lot of emphasis on quality packaging, which Mr. Sudarshan feel is as important as what is in the bottle. Mr. Krishna owned a boat that had been designed by a renowned architect and, this same gentleman approached him and asked to help design Crassile's first bottle. Instead of just labeling his drinks with boring names like lemon or honeydew, he decided to give each type a 'hip' moniker. The labels also have catchy copy: For best results, mix with individuals showing signs of sluggishness and laziness. Warning: if severe procrastination occurs, buy a whole case. The company's advertising and promotion activities are also unique. The company bought billboards in Delhi and advertisements in national magazines, including lifestyle like Cosmopolitan and business like Business India, Business Today. Mr. Krishna's strategy worked and according to a recent business article, we started to see the trendy people on the streets of Delhi with a bottle of VitaminTime in hand. The New Business Journal points out, however, that for all its goodwill, the stuff might not actually be very good for you. Each bottle (which sells for about INR 15) contains 125 calories and 32.5 grams of sugar, which is lot for something that claims to be a health drink. Skeptical nutritionists have questioned whether products like these can even be called 'water,' but the International Bottled Water Association, a trade group, allow companies to add flavors and colors not less than 1% of the content. In terms of the marketplace, Crassile is currently second to its nearest competitor and its success has attracted big-name competitors. Glacier was the first of the large beverage companies to enter the market, introducing its Propel Fitness Water in July 1999. Similarly, one company introduced its flavored Juliana Essentials in grocery stores this past June., and the newest entrant launched its Dasani NutriWater in three test markets in November.

PROSPECTS FOR FUTURE GROWTH

According to *New Business Journal*, Mr. Krishna welcomes such competition with good cheer. The fact that bigger companies are copying us means they think we know better than they do, he says, pausing to chuckle. The marketing buzz he's been able to generate should help too. Now that he has conquered Mumbai, Mr. Krishna's next step is completing the move into Bollywood. He enjoys offering his drinks at what he calls 'lifestyle events'. A recent ploy was to provide beverages for the Entertainment Tonight-sponsored Film Awards party at the Hotel Taj West End in Mumbai. Marketing executives at the company were concerned about the performance of their brand. They started a debate whether or not to adopt a new strategy for promotion and advertising. The executives felt that Golden-Jack brand felling to communicate its vitamin nutrition value which is a definite product attribute. According to them the best way to improve sales performance is by developing a more compelling advertising appeal. Focus group interviews conducted with consumers to evaluate the relative effectiveness of several alternative copy approaches making direct and implied comparisons between different competing brands with Gloden-Jack.

GOLDEN-JACK COMPANY PRIVATE LIMITED

Golden-Jack Company Private Limited's history goes back to 1987 when Ms. Aparna Chopra after getting divorce from his husband founded Chopra Distributors and began distributing fruit juices. She invested all the money she got from her husband as compensation. After so many years struggle in the field. In 1995, she created her own products and started marketing bottled water. Then, in August 2000, she merged with the Emoticon Soda Company to form the Golden-Jack Company. Today, Golden Jack is the largest brewer in the region in terms of volume, and it competes across a diverse range of markets. The company oversees more than 30 brands in different categories, including one of the domestic market leaders, a number of other alcoholic and nonalcoholic beverages, a group of theme parks, and a real estate enterprise. While retaining its brewing traditions, the company has adopted new technological traditions that improve its business and marketing effectiveness. In 1997, Chairperson Ms. Chopra vowed to make her company a leader in mining its customers' buying patterns.

GOLDEN-JACK COMPANY'S MARKETING STRATEGY

In 1995, the company began with six flavors (such as Lemon-Line and Strawberry) and later added additional flavors with memorable names such as Tango Lemon and Crushed Raspberry Blast. In 2000, the company introduced Fast Eddie Energy Drink and, the following year, a line of Emoticon Natural (Fun-Loving Carrot and Wu-Wu's Desire). With the exception of the energy drinks (which are sold in aluminum cans) and the natural teas and juices (glass bottles), the products are sold in bottles. As the web site states, while unique bottles and imported water have been successful in the past, Golden-Jack believes that these features increase production costs and reduce the ability of a manufacturer to respond quickly to any changes in the market. So, Golden-Jack provides a stock bottle that is both cost effective and convenient and its labels and support materials have been designed for efficient, low-cost production. According to Mr. Hoshiyar Singh, Executive Vice President says, "we are a fashion conscious refreshing beverage company. But fashion is beauty and beauty is in the eye of the beholder. We let our customers tell us what is cool. Our niche is the 12 to 24-year old Indian consumer who is into anything from photography to extreme sports and rock n roll. They are tech savvy, skeptical, educated, racially diverse, and have spending power." The unique aspect of the labeling, however, is that the labels are continually changed based on ideas generated and submitted by its consumers. According to Business Insights, Golden-Jack offers individuals and consumers a 'create-your-own-label' option for special occasions. These include weddings, birthdays, shareholder's meetings, trade shows, or just for the fun of it. As Mr. Singh explains, "Our photo program is vital. When one photo makes a bottle, that person will tell everyone they know about it. The people they tell will tell a few more and some will take the time to send in their own photo. That is an emotional connection. You inspire someone to get off their ass and become part of something fun. Furthermore, we have patented the right to customize and order branded merchandise over an Internet server." Distribution of Golden-Jack began with what it calls alternative distribution strategy. The company placed its own coolers, bearing its signature logo. In some truly unique venues such as skate, surf and sports shops, tattoo and piercing parlors, as well as individual fashion stores and national retail clothing and music stores. Following the execution of this strategy, Emoticon began an up and down the street attack on the marketplace, this time placing product in convenience and food stores. Finally, the company has now begun to achieve larger chain store listings with food retail giant companies and lifestyle stores. While the number of distributors nationwide is confidential, its products can be found in most major markets across the nation. In the same article, Business Insights identified Golden-Jack Company as collaborating with Fresh Bread Inc. to sell co-branded drinks at its specialty fresh bread and sandwich cafes. The custom labels feature black-and-white photos of bakery and related products and the text on the back pays tribute to the bakers who go to great measures every night kneading, scoring and baking. Golden-Jack doesn't do any traditional marketing. It displays its products at fancy food shows, convenience store shows, and surf and skate expos. The company also sponsors 'extreme' athletes, surfboarders, road shows and skateboarders. These athletes can be seen promoting Golden-Jack and sporting the Golden-Jack logo at extreme sporting events across the country. It also has a number of large orange vehicles covered in the company logo, which travel throughout cities in Northern India handing out products and talking to the people about the products. As far as pricing is concerned, Golden-Jack appears to be somewhere between big international players at one end to the scale and the bottlers who use expensive ingredients such as cane sugar, fruit juices, beers and squashes and unique glass bottles. "We like to be priced at INR 10 per bottle," Mr. Hoshiyar Singh observed, "a pragmatic pleasure."

PROSPECTS FOR FUTURE GROWTH

According to Mr. Singh, "the future is bright, energetic, flavored, and tasty for us as well as for our consumers." This shows Mr. Singh's concern for modern marketing practices with conviction. As part of Golden-Jack's growth strategy, emerging confectionery business in the country and region are now critical for driving growth. The growth trajectory across the category portrayed almost 35% growth annually. The company is coming up with highly standardized customized new flavors and product offerings with in the category and in different category as well. Mr. Singh says, "We are open to strategic or joint venture partnerships for the business expansion which come under way with some business giant and interested in exploring market, Management contracts and asset light strategy will be key to our growth.

In every company there are two distinct but interrelated environments: micro and macro respectively. The micro environment denotes those elements over which the company has control and attempts to manipulate in such a way as to optimize the profits. The macro environment concerns the elements outside the micro-environment but nevertheless influences it in many ways. The macro environment of a company consists of all the forces and agencies external to the company itself. Some of these elements are closer to the operation of the company than others e.g. company suppliers, distributive intermediaries and competing brands or companies. These closer macro elements are collectively referred as Proximate Macro Environment to distinguish them from the wider external environment such as demographic, socio culture, technological, political and economic environment. All of these are not an immediate part of the company yet they have a direct impact on the business of the company. As a marketing manager, one has to consider all above in order designing a fruitful and profitable marketing strategy.

TEACHING NOTE

The role of marketing is viewed as a discipline, function and set of activities to attract and retain customers in competitive market place. If marketing as an intellectual and operating discipline is to be institutionalized in organizations, it must not only pervade the minds of managers within the organization, but also infuse and energize their actions (Srivastava et al., 1999). The ever-increasing diversity in consumer tastes and habits as well as changing needs of business and organizational markets, coupled with cutthroat competition, structural changes in markets, continuous advancement in information, and production technologies do not only create new marketing approaches and methods but also threaten large companies and question the validity of their traditional marketing methods and practices (Hezar et al., 2006). Since this case would normally be discussed very early in a basic marketing course, it is suggested that the class begin with a very general question that allows all students to participate. Niche marketing caters to a very small group in a segment with some specific and distinct need, which the marketer satisfies through specific skills. Each discussion prompt or question will become progressively harder and begin to separate the students by capability. This case is written for use in a basic marketing course for arousing interest among students. More specifically it would be positioned at the point in the course during which niche marketing is discussed with its business implications. Information about five companies were chosen so that students can compare the dynamics and get better understanding about marketing decision making. All names of companies and individuals are fictitious and it is meant for avoiding endorsement during discussion. To stimulate brainstorming and learning deliberately used some company names but they do not have any relation with case. This case is prepared by the author for the sole purpose of aiding teaching and class room discussion in a hypothetical environment. This case is not meant to serve as an endorsement or a source of data or an illustration of effective or ineffective management practices of any company in any form or time. The data and situation described in the case is fictitious added just to arouse interest among students for discussion purpose only. All names of the organizations are fictitious in nature and character, or even used name do not have any relation to management of the respective organizations in part or full. This case does not have any relation with any corporation in any sense or mean and it is developed only for academic purposes. The references provided at the end of the case are merely suggestive in nature, the instructor can include some other references also. Some of the articles can be discussed in the class for better content delivery and understanding about the subject. Niche firms do not follow the regular Segmentation, Targeting, and Positioning (STP) process of marketing. The selection of customers and markets is the result of tradition, chance or the firm's production philosophy, and the firms make few attempts to position their products. The firms rely on resource-based advantages, high-quality products and personal relationships when competing in the marketplace (Toften & Hammervoll, 2009). A niche firm's marketing strategy is by and large based on a customer-valued competitive advantage and differentiation should be applied in terms of both intangible and actual use criteria. Niche firms always strive for long-term, personal relationships and customer commitment for its product offerings. Also, there seems to be some room for following one's own personal convictions and innovative ideas when crafting a marketing strategy, even though this approach certainly is not in line with the structured marketing strategy process suggested in textbooks (Toften & Hammervoll, 2009). Kids have taken a quantum leap in marketing as consumer segment, this means the marketers must self regulate attempts to exploit the potential of this growing segment.

CASE LEARNING OBJECTIVES

This case is intended to enable the student to:

1. Evaluate market segmentation with narrated well-defined niches and to develop understanding about role of niche marketing strategies with business processes for small firms.
2. Analyze different approaches to establishing a niche based on specific elements of the marketing mix for consumer satisfaction and evaluation.

3. Evaluate these company's niche marketing strategies against optimal niche characteristics enunciated in the basic marketing text course.
4. Review the prospects of the niche firms in an industry dominated by giants. What is the importance of industry analysis in the case?
5. Survival strategies which can be adopted by small firms in globalized marketing environment.
6. Consumer behavioral aspects need to be taken care of while formulating the niche marketing strategies, elucidate the statement with the help of case.

ACKNOWLEDGMENT

The author would like to thank anonymous reviewers including the editors of the case book for their constructive suggestions for improvement of the case. The author sincerely appreciate the contributions of Ms. Shalvi Sharma, Research Assistant in form of valuable time and efforts which she undertook in giving constructive suggestions, manuscript typing, collecting relevant references, proof reading the whole work and making it more lucid for end users.

REFERENCES

Biggadike, R. (1997). *Entering new markets: Strategies and performance*. Cambridge, MA: Marketing Science Institute.

Dalgic, T. (1998). Niche marketing principles: Guerrillas versus gorillas. *Journal of Segmentation in Marketing*, 2(1), 5–18. doi:10.1300/J142v02n01_02.

Dalgic, T. (2006). *Handbook of niche marketing: Principles, and practices*. New York: The Haworth Press Inc..

Dalgic, T., & Leeuw, M. (1994). Niche marketing revisited: Concept, applications, and some european cases. *European Journal of Marketing*, 28(4), 39–55. doi:10.1108/03090569410061178.

Dawar, N., & Frost, T. (1999). Competing with giants. *Harvard Business Review*, 77(2), 119–129. PMID:10387768.

Day, G. S., Shocker, A. D., & Srivastava, R. K. (1979). Customer-oriented approaches to identifying product-markets. *Journal of Marketing*, 43(4), 8–19. doi:10.2307/1250266.

Delaney, J. (1995). Minding your own niche business. *Nation's Business*, 83(5), 56–58.

Hammermesh, R. G., Anderson, M. J., & Hards, J. E. (1978). Strategies for low market share businesses. *Harvard Business Review, 50*(3), 95–102.

Hezar, I., Dalgic, T., Phelan, S., & Knight, G. (2006). Principles of global niche marketing strategies: An early conceptual framework. In Dalgic, T. (Ed.), *Handbook of Niche Marketing: Principles and Practices*. New York: The Haworth Press.

Leduc, B. (1998). *Target a niche market to increase your sales and profits*. Retrieved from http://www.smithfam.com/news/aug98j.html.

Linneman, R. E., & Stanton, L. Jr. (1992). Mining for niches. *Business Horizons, 35*(3), 43–51. doi:10.1016/0007-6813(92)90068-K.

Linneman, R. E., & Stanton, L. Jr. (1992). *Making niche marketing work: How to grow big by acting smaller*. New York: McGraw Hill.

Parrish, E. D., Cassill, N. L., & Oxenham, W. (2006). Niche market strategy for a mature marketplace. *Marketing Intelligence & Planning, 24*(7), 694–707. doi:10.1108/02634500610711860.

Raynor, M. E. (1992). The pitfalls of niche marketing. *The Journal of Business Strategy, 13*(2), 29–32. doi:10.1108/eb039478 PMID:10117142.

Shani, D., & Chalasani, S. (1992). Exploiting niches using relationship marketing. *Journal of Consumer Marketing, 9*(3), 33–42. doi:10.1108/07363769210035215.

Shani, D., & Chalasani, S. (1992). Exploiting niches using relationship marketing. *Journal of Services Marketing, 6*(4), 43–52. doi:10.1108/EUM0000000002532.

Sissors, J. Z. (1966). What is a market? *Journal of Marketing, 30*(3), 17–21. doi:10.2307/1249085.

Stanton, J. L., & Linneman, R. E. (1991). *Making niche marketing work*. New York: McGraw-Hill Inc..

Toften, K., & Hammervoll, T. (2008). Niche marketing and strategic capabilities: An exploratory study of specialized firms. *Marketing Intelligence & Planning, 28*(6), 736–753. doi:10.1108/02634501011078138.

Toften, K., & Hammervoll, T. (2009). Niche firms and marketing strategy: An exploratory study of internationally oriented niche firms. *European Journal of Marketing, 43*(11/12), 1378–1391. doi:10.1108/03090560910989948.

Varadarajan, P. R., Clark, T., & Pride, W. M. (1992). Controlling the uncontrollable: Managing your marketing environment. *MIT Sloan Management Review, 33*(2), 39–47.

Wade, J., & Goodman, S. (2005). Effective marketing of small brands: Niche positions, attribute loyalty, and direct marketing. *Journal of Product and Brand Management, 14*(5), 292–299. doi:10.1108/10610420510616322.

Whittaker, R. H., & Levin, S. A. (1975). *Niche: Theory and application.* Stroudsburg, PA: Dowden, Hutchinson & Ross Inc..

Chapter 15
Marketing of Tobacco Products in Australia:
Dealing with the Emerging Regulations

Rajeev Sharma
Charles Darwin University, Australia

EXECUTIVE SUMMARY

Liberal western, democratic traditions provide 'freedom of choice' to consumers. This doctrine is also extended to commercial organisations in developing their marketing and promotional strategies. Some products, tobacco in particular, have continued to attract a high level of social and legislative scrutiny in the industrialised countries. There is an argument that tobacco products are excessively harmful to the society–particularly the vulnerable and disadvantaged. As a result governments have a bigger responsibility and a significant role to play in regulating such goods and services. The Australian Federal Government has recently introduced a bill into Parliament. It aims to lay down very stringent guidelines and restrict the promotional options for tobacco product marketing in Australia. This real and evolving case study looks into the challenges faced by the marketers.

BACKGROUND

Tobacco is one of the most widely used addictive substances in the world. On April 6, 2011 Federal Health Minister of Australia Ms Nicola Roxon released the Government's draft legislation which would require tobacco companies to sell cigarettes in plain packaging (Jerga 2011). This has caused considerable anxiety within the tobacco industry.

DOI: 10.4018/978-1-4666-4357-4.ch015

Copyright ©2014, IGI Global. Copying or distributing in print or electronic forms without written permission of IGI Global is prohibited.

The initial assessment of the proposed legislation suggests that it will be an enormous threat to the tobacco industry which is still dealing with the stringent rules introduced by the previous governments. In brief, the proposed rules will not permit any company logos on cigarette packaging. Furthermore new rules also require all cigarette packages to prominently display large graphic photos of the physical damage caused by smoking. All cigarette packing irrespective of the manufacturer will be in 'olive green' colour. Research available to Federal Government has shown 'olive green' to be the least attractive colour for smokers. The warnings on cigarette packaging would cover more than 90 percent of space on the front of the packs, and 75 percent of the back.

TOBACCO INDUSTRY-A QUICK SNAPSHOT

The tobacco industry has had an interesting and often controversial history both globally and in Australia. Tobacco growing commenced during Australia's early years of settlement. By the 1820s tobacco was cultivated by farmers in the Hunter Valley region of New South Wales. In recent years the volume of commercial tobacco farming has declined quite considerably in Australia (Tobacco Industry In Australia).

Despite the predictions of 'doom and gloom' often reported in the western press, tobacco industry globally expects an expansion of the tobacco demand in the next few years. The increases in overall consumption are expected to emerge largely from the developing nations, while consumption in the industrialised countries will be static or in decline.

In all the countries surveyed, the biggest growth is expected to be in Zimbabwe, followed by Côte d'Ivoire, Brazil, Morocco, Venezuela, Pakistan, United Republic of Tanzania, and Bangladesh. The greatest decline is expected in New Zealand, followed by the UK, South Africa, Hong Kong, Australia, Singapore, and Finland (WHO, 2002).

On the supply side China, India, Brazil, and the US are the top four tobacco producers in the world. By global standards Australia was never a major tobacco producer by volume. The size of its consumer market in absolute terms also has been small. However it is important to note that per-capita consumption of tobacco in Australia has been consistently quite high. Despite the much publicised health risks associated with tobacco consumption, albeit mostly in the western countries, it is estimated that a billion adults worldwide make the choice to smoke.

Five firms dominate the global tobacco industry (apart from the state owned Chinese organization operating in China), Philip Morris International, British American Tobacco, Japan Tobacco, Altria, and Imperial Tobacco. In most countries these companies either have long established dominance, or have purchased the major domestic producer or producers. Due to cross ownership and other commercial arrangements, the big five often take a united stand on matters of common commercial interest.

According to IBISworld 2011, Australia has only two tobacco products manufacturers: Philip Morris (Australia) Limited and British American Tobacco (Australasia Holdings) Private Limited. In 2010 total industry revenues were in excess of one billion dollars. A large proportion of this revenue went to Government exchequer by way of taxes and excise duty.

SETTING THE STAGE

While it is widely acknowledged that smoking rates have been gradually declining in recent times (mostly in the western countries), the Australian Government believes that the incidence of smoking in Australia is still at an unacceptable level. It is confident that the new changes, particularly the 'olive green' packaging would discourage new people from smoking.

The new legislation is driven by two beliefs (1) cigarette smoking is the primary cause of half of all long-term smokers' death and (2) tobacco products are not normal consumer products and therefore should not be allowed to be marketed by the traditional tools of marketing and promotion. The Australian Government believes that the proposed change will take away the last opportunity that tobacco companies have in Australia, to try to market and promote their products by making them look luxurious or misrepresenting that they might be light and better for consumer health.

Tobacco companies, quite understandably view the packaging proposal as unhelpful, arbitrary, and illegal. They believe quite strongly that any additional restrictions in the display of their logo or trademark are unconstitutional and contrary to the spirit of 'World Trade Organisation' charter of free and unhindered use of legitimate intellectual property for trade. Any ban on the use of trademarks and logs on cigarette packaging therefore amounts to forcible acquisition of their intellectual property rights, a view also shared by Senator Barnby Joyce of the opposition party (Massola 2011). As a consequence the tobacco industry is prepared to challenge this action in the highest court of law as an attempt to deprive tobacco organisations to lawfully use their intellectual property (logos and trademark). It is the tobacco industry's view that the proposed packaging is unconstitutional and would cost the government and the taxpayers of Australia millions of dollars in compensation. Other legal experts however believe that the proposed changes are constitutional and well within the rules provided by the World Trade Organisation.

In view of the legislative framework, tobacco industry faces two challenges: 1.) how to convince the lawmakers that the proposed change is unlikely to deliver any tangible benefits to the community, and 2.) the need to devise an appropriate marketing strategy to differentiate competing tobacco brands in a highly cluttered product space–in case the law is eventually passed and implemented.

CURRENT CHALLENGE

Compared to the government's thinking, the main opposition party let by Mr Tony Abbott seems more sympathetic to tobacco industry's concerns and arguments. Mr Dutton the opposition health spokesman has an 'open mind' to any measures that help reduce smoking and maintains that there are other more effective measures to address the smoking problem in Australia. For example a more balanced measure to decrease smoking rates would be to further increase the excise on cigarettes, he said (Jerga, 2011).

As part of dealing with the immediate threat, tobacco industry has decided to highlight two major adverse consequences of the proposal. It argues that plain packaging of cigarettes will be confusing to both consumers and members of the distribution chain and cause unexpected errors and delays in service. In addition, and perhaps more seriously plain packaging will be a god-sent opportunity for counterfeiters. The entry of criminal elements into tobacco industry will also impose significant cost to the government.

The price of tobacco is identified as the single major factor influencing short term consumption of cigarettes. More importantly, price plays a major role in determining how young people will start smoking, and thus profoundly influences long-term consumption trends. According to Mackay and Eriksen of WHO, 2002 there is a clear inverse relationship between tobacco taxes and tobacco consumption. For every 10 percent increase in cigarette taxes, there is on average a four percent reduction in consumption.

THE WAY FORWARD

Historically tobacco companies have been free to promote their products everywhere-from television and cinema to sponsorship deals linking the names of cigarette brands with popular sporting events including cricket. It was not very long ago when the yearly triangular one-day cricket series was known as Benson and Hedges' series in Australia (Trembath 2011). Advertsing restrictions on tobacco products in western countries are a fairly recent development.

While forcing tobacco companies to use plain packaging has the potential to destroy one of their last advertising platforms, some commentators argue that tobacco industry has always been creative in devising ways to skirt advertising bans. For example, many blockbuster movies continue to present their key characters (often played by prominent stars) smoking well identified brands of cigarettes. It has been argued that this is another creative attempt of the tobacco industry to circumvent the regulations on advertising tobacco products. It is further claimed that this type of portrayal can indirectly promote smoking. As a consequence, the Federal Government's Preventative Task Force recommended that Australia follows the US and UK examples and require that smoking be taken into account when films are classified.

The Tobacco Plain Packaging Bill 2011 is due to be introduced during the winter sitting of the Australian Parliament following a 60-day period for public comment on the draft legislation. Australia will be the first country to take this drastic action to limit advertising options availability to tobacco industry. Governments and tobacco manufacturers in many countries around the world are following the developments with keen interest. If the proposed changes are successfully introduced in Australia, this will certainly have far reaching implications as other western countries re-assess their strategic options to manage tobacco induced health issues of their own populations.

The future of the tobacco industry in Australia appears immensely challenging. There are two imminent and plausible scenarios. Scenario 1: The proposed legislation is approved to make 'plain packaging' mandatory. This will make product differentiation excessively difficult. Scenario 2: The packaging 'status quo' is maintained for the time being but there is a hefty increase in taxes and excise duty on tobacco product-a move supported by the opposition party. In either case, marketing of tobacco products using the traditional marketing mix variables will be a huge challenge.

As Martin Broughton stated in defence of tobacco, "Most cultures and religions allow adults to make lifestyle choices, and to accept responsibility for their actions. Governments globally earn some ten times more revenue from tobacco than shareholders. The industry supports 100 million jobs. Tobacco is legal, and even the most vocal activists are at pains to stress that they are not abolitionists."

EPILOGUE

In November 2011, the Australian Senate passed the Federal Government's plain packaging laws for cigarettes, with amendments to the start date. The new packaging laws are now due to come into effect in December 2012, six months later than the original time frame.

The legislation bans the use of company logos and requires all cigarette packets to be a dark green colour. Pictures of diseased body parts, sickly babies, and dying people will cover 75 per cent of each cigarette packet, and tobacco industry logos, brand imagery, colours and promotional text will be banned.

It is too early to confirm if the legislated changes to cigarette packaging will deliver the desired changes in consumption patterns among the wider society. It is equally uncertain to assess the exact impact of these changes on the financial position of the tobacco industry in Australia.

REFERENCES

Broughton, B. (2001). The global tobacco industry: The real world choice for tobacco regulators., In *Proceedings of World Tobacco International Symposium and Trade Fair*. Hong Kong: British American Tobacco.

IBISWorld. (2011). Tobacco product manufacturing in australia. *Australian Industry Report*. Retrieved on http://www.ibisworld.com.au/industry/default.aspx?indid=120.

Jerga, J. (2011). More info needed on cigarette laws, says opposition health spokesman dutton. *The Australian*. Retrieved from http://www.theaustralian.com.au/news/breaking-news/more-info-needed-on-cigarette-laws-says-opposition-health-spokseman-dutton/story-fn3dxity-1226035388737.

Mackay, J., & Eriksen, M. (2002). *The tobacco atlas*. Geneva, Switzerland: World Health Organisation. Retrieved from http://www.who.int/tobacco/statistics/tobacco_atlas/en/.

Massola, L. (2011). Coalition split over cigarette packaging as barnaby joyce backs tobacco companies. *The Australian*. Retrieved from http://www.theaustralian.com.au/national-affairs/coalition-split-over-cigarette-packaging-as-barnaby-joyce-backs-tobacco-companies/story-fn59niix-1226061714807.

McGee, G. (2011). Cigarette packaging to go ugly olive green under proposed laws. *Herald Sun*. Retrieved from http://www.heraldsun.com.au/news/more-news/cigarette-packaging-to-go-ugly-olive-green-under-proposed-laws/story-fn7x-8me2-1226035141689.

Moerman, L., & Van Der Laan, S. (2005). Social reporting in the tobacco industry: All smoke and mirrors? *Accounting, Auditing & Accountability Journal*, *18*(3), 374–389. doi:10.1108/09513570510600747.

Tobacco in Australia Facts and Issues On line Resource. (n.d.). Retrieved from http://www.tobaccoinaustralia.org.au/chapter-10-tobacco-industry/10-8-the-tobacco-growing-industry.

Trembath, B. (2011). Tobacco industry gets creative to skirt ad bans. *ABC news.* Retrieved from http://www.abc.net.au/news/stories/2010/04/29/2886304.htm.

APPENDIX

Question

Consider yourself as a marketer of products that are becoming increasingly ostracised in most western countries. In view of the impending legislation, what marketing strategy will you recommend for tobacco products (cigarettes) in Australia and why? Please do remember tobacco industry and its products are entirely legal and well regulated. You are to take a professional rather than morally driven approach to marketing of cigarettes. Your personal preferences and moral dimensions should not influence your analysis and recommendations.

Answer to Question

It is important to acknowledge at the outset that there is no single best answer to this question. This is a wide ranging question. It links marketing strategy to environmental variations and forces students to consider a strategic response to a major change emerging from 'political-legal' environment of a country. This is obviously beyond the control of any particular organisation or industry. All cigarette manufacturing and marketing organisations in Australia that are affected by such changes have to re-think their strategy.

The proposed legislative change explicitly targets 'branding, packaging and labelling' aspects of marketing strategy. It limits the role these marketing tools can play in differentiating a particular brand from other competitors.

With this externally imposed constraint in mind, students are encouraged to explore how other elements of the marketing mix can be better applied to compensate for the legislative limitation.

The role of technology is worth exploring in assessing the strategic options. How to cultivate and sustain brand loyalty however should be the overarching consideration in making a strategic choice.

Chapter 16
Concentra BPO:
The Falling Customer Satisfaction

Shreya Dhingra
Jaipur National University, India

EXECUTIVE SUMMARY

This case study is about "Concentra", started by an entrepreneur along with his wife and colleagues who were later the part of the management. They started by providing BPO for financial services, contact center services, loyalty and customer retention. They started from a small company with limited manpower but grow up into big company spreading in many countries in lesser span of time. As the BPO expands, the management came across many problems in the company. One of the main problems which they came across was the employee dissatisfaction which resulted into lower customer satisfaction. The impact was so bad that they started loosing their customers and their business. This case study explains how a company can increase customer's satisfaction just by understanding and treating their employees as the first customers of the organization to be served.

INTRODUCTION

Arnab, MD of Concentra BPO is staying late in his office for a meeting with his friend, Vipin Khandelwal, Head of HR in a consultancy firm. Vipin enters his cabin with a surprised look on his face, and asked Arnab "What made you stay back in the office, is everything all right?" Arnab did not respond, he just stood near the window and looked towards him with a concerned look and said. "My company is running in losses. There is a decrease in customer satisfaction and there is also a high employee attrition rate from the last six months. The working environment of the company is not as it used to be."

DOI: 10.4018/978-1-4666-4357-4.ch016

Copyright ©2014, IGI Global. Copying or distributing in print or electronic forms without written permission of IGI Global is prohibited.

CONCENTRA BPO

Concentra BPO was started by Arnab Chakraborty in October, 2000 with 10 employees in New Delhi, India. He had 7 years of experience with Infoton BPO in Gurgaon before starting his own company. He left Infoton as a V.P. of Sales and Marketing. He travelled to many countries during this period and could bring 27 high value companies to Infoton for their outsourcing work. He was a high achiever there and won many awards for "Excellence in Service."

Seven employees of Infoton also joined him during the launch of Concentra. Concentra has done well over the last decade with the turnover touching ₹1,140 crores. They established 26 delivery centers in the year 2008 which are spread across India, UK, and Sri Lanka. The company has 70% of their employees in their onshore and 30% in offshore delivery centers. Concentra is one of the most highly preferred outsourcing partners by many MNCs across India and Europe. Concentra was ranked 365th in Fortune India 500 list of 2011 and their client lists include global Fortune 500 companies. The company provides services in the areas of customer management, collections, and data processing. They combine their expertise in Business Process Outsourcing (BPO), finance services, contact centre services, loyalty and customer retention, supply chain solutions, and public sector and citizen services to deliver innovative, individual solutions that help their clients to achieve their objectives. Their mission is to provide great service to their customers at economical costs. This is delivered by a team of well trained and highly experienced call center representatives. Concentra's dedicated staff at all levels listens to the customers, understand their problems, and provide high quality solutions fitting the customer's requirements with perfection.

Concentra's abilities in improving online customer service experiences, reducing service cost without making any compromises on Customer Satisfaction Index CSI scores, and value created thought technology transformation contributed to its growth in the initial years. This growth reflected its concentrated efforts to maximize efficiencies, drive innovation, and enhance business value for its customers. Concentra reported a 1.7% rise in net profit to ₹221.00 crores on a 3.5% increase in total income to ₹1,262 crores in financial year 2011-2012. The last 3 years after the recession in 2008-2009 have been bad for Concentra. It has also lost four of its main customers accounting for 25% of its business because of dissatisfaction of employees internally which effects the relation with the direct customers.

Concentra started with 10 employees and now has a team of 800 call center representatives with a team of five members in the top management along with Arnab. They had good management experience in different companies across the globe. Jatin Khurana joined as GM-communications after working as Senior Manager Communication with Customers First. Shraddha Mahajan joined as HR Head after working as an HR manager for seven years with Best BPO. Manoj Dewane joined as CIO after working as System In-charge with Miti group for six years. Sumit Jain joined as CFO after working with EWC as audit head in Delhi. Marketing function was handled by Arnab along with his wife Nupur Chakravorthy, who specialized in training and building strong client base. Arnab considers an excellent organization to be a combination of two very critical aspects: employee satisfaction and customer satisfaction.

CSI AT CONCENTRA

Customer Satisfaction Index (CSI) is simply an average of all attributes that are believed to contribute to customer satisfaction. Since different attributes can contribute differently to the overall customer satisfaction, the individual attributes are weighted to reflect this reality. This is the essence of a customer satisfaction index. Concentra enjoyed a CSI of more than 90% till 2009 but in the last 2 years post recession, the CSI has gone down and it was reported to be 78%. CSI of the last five years is shown in Table 1.

EMPLOYEE SATISFACTION AT CONCENTRA

Concentra is experiencing low employee satisfaction in the very demanding working environment with cost pressures and the falling rupee. Concentra achieved significant cost appreciation and development from its contact centers and employees in the earlier years. Post 2007, there is rise in the attrition rate and the reason was high declining employee satisfaction. Figure 1 shows the attrition rate in the last five years.

Some of the major challenges faced by Concentra due to employee dissatisfaction are:

Table 1. CSI from 2007 to 2011

Year	C.S.I (%)
2007	93
2008	96
2009	90
2010	84
2011	78

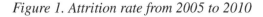

Figure 1. Attrition rate from 2005 to 2010

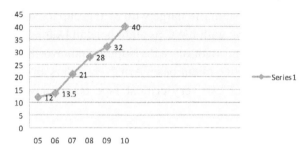

- Employee turnover is directly impacting the customer satisfaction, loyalty, and retention, which is leading to loss of potential customers.
- High turnover rate resulted into lower employee morale.

A survey was conducted with the help of HR Consulting firm of Vipin to study the employee satisfaction at Concentra. The findings of this research are shown in Figure 2.

Figure 2. Factors responsible for employee satisfaction

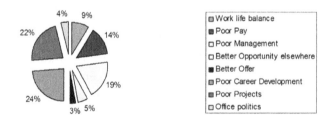

Figure 3. Points which should be considered for employee satisfaction

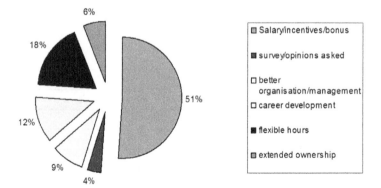

According to the survey which was conducted internally, they came to a conclusion that to control the attrition rate in their company the points in Figure 3 should be taken care of.

Although being very professional in his job life, Arnab learned one thing as an entrepreneur, which is for an employee, job satisfaction is extremely important and to achieve job satisfaction one must have the right skills and expertise to do the work. A high satisfaction level in employees always leads to a better customer satisfaction.

Arnab was concerned about the falling revenues, loss of customers, and high attrition rate. He is banking on Vipin's experience to get through this critical situation.

Chapter 17
A Case Study on Customer Experiential Management at High Five Hotels Pvt. Ltd, Nashik

Sonali Gadekar
MET's Institute of Management, India

Sushil Gadekar
MGV's Institute of Hotel Management, India

EXECUTIVE SUMMARY

Experiential Marketing is an extension of consumer orientation marketing. The organizations can use Experiential Marketing as one of models which has vast potential to serve as a link between improved customer satisfaction and brand loyalty. It can be described as one of the innovative ways of delivering the consumption experiences to the consumers before they buy a product or actually use the service. It works on the simple principle that the memories of experiences get preserved in the minds of prospective customers as well as repeat consumers which induces them to visit again and again for the same product or service. In this case study of High Five Hotel Pvt. Ltd., this innovative marketing strategy, known as experiential marketing, was applied by the management to establish itself in the market as a reputed brand. This case study presents various innovative promotional strategies followed in the hospitality industry. The ultimate outcome and the results after applying this 'experiential techniques' were excellent in terms of financial returns as well as customer satisfaction.

DOI: 10.4018/978-1-4666-4357-4.ch017

Copyright ©2014, IGI Global. Copying or distributing in print or electronic forms without written permission of IGI Global is prohibited.

INTRODUCTION TO THEME

The pleasure of experience can result in product procurement. Truly, experiential marketing or Customer Experience Management (CEM) is a new age marketing tactic to influence the customer's buying decision. The term "Experiential Marketing" refers to actual customer experiences with the brand/product/service that drive sales and increase brand image and awareness. It's the experience which is attracting the consumer towards a brand and ultimately a source for creation of brand loyalty.

ORGANIZATION BACKGROUND

The owner and promoter of chain group of hotels, Mr. Raj Malhotra had a vision of setting his dream project in Hospitality Industry in the Holy city of Nashik which is situated in Maharashtra state of India. Accordingly, a three star hotel, property named as High Five Hotels Pvt. Ltd, was established in January of 2011 on the Mumbai Agra National Highway. Mr. Malhotra had in mind that the Hotel will get a strategic locational advantage as it is situated on busy National Highway as well as within the proximity of Ambad Industrial area of Nashik city. His major target clients are affluent travelers who will be visiting Lord Sai Baba's Temple at Shirdi and the business clients from Mumbai's Corporate offices who regularly visit the companies in the industrial area. The 54 room luxurious hotel is equipped to provide world class staying and dining experience to the guests.

Mr. Gurucharan Singh, the General Manager (GM) has four efficient, enthusiastic, and energetic subordinates namely Mr. Alex D'souza as Food & Beverage Manager, Mr. Gupta as Front Office Manager, Ms. Kashmira as House Keeping In Charge, and Chef Vijay Kapoor as Food Production Manager. The organizational culture was healthy and everyone was working with the sole aim of giving best quality service to the customer with complete dedication and strong belief in "Atithi Devo Bhav" (Sanskrit words meaning *Guest is God*). It was of little difficulty for the management to get and retain skilled as well as qualified employees at operational level to work in restaurants and kitchen.

CURRENT SITUATION, CHALLENGES, AND GOALS

Mr. Malhotra had gauged the strong presence of competitors like Express Inn, Hotel Taj- Ginger, Hotel Sai Palace, and White Lily. He was worried over financial returns on investments made and also wanted to create unique identity of his Hotel. He decided to do what other hoteliers have neither done nor even thought of. He followed the new age marketing tool 'experiential marketing' to penetrate the market and to embark on effective pre-launch and post-launch strategies as suggested by the General Manager.

The drive-in guests had to face the parking problem as maximum space used to be occupied by the vehicles of staying guests. The management was ready to pay a high price to acquire the adjacent area for parking which was not readily available. Strong presence of established competitors and their sizable market share was another important concern.

Major goals which the organization hoped to accomplish were widening the market share, enhancing the number of repeat customers, and marketing the innovative idea of rendering an 'experience' of lavish and comfort staying to the guest even before they buy the service.

IMPLEMENTATION STRATEGY

Mr. Malhotra hired a consultant Mr. Aatish Rizvi from reputed Hospitality Consultancy Firm known as Welcome Services Pvt. Ltd. He conveyed the professional fees of $5000 which was nearing to the salary of General Manager, Mr. Singh. The consultant was not in favor of the experiential marketing tool as it involves relatively high cost factor and was instead more keen on traditional marketing. Mr. Singh, the GM was against the consultant's appointment. He had complete faith in experimental marketing tactics for which he submitted a plan of action to Mr. Malhotra. Realizing the probable and positive impact of the General Manager's plan of action, Mr. Malhotra took a pioneering decision to implement experiential marketing as his promotional strategy.

The plan of action designed and drafted by Mr. Singh included:

Pre Launch Strategy

1. He invited top industrialists, doctors, professional, consultants, tour planners, and journalists to a pre-launch Cocktail party. Winners of the various games played in the party were gifted with a free one night stay and morning breakfast on the next day.
2. He arranged the field visits of students of International Schools from Mumbai with free night stay in Hotel.
3. He put hoardings on highway depicting Hi fi Hotel as 2.5 km away or take 12 min drive to world class hospitality experience.

4. To attract corporate clients, he planned MICE (Meetings, Incentives, Conventions, and Exhibitions) event with complementary visit to Sula Winery. Nashik being famous for Grapes, it has many wineries and vineyards.

5. He also gave full page advertisement in leading *National Daily Times* of India.

Post Launch Strategy

1. He recruited a three member team of MBA marketing to undertake further market penetration activity.

2. An all new look was given for arranging theme parties to furniture, cutlery, equipment, and dance floors.

3. Special discounts and complementary cakes were announced for all children's parties, birthday parties, and college farewell parties.

4. Wine, chocolates, dry fruits, and fruit baskets were made complementary for every room occupied.

5. Specialty restaurants with Thai, Mexican, Italian, Chinese, and Spanish menu with authentic recipes were planned.

Experiential Marketing Strategy

1. It was advertised that those corporate clients arranging 'Product launch', such as Designer fashion shows, television cookery shows, musical nights, and so forth will get a one night and one day free stay with their family.

2. The external stakeholders of the hotel, such as the suppliers, auditors, lawyers, architects, and so forth, were given complementary dinners with family to market the experience.

3. Venue partner for various exhibitions and property fairs.

4. Dinner with celebrities and national players.

5. Complementary snacks for the students of hotel management colleges for industry visits were also arranged to the hotel.

THE PROMOTIONAL STRATEGIES

As a part of efforts to enhance the number of repeat clients, a plethora of promotional activities were decided to be undertaken. Ticket booking services, loyalty discounts, toys for the kids, babysitting services, free mehendi (hand decoration) to ladies, spa and ayurvedic massage, free health checkup, free astrology services, and free guide service for tourists, to name few.

Other specialty services were given to the regular clients. Chocolate bouquets were given to the guests while checking out. Standardized recipes, quantity, and presentation style of international standards were followed. Free movie tickets for multiplex cinema theatre were given to regular visitors. Advertisement at similar cinema theatre were given–"Have dinner at HI FI and get 2 tickets free."

Apart from basic amenities, free mini bar in every room, mini buffet for kids, magic shows, and fire shows at fixed intervals were also part of experimental promotion strategies. Roof-top open theatre, cultural shows, and cricket matches on the big screen were the real crowd pullers.

Coffee bar, wine bar, pastry shop, jewelry and antique piece outlet, currency exchange facility, and a travel desk were also established on the basis of client feedback.

OUTCOME OF IMPLEMENTATION STRATEGY

Due to above promotional strategies, repeat clients rate was increased by 48% and monthly turnover was more than double. It could establish itself as a reputed brand in the corporate sector as well as in the next two quarters. Competitors started to reframe their promotional strategies.

LESSONS LEARNED

Experience teaches more than mere information provided to the guests. This entire episode stood as a motivating factor for the competitors in the same industry as well as acting as a source of inspiration to new comers in the industry. It created awareness and importance of experiential marketing strategy amongst staff and localities.

CONCLUSION

With the emergence of the global knowledge economy, marketers have started witnessing the profound potential of unique marketing phenomenon known as "experiential economy." It can be proven that the personal experiences of the consumers shapes the opinions and buying preferences more strongly than the promotions through advertising or even word of mouth publicity. Experiential marketing is also about identifying the right customers and selling the dreams. Here the dream is not a product, it is all about the experience.

REFERENCES

Pine & Gilmore. (1999). *The Experience Economy.* Boston: Harvard Business School Press.

Shrivastav. (2009). *Experiential marketing: Buy it or leave it, but try it with pleasure.* Retrieved from www.televisionpoint.com.

Zhao & Zhang. (2009). The application of experiential marketing in china's real estate. *International Journal of Business Management, 4*(5), 222–225.

Chapter 18

Case Study on Customer's Ambidextrous Nature of Trust in Internet Banking:
Australian Context

Sujana Adapa
University of New England, Australia

Fredy Valenzuela
University of New England, Australia

EXECUTIVE SUMMARY

This case study provides information related to the Australian retail-banking sector and specifically about the electronic banking service delivery channels. As a Western nation, Australia is classified as a developed country with well-developed infrastructure, gross domestic product, per capita income, and economic status. A cross-sectional mall intercept survey was conducted in order to explore the trust related perceptions of the Australian consumers' towards the internet banking service delivery channel. Trust is an important variable because of its high relevance to the success and/or failure of many businesses, products, and service offerings. Although there exists several benefits attached to the internet banking transactions, the survey carried out, indicates that there are a significant number of customers in Australia, who do not perform internet banking transactions due to lack of trust in the bank (or bank personnel or internet service delivery channel etc.). Consequently, results also indicate that a majority of the customers preferred to use internet banking

DOI: 10.4018/978-1-4666-4357-4.ch018

Copyright ©2014, IGI Global. Copying or distributing in print or electronic forms without written permission of IGI Global is prohibited.

transactions due to the trust that they have in carrying out these electronic banking methods. Therefore, this study provides information related to the ambidextrous nature of the trust component and how the aforesaid affects the consumer's perception levels towards the adoption/non-adoption of internet banking in the Australian context. Moreover, this study provides results obtained through a cross-sectional mall intercept survey carried out in the Australian context and verbatim quotes obtained from the respondents in the form of open-ended comments. Furthermore, the implications related to bank managers, government, and policy-makers are presented.

INTRODUCTION

Many businesses irrespective of their size, seem to operate in physical and/or electronic environments due to benefits such as gaining market share, maintaining competitive advantage, meeting consumer's needs, and so on. As a result, modern businesses have a combination of bricks and mortar and clicks and mortar presence party to retain their existing customer base and partly to differentiate their business from the competitors. One such business entity is the retail-banking sector that has successfully ventured into online banking transactions whilst complementing its physical bank branches. Thus, banks throughout the world have taken the advantage of the advent of the internet and various technological advancements. As such, there has been a proliferation of electronic service delivery channels in the retail-banking sector. Consumers' are also exhibiting greater interest to use electronic service delivery channels due to convenience, 24/7 service delivery, self-service options etc., Therefore, published global academic and business reports indicate the uptake of internet banking by customers in a phenomenal manner across many countries. Yet, in many countries the uptake of internet banking by customers has not reached the projected statistics due to lack of infrastructure, speed of internet connectivity, customer awareness, and so forth. Customers' perception of trust is one such factor that may/may not influence their adoption/non-adoption of internet banking.

The concept of trust in a more general sense is related to psychological and sociological perspectives, which pave the way to better understand consumer-based trust, and consumers' association with the trust construct in an online or electronic environment. General trust identified in the existing literature is internal in nature and attempts to explain business-to-business relationships. The psychological perspective identifies trust as a generalised expectancy and relates to interpersonal trust relationships. The sociological perspective relates to communal trust and social capital (Kramer, 1999). Trust in general is defined as 'a belief or expectation about the trusted party or as a behavioural intention or willingness to depend or rely on another party' (Grabner-Kraeuter & Kaluscha, 2003). Mayer et al. (1995) stated that trust is 'the willingness of a party to be vulnerable to the actions of another party based on the expectation that the others will perform a particular action important to the trustor, irrespective of the ability to monitor or control that other party'. To date neither researchers nor practitioners agree on a single definition of trust which is applicable unanimously either to business-to-business or business to consumer contexts. Lack of conclusive evidence might be attributed to the difficulty in measuring trust, which is an arbitrary and abstract concept.

Trust has been identified as a potential driving force for the development of electronic commerce applications as it determines the consumers' acceptance and willingness to engage in various transactions. Proper maintenance of trust between buyers and sellers is important for the success of E-commerce. Consumers' perception towards trust reduces their uncertainties and increases their transactional activities. The concept of trust plays a crucial role in the online environment due to its impersonal nature and extensive use of technology. Several researchers identified lack of trust as an important feature related to consumers' reluctance to perform online transactions. Online trust is defined as a belief or expectation about the website or the web vendor and/or the internet as a trusted party or object of trust or as a behavioural intention or willingness to depend or rely on the trusted party. Willingness to perform internet-based transactions depends on consumers' trust in a specific party, such as the bank, and in the internet as an underlying transaction medium. In the internet banking context, the trustor is typically identified as a consumer and the trusted party is the bank or the internet.

Several researchers identify trust as a multidimensional concept and the specific dimensions relate to disposition to trust, institutional based trust, trusting belief and trusting intention. Disposition to trust is identified as individuals' faith or trust in others. Institutional trust consists of structural assurance and situational normality enabling interactions between the parties to be successful. Trusting belief refers to three beliefs of competence, integrity and benevolence. Competence is the trustors' belief in the ability of the trustee. Integrity is the belief of the user that the services provided by the trustee are ethical, honest, and complete. Trusting intention relates to the user's aim to access the services provided by the trustee. The component of trust in the use of internet-based transactions enables further perceived consequences such as favourable expectations by consumers that the internet is reliable and will not result in any of the negative consequences.

The disposition to trust dimension is not considered in the present study as there is no interaction of the consumers with any other bank personnel in performing internet-based transactions. Often trusting beliefs are affected by institutional-based trust and form an integral part of electronic environment. Consumers' trust in online transactions is affected by the characteristics of the bank, website and underlying technology infrastructure. Internet trust in the present study is conceptualised as consumers' trusting beliefs in the reliability and predictability of the internet and the willingness of the consumer to depend on the internet medium with regard to their economic transactions and did not include any characteristics of the banks or bank websites.

This case study provides information related to the Australian retail-banking sector and specifically about the Australian internet banking environment. Taking into consideration the economic wealth of the country, Australia is a developed country with well-developed infrastructure. However, the survey carried out, indicates that there are a significant number of customers in Australia, who do not perform internet banking transactions due to lack of trust in the bank or bank personnel or internet service delivery channel etc., Consequently, results also indicate that a majority of the customers preferred to use internet banking transactions due to the trust that they have in carrying out these electronic banking methods. Therefore, this study provides information related to the ambidextrous nature of the trust component and how the aforesaid affects the consumer's perception levels towards the adoption/ non-adoption of internet banking in the Australian context. Moreover, this study provides results obtained through a cross-sectional mall intercept survey carried out in the Australian context and verbatim quotes obtained from the respondents' in the form of open-ended comments. Furthermore, the implications related to bank managers, government and policy-makers are presented.

AUSTRALIAN BANKING SECTOR

The financial services sector includes banking and non-bank financial services such as building societies, the securities exchange and services to finance and insurance businesses. Growth in the industry has been driven by the globalisation of financial transactions, development of new and more sophisticated financial services and products, increased international activity and significant growth in the funds management industry (Gyptra & Dixon, 2002). Commercial banking in Australia began in the 1800s with the formation of British banks by colonists (Unnithan & Swatman, 2001). The first central bank established was the Commonwealth Bank in 1901 (Lyell et al., 1997). The Reserve Bank of Australia (RBA) emerged as a separate entity in 1959 and attained the status of the national regulatory body. The Non-Bank Financial Intermediaries (NBFIs) in Australia were formed and developed in the 1960s and 1970s (Carew, 1998). The decrease in the influence of the RBA was evident in 1979 and 1983 following the recommendations of the Campbell and Martin Committees (Carew, 1998). Australian banks were even more open to service innovations due to the floating of the exchange rate in 1983 and the opening of the Australian banking system to foreign competitors in 1984 (Unnithan & Swatman, 2001). In the past two decades the financial services sector has developed rapidly in terms of size, industry and the introduction of innovative products and services oriented towards consumers and businesses (Al-Hawari et al., 2005).

The Australian financial sector has been transformed from a relatively closed system in the 1950s and 1960s based on a conventional mode of banking to a modern and competitive system offering a wide range of products and services (Gardener et al., 1999). An upsurge in the Australian retail banking sector's productivity was evident during the period 1986 to 1995 (Avkiran, 2000). The Australian financial market is currently dominated by principal regulators such as the RBA regulating monetary policies, the Australian Prudential Regulation Authority (APRA) overseeing the banking and financial institutions and the Australian Securities and Investments Commission (ASIC) regulating shares trading. The modern Australian banking system is characterised by four major banks garnering a significant proportion of the market share as a result of a series of bank mergers, credit unions formed by the unions and co-operatives, building societies predominantly created by the housing finance demand, and funds management institutions involved in superannuation and funds (Unnithan & Swatman, 2001). Additionally, the Australian Banker's Association (ABA) is the national organisation representing licensed banks in Australia (Avkiran, 2000).

These rapid changes encouraged banks to acquire essential knowledge regarding future trends in order to compete effectively (Al-Hawari et al., 2005). The advent of internet and related technological innovations has demonstrated a remarkable influence on services, as exhibited by the proliferation of service delivery channels (Bitner et al., 2000; Dabholkar & Bagozzi, 2002). Australia's retail banking sector exhibits certain similarities and differences with those of Canada, New Zealand, United Kingdom and the United States of America (Worthington & Edwards, 2000). Historically, financial institutions and financial systems have strong associations with rural towns and a strong sense of community building, which is unique to the Australian banking system (Wallis Report, 1997). Approximately 80-85 percent of the Australian banking market is controlled by four major banks and the remainder is shared by the regional banks and credit unions (IBIS World, 2005). Also, IBIS World (2005) noted that consolidation of these major banks is unlikely due to the intervention of the Australian Consumer and Competition Commission (ACCC).

Retail banking includes all forms of banking undertaken by individuals and often encompasses any type of relationship that a consumer has with the bank from performing transactions, maintaining various accounts, dealing with the credit and debit cards, as well as mortgage and investment banking. There is a multitude of retail banking services available for consumers but their classification and total number may vary across different target markets (Akinci et al., 2004). Broadly speaking, retail banking services can be classified into the following four groups: current account, insurance-based, credit-based and investment-based services (Howcroft et al., 2002). In relation to internet banking, five basic services have been listed by researchers: viewing account balances and transaction histories, paying bills, transferring funds between accounts, requesting credit card advances, and ordering cheques (Chou & Chou, 2000).

THEORETICAL CONCEPTS OF TRUST

The concept of trust in a more general sense is related to psychological and sociological perspectives, which pave the way to better understand consumer-based trust, and consumers' association with the trust construct in an online or electronic environment. General trust identified in the existing literature is internal in nature and attempts to explain business-to-business relationships. The psychological perspective identifies trust as a generalised expectancy and relates to interpersonal trust relationships (Grabner-Kraeuter & Kaluscha, 2003). The sociological perspective relates to communal trust and social capital (Kramer, 1999). Trust in general is defined as 'a belief or expectation about the trusted party or as a behavioural intention or willingness to depend or rely on another party' (Grabner-Kraeuter & Kaluscha, 2003). Mayer et al. (1995) stated that trust is 'the willingness of a party to be vulnerable to the actions of another party based on the expectation that the others will perform a particular action important to the trustor, irrespective of the ability to monitor or control that other party'. To date neither researchers nor practitioners agree on a single definition of trust which is applicable unanimously either to business-to-business or business to consumer contexts (Grabner-Kraeuter & Kaluscha, 2003). Lack of conclusive evidence might be attributed to the difficulty in measuring trust, which is an arbitrary and abstract concept. However, existing literature focuses on the definitions of general trust presented in Table 1.

These definitions of "trust" are applied in numerous studies across a number of academic disciplines, but several researchers contend that the concept of trust needs

Table 1. Definitions of general trust

Hardin (2002)	'Trust is inherently a rational or intentional commitment or judgment' (p.186)
Kramer (1999)	'Trust entails a state of perceived vulnerability that is derived from individuals' uncertainty regarding the motives, intentions, and prospective actions of others on whom they depend' (p.571)
Ruscio (1999)	Trust is defined as 'merely another strategy to achieve ones' interests and springs not from duty or obligations to others but from a calculation that it is in ones' personal interest to trust others' (p. 645)

further research because it is a multidimensional and complex construct. The five types of trust emerged from the general conceptualisation of trust as a construct and are presented in Table 2.

Existing business and marketing literature refers to consumer-based trust which relates largely to a psychological construct and, to a lesser extent, a sociological construct. Moorman et al. (1992) defined consumer based trust as 'the willingness to rely on an exchange partner in whom one has confidence.' Fukuyama (1995) described trust as 'the shared norms of ethical behaviour between network members'. Thus the concept of trust is often ambiguous and highly context dependent (Egger, 2003; Suh & Han, 2003). For the success of any business, trust is vital and as such it plays an important role in the banking industry (Yousafzai et al., 2005). Trust has been identified as a potential driving force for the development of electronic commerce applications as it determines the consumers' acceptance and willingness to engage in various transactions (Herrmann & Herrmann 2004). Proper maintenance of trust between buyers and sellers is important for the success of e-commerce (Gulati & Sytch, 2008; Chang et al., 2005). Suh & Han (2003) reported that consumers' perceptions towards trust reduces their uncertainties and increases their transactional activities.

Research indicates the delineation of online trust from offline trust (Yousafzai et al., 2005). The concept of trust plays a crucial role in the online environment due to its impersonal nature and extensive use of technology (Grabner-Kraeuter & Faullant, 2008; Gan et al., 2006; Yousafzai et al., 2003). Offline trust, characterised by attributes such as eye contact, tone of voice, appearance and behaviour of people, does not seem to be valid in an electronic environment (Yousafzai et al., 2005). Several researchers identified lack of trust as an important feature related to

Table 2. Types of trust emerged from general trust

Characteristic-based trust	Fenton (2000)	Relates to an individual's social and cultural background.
Process-based trust	Fenton (2000)	Associated to past and present exchanges and reputation and identified as relevant in maintaining long-term relationships.
Institutional-based trust	Pavlou & Gefen (2004) Walczuch & Lundgren (2004)	Cover the aspect of trust in terms of certification and legal constraints and includes other embodiments of institutions with social and communal importance.
Cognition-based trust	Kumar & Paddison (2000)	Characterised by competence, responsibility, reliability, predictability and dependability as attributes of a potential trustee.
Affect-based trust	Kumar & Paddison (2000)	Formed on the basis of emotional bonds between the potential trustor and trustee.

consumers' reluctance to perform online transactions (Flavian et al., 2006; Luarn & Lin, 2004; Mukherjee & Nath, 2003). Trust is of an important concern in many social interactions (Pavlou & Fygenson, 2006; Gefen & Straub, 2003). Online trust is defined as a belief or expectation about the website or the web vendor and/or the internet as a trusted party or object of trust or as a behavioural intention or willingness to depend or rely on the trusted party (McKnight et al., 2002; McKnight & Chervany 2002). Electronic trust is defined as 'the assured confidence a trustor (the user) has in the trustees' (the form of electronic banking) ability to provide reliable banking services' (Yousafzai et al., 2005). Willingness to perform internet-based transactions depends on consumers' trust in a specific party, such as the bank, and in the internet as an underlying transaction medium (McKnight et al., 2002). In the internet banking context, the trustor is typically identified as a consumer and the trusted party is the bank or the internet.

Several researchers identify trust as a multidimensional concept and the specific dimensions relate to disposition to trust, institutional based trust, trusting belief and trusting intention (Riegelsberger et al., 2005; Wang & Emurian, 2005; Yousafzai et al., 2005; Patton, 2004; McKnight et al., 2002). Disposition to trust is identified as individuals' faith or trust in others. Institutional trust consists of structural assurance and situational normality enabling interactions between the parties to be successful. Trusting belief refers to three beliefs of competence, integrity and benevolence. Competence is the trustors' belief in the ability of the trustee. Integrity is the belief of the user that the services provided by the trustee are ethical, honest and complete. Trusting intention relates to the user's aim to access the services provided by the trustee. The component of trust in the use of internet-based transactions enables further perceived consequences such as favourable expectations by consumers that the internet is reliable and will not result in any of the negative consequences (Pavlou & Fygenson, 2006).

The disposition to trust dimension is not considered in the present study as there is no interaction of the consumers with any other bank personnel in performing internet-based transactions. Often trusting beliefs are affected by institutional-based trust and forms an integral part of electronic environment (Yousafzai et al., 2005). Consumers' trust in online transactions is affected by the characteristics of the bank, website and underlying technology infrastructure. Internet trust in the present study is conceptualised as consumers' trusting beliefs in the reliability and predictability of the internet and the willingness of the consumer to depend on the internet medium with regard to their economic transactions and did not include any characteristics of the banks or bank websites.

The prevailing view of consumer trust in the e-commerce literature contends that trust has a direct positive effect on consumers' attitude and behaviour (Teo & Liu, 2007; Jarvenpaa et al., 2004; Suh & Han, 2003; Pavlou, 2003). Jarvenpaa et al.

(1999) reported that consumers' willingness to purchase in an internet store is affected by their perceptions regarding trust. Bhattacharjee (2002) noted that trust and familiarity of the consumers plays a predominant role in influencing their willingness to transact online. Consumers' purchase intentions are influenced by integrity and benevolence components of trust (Gefen, 2002). Also, Gefen et al. (2003) concluded that trust is a significant predictor of potential and repeat customer purchase intentions. George (2004) revealed that consumers' purchase intentions in an electronic environment are determined by their perceptions regarding internet trustworthiness. Trust in one's bank is a key determinant in directly influencing consumers' use of internet banking (Sohail & Shanmugam, 2003). Pavlou (2003) reported that trust has a positive direct effect on consumers' attitude towards internet banking.

Ratnasingam et al. (2005) reported that 'whereas the traditional notion of trust primarily focuses on trust in a trading partner, trust in e-business also incorporates the notion of trust in the infrastructure and the underlying mechanism (technology trust) which deals with transaction integrity, authentication, confidentiality, and non-repudiation'. Lee & Turban (2001) state that 'human trust in an automated or computerised system depends on three factors: (1) the perceived technical competence of the system, (2) the perceived performance level of the system, and (3) the human operator's understanding of the underlying characteristics and processes governing the system's behaviour.' A plethora of studies acknowledge the importance of trust in the internet medium (McCole & Ramsay, 2009; Eastlick et al., 2006; McKnight et al., 2002). Thus, the trust component associated with the internet-based channel stresses the perceived ability of the internet to perform the task, as well as the speed, reliability and availability of the system (McCole & Ramsay, 2009). The component of trust was identified as critical in facilitating electronic transactions in the existing literature (Grabner-Kraeuter & Kaluscha, 2003).

Researchers also contend that, in order to attain the true electronic transactions potential, the internet has still some way to go and often lack of trust between transacting parties and the system facilitating the exchange impedes the speed at which this potential has yet to be realised (Gupta & Kim, 2007; Dinev et al., 2006). Electronic transactions recognise the role of the consumer as a key 'stakeholder' in these interactions, as the ultimate decision of whether a transaction will take place or not depends on the consumer (McCole & Ramsay, 2009). Therefore, the present study stresses the importance of internet channel based trust and further intends to identify the influence exerted on consumers' continued use and frequency of use of internet banking by Australian consumers.

CHANNEL FACTORS

Channel factors were operationalised in accordance with work by Hernandez & Mazzon (2007), Chan & Lu (2004), Tan & Teo (2000), Rhee & Riggins (1997), Bhimani (1996), Cockburn & Wilson (1996), and Lee (1996). For the purpose of this study, channel factors were measured using the 15 item scale consisting of four sub-dimensions (Hernandez & Mazzon, 2007; Tan & Teo, 2000). Data were collected from the respondents who were current internet banking users, using 15 items from CD1 to CD15, which used a six-point Likert scale defined as (1) Strongly Agree, (2) Agree, (3) Neither Agree nor Disagree, (4) Disagree, (5) Strongly Disagree, and (6) Unable to Rate. As shown in Table 3, the sub-dimensions measured with regard to the channel factors included:

- **Perceived Self-efficacy:** Consisted of five items (CD1, CD2, CD3, CD4, and CD5)
- **Perceived Risk:** Consisted of four items (CD6, CD7, CD8, and CD9)
- **Perceived Trust:** Consisted of three items (CD10, CD11, and CD12)
- **Perceived Personalisation:** Consisted of three items (CD13, CD14, and CD15)

The items included in the sub-dimensions were obtained from scales already validated in the existing literature related to the adoption, intention to adopt and internet banking contexts. The items included in the perceived self-efficacy, perceived risk, perceived trust and perceived personalisation sub-dimensions were identified from the existing literature associated with work by Chan & Lu (2004), Gan et al. (2006), Herington & Weaven (2007), and Srinivasan et al. (2002).

The items included in the self-efficacy sub-dimension were adapted from previous studies (Hernandez & Mazzon, 2007; Chan & Lu, 2004; Tan & Teo, 2000; Compeau & Higgins, 1995). In a study by Tan & Teo (2000), self-efficacy was found to influence the adoption of internet banking in Singapore (N = 454). Cronbach's coefficient alpha values were computed to test for construct reliability and were identified as adequate (0.8767). The factor analysis conducted satisfactorily and met the conditions of convergent and discriminant validity with a minimum reported factor loadings of 0.4. In another study comprised of a sample of 183 internet banking users in Hong Kong by Chan & Lu (2004), the maximum likelihood method was employed using the varimax rotation. All the items exhibited factor

Table 3. Channel factors including theorised sub-dimensions and various items

Theorised Sub-Dimensions	Items Included	Item Numbers	Reverse Coding Required
Perceived Self-efficacy	I am confident of using internet banking even if there is no one around to show me how to use it.	CD1	No
Perceived Self-efficacy	I am confident of using internet banking if I have built-in online "help" function for assistance.	CD2	No
Perceived Self-efficacy	I am confident of using internet banking even if have only the online instructions for reference.	CD3	No
Perceived Self-efficacy	I am confident of using internet banking if I see someone else using it before I try it myself.	CD4	No
Perceived Self-efficacy	I am confident of using internet banking if I could call someone for help if I got stuck.	CD5	No
Perceived Risk	I am confident that internet banking in Australia is secure.	CD6	No
Perceived Risk	Information concerning my internet banking transactions can be accessed by others.	CD7	Yes
Perceived Risk	Performing internet banking transactions makes me feel psychologically uncomfortable.	CD8	Yes
Perceived Risk	Internet banking transactions could lead to an inefficient use of my time.	CD9	Yes
Perceived Trust	Internet banking is trustworthy.	CD10	No
Perceived Trust	I trust in the ability of internet banking to protect my privacy.	CD11	No
Perceived Trust	Using internet banking is financially secure.	CD12	No
Perceived Personalisation	Performing internet banking makes me feel that I am a unique customer.	CD13	No
Perceived Personalisation	Internet banking websites provide information that is tailor-made for me.	CD14	No
Perceived Personalisation	The promotional offers that I receive through internet banking transactions are attractive to me.	CD15	No

loadings of more than 0.8 and a construct reliability of 0.938. In a study by Hernandez & Mazzon (2007) involving a Brazilian sample, the self-efficacy measure was validated by means of exploratory factor analysis using principal components extraction and varimax rotation. The communalities extracted from all the items were higher than 0.7 and there were no cross-loadings superior to 0.3. Bartlett's Sphericity test was significant at one percent and the resulting Cronbach's alpha coefficients were more than 0.7.

The items included for the perceived risk dimension were obtained from existing studies (Gan et al., 2006; Tan & Teo, 2000; Rhee & Riggins, 1999; Bhimani, 1996; Lee, 1996; Cockburn & Wilson, 1996). Gan et al. (2006) examined the factor structure of the perceived risk sub-dimension using a maximum likelihood factor analysis. In that study, consistent with Zeithaml & Bitner's (2003) study of the theoretical framework related to the consumer decision-making process related to the services, Gan et al. (2005) found that all the items included under the perceived risk dimension exhibited satisfactory internal consistency reliability with a Cronbach's alpha value of 0.6 and above. Gabriel & Nyshadham (2008) studied the risk characteristics as well as perceived risks associated with USA consumers using factor analysis with varimax rotation. Reliability was assessed on the basis of the internal consistency by obtaining the Cronbach's alpha coefficients (more than 0.8).

Items included in the trust sub-dimension were obtained from well established scales used in the existing literature (Herington & Weaven, 2007; Ribbink et al., 2004; Mukherjee & Nath, 2003; Wang et al., 2003; Black et al., 2001; Hoffman et al., 1999; Sathye, 1999). In a study by Herington & Weaven (2007), the impact of online service quality on the level of customer relationship development was explored using a convenience sample of 200 Australian respondents and using an online banking trust component measured with items previously used by Ribbink et al. (2004). A single factor was to represent the trust measure which explained 55 percent of the variance. In a study in Doha, Qatar using the trust-relationship commitment model and its influence on internet banking, Kassim & Abdulla (2006) used 276 bank customer responses. The research focused on Gronroos (2001) theoretical framework and employed confirmatory factor analysis. The reliability, convergent and discriminant validity were estimated by Cronbach's alpha coefficient, composite reliability and average variance. Cronbach's alpha values obtained were adequate (> 0.70) and factor loadings obtained were relevant except for one item which was subsequently dropped from further analysis.

The items included in the perceived personalisation construct were obtained from the existing studies (Huang & Lin, 2005; Coner, 2003; Srinivasan et al., 2002; Winsor et al., 2002; Mittal & Lassar, 1996). In a study related to customer-oriented financial service personalisation by Huang & Lin (2005), the items included in the perceived personalisation construct were confirmed by adopting a Delphi study. In another study by Mittal & Lassar (1996) focusing on the role of personalisation in service encounters, data obtained from USA respondents (N = 233) were subjected to factor analysis for validation of the scale items. Factor analysis of four items of personalisation yielded a single factor with eigenvalues greater than one. This single factor captured 73.9 percent of the variance. Factor loadings reported for the four items were greater than 0.75 and Cronbach's alpha value was greater than 0.90.

PRINCIPAL COMPONENT ANALYSIS OUTPUT FOR THE CHANNEL FACTORS

The results of the principal component analysis output for the channel factors are presented in Table 4. It is evident from the table that the KMO measure of sampling adequacy (0.773) and Bartlett's test of Spherecity (p < 0.001) were satisfied. Using the Kaiser-Guttman retention criterion of eigenvalues greater than one, a two component solution provided the clearest extraction. These two components accounted for 36.593 percent of the total variance. The two component model was deemed to be the best solution because of its conceptual clarity and ease of interpretation. Also, the component correlation matrix reveals that the two emerged components of the channel-related factors to be moderately positively correlated (0.341) and are well discriminated.

The two channel factors components were labelled based on a review of the thematic content of the different items of their defining items. Considering the different scale items aligned to each component, the components were labelled as following.

Component 1: Perceived Safety

This component relates to the safety of internet banking with regard to the risk, security and trust associated by the consumers with internet banking as a service delivery channel. Moreover, the component included items related to the internal component of self-efficacy, indicating that internet banking users were confident that they can perform their transactions without any help. The component was thus labelled as perceived safety.

Component 2: Perceived Specialty

This component is related to the personalisation component perceived by the consumers as unique and special customers due to internet banking. Also the component consists of the external component of self-efficacy, indicating less confidence associated with the internet banking consumers without the presence of a role model or online help functions. Thus the component was labelled as perceived specialty.

The open-ended questions relating to the qualitative data were developed alongside the quantitative scales. Most of the theoretical perspectives that emerged from existing studies on internet banking research were a result of quantitative studies involving testing of questionnaire data. In order to gain an in-depth understanding of the opinions of respondents about their internet banking experience, qualitative open-ended questions were developed. The open-ended question included in the

Table 4. Summary of principal component analysis for channel factors measure (N = 372)

Scale Items	Factors	
	1	**2**
LCD10 Internet banking is trustworthy	0.70	
LCD11 I trust in the ability of internet banking to protect my privacy	0.66	
LCD12 Using internet banking is financially secure	0.62	
LCD1 I am confident of using internet banking even if there is no one around to show me how to use it	0.62	
LCD3 I am confident of using internet banking even if I have only the online instructions for reference	0.58	
LCD9 Internet banking transactions does not lead to an inefficient use of my time	0.55	
LCD6 I am confident that internet banking in Australia is secure	0.53	
LCD7 Information concerning my internet banking transactions cannot be accessed by others	0.43	
LCD5 I am confident of using internet banking if I could call someone for help if I got stuck		0.74
LCD4 I am confident of using internet banking if I see someone else using it before I try it myself		0.67
LCD14 Internet banking websites provide information that is tailor-made for me		0.54
LCD2 I am confident of using internet banking if I have the built-in online "help" function for assistance		0.49
LCD13 Performing internet banking makes me feel that I am a unique customer		0.44
LCD15 The promotional offers that I receive through internet banking transactions are attractive to me		0.40
Eigenvalues	3.425	1.698
Factor Correlation Matrix		
	Factor 1	**Factor 2**
Factor 1	1.000	0.341
Factor 2	0.341	1.000

present study is exploratory in nature and arose mostly out of the existing literature which elicits the need for qualitative responses and makes an attempt to shift the focus of the existing literature by seeking the opinions of the respondents in their own words.

Raw data obtained from the open-ended question was categorised into a series of conceptually clustered matrices. Actual responses obtained from the open-ended question were reduced to meaningful themes. Themes that were identified either supported the existing theory on internet banking research or introduced new themes specific to internet banking research in the Australian context from the consumers' perspective. The themes identified were displayed in the form of count summaries and frequencies of 'themed' responses.

THEMATIC MATRIX DISPLAYS

Miles & Huberman (1994) reported the use of conceptually clustered matrix displays while reducing data into thematically similar categories. Also Miles & Huberman (1994) recommended the application of thematic matrix displays where several research questions are clustered 'so that meaning can be generated more easily', and it is of primary interest when the researcher has 'a priori ideas about items that derive from the same theory or relate to the same overarching theme'. Miles and Huberman (1994) also reported the possible occurrence of 'conceptual coherence' when the responses given by the respondents are more or less similar.

Subsequently, all the responses were manually transcribed for the analysis. Responses obtained for each open-ended question were systematically analysed for the presence of thematically similar words and phrases. Later these themes were compared with the selected demographic characteristics in order to investigate whether any similarities or differences occurred. Some actual quotes in the respondent's own words, which in a broader sense indicated what the majority of the respondents had written while filling out the questionnaire, are presented.

ANALYSIS OF RESPONSES TO OPEN-ENDED QUESTION: REASONS FOR NOT USING INTERNET BANKING

298 valid responses were analysed into common themes for the purpose of the present study from the effective sample size of 311. Out of these 298 responses, 98 were male respondents and 200 were female respondents. The majority of the respondents that provided reasons for not using internet banking transactions were within the age categories of 41-50 years and 51-60 years. Moreover, the majority of the responses for the open-ended question asking respondents the reasons for not using internet banking were provided by those with Asian and Anglo-Australian ethnic background, administration and self-employment categories, and with vocational education.

CONTENT-ANALYTIC SUMMARY TABLE DISPLAYING REASONS FOR NOT USING INTERNET BANKING

Table 5 shows a hierarchy of macro and micro thematic categories in the second and third columns that emerged from the analysis of respondents' reasons for not using internet banking. These themes are then presented as the raw verbatim responses given by respondents and presented in the fourth column. The table also provides, in parentheses, the number of times a certain response was mentioned by respondents. For the purpose of this case study only results related to the trust variable are presented.

'Trust' has been identified as the second important macro theme based on the actual response counts offered by the internet banking non-users. Under the macro theme of trust, four micro themes arise in descending: lack of trust in the channel, lack of trust in the internet, lack of trust in the bank and lack of trust in the bank personnel. Lack of trust in the channel was related to the 'financial transactions' and 'electronic channels' in a more specific and general manner. Lack of trust in the internet was related to the non-users past experiences with 'multi level marketing' and 'fake websites'. Some of the non-users associated their lack of trust in the bank with regard to possible 'financial loss' and 'banks no assurance'. Lack of trust in the bank personnel was reported most often by male respondents who were self-employed and dealing with vast amounts of money in their usual transactions. Also

Table 5. Conceptually-clustered matrix display: reasons for not using internet banking

Number	Macro Theme	Micro Theme	Responses
1	Trust (47)	Lack of trust in the channel	"do not believe internet banking transactions/I don't trust electronic channels/do not trust this channel of service as there is no assurance that it is tamper free" (24)
		Lack of trust in the internet	"had bad experience with multi level marketing in internet/cannot trust internet/fake websites similar to those of banks may appear on internet which cannot be trusted" (18)
		Lack of trust in the bank	"no trust in the bank/banks do not follow any ethical procedures and I have no trust in them" (3)
		Lack of trust in bank personnel	"I have no trust in the bank personnel/when dealing with big amount of money I do not trust bank staff/ bank personnel are not safe though" (2)

lack of trust in the bank personnel by non-users of internet banking was associated with their familiarity with the technological advancements and possibly the fear associated with any financial loss.

IMPLICATIONS

Overall the information presented in this case study exhibits the ambidextrous nature of the variable trust. Results obtained from the internet banking users indicate that trust is an important variable in influencing Australian consumers' adoption, continued and frequent use of internet banking activity. Results obtained also highlighted the fact that consumers are oriented towards the safety and specialty components of trust in performing internet banking transactions. Consumers performing internet banking transactions trust the channel delivery option as safe and secure. Also these consumers consider internet banking as special due to the confidence in their self-efficacy related abilities and personalisation aspects of the service delivery option. Consequently, the qualitative thematic categories emerged from the non-users of internet banking revealed that lack of trust is the main factor that hinders them from adopting and performing internet banking related transactions. This major theme identified as lack of trust is further categorised into several micro themes such as lack of trust in the channel, lack of trust in the internet, lack of trust in the bank and finally lack of trust in bank personnel. Thus the results presented in this study highlight that trust is an important factor that invariably influences both the users as well as the non-users of internet banking. Therefore retail banking managers need to formulate effective channel management strategies that enhance the trust levels of the existing and potential consumers in promoting internet banking transactions. Also bank managers need to assure and highlight the fact that internet banking is safe and secure and will not result in the loss of private information related to the consumers. Similarly the bank management may need to focus on offering minimal training to novice consumers about performing internet banking transactions in order to increase their level of confidence with this service delivery option. Banks may also need to focus on frequently highlighting the advantages and convenience associated with the internet banking service delivery channel to the consumers through effective marketing communication tools.

REFERENCES

Akinci, S., Akoy, S., & Atilgan, E. (2004). Adoption of internet banking among sophisticated consumer segments in an advanced developing country. *International Journal of Bank Marketing, 22*(3), 212–232. doi:10.1108/02652320410530322.

Al-Hawari, M., Hartley, N., & Ward, T. (2005). Measuring banks automated service quality: A confirmatory factor analysis approach. *Marketing Bulletin, 16.*

Avkiran, N. K. (2000). Rising productivity of australian trading banks under deregulation 1986-1995. *Journal of Economics and Finance*. Murfreesboro, TN: Middle Tennessee State University.

Bhattacharjee, A. (2002). Individual trust in online firms: Scale development and initial test. *Journal of Management Information Systems, 19*(1), 211–241.

Bhimani, A. (1996). Securing the commercial internet. *Communications of the ACM, 39*(6), 29–36. doi:10.1145/228503.228509.

Bitner, M. J., Brown, S. W., & Meuter, M. L. (2000). Technology infusion in service encounters. *Journal of the Academy of Marketing Science, 28*(1), 138–149. doi:10.1177/0092070300281013.

Black, N. J., Lockett, A., Winjklhofer, H., & Ennew, C. (2001). The adoption of internet financial services: A qualitative research. *International Journal of Retail and Distribution Management, 29*(8), 390–398. doi:10.1108/09590550110397033.

Carew, E. (1998). *Fast money 4: The best selling guide to australia's financial markets*. Sydney: Allen Unwin.

Chan, S., & Lu, M. (2004). Understanding internet banking adoption and use behaviour: A hong kong perspective. *Journal of Global Information Management, 12*(3), 21–43. doi:10.4018/jgim.2004070102.

Chang, I. C., Li, Y. C., Hung, W. F., & Hwang, H. G. (2005). An empirical study on the impact of quality antecedents on tax payers' acceptance of Internet tax-filing systems. *Government Information Quarterly, 22*, 389–410. doi:10.1016/j.giq.2005.05.002.

Chou, D., & Chou, A. Y. (2000). A guide to the internet revolution in banking. *Information Systems Management, 17*(2), 51–57. doi:10.1201/1078/43191.17.2.2 0000301/31227.6.

Cockburn, C., & Wilson, T. D. (1996). Business use of world wide web. *International Journal of Information Management, 16*(2), 83–102. doi:10.1016/0268-4012(95)00071-2.

Compeau, D. R., & Higgins, C. A. (1995). Application of social cognitive theory to training for computer skills. *Information Systems Research, 6*(2), 118–143. doi:10.1287/isre.6.2.118.

Compeau, D. R., & Higgins, C. A. (1995). Computer self-efficacy: Development of a measure and initial test. *Management Information Systems Quarterly, 19*(2), 189–211. doi:10.2307/249688.

Coner, A. (2003). Personalisation and customisation in financial portals. *Journal of American Academy of Business, 2*(2), 498–504.

Dabholkar, P. A., & Bagozzi, R. P. (2002). An attitudinal model of technology-based self service: Moderating effects of consumer traits and situational factors. *Journal of the Academy of Marketing Science, 30*(3), 184–201.

Dinev, T., Bellotto, M., Hart, P., Russo, V., Serra, I., & Colautti, C. (2006). Privacy calculus model in e-commerce–A study of italy and the united states. *European Journal of Information Systems*, 389–402. doi:10.1057/palgrave.ejis.3000590.

Eastlick, M. A., Lotz, S. L., & Warrington, P. (2006). Understanding online b-to-c relationships: An integrated model of privacy concerns, trust, and commitment. *Journal of Business Research, 59*(8), 877–886. doi:10.1016/j.jbusres.2006.02.006.

Egger, F. N. (2003). *Evaluating the customer trust experience in business to consumer ecommerce environments*. Retrieved from www.scholar.google.com.

Fenton, N. (2000). Trust, confidence, and risk. In: F. Tonkiss., A. Passey., N. Fenton, & L. C. Hems (Eds.), Trust and Civil Society. London: MacMillan.

Flavian, C., Guinaliu, M., & Torres, E. (2006). How bricks-and-mortar attributes affect online banking adoption. *International Journal of Bank Marketing, 24*(6), 406. doi:10.1108/02652320610701735.

Fukuyama, F. (1995). *Trust: The social virtues and the creation of prosperity*. New York: Free Press.

Gabriel, I. J., & Nyshadham, E. (2008). A cognitive map of people's online risk perceptions and attitudes: An empirical study. In *Proceedings of the 41st Annual Hawaii International Conference on System Sciences*, 274. Washington, DC: IEEE Press.

Gan, C., Clemes, M., Limsombunchai, V., & Weng, A. (2006). A logit analysis of electronic banking in new zealand. *International Journal of Bank Marketing, 24*(6), 360–383. doi:10.1108/02652320610701717.

Gan, C., Limsombunchai, V., Clemes, M., & Weng, A. (2005). Consumer choice prediction: Artificial neural networks versus logistic models. *Journal of the Social Sciences, 1*(4), 211–219. doi:10.3844/jssp.2005.211.219.

Gardener, E., Howcroft, B., & Williams, J. (1999). The new retail banking revolution. *The Service Industries Journal, 19*(2), 83–100. doi:10.1080/02642069900000020.

Gefen, D. (2002). Reflections on the dimensions of trust and trustworthiness among online consumers. *The Data Base for Advances in Information Systems, 33*(3), 38–53. doi:10.1145/569905.569910.

Gefen, D., Karahanna, E., & Straub, D. W. (2003). Trust and TAM in online shopping: An integrated model. *Management Information Systems Quarterly, 27*(1), 51–90.

Gefen, D., & Straub, D. W. (2003). The relative importance of perceived ease of use in IS adoption: A study of e-commerce adoption. *Journal of the Association for Information Systems, 1*(8), 1–28.

George, J. F. (2004). The theory of planned behaviour and internet purchasing. *Internet Research, 14*(3), 198–212. doi:10.1108/10662240410542634.

Grabner-Kraeuter, S., & Faullant, R. (2008). Consumer acceptance of internet banking: The influence of internet trust. *International Journal of Bank Marketing, 26*(7), 483–504. doi:10.1108/02652320810913855.

Grabner-Kraeuter, S., & Kaluscha, E. A. (2003). Empirical research in on-line trust: A review and critical assessment. *International Journal of Human-Computer Studies, 58*, 783–812. doi:10.1016/S1071-5819(03)00043-0.

Gronroos, C. (2001). *Service management and marketing: A customer relationship management approach*. Chichester, UK: Wiley.

Gulati, R., & Sytch, M. (2008). The dynamics of trust. *Academy of Management Review, 33*(1), 276–278. doi:10.5465/AMR.2008.27753143.

Gupta, S., & Kim, H. W. (2007). The moderating effect of transaction experience on online purchase decision calculus. *International Journal of Electronic Commerce, 12*(1), 127–158. doi:10.2753/JEC1086-4415120105.

Gyptra, P., & Dixon, P. (2002). Future of banking expectation. *Global Change*. Retrieved from www.globalchange.com/futurebank.htm.

Hardin, R. (2002). *Trust and Trustworthiness*. New York: Russell Sage Foundation.

Herington, C., & Weaven, S. (2007). Can banks improve customer relationships with high quality online services? *Managing Service Quality, 17*(4), 404–427. doi:10.1108/09604520710760544.

Hernandez, J. M. C., & Mazzon, J. A. (2007). Adoption of internet banking: Proposition and implementation of an integrated methodology approach. *International Journal of Bank Marketing, 25*(2), 72–88. doi:10.1108/02652320710728410.

Hoffman, D. L., Novak, T. P., & Peralta, M. (1999). Building customer trust online. *Communications of the ACM, 42*(4), 80–85. doi:10.1145/299157.299175.

Howcroft, B., Hamilton, R., & Hewer, P. (2002). Consumer attitude and the usage and adoption of home banking in the united kingdom. *International Journal of Bank Marketing, 20*(3), 111–121. doi:10.1108/02652320210424205.

Huang, E. Y., & Lin, C. Y. (2005). Customer-oriented financial service personalisation. *Industrial Management & Data Systems, 105*(1), 26–44. doi:10.1108/02635570510575171.

Jarvenpaa, S. L., Shaw, T. R., & Staples, S. (2004). Toward contextualised theories of trust: The role of trust in global virtual teams. *Information Systems Research, 15*(3), 250–267. doi:10.1287/isre.1040.0028.

Jarvenpaa, S. L., Tractinsky, N., & Saarinen, L. (1999). Consumer trust in an internet store: A cross-cultural validation. *Journal of Computer-Mediated Communication, 5*(2).

Kassim, N. M., & Abdulla, A. K. M. A. (2006). The influence of attraction on internet banking: An extension to the trust-relationship commitment model. *International Journal of Bank Marketing, 24*(6), 424–442. doi:10.1108/02652320610701744.

Kramer, R. (1999). Trust and distrust in organisations: Emerging perspectives, enduring questions. *Annual Review of Psychology*, 569–598. doi:10.1146/annurev. psych.50.1.569 PMID:15012464.

Kumar, A., & Paddison, R. (2000). Trust and collaborative planning theory: The case of the Scottish planning system. *International Planning Studies, 5*(2), 205–223. doi:10.1080/13563470050020194.

Lee, M. K. O., & Turban, E. (2001). A trust model for consumer internet shopping. *International Journal of Electronic Commerce, 6*(1), 75–91.

Lee, P. (1996). The cutting edge: So far, online banking is mostly wishful thinking. *Los Angeles Times*. Retrieved from http://articles.latimes.com/1996-09-30/business/fi-48990_1_online-bank-customers.

Luarn, P. & Lin, L. H. (2004). Towards an understanding of the behavioural intention to use mobile banking. *Computers in Human Behaviour*, 1-19.

Lyell, D., Crane, R., Crowley, M., & Fraser, I. (1997). *Financial institutions and markets*. Sydney: LBC Information Services.

Mayer, R. C., Davis, J. H., & Schoorman, F. D. (1995). An integrative model of organisational trust. *Academy of Management Review*, *10*(3), 709–734.

McCole, P., & Ramsey, E. (2009). A profile of adopters and non-adopters of ecommerce in SME professional service firms. *Australasian Marketing Journal*, *13*, 36–45. doi:10.1016/S1441-3582(05)70066-5.

McKnight, D. H., Choudhury, V., & Kacmar, C. (2002). Developing and validating trust measures for e-commerce: An integrative typology. *Information Systems Research*, *13*(3), 334–361. doi:10.1287/isre.13.3.334.81.

McKnight, H. D., & Chervany, N. L. (2002). What trust means in e-commerce customer relationships: An interdisciplinary conceptual typology. *International Journal of Electronic Commerce*, *6*(2), 35–59.

Miles, M. B., & Huberman, A. M. (1994). *Qualitative data analysis: An expanded source book* (2nd ed.). Thousand Oaks, CA: Sage Publications.

Mittal, B., & Lassar, W. M. (1996). The role of personalisation in service encounters. *Journal of Retailing*, *72*(1), 95–109. doi:10.1016/S0022-4359(96)90007-X.

Moorman, C., Zaltman, G., & Deshpande, R. (1992). Relationships between providers and users of marketing research: Dynamics of trust within and between organisations. *JMR, Journal of Marketing Research*, *29*, 314–329. doi:10.2307/3172742.

Mukherjee, A., & Nath, P. (2003). A model of trust in online relationship banking. *International Journal of Bank Marketing*, *21*(1), 5–15. doi:10.1108/02652320310457767.

Patton, M. A. (2004). Technologies for trust in electronic commerce. *Electronic Commerce Research*, *4*, 9–21. doi:10.1023/B:ELEC.0000009279.89570.27.

Pavlou, P., & Fygenson, M. (2006). Understanding and predicting electronic commerce adoption: An extension of the theory of planned behaviour. *Management Information Systems Quarterly*, *30*, 115–143.

Pavlou, P. A. (2003). Consumer acceptance of electronic commerce: Integrating trust and risk with the technology acceptance model. *International Journal of Electronic Commerce, 7*(3), 101–134.

Pavlou, P. A., & Gefen, D. (2004). Building effective online market places with institution-based trust. *Information Systems Research, 15*(1), 37–59. doi:10.1287/isre.1040.0015.

Ratnasingam, P., Gefen, D., & Pavlou, P. A. (2005). The role of facilitating conditions and institutional trust in electronic marketplaces. *Journal of Electronic Commerce, 48*(3), 69–82. doi:10.4018/jeco.2005070105.

Report, W. (1997). *The financial system inquiry final report.* Canberra, Australia: AGPS..

Rhee, H. S., & Riggins, F. (1999). *GVU's WWW user surveys: High level summary of internet banking survey.* Retrieved from www.gvu.gatech.edu/user-survey/survey-1997-04/graphs/banking/report.html.

Ribbink, D., Riel, A., Liljander, V., & Streukens, S. (2004). Comfort your online customer: Quality, trust, and loyalty on the internet. *Managing Service Quality, 14*(6), 446–456. doi:10.1108/09604520410569784.

Riegelsberger, J., Sasse, A. M., & McCarthy, J. D. (2005). The mechanics of trust: A framework for research and design. *International Journal of Human-Computer Studies, 62*, 381–422. doi:10.1016/j.ijhcs.2005.01.001.

Ruscio, K. P. (1999). Jay's pirouette, or why political trust is not the same as personal trust. *Administration & Society, 31*(5), 639–657. doi:10.1177/00953999922019274.

Sathye, M. (1999). Adoption of internet banking by Australian consumers: An empirical investigation. *International Journal of Bank Marketing, 17*(7), 324–334. doi:10.1108/02652329910305689.

Sohail, M. S., & Shanmugam, B. (2003). E-banking and customer preferences in malaysia: An empirical investigation. *Information Sciences, 150*, 207–217. doi:10.1016/S0020-0255(02)00378-X.

Srinivasan, S. S., Anderson, R., & Ponnavolu, K. (2002). Customer loyalty in e-commerce: An exploration of its antecedents and consequences. *Journal of Retailing, 78*(1), 41–50. doi:10.1016/S0022-4359(01)00065-3.

Suh, B., & Han, I. (2003). The impact of consumer trust and perceptions of security control on the acceptance of electronic commerce. *International Journal of Electronic Commerce, 7*(3), 135–161.

Tan, M., & Teo, T. S. H. (2000). Factors influencing the adoption of internet banking. *Journal of the Association for Information Systems*, *1*, 1–42.

Teo, T. S. H., & Liu, J. (2007). Consumer trust in e-commerce in the united states, Singapore, and china. *Omega–The International Journal of Management Science*, *35*, 22–38. doi:10.1016/j.omega.2005.02.001.

Unnithan, C. R., & Swatman, P. M. C. (2001). eBanking adaptation and dot.com viability–A comparison of Australian and Indian experiences in the banking sector. In *Proceedings of the 11ᵗʰ BIT 2001 Conference*. Manchester, UK: AES Press.

Walczuch, R., & Lundgren, H. (2004). Psychological antecedents of institution-based consumer trust in e-retailing. *Information & Management*, *42*, 159–177. doi:10.1016/j.im.2003.12.009.

Wang, Y. D., & Emurian, H. H. (2005). An overview of online trust: Concepts, elements, and implications. *Computers in Human Behavior*, *21*, 105–125. doi:10.1016/j. chb.2003.11.008.

Wang, Y. S., Wang, Y. M., Lin, H. H., & Tang, T. I. (2003). Determinants of user acceptance of internet banking: An empirical research. *International Journal of Bank Marketing*, *14*(5), 501–519.

Winsor, R. D., Sheth, J. N., & Manolis, C. (2002). Differentiating goods and services retailing using form and possession utilities. *Journal of Business Research*, *57*(3), 249–255. doi:10.1016/S0148-2963(02)00324-7.

World, I. B. I. S. (2005). *National and regional commercial banks in australia (k7325)*. Retrieved from www.ibisworld.com.au.

Worthington, S., & Edwards, V. (2000). Changes in payments markets, past, present and future: A comparison between australia and the UK. *International Journal of Bank Marketing*, *18*(5), 212–221. doi:10.1108/02652320010356771.

Yousafzai, S. Y., Pallister, J. G., & Foxall, G. R. (2003). A proposed model of e-trust for electronic banking. *Technovation*, *23*, 847–860. doi:10.1016/S0166-4972(03)00130-5.

Yousafzai, S. Y., Pallister, J. G., & Foxall, G. R. (2005). Strategies for building and communicating trust in electronic banking: A field experiment. *Psychology and Marketing*, *22*(2), 181–201. doi:10.1002/mar.20054.

Zeithaml, V. A., & Bitner, M. (2003). *Services marketing: Integrating customer focus across the firm* (3rd ed.). Boston: McGraw Hill.

Chapter 19

Should Corporate Political Lobbying Come under Scanner by Regulatory Mechanism?
Vaishnavi Corporate Communication and 2G Spectrum Scam:
A Political Lobbying Case

S. Jayachandran
IIT Madras, India

EXECUTIVE SUMMARY

Marketing is more political in the free market economy today than ever and firms need to apply social power and public relations either to enter into a new market or to operate more successfully in the existing market. Often, they apply reward power and political lobbying as marketing strategic tools. The Indian telecom market is booming fast and becoming highly competitive. Accordingly, there is an aggressively, rushed bid for 2G spectrum license. In the mean time, the telecom ministry's decision of, "First come, First serve," instead of an auction method, paved the way for political lobbying. At the end of 2G spectrum allocation, there was widespread allegation that the cellular operators fraudulently secured licenses from the telecom ministry by using power and public relations and in doing so played an important role on behalf of its clients. The apex court monitored the investigation of 2G scam

DOI: 10.4018/978-1-4666-4357-4.ch019

Copyright ©2014, IGI Global. Copying or distributing in print or electronic forms without written permission of IGI Global is prohibited.

and ordered cancelling of all licenses granted in 2008. This case raises four vital points for discussion as the backdrop of the changing marketing environment: 1.) Should marketing facilitating agents bother with the ideals of morality? 2.) Is it wrong that Vaishnavi Corporate Communication exploited weak and corrupt system of governance in favor of its clients? 3.) Are the actions of government watchdog agents justifiable, when an issue is concerned with public interest? 4.) Should political lobbying come under scanner by a regulatory mechanism to contain adverse implications of firms' marketing strategy? If so, what should be the modus operandi of the regulatory mechanism?

TODAY'S MARKETING IS A POLITICAL EXERCISE

In the current competitive environment, marketing is increasingly becoming a political exercise. A firm has to manage different stakeholders in order to market successfully and it seems sometimes a tough task. Often, there is a need for applying power and public relations skills either to enter a new market or to operate more successfully in the existing market. It becomes obvious that the traditional assembling of marketing mix strategy is not sufficient when there is a certain extraordinary market situation and marketing executives may be lacking skills of handling such market forces, which warrant application of power and public relations. So, corporate houses seek the services of facilitators who include agents, brokers, market research firms, advertising agencies, public relations consultants, event organizers, freelancers, experts, professionals, and so forth. The facilitating agents charge commission for the service they render.

One significant development in the post liberalization era is the tremendous boom in the services sector, which includes banking and financial services, telecom services, tourism and hospitality services, health services, retailing services, and more. All of these service providers need the services of some professionals/specialists/experts/consultants in one way or other and most often the service providers are clients of these facilitators for successful marketing of their services.

The facilitators often use *power* and public relation skills to achieve the desired result on behalf of their clients. Generally, they apply a power base appropriate to the situation in order to influence the party involved in a buying-selling relationship. Such power bases have been identified as reward power, coercion power, legitimate power, referent power, and expert power (French & Raven, 1959).

Reward power is most often used in marketing of products/services and this may be in the form of fabulous gifts including kickbacks, valuable items, and so on. *Coercion power* involves intimidating the other party for compliance and this includes social boycotting, financial harming, and physical threatening. *Legitimate power* is applied by legal authority to secure the compliance of the other party. Usually, a state authority is exercising such power to extract compliance from its citizens. *Referent power* is also known as attraction or status power and the one who enjoys such referent power obtains compliance from the other party by his/her very presence or involvement in a social relationship or buying-selling relationship. *Expert power* is based on the wide recognition of an individual's expertise in a particular field and such expert's opinion or views will prevail in an issue. In other words, the other party simply yields to an expert's views as there is widespread recognition for his/her expertise in the particular field. Possession of information/knowledge with regard to a specific issue/subject is also considered as expert power.

Applying a power base alone may not help a company to get access into a market if it fails to cultivate appropriate public relations. Before entering a market, a firm must understand the structure of different stakeholders of a business (different publics) and how power is being distributed in the target community. In the Indian democratic polity, for example, single party rule has ended long ago. A coalitional form of government has come to exist at the centre and the same will continue in the coming years as there is no hope for single party rule. When power is vested among coalitional partners (political parties which have formed the government jointly at either the centre or state), a corporation has to work through the coalition to achieve its business goal. Therefore, marketing firms need to assess the relative power of each political party and forge a grand strategy by applying power and public relation skills.

INDIAN TELECOM INDUSTRY AND THE MARKET

The Indian telecom industry is booming phenomenally and it is not only growing fast but also as the second largest in the world after China. Currently, the GSM (Global Standard for Mobile) operators occupy 80 per cent of the total mobile telephony market and the CDMA (Code Division Multiple Access) services account for 20 per cent of the wireless market.

Until the middle of 2008, there were about seven operators including the government owned BSNL (Bharat Sanchar Nigam Ltd) and MTNL (Mahanagar Telephone Nigam Ltd). Almost all competitors have their presence in each of the 23 telecom circles in the country. At the end of 2009, the number of operators has swelled to 14. With so many operators, the Indian telecom market is overcrowded and became highly competitive. The situation has led to price wars without any perceptible difference in the service quality of the operators.

The Indian telecom business has reached a stage where mobile operators have to grab customers. Big operators like Tata Telecom and Reliance, who started off in the CDMA segments, later attempted to secure GSM license. Further, as the markets in towns and cities have been fast saturating, operators need to focus more in the rural areas, where the investment cost is much higher due to laying new networks and marketing promotions.

Because of heavy competition slugging out in the telecom industry, there was rush and aggressive bidding for 2G spectrum. Meanwhile, the telecom ministry's decision, 'first come, first serve,' instead of an auction method, paved the way for corporate lobbying and as a result it was alleged a large scale corruption in the 2G spectrum allocations.

VAISHNAVI CORPORATE COMMUNICATION

Vaishnavi Corporate Communication is a corporate lobbying agency which was founded on November 1st 2001 by the 2G (second generation mobile services) Spectrum fame Niira Radia, a most powerful and enterprising political lobbying professional. It attained phenomenal growth in terms of revenue and number of clients in the past nine years. In 2007, its client number rose to fifty corporate including the high profile Tatas on the one side and the formidable Reliance group on the other. The gross revenue of Vaishnavi touched to Rs 300 crore in the year 2009. All the credit for Vaishnavi's growth in a short span of time goes to its founder, who is known for her powerful lobbying skill.

Before venturing into the Public Relations (PR) business, Niira Radia made two attempts of her own at starting an airline service. First, she decided to float Crown Express and then Magic Air. She was unsuccessful in both due to her British citizenship. So, ultimately she founded PR lobbying–Vaishnavi Corporate Communication and her corporate office was set up in a half white building in New Delhi's South extension.

The client list first began with Indian hotels, the Tata Group which runs the Taj Chain of hotels. Soon, it was serving 14 companies of the Tata Group and then eventually the number swelled to 90. Each Tata company signed annual contracts with Vaishnavi corporate communications. The Tata Teleservices was paying Rs 45 lakhs a month. In comparison, an MNC telecom giant was known to pay a third of that to its PR firm. Many industry experts viewed that the billings that Vaishnavi declared were nowhere close to industry standards. The companies that required more interface with government policy makers, the media and the public, may have paid more. Tata Group contracts were renewed every year without any competitive bids being called. Later on, Vaishnavi had non-Tata clients like ITC Foods, Hindustan Construction Company, Punj Lloyd, Ascendas, Haldia Petrochemicals, JK tyres, the Confederation of Indian Industries, and Bennett, Coleman &Co. PR business has become a very big business and Vaishnavi has emerged as the big fish in the lobbying bond. "Vaishnavi is unique and it has unprecedented concept, unprecedented clients," said Vishal Mehta, a trusted aide to Niira Radia, before pausing to add, "unprecedented crises."

The lobbying skill has helped her to cultivate personal contacts, relations and friendship with corporate people and others. Her network of friends include politicians, bureaucrats, and corporate and media journalists. With this network she has proved to the world that a PR lobbyist could do havoc in a democracy. In a recent conference held at the Asian College of Journalism, New Delhi, the speakers pointed out that Radia is a powerful lobbyist and she wielded influence over sixty per cent of Indian Advertising industry.

VAISHNAVI CORPORATE COMMUINCATION AND 2G SPECTRUM ALLOCATIONS

Spectrum is an electromagnetic wave that facilitates wireless communication–SMSes and voice data can be transmitted between phone to phone or phone to computer. So, the 2G scam, which has become the current political issue in India, involves the sale of second generation spectrums by the Indian Telecommunication Ministry to cellular operators in the country. The Comptroller and Auditor General (CAG) of India has alleged, in its report, that the Telecommunication Ministry has caused a huge loss of Rs 176,459 crore to the exchequer by selling the spectrum licenses at 2001 price in 2008. The CAG has estimated the revenue loss in terms of 2008 price. It is just like selling a housing plot in a metro city at 2001 price without bothering the current market value of the land in 2008.

CAG. In its report, further alleged that several ineligible companies have secured 2G licenses and such companies (like S-Tel, Uninor, Videocon, Loop) have failed to conform to the prescribed norms under the 2G Spectrum allocation process. Therefore, the 2G Spectrum deal seems to be a messy issue which brings out a stench nexus of politicians, bureaucrats, journalists and lobbyists.

Radia's involvement in the 2G Spectrum deal. In the process of lobbying on behalf of her clients, seems highly spicy, sensational and serious. Many in the corporate and public raise their eyebrows about her lobbying skills and networks. Sensed her dangerous political lobbying, the Income Tax department (IT) has legally taped all the nine telephone lines of her on the basis of advice of the Central Bureau of Investigation (CBI) and the telephone tape recording continued for about 180 days from 20ᵗʰ August in 2008 and again from 11ᵗʰ May 2009 to July in 2009.

The CBI began its probe in the 2G Spectrum scam from October 2009 and it requested the IT department to provide a part of the recordings (total number of tape recording of conversation is about 5800).

It has been widely alleged that the transcripts in the conversation revealed many startling facts including Niira Radia's powerful role in deciding the ministerial berth for the then minister for telecommunication and her involvement in getting 2G licenses for her three clients viz Unitech, Swan, and Datacom. In a conversation with the then minister for telecom, it has been alleged that she confirmed that his name has been cleared as minister for telecom, even before the official announcement of the government. Again, it was alleged that her involvement in the conversation as she advised her clients to resell the shares for higher margin.

When 2G spectrum scam became everyday news, the opposition parties stalled the parliament to sack the then telecom minister. Meanwhile, Radia escaped to a foreign country to avoid facing questions from investigating agencies. However, she was summoned to confirm the transcripts in the conversation and she assured the investigating agencies to extend full co-operation. In her confession, she has stated that she has not made any money out of 2G Spectrum deal except the consulting fee charged from her clients.

AUTHOR'S RECOMMENDATION AND SUGGESTION

The four questions/points presented above for discussion are in the light of the Vaishnavi Corporate Communication's political lobbying in the 2G spectrum allocation. The intention of the questions/points is to generate thinking in terms of 'for and against' of the political lobbying in a free market and its implications on the economy and society. In other words, the questions/points aim to bring into a serious discussion among management students in the context of public policy making and political lobbying. Again, political lobbying cannot be done away and it is a necessary evil in any marketing. Therefore, the author suggests the following in addition to the questions/points, as a method for avoiding adverse impact of political lobbying on the society and economy:

In any industrial/organizational buying-selling, the government department or government –owned enterprise is supposed to constitute a committee to solicit competitive bids from eligible suppliers/bidders. This is mandatory in any central or state government purchasing and the constitution of buying committee depends upon the volume of business. A buying/selling committee evaluates and selects the eligible supplier finally in terms of certain norms. In the competitive bids' process, there are lot of chances for commissions and omissions. Powerful lobbyists would always influence the decision process in their favor. It is a well-known fact that the successful bidder would be the one who enjoys the backing of stalwarts of the ruling elite/party.

The crux of the 2G Spectrum case is that the telecom ministry has failed to constitute a competent committee for spectrum allocation. The first-come, first serve is contrary to the existing norms and practices and the telecom ministry 's arbitrary decision cleared the way for powerful lobbying in the spectrum allocation. As a result, Vaishnavi corporate communication exploited the telecom's decision in favor of its clients.

The government decision-makers/policy makers should opt for joint/collective decision-making when the volume of business involves multi-crores. In a dealing like 2G spectrum allocation, for example, the ministry's decision seems to be highly arbitrary and contrary to the established norms. Therefore, the author suggests the following method to constitute committees when the government departments or their agents decide to go for purchase or allocation of resources to private enterprises, particularly, when the volume of business involves multi-crores and of extraordinary national important scarce resources like the one viz 2G spectrum or in the case of allocating natural resources like minerals including coal, iron ore, oil, and so forth:

1. The government at the centre or state must maintain panel of experts from different fields – Science and Technology, Administration, Judiciary and others.
2. In constituting purchasing/sale committees, an independent government agency like Central Vigilance Commission (CVC) or any other constitutional body deemed to be independent of political influence can constitute such committees drawing experts from the panel.
3. The agency that constitutes such committees must ensure high independence of such committees from political lobbying. A committee should be vulnerable to political lobbying.
4. The committee must not have more than seven members including the chairman and the chairman of the committee should not be a politician.
5. The members must be well known for their expertise, honesty and integrity at national level in the relevant field.
6. The committee shall have maximum of two members from the concerned ministry.
7. The committee must be fair and free in decision –making and the outcome of the decision must be a consensus.
8. The committee must be held responsible for answering any allegations/charges.
9. The committee may have social activists, media specialists as members if it is warranted, apart from the experts drawn from the panel.

10. The ministry concerned must submit all details of the competitive bidders including the background, expertise and the credibility of the bidder in the relevant field.
11. The constitution of the committee must be open and transparent to the public.
12. The committee constituted for the purchasing/sale must get the approval of the cabinet of the respective government and the apex court of the country.

STATEMENT FROM VAISHNAVI CORPORATE COMMUNICATIONS PVT LTD

We strongly condemn the unsubstantiated, baseless and reckless allegations being indiscriminately leveled by some media properties against our group, Chairperson, officers and our only client in the telecom space, Tata Teleservices.

For nearly a year now, there have been transcripts of purported conversations between our Chairperson, Ms Niira Radia with some reputed personalities from various walks of life. These unverified transcripts and tapes have been widely circulated in the media by motivated and vested interests intent on maligning us, and deflecting public attention from their own wrongdoing in the telecom sector. Indeed, many of the purported transcripts being circulated have absolutely no relevance to telecom at all, and are merely being used for dramatic effect, and to create the illusion of wrongdoing on our part. The CAG report on telecom clearly states and shows that our client Tata Teleservices has been unfairly discriminated against in the allotment of spectrum. The CAG report also clearly identifies the telecom operators who have extracted undue benefits and advantages from the government and people of India in the telecom space. Now, when media and national attention is focusing on these wrongdoings, some vested interests are seeking to create a smokescreen behind which they can hide their own wrongdoings and misdeeds.

By once again distributing tapes and attributing alleged conversations to Ms Niira Radia at a time when there is a media frenzy over telecom, these vested interests seek to divert public attention from the key issues outlined in the CAG report, and companies that CAG has directly accused of extracting undue benefits from the government. While many media properties have desisted the efforts of these vested interests, others have fallen into the trap of using their unverified and unsubstantiated allegations against us, apparently without conducting their own due diligence or adhering to ba journalistic norms. A simple illustration of such false reporting has been a statement published in the DNA newspaper, which said Ms Radia is in London and implied our Chairperson is evading the law, when the fact is that she is very much in India and committed to fully cooperating with any of the agencies currently investigating the telecom industry.

For the record, we would like to state that we had been asked by one single agency for some information and we have been complying and cooperating fully with them. It is also a matter of concern to us that the names of some of our senior colleagues and former associates have also been dragged in to controversy through an unprovoked and unabashed trial by media.

The reputations of these eminent persons has been built painfully over years of dedicated and sincere national service, and are now being tarnished by this vicious campaign without any corroboration of facts and verification.

We are proud of our clients and the relationships we have shared with them. Together, we have worked to create a more level playing field in telecom for our client Tata Teleservices and have always conducted ourselves with the highest levels of probity and maintained the highest standard of professional behavior.

We sincerely hope that the media will exercise caution and discretion in their reporting while continuing their pursuit of the truth.

Spokesperson, Vaishnavi Corporate Communication Pvt. Ltd.

REFERENCES

Benjamin, J. (1996). *Principles, elements, and types of persuasion.* Fort Worth, TX: Harcourt Brace.

French & Raven. (1959). *The bases of social power. Studies in Social Behavior.* Ann Arbor, MI: University of Michigan Press.

Grunig & Hunt. (1984). *Managing public relations.* New York: Holt, Rinehart, and Winston.

Grunig. (1992). Excellence in public relations and communication management. Mahwah, NJ: Erlmbaum.

Kendall. (1997). Public relations campaign strategies: Planning for implementation (2nd Ed.). New York: Addison-Wesley.

Kotler, P. (1986). Mega marketing-Strategies to enter blocked markets. *Harvard Business Review.*

Nager, N. R., & Allen, T. H. (1984). *Public relations managed by objectives.* Lanham, MD: University Press of America.

Seitel, F. P. (2006). *The practice of public relations.* Upper Saddle River, NJ: Prentice Hall.

Shelby & Nevin. (1974). Power in a channel of distribution: Sources and consequences. *JMR, Journal of Marketing Research, 9*(1).

APPENDIX

Anecdote of 2G Spectrum Scam

August 2007: Process of 2G spectrum allotment began along with Universal Access Service (UAS) License by the Department of Telecommunication, Govt. of India.

September 2007: Telecom Ministry issued notification fixing the deadline date for application as 01/10/2007 and it received 575 applications for UAS License.

November 2007: Prime Minister directed the telecom minister to ensure fair and transparence in the revision of license fee for 2G spectrum allotment.

November 2007: Finance ministry too raised concerns over the method adopted by the Telecom ministry.

January 2008: Telecom ministry decided to issue UAS license on first-come-first basis and advanced the cut- off date to 25/09/2007. The same was announced in the telecom official website.

January 2008: Tata Teleservices, Swan Telecom and Unitech sold off a part of their stakes at much higher rates.

November 2008: Media alleged something wrong in the 2G spectrum license deal. Mr Subramanian Swamy sought the sanctioning of the Prime Minister for prosecuting the Telecom minister under the provisions of Prevention of Corruption Act.

July 2009: The Delhi High court pronounced advancing of cut-off date as illegal on a Governmental complaint by S-Tel, one of the telecom applicants for UAS license.

May 2009: Central Vigilance Commission (CVC) directed the Central Bureau of Investigation (CBI) to probe the 2G spectrum allocation on the basis of a complaint by an NGO (Non- Government Orgaisation).

November 2009: The CBI sought the details of tapped conversation of corporate lobbyist Niira Radia to find out the involvement of middlemen in the allotment of 2G spectrum UAS license.

May 2010: The Comptroller and Auditor General (CAG) of India reported a large scale irregularities (A mindboggling figure of Rs 1,76,465 crores revenue loss to the exchequer) in the 2G spectrum allotment.

October 2010: The Supreme Court (SC) asked the central government to respond to the CAG's report.

November 2010 (14/11/2010): The telecom minister resigned.

November 22nd 2010: CBI examined the role of Niira Radia, Chief of Vaishnavi Corporate Communication under the instruction of the apex court.

December 2010: The Supreme Court ordered probe in to spectrum allocation since 2001 and setting up of a Special Court to try 2G spectrum scam.

February 2011: The former telecom minister was arrested and the Supreme Court directed the CBI to probe the corporate houses, specifically the alleged beneficiaries of 2G scam.

September 2011: The CBI issued a clean chit to Tata and Videocon group.

October 2011: The special court for 2G scam framed charges against the former telecom minister and sixteen others.

October 31ˢᵗ 2011: *Ms. Niira Radia, the founder of the Vaishnavi Corporate Communication (VCC), announced the shut down of her corporation and decided to exit from the Public Relations communication consultancy business. She mentioned personal priorities of family and health as reasons for the painful decision to close down. Radia's decision spelled the end of Vaishnavi's account with both Tata Group and Reliance Industries.*

December 2011: The CBI filed a third charge sheet accusing three companies – Loop Telecom Pvt Ltd, Loop Mobile India Ltd and Essar Telecom in the 2G case.

January 2012: The Supreme Court directed the CBI to submit a status report in co-ordination with the CVC with regard to 2G scam investigation.

February 2012: The Supreme Court ordered cancelling of all 122 licences granted in 2008 by the then telecom minister and further directed the government to issue 2G license through auctioning within four months of time.

Chapter 20

Tata GoldPlus:
Adoption of Customer Oriented Strategy for Penetrating Market Opportunity

Salma Ahmed
Aligarh Muslim University, India

EXECUTIVE SUMMARY

The TATAs entered the jewelry market with a retail chain, Gold Plus, which was engaged in selling branded jewelry. Their focus was on the mass market with a presence in small towns and in rural India. The sale of jewelry is based on trust which cannot be established in a day and the jewelry market has been the domain of local players who have dominated for years and have developed strong bonds with their customers over many decades. Further, there are also many players in the branded jewelry segment such as Gitanjali, D'damas, Asmi, to name a few and many other multi-national firms. These would provide stiff competition to Gold Plus. Therefore it remains to be seen how far Tata Goldplus is able to make a place for itself in the crowded market.

INTRODUCTION

The Gems and Jewelry (G&J) market has grown fast and what was considered unaffordable and out of reach of a common man has suddenly made a common housewife visit this market. The growth of this market could be one of the highest in consumer sector. What was thought to be worn by those who were the rich and the suave has suddenly come within the reach of the common man. This has become possible with a strong marketing strategy, development of the retail chain, and a change in

DOI: 10.4018/978-1-4666-4357-4.ch020

Copyright ©2014, IGI Global. Copying or distributing in print or electronic forms without written permission of IGI Global is prohibited.

the philosophy and style of sale of products. The growth in this sector could also be attributed to striking the chord with the consumer and challenging the buying power of the consumer. TATAs made a foray into this sector with Gold Plus-a retail chain engaged in retailing of branded jewelry focused at the mass market.

Indeed an innovative venture. But how successful would they be in their venture remains to be seen. Would they be able to penetrate this sector? This is because on one hand this is a playfield of the local jewelers who have come a long way in developing strong bonds with their customers over many decades. On the other, there are some major competitors to face in the branded jewelry segment such as Gitanjali, D'damas, Asmi, to name a few and many other multi-national firms that may provide stiff competition to Gold Plus.

INTRODUCTION TO TATA GROUP, TANISHQ, AND GOLD PLUS

The Tata Group is a multinational conglomerate based in Mumbai, India. Tata Group is the largest Company in India expressed in terms of market capitalization and revenues. It started with manufacture of steel and today it has presence not only in steel but in almost every field; from automobiles to information technology, communication, power, tea, and hotels. In fact, it has presence across seven business sectors. It has operations in more than 85 countries.

The Tata Group owns the Titan Industries. Titan Industries is India's leading manufacturer of watches and jewelry. It is the world's sixth largest manufacturer brand of watches. It was established in 1984 as a joint venture between the Tata Group and the Tamil Nadu Industrial Development Corporation. The company is said to have transformed the Indian watch market, offering quartz technology with international styling. These watches are manufactured at its state-of-the-art factory at Hosur, Tamil Nadu. In 1995, the company diversified into jewelry under the brand Tanishq. Tanishq is a branch of the TATA Group which retails in jewelry and it is said to be India's largest business house. It came into operations in 1996 and is today India's largest brand of jewelry. It is said to be India's most admired brand of jewelry and an *elitist class brand* of jewelry.

Gold Plus, on the other hand, is a *mass-market* jewelry *brand* from the TATA Group. It is a chain of jewelry outlets from Titan Industries focused at the small towns. It launched its first store at Bheemavaram and later at 15 places across Tamil Nadu, Madhya Pradesh, Andhra Pradesh and Maharashtra. Goldplus has a commitment to provide customers in smaller towns and rural India gold jewelry *in assured purity.* It has received huge acceptance from consumers. It is basically targeted at semi-urban and rural areas.

There are so far over 29 Gold Plus stores spread in 6 states across India. It is also the pioneer in India in offering branded jewelry to rural and semi-urban customers. It focused on tapping on the immense opportunity existing in the small towns and rural India. Reports suggest that 60% of gold in India is bought in towns and villages (TOI, Aug 17, 2012).

GOLDPLUS RETAIL-AN INNOVATIVE RETAIL VENTURE

The company first undertook a pilot study in Erode in August 2005 and Rathlam in Madhya Pradesh to test their concept of retail in jewelry. Satisfied with the results of the study, it set up retail chains in different parts of the country. It has set up 97 showrooms in 68 cities providing the comfort and ambience that the consumer looks for. These showrooms have warm and professional salesmen and provide a different and superior shopping experience.

A Karigar Room?

Within their store they also have an attached Karigar room with the latest technology to cater to the servicing facilities of customers. Further, these showrooms have a completely localized front end as well as a back end. Here, Gold Plus has the advantage of using the design and retail expertise of Titan Industries to bring to the consumers products with local taste and preferences. In fact the products and showroom ambience is created in such a manner that on one hand the consumers get the comfort and ambience of any retail centre and on the other they do not feel uncomfortable as the interior is *localised*. In other words, *the display of shops is local*, that is, it takes the appearance of any other local jeweler. The consumers, therefore, do not feel the shop is *up-market* and therefore prices would be high. The initial hesitation that a consumer would have in entering a retail center which is associated with high costs is totally lost.

STRATEGY OF GOLD PLUS

First the company identified the gap that existed in the market. It identified that there existed a huge market for jewelry in rural and semi-urban India and that there is also a lack of a branded jeweler in the mass market.

The Jewelry market in India can be classified into three tiers. (Figure 1) Gold Plus wants to be in the middle crust.

In India, Gold has immense historical, religious, cultural, social, and economic significance. However, there is an absence of standardization and as such there is always a fear prevailing among the consumers about the purity of gold. Reports suggest that there is approximately 5% adulteration in gold sold across stores in the unorganized market. (commodityonline.com) Gold Plus brings with it the assurance of purity and being a Tata group company, it is symbolic. Therefore, it communicates the *core values of the Tatas, that is, of trust, transparency and honesty.*

Gold Plus has introduced professional retailing in the otherwise disorganized Indian jewelry market. It stressed on facts like:

- Impurity of gold when purchased from local jewelers
- Offering of standardized products in undifferentiated market
- Establishing of quality benchmarks
- Creating awareness about purity of gold
- Identification of major seasons for purchase of jewelry
- Establishing of an emotional bonding with the customers
- Offering a range of designs-over 5,000 designs in 22 kt plain gold and diamond jewelry

IDENTIFICATION OF SEASONS FOR GOLD PURCHASE

The major drivers of gold purchase in India are the *harvest, marriage and festival seasons.* Gold Plus has attempted to establish an emotional bonding with the custom-

Figure 1. Tata Goldplus targets semi-urban and urban markets

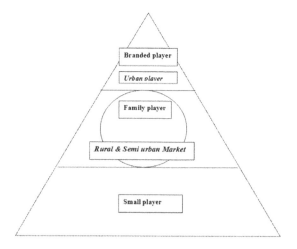

ers by participating in every such occasion of gold purchase by offering innovative schemes during these occasions.

One such scheme of Gold Plus is a monthly saving scheme called *Golden Future Savings Scheme* (Business Standard, 2008 & Financial Express, 2006). This offers the buyers the opportunity to buy ornaments in easy installments by paying small sums in advance. Attractive gifts are also made available to all those who have enrolled for such initiatives.

Innovation

Gold Plus provides its consumers designs in contemporary and ethnic styles which have been inspired from India's rich heritage. These designs are in modern as well as traditional forms, and they are available at an affordable price. It also introduced the *Karatmeter* (Pradhan, 2012) the only non destructive means to check the purity of gold. This further ensures confidence of the customers.

Gold Plus has introduced the concept of *Karigarpaar*. It has twenty such vendors. These vendors follow a hub and spoke model. Each Karigar serves five stores. Each region gives its demand and this is further given to the Karigar. In this way, apart from ensuring quality, the turnaround time works out to be less.

Consumer Connect and Customer Retention Initiatives

The company connects with the customers by connecting with the cultural nuances of India. Therefore a store in Erode looks totally different from a store in Rathlam. In this way it tries to connect with the local gold seller and provides comfort to the consumers. Further, it has also undertaken many customer relationship initiatives. These initiatives are the *Golden Chariot* and *Golden Future Savings Scheme* (commodityonline.com). In the first scheme, a vehicle from Gold Plus which has a karatmeter goes to consumers' homes and consumers are encouraged to come to check the purity of gold they already have in their homes. They also clean and polish the ornaments that the consumers hold free of cost. In the second scheme, consumers are allowed to plan future purchase of gold and pay for them in easy installments. In yet another scheme, a 24.5 kg gold bangle was taken across different roads in a road show across 17 towns and consumers were invited to guess the weight of the bangle (commodityonline.com).

Market Segmentation

Gold Plus has adopted a unique strategy for segmenting the market. It has segmented the market into two. It segments the market *by occasions of wear* and *by purchase*.

First taking the case of *segmentation by occasions of wear*, typically, the traditional segmentation of the Indian jewelry market would be gold, diamond and platinum. This is segmentation by material. Another typical segmentation could be wedding, fashion and trinket jewelry. However, at Tanishq the traditional approaches are discarded and segmentation is seen from a new and a totally consumer-driven perspective.

Goldplus also segmented by purchase. The consumer buying habits were divided into three clear segments: *everyday-wear* jewelry, *special-occasion wear* jewelry *and wedding-wear* jewelry. *Everyday wear* jewelry consist of jewelry for work or home. *Special occasion wear* could either be contemporary or traditional Indian styles. *Wedding* jewelry could either be the trousseau, which is worn to the wedding hall, or *mandap*, or it could be fashion jewelry. Earlier jewelry was seen as a commodity. This however gives a new perspective to jewelry and its use. The advantage of looking at the consumer this way is to have a new marketing approach which was not possible earlier.

The second strategy that the company followed was to create more occasions of jewelry purchase. For this it identified the traditional festivals and these became the key occasions of jewelry purchase for the consumers. Gold is purchased on occasions like *Akshaya Tritiya*, a Sanskrit name for a festival in April; *Karva Chauth* in October; and *Varalakshmi Vrat*. (Indian Express, 2009). These occasions were not associated with jewelry purchase four years back as much as they are today. These are also the result of marketing efforts undertaken by the company. Region specific occasions also exist. For instance, during Dussehra, jewelry is bought in the eastern parts of the country, purely because of marketing efforts; while in Kerela jewelry is purchased during festivals like Onam and in Tamil Nadu the occasion is Pongal. One can see that brands such as Tanishq which is actively working in India have engineered a peak in jewelry purchase virtually in every month of the year. Therefore the company has been successful in creating more occasions of jewelry wear. In order to do this the company segmented the market differently by consciously putting those occasions into the minds of consumers. And this strategy worked successfully.

Advertising or Customer Relationship?

The company adopts a no-frill approach to advertising. Therefore the advertising cost is very low. It has devised its unique method for developing customer contact. The company visits card sellers (card houses where wedding cards are published) and band group agencies from here they track the weddings that take place through visits to card houses and band group agencies. Once they have identified the residences where marriage is to take place, the representatives from the retail store visits the customer house with a box of sweet. The customer is further given a catalogue of designs and invited to the showroom to make a selection and place an order. The customer in return is motivated to visit the store. If the visit culminates into a purchase, the company, on the day of the marriage, puts a banner of Gold Plus congratulating the couple. This makes the customer feel good and this also works like a very effective form of advertising. Also, a gift from Titan consisting of Sonata watch for men and women is also given to the couple. In fact, the company has been able to make a business of Rs 446 lakhs in this manner.

Many other such events are organized. For instance, on mothers day mothers are invited to the store and a gift and photo frame is given to them.

To make their presence felt, and also to create a bond with the customer, many other local events are also organized. It organized rangoli competition in which 300 families participated. State level painting competition was also organized during summer vacations entitled *Shabash Chutti* to carry on communicating with the consumer.

Educating the Customer

The company officials also educated the customer regarding purity of gold. The concept of 22 carat and use of karatmeter was communicated to them which were unheard of earlier. Also every Goldplus product is endorsed with a certificate of purity of gold and a perfect finish.

Customised Designs

Earlier the jewelry sold had fixed designs. For instance, a neck-chain would have a standard set of patterns to choose from. Gold Plus introduced the *concept of customization in ornaments*. Earlier the karigars produced one complete set; however now he manufactures modules. They modularized the product and customer was given the option to design his own product by selecting different options from these modules, and combining them to create their unique design. A customer therefore can be very creative in creating its own masterpiece, which would be unique and different, from those of others.

Supply Chain Initiatives

The supply chain of Tanishq and Gold Plus is the same. Titans investment in IT and retail enables Gold Plus to achieve cost-effective and responsive supply chain logistics which helps to deliver greater value for the customers.

Benefits to Customers

There are immense benefits that the customer gets by purchasing jewelry from Gold Plus stores. First, they come across transparent operations, get value for money, and also better and standardized products. There are immense benefits to the society as well. These are through improved practices, increased awareness amongst consumers, and employment generation through karigar and also through retail employment. So far it has 29 stores across 6 states but plans to increase by another 6-7 in Tier I and Tier II towns (2010).

Future Growth through Franchise Model

The company plans to grow by following a franchise model. The interior, people and real estate would belong to the franchise while Tata would hold ownership to stocks.

MANAGERIAL DILEMMA

The jewelry market in India is currently dominated by local jewelers who have developed strong mutual relations with their customers over the decades. How can the big players in the market find a place for them in such a scenario is a pertinent question that needs to be answered. This is because these local jewelers help the customers develop a sense of belonging, and they have been doing so over decades, thereby resulting in a mutually satisfying and fruitful relationship for both.

There are some good names in the jewelry business such as P. C. Jewelers, P. C. Chandra, Nathumal Jewelers, and Subhash Jewelers, who have a dominant presence in different regions, and who ensure that their customers have a rewarding experience while visiting the showrooms. Because of the less professional attitude, these jewelers offer tailor-made services specially designed for their hard-core loyal customers.

The customers, while visiting these showrooms, experience a homely environment in terms of recognition they receive. Further, the customers may get the smallest of jobs and repair work done easily, and that too, free of charge on certain occasions. Such services cannot generally be availed of at Gold Plus. Moreover, the customers prefer to visit those jewelers where their parents used to, thereby resulting in relationship building over generations.

An element of trust that has been developed between traditional jewelers and the customers after interaction and communication over years is that they cannot phase out very soon which might prove to be a hindrance for Gold Plus as reliability of promises, honesty, and mutual interests serve as indicators of trust in buyer-seller relationships. And this the traditional jewelers have carved out over the years very beautifully. Without trust, a vacuum is created in the way the deals are concluded. *Gold Plus might take a significant amount of time before it could develop trusted relationships with its customers.*

Another important aspect is the commitment from both ends. If the traditional jewelers are committed towards quality, latest designs and the most client oriented services at competitive prices, they can easily ensure retention of customers which is another area to be looked upon by Gold Plus. Commitment reduces the risk of uncertainty and the buyer can be assured of quality and prices which in turn might help the retailer in getting a committed customer.

Another parameter as a top most priority of the retailers today is *satisfaction.* For the jeweler, the opportunity to improve the customer relationship is through customer satisfaction. The traditional (local) jeweler has succeeded in creating a satisfied customer, it is most unlikely that the customer would ever leave him (the jeweler).

Another aspect is the dependence of both parties on each other. The dependence is required in order to achieve desired goals. Today's business scenario has changed from product oriented business to customer oriented business and the traditional jewelers are trying to implement such schemes that cater to the basic needs of the customers by providing them with the latest designs at an affordable price. The customer depends on the jeweler for buying the best jewelry in the market at the lowest rates while the jewelers depend on their customers for their sales. This dependence of the customers on the age-old traditional jewelers and vice-versa can be another hurdle that Gold Plus should be paying attention to.

The traditional jewelers enjoy major share of the jewelry market due the concept of relationship marketing. Instead of emphasizing on short term transactions, relationship marketing considers the development and maintenance of long-term relationships with customers. These jewelers have developed a strong bonding with their customers over decades which has given them an opportunity to easily dominate the market by catering to the needs of their loyal and trustworthy customers who in turn have a sense of belonging in this relationship with the jewelers.

This satisfied group of customers would always like to visit only those jewelry stores where they are satisfied and where they get some recognition which is an important ingredient in the relationship building. Further, the customer would like to have its problem solved without much hassle and in a fairly lesser amount of time which can be provided by traditional jewelers and not big firms like Gold Plus who have a much professional attitude.

THE MARKET FOR JEWELRY

The market for Gems and Jewelry is a fast growing market in the world, and India is no exception. Infact, the Indian Gems and Jewelry industry is one of the fastest growing segments in the Indian economy with an annual growth rate of approximately 16 percent (CII Report).

Indian jewelry is manufactured and designed keeping in mind the current situation and prevailing trends and the latest fashion trends. Because of their curvaceous designs, exotic styles and aesthetic appeal, Indian jewelry attracts the attention of people. It is usually believed that Indian jewelry is capable of pleasing the eye and also enhancing the charm of anyone's overall personality. Today, Indian jewelry is available in the market in various exquisite designs and awe-inspiring finishing.

The Gems and Jewelry (G&J) market comprises of sourcing, processing, manufacturing and selling of precious metals and gemstones, such as, Gold, Platinum, Silver, Diamond, Ruby, and Sapphire to name a few. The market size in India is estimated to be of Rs 80,000 crores. Of this, 60% consists of consumers in the semi-urban and rural sectors and the remaining 40% constitutes of consumers in the Tier-1 and Tier-2 cities.

In India there are two major segments of the jewelry *sector.* The first is the gold and the second is diamond. Gold jewelry constitutes 80% of the jewelry market, and the remaining 20% comprises of fabricated studded jewelry (KPMG Report). Fabricated studded jewelry constitutes diamonds and gemstone jewelry. India is said to be the largest diamond cutting and polishing center in the world. It enjoys 60 percent value share, 82 percent carat share, and 95 percent share of the world market in terms of pieces. It is said that 9 out of 10 diamonds sold worldwide are cut and polished in India.

The Gems and Jewelry (G&J) market contributes significantly to the Indian economy and a large chunk of its income comes from exports. Gems and jewelry also account for more than 15% of India's total exports. The main drivers of this sector are a highly skilled and low cost manpower that is available in India. Apart from this, the strong government support in the form of incentives and establishment of SEZs have also been instrumental for its growth (Indian Gems and Jewelry Market-Future Prospects to 2011, a report by RNCOS).

There is increased consumption of gems and jewelry and the sale is estimated to be at a CAGR of around 14% from 2007-08 to 2010-11. India is the largest consumer of gold (around 20 percent of global consumption which is estimated to be 800 tonnes of gold) (IBEF report, 2012)and also the largest diamond processor (around 90 percent by pieces and 55 percent by value of the global market). It is said to be worth over $10 billion a year.

PRESENT MARKET STRUCTURE FOR JEWELRY RETAIL

Presently the market for jewelry is disorganized, fragmented, and provides a poor shopping experience to its consumers. Transactions are primarily driven by relationships; that is, because grandparents purchased their requirement of jewelry from a particular shop, one would also fulfill his requirements from the same place. Also many a time it is the religious flavour, that is, as the jeweler follows a particular religion, and the buyer is also a follower of the same religion; therefore, he would go there to purchase his requirements of gold.

JEWELRY RETAIL

It is estimated that there are about 3 lakh traditional retail jewelers (family jewelers) who hold 96 per cent of the market share. Of late, the jewelry market has recorded tremendous change. The old and traditional ornaments are being replaced by branded designs; and gold is replaced by diamonds and precious stones. The buying pattern of consumers is also fast changing. Indians are largely opting for branded jewelry than buying from a 'family jeweler.' This change has created ample opportunity for the retailers. Though growing at 30-40 percent annually, currently the organized jewelry retail has therefore caught up though at present it constitutes only 3 per cent of the overall market (which is estimated to be less than 2% by value). (Business Standard, 2013)

The main two factors that are stimulating the growth of branded jewelry retail. On one hand, it is the spread of organized retail culture and on the other it is the huge consumption of jewelry in India. Other factors that are stimulating sales are: a critical awareness of quality, preference for brands, and increasing consciousness of purity of product among buyers (which is often not guaranteed by the on the disorganized players). Further, factors like convenience, good shopping ambience are yet other reasons cited. Yet another reason oft quoted is that earlier consumption of gold was seen as an investment product; however, today it is being seen as a luxury product and thus needs innovation.

Also new formats such as boutiques, supermarkets and gold souks are also expected to emerge in jewelry retail further, going forward, jewelry would be seen as a fashion and lifestyle product. Branded jewelry retailers would then play a more important and greater role.

Export Status of Gems and Jewelry

The Indian Gems and Jewelry (G&J) sector contributed to 15 percent of India's total merchandise exports during 2005-2006 and it was about 13.7 per cent of the country's total merchandise exports in 2006-2007. The demand for retail jewelry (both branded and unbranded) in the domestic market was estimated to be Rs 490 billion in 2005, with diamond jewelry comprising Rs 80 billion. By 2010, according to a study by McKinsey, the branded jewelry market is expected to reach Rs 100 billion by 2010 (report of McKinsey). The sale of diamond jewelry in India has been increasing at a rapid pace of 25% every year over the last two years. The branded jewelry segment has grown at a much higher rate.

Growing Competition

The branded jewelry segment is anticipated to grow at a very fast rate-at a much faster rate as compared to other segments in near future. India holds the position of being the world's largest consumer with gold consumption being assessed to be as high as 20% in India. There are many companies which have already made a presence. Though today there only a few players in the organized segment, more are expected to enter soon.

Gitanjali

The Gitanjali group has a presence in this segment. This poses formidable competition to GoldPlus. This is one of the largest integrated diamond and jewelry manufacturers and retailers in India. It plans to expand its outlets to 1,500 from 840 in the next couple of years. It further intends to set up a diamond processing Special Economic Zone (SEZ) near Bangalore.

The Gitanjali Group, has tied up with ICICI Bank to launch the ICICI Bank-Gitanjali Card, a comprehensive credit card that allows cardholders to avail of benefits across 2,000,000 merchants in India and more than 22 million merchants internationally.

It owns the famous brands Nakshatra, Gili, Asmi, Sangini, D'damas, and Desire.

Gili

Gili's primary brand value is "Genuine diamond and gold jewelry at affordable prices. In fact, this is the first jewelry brand that brought diamond jewelry within the reach of the masses.

Nakshatra

Nakshatra, is a premium brand which is primarily positioned as a lifestyle statement for women. It tries to blend mystique with glamour and was declared a Superbrand in 2004.

Asmi

Asmi, in Sanskrit means "I". It is indicative of a passionate exposition of the intensity and drive with which she lives her life. Gitanjali Gems' Asmi line also has a collection called the "Corporate and Graduate" which accounts for 50-60 percent of the sales of the entire line.

Sangini

Sangini, yet another brand of the Gitanjali Group, is positioned as a brand that glorifies women in a relationship.

D'damas

D'damas is a generic brand which combines international quality with Indian values. It represents luxury and aspiration, innovativeness, assurance, and dynamism. It has been recognised and awarded as a Jewelery Masterbrand. There are many brands under D'damas like Forevermark Solitaire, Damas Solitaire, Glitterati, Collection G, Gold Expressions, Vivaaha, Ballerina, Bollywood Gold and Insipration.

Desire

Desire Lifestyle is a diversified product range which targets the lifestyle needs to reflect the style and upcoming trends amongst the masses.

Reliance

Reliance already has a presence. It has stepped in retail of jewelry under the name Reliance Jewels. It set up its first retail store in Bangalore in November 2007 followed by another in Hyderabad in 2008. It has targeted to capture a 10% market share in India's jewelry market within the five years. (Reuters reports). Its plans are to open a mix of both own-and-operate and franchise stores. It plans to set up seven outlets in Ahmedabad, Ludhiana and Dhanbad within the year and further has plans to set up 300 stores across India by 2012 out of which 100 are expected to follow the franchise model. Reliance retail enjoys good brand goodwill. It wants to leverage this goodwill to earn market share, provide competitive pricing, jewelry assortment and demand for hallmarked jewelry. It also has tied up with 37 manufacturing partners for various kinds of jewelry.

Scintillating

Scintillating is also in gems and jewelry. It has 14 retail outlets primarily across North India and is looking for a pan-India presence.

Flawless

Flawless Diamond India Ltd has planned to open 75 additional outlets in the next two years.

Rajesh Exports

There are a few major players in the G&J segment, with Rajesh Exports being the most dominant name. Other key players in the field include Gitanjali Gems, Suhash-ish Diamonds, Su-Raj Diamonds, Vaibhav Diamonds and Tanishq. The company also faces competition from these players.

Competition from Foreign Players

This sector is gradually becoming more organized and foreign players are also expected to enter the market more aggressively. There are also many Multi-National branded jewelry retailers such as Tiffany, Cartier, Zales, and Harry Winston who have either set up shops or are keen to set up shops in India. Further, the government's decision to allow 51 percent FDI in single brand retail store also helped many foreign retailers to enter into India.

Damas

One of the world's leading jeweler Damas entered India way back in 2003 with a 50-50 joint venture with Gitanjali Gems Ltd. It opened its first retail store in Bangalore in 2005 and has increased its presence by another seven showrooms.

Swarovski

Swarovski, the Austria-based crystal goods manufacturer and marketer, is an early starter in the Indian market. It plans to set up 30 stores by 2009 and several other stores in the shop-in-shop format. It has on offer a line called Passages of the Night which has grown over 70 percent in the last year.

Pranda Jewelry

There are other international players such as Thailand-based Pranda Jewelry who are also expected to enter the retail segment in India. This company plans to invest US $ 21.15 million towards retail expansion in India. Arens Gold Souk International Limited has opened a special shopping mall for branded jewelry. The company is further planning to open about 100 Gold Souks in India in near future.

Grisogono

Geneva-based luxury watch and jewelry brand Grisogono also has plans to have a strong presence in India. It has set up its first boutique for US $ 5.29 million and plans top add six more mono-brand outlets by 2011.

Kiah

Kiah, also a retailer in diamond jewelry already has 15 stores in India and plans to expand the network to 30 by the end of 2009.

Damas India

Damas India is an integrated jeweler and watch retailer having a market presence with 450 stores. It was started in Syria in early 1900 by Mr Mohammed Tawfique Abdulla, who undertook the total responsibility of designing, crafting and selling jewelry himself. The Group sells jewelry and watches through three distinctive stores which are targetted to different groups of consumers-The *Les Exclusive* stores which caters to the high net worth consumers, the *Semi-Exclusive* stores caters to the upper middle class such as tourists and expatriate professionals and office workers, and the Damas 22K stores which cater to the middle income and working population.

There are also other prominent brands in the market like Adora, D'Damas, Oysterbay, De Beers, and Carbon. There are in all about 30 major players marketing about 50 brands in India.

QUESTION

With competition picking up soon and fast, evaluate the strategy that Tata Gold Plus has adopted to make its position in the market? Also suggest the strategies that it should adopt to retain market share and also remain at the top?

REFERENCES

Bharat Book Bureau. (2008). *Indian gems and jewelry market.* Retrieved from www.Bharatbook.com.

Business Standard. (2008). *Brand managers need to connect with rural consumers.* Retrieved from http://www.Business-Standard.com/india/storypage. php?autono=340384.

Business Standard. (2013). *Organised retail jewelry sector growing by 40%.* Retrieved from http://www.business-standard.com/article/companies/organised-retail-jewelry-sector-growing-by-40-111041300065_1.html.

Commodity Online. (2009). *Goldplus from tata banks on rural buyers.* Retrieved from http://www.commodityonline.com/news/goldplus-from-tata-banks-on-rural-buyers-15291-3-15292.html.

Confederation of Indian Industry. (2013). *Gems and jewelry.* Retrieved from http://www.cii.in/Sectors.aspx?enc=prvePUj2bdMtgTmvPwvisYH+5EnGjyGXO9hLEC vTuNt+KvFl5tZninrd2RhXtdzu.

Diamond World. (2008). *Reliance jewels targets 10% of india's jewelry market.* Retrieved from http://www.DiamondWorld.net/contentview.aspx?item=1938.

Fibre2Fashion. (2008). *Tanishq bags retail chain of the year award.* Retrieved from http://www.fibre2fashion.com/news/fashion-news/newsdetails.aspx?news_ id=61754.

Financial Express. (2008). Tanishq bags retail chain of the year award. Retrieved from http://www.ibef.org/exports/Gems-and-Jewelry.aspx.

Goldplus. (2010). *Goldplus launches diamantine india.* Retrieved from http://www. goldplus.in/goldplus-launches-diamantine-india.

Gorpade & Goswami. (2011). After gold prices fall, goldsmiths take to adulterating. *DNA India.* Retrieved from http://www.dnaindia.com/bangalore/1593656/report-after-gold-prices-fall-goldsmiths-take-to-adulterating.

IBEF. (n.d.). *KPMG report*. Retrieved from http://www.ibef.org/download/ibef_%20 jewellery_06.pdf.

Indian Jewelers New Service. (2012). *Industries plans to increase number of gold-plus, tanishq stores*. Retrieved from www.indianjeweller.in/contentview.aspx/ Titan.

JustStyles. (2011). *Indian gems and jewelry market-Future prospects to 2011*. Retrieved from http://www.Juststyle.com.

Kannan, S. (2009). Tanishq hopes to raise the bar for jewelry artisans. *The Hindu Business Line*. Retrieved from http://www.thehindubusinessline.com/todays-paper/tp-marketing/tanishq-hopes-to-raise-the-bar-for-jewellery-artisans/article1066398.ece.

Mahesh, R. (2006). Despite volatile price, tanishq gold sales up. *Financial Express*. Retrieved from http://www.Financial-Express.com/old/latest_full_story.php?content_id=136052.

Money Contorol. (1970). Tata gold plus promises to offer pure gold. Retrieved from http://www.moneycontrol.com/news/business/goldplustata-promises-to-offer-pure-gold-jewellery_190784.html.

New Indian Express. (2009). Unique offers for this akshaya tritiya. Retrieved from http://newindianexpress.com/cities/chennai/article62157.ece?service=print.

Newsonproject.com. (2012). *Tata industries plans to increase the retail presence*. Retrieved from http://www.newsonprojects.com/story.asp?news_code=13254.

Pradhan, S. (2012). *Retailing management text and cases*. Noida, India: Tata McGraw.

Subramanian, S. (2007). Golden management lessons from titan. *Rediff Business*. Retrieved from http://www.rediff.com/money/special/titan/20070328.htm.

TATA Group. (2001). Tanishq in talks with US Group to market jewelry. Retrieved from http://www.tata.in/company/Media/inside.aspx?artid=us2gxa6D+rY=econo mictimes.

TATA Group. (2008). *The world's biggest gold bangle unveil by the gold plus jewelry*. Retrieved from http://www.IndiaPRwire.com/pressrelease/fashion/2008080711862.htm.

The Times of India. (2012). *Gold demand falls for 2nd straight quarter*. Retrieved from http://articles.timesofindia.indiatimes.com/2012-08-17/india-business/33248673_1_gold-demand-world-gold-council-investment-demand.

World News Service. (2008). *The changing retail formats are changing the way jewelry is sold*. Retrieved from http://wwwdaimondworld.net/contentview.aspx?item=2465.

Chapter 21
When Citi was Found Sleeping

Suresh Chandra Bihari
IBS Hyderabad, India

EXECUTIVE SUMMARY

"Citi never sleeps" is the famous signature claim of Citi bank. But their claim was made a mockery in a high profile branch in India where several depositors and high-net worth individuals were duped in a fraud to the tune of Rs 460.91 crore, engineered by their Global Wealth Manager Shivraj Puri who was working at Gurgaon branch of the bank. Corporate houses like the Hero group and 20-odd people invested in schemes which were sold to them by showing them a forged letter of the market regulator, Sebi. The clients were offered super normal returns and were lured by the Relationship Manager who enjoys a special relationship of trust and confidence with the clients. The clients were cheated understandably for their lack of understanding of the nuances of the product. But the greater issue at stake was the onerous practices of Wealth Management by banks in India and the lack of regulatory control in this fast developing area that allowed the incident to happen in the first place.

LEARNING/TEACHING OBJECTIVES

1. To examine the various underlying issues relating to the fraud that took the industry observers, market players and regulators by surprise and shock.
2. To understand the various issues relating to Wealth Management in general and the practices in India, in particular.

DOI: 10.4018/978-1-4666-4357-4.ch021

Copyright ©2014, IGI Global. Copying or distributing in print or electronic forms without written permission of IGI Global is prohibited.

3. To understand the implications of the case for the future of Wealth Management, with special reference to India, in the greater interests all the stakeholders, particularly the investors at large.

THE CASE SYNOPSIS

A fraud involving more than Rs. 460 crore was unearthed at the leading multinational lender Citibank's Gurgaon (Haryana) branch (*NDTV Profit*, 2013a). Gurgaon Police lodged an FIR under sections of cheating and forgery against a bank employee and three others and 18 accounts having close to Rs. 4 crore belonging to them was frozen. The fraud is said to be a handiwork of Shivraj Puri, the employee who is alleged to have sold investment products to high net worth clients claiming that they would generate unusually high returns. It is also alleged that Puri, who is named in the FIR, showed a forged notification of market regulator Securities and Exchange Board of India for obtaining funds from customers. He is also accused of claiming that these products were authorized by the bank's investment product committee. Puri allegedly sought deposits from high net worth customers in lucrative schemes but transferred the funds to some fictitious accounts. Funds amounting to Rs. 460.91 crore belonging to about 20 customers were transferred to such accounts, it was revealed.

Industry observers, management of the company, and all stakeholders including regulators were taken by surprise. But the fraud has opened a Pandora's Box and the whole host of issues is being debated such as the role of a Relationship Manager, Product Development in Wealth Management, Regulation of Wealth Management Business in India, among others. The case is aimed at highlighting the issues and the action being taken/contemplated over the issues. As the matters, reported in December 2010, is still under the process of investigation and follow up action at certain quarters, the case is updated till the date of completion, 25th May 2011.

FULL CASE STUDY-THE GURGAON FRAUD AT CITIBANK

The Incident

Gurgaon police on 30th December 2010 arrested Citibank Relationship Manager Shivraj Puri, who allegedly masterminded a major fraud in the Gurgaon branch of the Bank. Puri was alleged to have opened 78 accounts in his name and in the names of his grandparents, Premnath Puri and Sheela Premnath Puri besides an account in the name of his mother, Deeksha Puri. These accounts are with different financial institutions including banks and brokerage houses spread across Gurgaon, Delhi and Kolkata among which Religare, Bonanza and India Info line also figure in the list. The banks include SBI, HDFC, Standard Chartered, PNB, Axis and ABN-Amro (IBTimes Staff Reporter, 2010). According to sources (SmartInvestor.In., 2010), Shivraj Puri used to seek deposits from high-net worth customers in lucrative schemes. However, he used to transfer the funds to some other accounts. Funds amounting to Rs 400 crore belonging to about 20 customers, according to sources, were transferred to fictitious accounts. Shivraj is charged with selling investment products to clients claiming that these would generate unusually high returns. It has been alleged that the employee also showed a forged notification of market regulator Securities and Exchange Board of India for garnering funds from customers. Shivraj also claimed that the products were authorized by the banks investment product committee. The incident almost stirred the entire financial sector in India and the regulators including the Securities and Exchange board of India (SEBI), the Reserve Bank of India(RBI) and the Ministry of Finance are seized with the matter and the Bank in question has geared up the process of damage control by taking action against the erring employees.

The Aftermath

Citibank has terminated services of 7 employees at its Gurgaon branch, where Rs 460 crore frauds were detected last year, as per Press Trust of India report released on August 3, 2011.

"Following disciplinary procedures, services of a few employees of our Gurgaon branch have been terminated," a Citibank spokesperson said on March 8, 2011. These employees were reportedly under suspension ever since the fraud came to light. The government on Friday, March 4, 2011 (*NDTV Profit*, 2013a), had also said that Reserve Bank of India (RBI) has conducted a special inquiry into Rs. 460-crore Citibank fraud case and was in the process of completing its final report. "RBI has conducted a special scrutiny of the related accounts at Citibank, Gurgaon (branch) and other connected accounts at other banks. The final report is being completed," Minister of state for Finance Namo Narain Meena told the Lok Sabha in a written reply (SmartInvestor.In., 2013b). Pointing out that the fraud in the Citibank's Gurgaon branch was going on since September 2009, the minister said, "the major transactions took place between May 2010 and November 2010. The bank has furnished details of the fraud to the RBI in the Fraud Monitoring Report."

Citibank's manager Puri, Meena said, "Perpetrated the fraud by mobilizing funds to the tune of Rs. 460.91 crore unauthorisidely from High Net worth Individual (NHI) customers and certain corporate for the purpose of investing in stock market, assuring them high returns." While providing details of the modus operandi, the minister said, Puri fabricated a circular of the Securities and Exchange Board of India to lure people into investing into accounts held by his accomplices Premnath, Shiela Premnath, and Deeksha Puri.

The investors, Meena added, were even issued fake receipts/acknowledgements on Citibank's stationary. The funds thus collected through the "Premnath Account" were transferred to various brokerage houses for making investment in the securities market. "There were 27 other accounts which had been opened in the (Citibank's Gurgaon) branch in the names of Puri's relatives..", the minister added. Besides, he said, the fraudulent transactions also took place in the accounts of broker firms like BG Financial Services, G 2S Management consultants and Normans Martin Broker. The fraud came to light after the bank look into a query from a customer at Citibank's Nehru Place branch about its scheme offering high returns. After discovering the fraud, the Citibank on December 5, 2010, filed a complaint with the Gurgaon police which is investigating the case. The recent Citibank fraud has made the government review the regulatory issues regarding wealth management and private banking services offered by the banks (The Business Standard, 2011a). The sub-committee of Financial Stability and Development Council (FSDC), which met in New Delhi on Friday, March 4, 2011, has discussed the issue of wealth management services by banks. The sub-committee is headed by the governor of Reserve Bank of India. This was the first meeting of the subcommittee since the formation of FSDC in December. Banks have to take the RBI's approval for offering portfolio management services. However, bank sponsored non-banking financial services companies are allowed to offer discretionary PMS.

RBI guidelines also mandate that PMS should be entirely at the customer's risk, without guaranteeing, either directly or indirectly, a pre-determined return. Funds for portfolio management cannot be for less than one year. Portfolio funds are not be deployed for lending in call money, inter-bank term deposits and bills rediscounting markets and lending to corporate houses. The Securities and Exchange Board of India (Sebi) is jointly working with other regulators to enhance norms for wealth management, which has been under the regulatory scanner since the 400-crore Citibank India scam was exposed in December last year. According to a Sebi official, there is an urgent need for regulators to integrate at both operating and surveillance levels, to counter harmful product innovation (The Business Standard, 2011b). "We are all on-board to look into this business (wealth management)," said K N Vaidyanathan, executive director, Sebi. "From our (Sebi's) side, we first took the step of advising asset managers to start implementing additional due diligence measures for institutional distribution. We need to get together to have a common set of rules. The process is in progress. We will come out with it soon," he said on sidelines of a management seminar. Vaidyanathan, who looks after regulations related to mutual funds, foreign institutional investors and collective investment schemes, added that while various regulators collaborated at the policy level, there was a strong case for moving beyond these efforts.

"I think we made a great step with the Financial Stability and Development Council, but we need to integrate with regulators—not just at policy, but also at operating and surveillance levels," he said when asked whether inter-regulatory coordination is a challenge. "Markets are far too advanced. Wealth managers today straddle products which cut through banking, capital market and insurance regulatory frameworks. We can't remain silent. We need to come together and address how to regulate wealth managers better," he said. He also added a relationship manager's remuneration was not fully aligned with the investor's interest. "The institution guards its risk by getting certain documents from the customer. So, the risk of the relationship manager is actually borne by the customer," he said. Incidentally, high net worth individuals often give the power of attorney to relationship managers. On a different note, Sebi will soon come out with guidelines to allow foreign individuals to invest in mutual fund schemes in India. In Union Budget 2011-2012, finance minister Pranab Mukherjee allowed mutual funds to accept subscription from foreign investors, who comply with KYC (know your customer) norms.

"We are working on it. I would say it is a matter of weeks, not months," said Vaidyanathan. "We are in the process of working with the Reserve Bank of India and ministry. Hopefully, we will come out with those guidelines soon," he added. "Wealth managers today straddle products, which cut through banking, capital market and insurance regulatory frameworks."

One of the key reasons for the global financial crisis was that there were too many inadequately monitored financial products in the market (Business Line, 2010). As per an editorial analysis in the Business daily, The Hindu Business Line dated December 31, 2010, a fraudulent product or scheme is more likely to succeed when there are 50 such products/schemes on offer than, say, 20. Let it not be forgotten that one of the key reasons for the global financial crisis, of which Citibank was a prominent victim, was that there were far too many financial products in the market which could not be monitored properly (Business Line, 2010). According to a report by international consultancy firm Celent, India is set to become a huge hunting ground for wealth managers with the number of their potential clients and size of manageable wealth both expected to grow four-times through 2012. The wealth management market will have a target size of 42 million households by 2012, as against just about 13 million in 2007, noted the report titled "Overview of the Wealth Management Market in India."

"The wealth management sector is poised to witness tremendous growth. India's economic growth is making larger sections of the population prospective customers of wealth management providers," Celent said. The growth would be seen across all income-levels, but the lower-income segment would record the maximum growth in terms of volume, while high-net worth households would contribute the most in terms of wealth size, it noted. Celent has defined a household with a minimum income of $5,000 (Rs2 lakh) as the lowest end of the target market for wealth managers, while one with at least $30 million (Rs120 crore) of investible income has been put in the category of ultra-high net worth. "The market would see different products being launched for catering to different client segments," Celent's banking practice and author of the report Ravi Nawal said. "There is an increasing momentum towards structure in this previously chaotic domain. We should expect some very India specific innovations in the near future," Nawal added.

The market is currently dominated by unorganized players, whose share is 1.5 times that of the organized market. However, a structural change is taking place and organized players are drawing clients away from the unorganized players. Wealth management revenues are expected to contribute 32-37% of the total revenue of full-service financial institutions by 2012, Celent said. According to the report, mass-market (Rs2-10 lakh of disposable income) would be a key driver, accounting for 40% of the overall growth in the number of households. A majority of wealth managers, except niche players, would target the mass market because of its youth-dominance and this market would see more service providers entering the fray with a 'own them young' policy. The ultra-high net worth households with wealth in excess of $30 million would have a total population of 10,500 households by 2012, while the super high net worth households ($10-30 million) are expected to grow to 42,000. The population of high net worth households ($1-10 million) would grow to 3,20,000, while there would be 3,50,000 households in the super-affluent category (Rs50-400 lakh). Besides, 10 lakh new households would join mass-affluent category (Rs10-50 lakh), taking their population to 18 lakh by 2012. However, a vast majority of 39 million households, out of the total 42 million target market population in 2012, would belong to the mass market (Rs2-10 lakh). Private Banks, independent financial advisors and full service brokerages would serve the high net worth segment, while ultra high net worth households would be served by private banks and family offices.

REGULATORS PLAN NEW RULES TO MONITOR WEALTH MANAGERS

The Securities and Exchange Board of India, along with the Reserve Bank of India and the government of India, is working on new rules to regulate the flourishing wealth management business, a senior official from Sebi said on October 3, 2011 (The Business Standard, 2011b). The wealth management industry, estimated to be at $1 trillion, offers investors a range of financial products across different asset classes cutting across regulatory turfs. We need to integrate with regulators not just at the policy level but at the operating and surveillance level as well, said KN Vaidyanathan, executive director of the investment management department in the Securities and Exchange Board of India. Markets are far too advanced, the wealth managers of today straddle products which cut through banking, capital markets and insurance regulatory framework. We can't remain silent. We need to come together, better address how to regulate wealth managers. That process is in progress and we will come out with it soon, he said. Mr Vaidyanathan said from an investor's standpoint, the risk in the wealth management business is the relationship manager. His remuneration is not fully aligned with investor interest, he said. The institution guards its risk by getting certain documents from the customer, so the risk of the relationship manager is actually borne by the customer, he said. Adding that one of the challenges facing regulators is the cost of non-compliance as a lot of people want light-touch and tissue paper-thin regulation. People will respect when there is a fear of non-compliance. Till the time you establish that cost of non-compliance clearly in the system, you can't afford to be a light touch regulator. But there is a risk in this non-compliance and I must say it is tempting to confuse socialism with capitalism. Sebi will soon come out with the guidelines to allow foreign nationals to invest in domestic mutual funds.

RULES IN THE OFFING

A new set of rules are underway for the $1-trillion wealth management industry and the Reserve Bank of India (RBI) the Securities and Exchange Board of India (SEBI) may be made responsible for implementing these regulations and keeping a close watch on any violations. The government has pooled in various regulatory resources to frame a comprehensive rule-book for wealth management practices by seeking inputs from the RBI, SEBI and other financial sector regulators, a senior official said.

Given the size of the industry and therefore a higher risk of large-scale frauds or manipulations, the new rules could comprise of SEBI and RBI being given powers to impose strict penalties.

While the RBI and SEBI would be primarily responsible for compliance of the rules, help would be sought from other regulators, namely commodity regulator Forwards Markets Commission (FMC), the Insurance Regulatory and Development Authority (IRDA) and Pension Fund and Regulatory Development Authority (PFRDA), whenever needed, the official said.

The proposed regulations are currently being given final touches and would soon be announced by the government, he added. The new set of rules are being framed under the aegis of the Financial Stability and Development Council (FSDC), a high-level regulatory body chaired by the finance minister that was set up by the government in December 2010 in place of erstwhile high-level coordination committee on financial markets.

The FSDC has held two meetings so far-the first in December 2010, and the second, earlier this year-and the issue of the proposed wealth management regulations was discussed on both occasions. Besides, a sub-committee of FSDC held its first meeting last week, which was chaired by RBI governor D Subbarao and was attended by SEBI chairman UK Sinha, besides other regulators and finance ministry officials.

The sub-committee also discussed regulatory issues relating to wealth management and private banking businesses undertaken by banks.

In a latest meting in Mumbai on May 25, 2011, the sub-committee of the Financial Stability Development Council (FSDC) has agreed to strengthen the regulatory framework for wealth management companies.

The meeting of the high-level committee of financial regulators and top government officials discussed the need to regulate the wealth management segment better in the background of increasing instances of frauds being committed by wealth managers.

TEACHING NOTE ABOUT CITIBANK

Citibank

Citibank, a major international bank, is the consumer banking arm of financial services giant Citigroup. Citibank was founded in 1812 as the *City Bank of New York*, later *First National City Bank of New York*. Citibank has retail banking operations in more than 100 countries and territories around the world. More than half of its 1,400 offices are in the United States, mostly in New York City, Chicago, Los Angeles, the San Francisco Bay Area, Washington, D.C. and Miami. More recently, Citibank has expanded its operations in the Boston, Philadelphia, Houston, and Dallas metropolitan areas. In addition to the standard banking transactions, Citibank offers insurance, credit cards and investment products. Their online services division is among the most successful in the field, claiming about 15 million users.

Citibank India

Established in the beginning of 20th century in Kolkata, Citibank has a long history in India. Currently it is the largest foreign direct investor in financial service providers in India with a total capital commitment of approximately US$ 4 Billion in its onshore banking and financial services business and its principal and alternate investment programs. It operates 42 full-service Citibank branches in 30 cities and over 700 ATMs across the country. Citibank is an employer of choice to about 7,500 people.

Products and Services

Citi offers consumers and institutions a broad range of financial products and services, including consumer banking and credit, corporate and investment banking, securities brokerage, and wealth management. Citi's franchise in India includes businesses such as equity brokerage, equities distribution, private banking (Citi Private Bank) and alternate investments and private equity (CVCI).

Corporate Organizational Structure

Since March 31, 2008, Citibank is following a comprehensive organization structure to achieve greater client focus and connectivity, global product excellence, and clear accountability. The new organizational structure will allow Citi to focus its resources towards growth in emerging and developed markets and improve efficiencies throughout the company.

Citi has established a regional structure to bring decision-making closer to clients. It is empowering the leaders of the geographic regions with the authority to make decisions on the ground. These geographic regions are each led by a single chief executive officer. In addition, Citi has reorganized its consumer group into two global businesses-Consumer Banking and Global Cards. Institutional Clients Group and Global Wealth Management, which are already organized as global businesses. The four global businesses will allow Citi to deliver on product excellence in close partnership with the regions.

Business Summary

Citigroup Inc., a diversified financial services holding company, provides a range of financial products and services to consumers, corporations, governments, and institutions worldwide. The company operates through two segments: Citicorp and Citi Holdings. The Citicorp segment operates as a global bank for businesses and consumers with two primary businesses, Global Consumer Banking and Institutional Clients Group. The Global Consumer Banking business provides retail banking and Citi-branded cards in North America; Asia; Latin America; and Europe, the Middle East, and Africa (EMEA). The Institutional Clients Group business provides securities and banking services comprising investment banking and advisory services, lending, debt and equity sales and trading, institutional brokerage, derivative services, and private banking; and transaction services consisting of treasury and trade solutions, and securities and fund services. The Citi Holdings segment operates Brokerage and Asset Management, Local Consumer Lending, and Special Asset Pool businesses. The Brokerage and Asset Management business, through its Morgan Stanley Smith Barney joint venture, offers retail brokerage and asset management services. The Local Consumer Lending business provides residential mortgages, retail partner card loans, student loans, personal loans, commercial real estate, and other consumer loans and assets, as well as western European cards and retail banking services. The Special Asset Pool business consists of a portfolio of securities, loans, and other assets. The company has approximately 200 million customer accounts and operates in approximately 160 countries and jurisdictions. As of December 31, 2011, it had 1,016 retail bank branches in North America; 292 retail branches in EMEA; 2,221 retail branches in Latin America; and 671 retail branches in Asia. Citigroup Inc. was founded in 1812 and is based in New York, New York. See Tables 1 and 2 for Citi's balance sheet and income statement.

Technology

Citibank is redirecting much of its technology spending to outside IT organizations that provide commercially available, nonproprietary software applications for specific business processes and manage systems for data distribution, transaction processing, voice, and imaging services-freeing up the bank to focus on banking-not technology competencies.

Citiprivatebank.com is a private, restricted-access Internet based service. They use encryption technology to protect the transmission of account data to or from customers via citiprivatebank.com. For security reasons and to safeguard the security of data, access to citiprivatebank.com is limited to browsers that can support a minimum of 128-bit encryption technology. Nevertheless, because information about customers, their accounts, and relationships can be accessed through a public network, there can be no assurance that the account information will remain secure and customers accept the risk that unauthorized persons may view such information.

About Wealth Management

A host of wealth managers globally have found this to be a thriving business and made good inroads like, Citibank, UBS, HSBC, Credit Suisse, Merrill Lynch, J.P. Morgan, BNP Paribas, Deutsche Bank, Morgan Stanley, and others, globally offer their clients wealth management services. Private Banks like Pictet, Julius Baer, Coutts, Sal Oppenheim, Lombard Odier Darier Heutsch, BMO Harris, Unicredito etc., offer specialized and niche private banking offerings in their respective domestic

Table 1. Balance sheet

Period Ending	Dec 31, 2011	Sep 30, 2011	Jun 30, 2011	Mar 31, 2011
Assets				
Current Assets				
Cash and Cash Equivalents	460,334,000	478,933,000	467,923,000	452,565,000
Short Term Investments	-	-	-	327,257,000
Net Receivables	27,777,000	37,992,000	40,695,000	40,901,000
Inventory	-	-	-	-
Other Current Assets	-	-	-	-
Total Current Assets	-	-	-	-
Long Term Investments	1,202,274,000	1,212,481,000	1,245,061,000	923,678,000
Property Plant and Equipment	-	-	-	-
Goodwill	25,413,000	25,496,000	26,621,000	26,339,000
Intangible Assets	6,600,000	6,800,000	11,394,000	7,280,000
Accumulated Amortization	-	-	-	-
Other Assets	151,480,000	174,290,000	164,932,000	169,795,000
Deferred Long Term Asset Charges	-	-	-	-
Total Assets	1,873,878,000	1,935,992,000	1,956,626,000	1,947,815,000
Liabilities				
Current Liabilities				
Accounts Payable	56,696,000	56,093,000	57,245,000	50,394,000
Short/Current Long Term Debt	252,814,000	289,430,000	276,732,000	266,447,000
Other Current Liabilities	865,936,000	851,281,000	866,310,000	865,863,000
Total Current Liabilities	-	-	-	-
Long Term Debt	449,587,000	482,675,000	504,765,000	522,887,000
Other Liabilities	69,272,000	77,171,000	72,929,000	68,792,000
Deferred Long Term Liability Charges	-	-	-	-

continued on following page

Table 1. Continued

Period Ending	Dec 31, 2011	Sep 30, 2011	Jun 30, 2011	Mar 31, 2011
Minority Interest	1,767,000	1,970,000	2,281,000	2,356,000
Negative Goodwill	-	-	-	-
Total Liabilities	1,696,072,000	1,758,620,000	1,780,262,000	1,776,778,000
Stockholders' Equity				
Misc Stocks Options Warrants	-	-	-	-
Redeemable Preferred Stock	-	-	-	-
Preferred Stock	312,000	312,000	312,000	312,000
Common Stock	29,000	294,000	293,000	293,000
Retained Earnings	90,520,000	89,602,000	85,857,000	82,554,000
Treasury Stock	(1,071,000)	(1,089,000)	(1,087,000)	(878,000)
Capital Surplus	105,804,000	105,297,000	103,211,000	102,740,000
Other Stockholder Equity	(17,788,000)	(17,044,000)	(12,222,000)	(13,984,000)
Total Stockholder Equity	177,806,000	177,372,000	176,364,000	171,037,000
Net Tangible Assets	145,793,000	145,076,000	138,349,000	137,418,000

Currency in USD.
(Source: Yahoo Finance)

markets. Private Banking and Wealth Management typically constitute about 5 to 10% of the profitability of most of the banks offering wealth management solutions, obviously large part of the revenues and profitability for the specialized private banks are derived from the wealth management activity. The cross selling of solutions to wealth management clients also generate significant revenues for banks and hence wealth management is a value proposition for most banks."

Wealth Management Defined

- Professional service providers of *wealth management* view it as a new distinct orientation in the provisions of financial services to "super wealthy" clients having a $I million plus investments and even to mass effluents having investible wealth between $1,00,000 to $1 million.

Table 2. Income statement

Period Ending	Dec 31, 2011	Dec 31, 2010	Dec 31, 2009
Total Revenue	65,814,000	59,559,000	40,933,000
Cost of Revenue	-	-	-
Gross Profit	65,814,000	59,559,000	40,933,000
Operating Expenses			
Research Development	-	-	-
Selling General and Administrative	51,905,000	48,340,000	49,193,000
Non Recurring	16,694,000	14,456,000	15,414,000
Others	11,824,000	25,077,000	39,004,000
Total Operating Expenses	-	-	-
Operating Income or Loss	12,627,000	10,773,000	(9,795,000)
Income from Continuing Operations			
Total Other Income/ Expenses Net	1,997,000	2,411,000	1,996,000
Earnings Before Interest And Taxes	38,858,000	38,280,000	20,103,000
Interest Expense	24,234,000	25,096,000	27,902,000
Income Before Tax	14,624,000	13,184,000	(7,799,000)
Income Tax Expense	3,521,000	2,233,000	(6,733,000)
Minority Interest	(148,000)	(281,000)	(95,000)
Net Income From Continuing Ops	11,103,000	10,951,000	(1,066,000)
Non-Recurring Events			
Discontinued Operations	112,000	(68,000)	(445,000)
Extraordinary Items	-	-	-
Effect Of Accounting Changes	-	-	-
Other Items	-	-	-
Net Income	11,067,000	10,602,000	(1,606,000)
Preferred Stock And Other Adjustments	-	-	-
Net Income Applicable To Common Shares	11,067,000	10,602,000	(1,606,000)

Currency in USD.
(Source: Yahoo Finance)

- In simple words, wealth management can be defined as the complete blend of various asset classes, tax consultancy and risk management strategies molded into a single cast.
- A comprehensive service to optimize, protect and manage the financial well–being of an individual, family or corporation, both in the home country (on-shore) and at the large international financial centers (offshore).
- Wealth management normally addresses certain critical issues such as asset allocation, retirement planning, estate and trust planning, business succession planning as well as equity planning.

Primary Reasons for the Growth in HNWIs

- There are two primary reasons for the increase in the wealth of HNWIs and the number of HNWIs across the world:
  - ○ Firstly, it is because of a continuous high growth rate in the economies.
  - ○ Secondly, with increase in market capitalization, the existing HNWIs are benefited resulting in increased wealth.

Drivers of Wealth Management Business

- **Financial Liberalization and deregulation:** One of the primary reasons for the increasing attention towards wealth management is the economic liberalization that was initiated way back in the 1990s Over the past few decades, the trend towards deregulation and financial liberalization has contributed significantly to the wealth management industry's expansion. It has triggered considerable improvements in the quality and variety of services being offered.
- **Wealth Accumulation:** In many economies, a notable shift is taking place away from labor-intensive production to more capital-intensive activity. Based on this development, a clear secular trend towards wealth accumulation is likely to continue over the next decade, with wealth expected to grow faster than GDP in most developed countries.
- **Equtisitation:** The developments over the past ten years indicate that global equity markets will continue to grow. Institutional and individual market participants will tend to invest a greater share of their assets into equity and related products and the corporate sector will increasingly rely on equity financing.
- **Retirement Provisioning:** In coming decades, most developed countries will be confronted with significant demographic shifts. Thus, pension reform

271

is on the agenda of many governments across the world. The strong reliance in Continental Europe and Japan on unfunded schemes will make reform increasingly inevitable.

- **Corporate Restructuring:** Despite the drastic market setbacks experienced in the corporate finance sector over the last few years, some long-term secular trends pointing towards an ongoing demand for advice on corporate restructuring are visible. Liberalization of trade and technological progress will increase global competition for corporations, pressuring them to restructure and consolidate their activities and structures.
- Others
  - Knowledge-based economy
  - Employee stock option plans
  - Government regulations
- There are 70,000 HNWIs in India according to the 2005 world wealth report published by Merrill lynch and Capgemini.
- The report considers HNWIs as those individuals who have financial assets of at least US$1 mn, excluding their primary residence.

Understanding Wealth Management

- The wealth management industry in India is on a remarkable growth path.
- It is the integration of asset, debt, tax, and risk management strategies into one seamless financial solution.
- Ability to set a trend and provide investment advice to their clients.
- Investment areas in India usually include equities, derivative instruments, mutual funds, bonds and of late, commodities.
- The suite of wealth management products is expanding and includes today art, real estate and jewellery advisory services.
- Wealth management and financial planning are useful from a cost-benefit perspective of the financial institutions.
- Involves more sophisticated risk management strategies.
- Possibly a wider variety of investment options such as hedge funds.

Need for Wealth Management

- Inclination to maximize the investment returns
- Planning for retirement
- Saving for children's education
- Arranging enough liquidity to buy a house

- Housing finance, mortgages
- Financial planning for unmarried couples
- Solutions for asset management after the death
- Legal management of will and health care planning

Advantages of Wealth Management

- It is better way to manage the wealth.
- Investors need not to spend their valuable time.
- Investors do not have to endure complicated transactions and a lot of paperwork.
- It is the most efficient and profitable use of one's resources (through trust).
- It provides proper planning of estate.
- It can provide a strategy for your financial affairs.
- It enables you to evaluate where you are now (current situation), where you want to get to (identifying future goals) financially in the future and how you can achieve your goals (provides direction).
- The HNWIs face complexity and need tailored solutions to manage their wealth by a specialist.
- Increase in foreign investments.
- Understanding the local market.
- Building for sound financial planning through experience.
- Changing requirement of the client.
- Bringing trends and standards of living.
- Revaluation and restructuring the investments.

The Indian Experience

- HNIs has boosted the demand for the professional wealth managers.
- The array of wealth management products has even extended towards art & craft, real estate and jewellery.
- The estimated market size of wealth management in India is approximately around Rs. 20,000 crores to Rs. 2,00,000 crores.
- The minimum level of wealth that one need to have in order to avail the wealth management services is much lower with the average size of the client's corpus around Rs.1.5 crores.
- In Asia, and particularly in India, the ratio of the self-managed to the professionally managed wealth is much higher when compared to the US and other developed countries.

- The critical wealth level is a turning point in the individual's life where he or she must focus more on wealth management i.e. Preserving wealth than on accumulating wealth or financial planning.
- Wealth management services typically include more risk management strategies for individuals with higher net worth.
- Wealth is relative to the individual's standard of living, retirement goals and earnings.
- Every individual should be cognizant of their critical wealth level and focus on wealth management more beyond a critical point.

Recent Trends in Wealth Management

- The survey of wealth management by Citigroup private bank has revealed the following trends in wealth management.
- The abundance of financial news, data and analysis and the dramatic growth of alternative investment opportunities have increased the financial sophistication of ultra affluent individuals around the world giving them an edge over important aspects of modern investment management and alternative asset classes.
- Ultra affluent investors are sought after by all sorts of wealth advisors from private banks and investment banks to alternate asset firms. Given the proliferation of information and financial news the investors does not add sufficient value to the advice from the financial manager on access to investment products.
- The survey includes most affluent groups from five regions; The US, Latin America, Europe, the middle east and Asia pacific.

Ethical Issues

- An advisor should be a symbol of integrity.
- The advisor's opinion and advice should be honest.
- Most of the advisors have a professional edge and they work in tandem with the standards of their respective institutes.
- Hence, a wealth manager has to be very careful when guiding an investor.

Position of India in Wealth Management

In the annual survey done by Cap Gemini, SA and Merrill Lynch it was found that ranks of millionaires grew 6% in the previous year, because the number of richer people grew in India & China where India is competing China. India & China posted the biggest gain in millionaires advancing by 23% & 20% respectively.

When we are watching the world wide increase in number of millionaires the facts collected by Cap Gemini, S.A. and Merrill Lynch survey report. India has 23% growth in the last year. The biggest Asian economy China stands on second position with 20%, west Asia 16%, United States 4% and United Kingdom (UK) 2%.

Limitations of Wealth Management

WM Reduces the Scope of Management

The term wealth management is only related with the higher level means rich people and is not having any plans and provisions for poor and lower and middle level of society.

Chances of Fraud

Another demerit or limitation of the concept is that it does not reflect the actual position. The customer doesn't know about the things going on with using his wealth and there may be chances of forgery and fraud with customers.

Actual Picture vs Inflation

The actual position of market may not be known to the investor because every thing is done by some professionals. There may be chance that the customers are in risk but they are showing the false return and vice-versa.

REFERENCES

Angelbroking. (2013). Retrieved from angelbroking.com.

Anita. (2010). Scam hits citibank india; fraud worth 400 crore. *One India.* Retrieved from http://news.oneindia.in.

Bhatnagar, S., & Bhalla, M. (2010). Citibank fraud: Rs 400 cr allegedly siphoned off. *India Times.* Retrieved from http://articles.economictimes.indiatimes.com

Business Line. (2010). *Why Citi can never sleep.* Retrieved from http://www.the-hindubusinessline.in/2010/12/31/stories/2010123150230600.htm.

Citibank. (2013). Retrieved from http://www.online.citibank.co.in/.

Ernst & Young. (2011). *Wealth-management-study-investing-in-the-future.* Retrieved from http://www.ey.com

Fitch. (2011). Fraud may impact Citi's wealth management biz, but not short-term rating. *Hindu Business Line.* Retrieved from http://www.thehindubusinessline.in

Ghosh, J., & Lele, A. (2010). Citi scam puts wealth managers under lens. *The Business Standard.* Retrieved from http://www.business-standard.com.

Gopakumar, G., & Shukla, T. (2011). Citi fraud highlights regulatory gap in wealth MGMT service. *Money Control.* Retrieved from http://www.moneycontrol.com.

IBTimes Staff Reporter. (2010). India's citibank fraud case: Gurgaon police arrest key suspect shiv raj puri. *International Business Times.* Retrieved from http://www.ibtimes.com/articles/96175/20101230/india-s-citibank-fraud-case-gurgaon-police-arrest-key-suspect-shiv-raj-puri.htm#ixzz1HWv6BVeG.

Investopedia. (2013). *High net worth individual-HNWI.* Retrieved from http://www.investopedia.com.

Kulkarni, P. (2011). RBI seeks wealth management details post citibank scam. *India Times.* Retrieved from http://articles.economictimes.indiatimes.com.

NDTV Profit. (2013a). Retrieved from http://profit.ndtv.com/news/show/rs-400-crore-fraud-uncovered-at-citibank-s-gurgaon-branch-132352?cp.

NDTV Profit. (2013b). Retrieved from http://profit.ndtv.com/news/show/probe-into-citibank-fraud-to-complete-soon-govt-143568?cp.

Parekh. (2011). Lack of wealth MGMT guidelines caused citibank fraud. *Press Trust of India.* Retrieved from http://www.business-standard.com.

PTI. (2011) Citi fraudster took exposure of Rs 1.13 lakh cr on nifty:sebi. *One India.* Retrieved from http://news.oneindia.in

Reporter, B. S. (2011, March 06). Wealth management under FSDC radar. Retrieved from http://www.business-standard.com

SmartInvestor. In. (2010). *Rs 400 cr fraud uncovered at citibank's gurgaon branch.* Retrieved from http://smartinvestor.in/market/story-54488-storydet-Rs_400_cr_fraud_uncovered_at_Citibanks_Gurgaon_branch.htm.

Swagata Gupta And John Satish Kumar. (2011, January 07). Indian Regulators Investigating Citi Case. Retrieved from http://online.wsj.com

The Business Standard. (2011a). E-paper dated 6th March 2011. Retrieved from http://www.business-standard.com/todays-paper.

The Business Standard. (2011b). E-paper dated 3rd December-2011. Retrieved from http://www.business-standard.com/todays-paper.

Wikipedia. (2013a). *High-net-worth individual.* Retrieved from http://en.wikipedia.org.

Wikipedia. (2013b). *Wealth management.* Retrieved from http://en.wikipedia.org.

Chapter 22

Triumph Charter School Service Provider

Verneshia (Necia) Boone
University of Phoenix, USA

EXECUTIVE SUMMARY

Charter schools are perhaps known to many people as community schools that are publicly funded. Educators and policy makers of the United States consider public schools in which tuition for primary and secondary students is free. A few community leaders and public officials have disclosed that selected charter school providers have too much flexibility in how they operate the schools. Perhaps their beliefs are such because most of the charter or community schools are operated under a contract in partnership with a sponsoring entity (Center for Education, 2008). According to educators and political leaders located in the Midwest region of the United States, charter schools were designed to address the current state of educational programs and to introduce an alternative model to traditional public education for economically disadvantaged students. For the last decade, research has shown that the goals and objectives of charter schools and charter school providers and leaders have been a contentious subject matter for United States educators and policy makers (Center for Education, 2008). The reason is perhaps linked to personal beliefs that charter school providers or leaders drain funding from local public school districts and do not offer disadvantaged students a better education. The case study provides an overview about Duke and Duchess Technology Centers as well as Triumph Management Company and their, products and services, competition, management structure, leadership styles, and recent challenges. Questions appear at the end of the case study for students to discuss and debate.

DOI: 10.4018/978-1-4666-4357-4.ch022

Copyright ©2014, IGI Global. Copying or distributing in print or electronic forms without written permission of IGI Global is prohibited.

THE EVOLUTION: TRIUMPH CHARTER SCHOOL SERVICE PROVIDER

A charter may be considered as a written agreement that empowers local leaders of school districts, the State Department of Education, parents and other authorized sponsors to govern areas such as curriculum standards, performance measures, governance and financing (State Department of Education, 2010). According to Center for Education (2008), Charters schools in the United States have been designed to address the current state of education and to introduce an alternative model to traditional public education for economically disadvantaged students in the United States.

In the 21st century, the purpose of charter schools and charter school providers has been a contentious subject matter for United States educators and policy makers. The reason is perhaps linked to their beliefs that charter school providers or leaders drain funding from local public school districts and do not offer students a better education. According to data released by the State Department of Education (2010), charter schools are independent public schools that provide an alternative learning experience based on various state laws. The purpose of this case study is to provide a historical overview about The Duke and Duchess Training Centers as well as Triumph Management Company. Triumph is owned by Veronica Walton. Triumph is the service providers responsible for the complete operations of Duke and Duchess Training Centers. This case study will provide a historical overview including information about Triumph Management Company, the training centers, products/services, organizational structure, competition, current issues and challenges.

HISTORY

The popularity of charter schools commenced in the 1990s and are often started by public school teachers, concerned parents, or local activists and sponsored by traditional school districts, non-profit agencies, local universities, and government entities. In a survey of United States charter schools, 59% of the charter school leaders reported that they had a waiting list, averaging 198 students (Center for Education, 2008). The curriculum for each charter school may vary. Some schools are designed to offer general education courses whereas others schools specialize in specific subject matters (e.g. technology, math, science). A few of the community school leaders have not implemented specialized programs to addresss the needs of the students. They have implemented computers as teachers allowing teachers to function as personal tutors. For example, Veronica Walton who is the owner of Triumph Management Company, stated that, "As we journey through the 21st

century, we have discovered that the further you go down the academic achievement continuum, the more effective the computer is as teacher." Regardless of the school curriculum, students are required to complete and pass a state-mandated exam (Ibid, 2008).

CHARTER SCHOOL OWNERSHIP AND SERVICES

The comprehensive and rigorous application process to gain specific approval to open a charter school can be time consuming. Specific programs exist to guide applicants through the application and grant processes for the authorization of their charter. The grant process pertains only to applicants interested in government or private funding to move the school in the right direction.

Two ownership models exist today. An individual owner(s) is one model. The model is designed to allow experienced school administrators, teachers, community leaders, or political leaders to have complete ownership and management responsibilities of a school(s). The second model is an organization. This model is designed to allow an offsite administrative team to manage the back-office responsibilities of the school, while skilled teachers and support staff manage the students and the schools. For either model, a designated person is responsible for the completion of a comprehensive and rigorous application process. Once the application is completed, it is submitted to the Board of Trustees of a local sponsor (e.g. a university, an educational institution, or a 501C [3] non-profit agency). Once a partnership is established with the local sponsor, and the application process is approved, charter school owners are eligible to receive state and federal funding. The designated owners have the authorization to enroll students while adhering to strict local, state, and federal guidelines. The sponsor also requires the charter school founders, to establish a school board comprised of at least five members, administrator/principal, teachers, and staff.

CASE STUDY

Ten years ago, Ms. Veronica Walton of Columbus, Ohio observed that employees who worked for her father lacked basic math and technology skills. She decided to open a technology center in the lower level of her father's company. The technology school was very successful. Within 10 years she started an company called The Triumph Management Company and was operating more than 21 community technology schools in two states under the auspices of two separate educational ventures. The training centers are tuition-free and are open to students in grades K-8 throughout the state of Ohio. The technology centers are alternative education charter schools serving students between the ages of 16 and 21. This program is designed for students who have dropped out, or who may be at risk for dropping out, a traditional high school program. Veronica also opened a web-based school that served students in grades K-12. The home-based distance learning model is designed to accommodate any student. The Duke and Duchess Technology Centers are entirely funded with state and federal tax dollars through the Ohio Board of Education based on student population. Students who complete the 12th grade and pass the graduate tests will receive a high school diploma, not a Graduate Equivalency Diploma (GED).

TRIUMPH MANAGEMENT STRUCTURE

Veronica and her staff are state certified and professional educators and leaders. The executive staff of the Triumph Management Company is located in Columbus, Ohio. The various Duke and Duchess Technology Centers are managed by state certified principals who report to the executive staff members of Triumph Management Company. Each school is staffed by certified educators, counselors, and technicians whom deliver the alternative learning programs to disadvantaged students.

The leaders have established a rapport with their public authorities who have authorized and sponsored each of Veronica's K-12 school charters. The public authorities or sponsors are charged with monitoring the performance of the schools, the teachers and the students. The sponsors also have the authority to close a school or center if the staff at Duke and Duchess fails to produce satisfactory results.

TRIUMPH COMPANY LEADERS

In year 2013, Sonja Roy, a reporter, of The Leaders Newspaper published an article about Triumph Management Company. Roy stated that Veronica's first technology center was founded in 2003 and The Triumph Management Company is headquartered in Columbus, Ohio. The article detailed that the management company operates in Dayton and Cincinnati, Ohio. The company leaders provide services that include general operations management, human resources, financial reporting, board relations, facilities acquisition, development and management, and student-data reporting to state education authorities. The executive team builds and develops education programs that include technology and leadership. The management company also offers tuition-free home-based distance learning and alternative education programs for traditional students.

Roy also stated that Veronica's team appears to demonstrate the core principles of effective management and consistently hire diverse team of qualified individuals to remain competitive and succeed in the industry. In year 2010, the executive team was comprised of the following individuals:

- **Marlon Brandon:** Chief Executive Officer-25 years of experience
- **Mercedes Scott:** Chief Financial Officer–15 years of experience
- **Lena Allen:** Vice President of Technology Centers–20 years of experience
- **Ronald Walton:** Vice President of Web-based Programs–10 years of experience
- **Sougata Mukherjee:** Chief Information Officer–10 years of experience
- **William Fox:** Executive Director of Implementation Division–22 years of experience and a family member
- **Brenda Nizer:** Executive Director of Business Development & Community Engagement-5 years of experience and a political friend

SOCIAL RESPONSIBILITIES

Dwayne Lamont, the president of a local *Charter Schools Concerned Parents Organization*, read and vehemently responded to the article. He stated that the owner of the management company has become very rich operating the technology centers for a profit. Lamont declared that the disadvantaged students who attend the schools are (a) being educated in old and substandard buildings, (b) using outdated technology and other related equipment, and (c) lacking the critical skills to enroll into a local college or to obtain entry-level positions in their specific educational field. Lamont also disclosed that Veronica, and her husband, Earnest make limited contributions to local community events and very seldom attend local community functions. In other words, they are not a socially responsible company. Lamont advocated that the couple is a major Republican political contributor because they have ties to the current legislature who has dealt with the charter school issues in recent years that worked in their favor. In 2000, for example, the couple gave a combined contribution of $532,300 to state candidates and Republican organizations, including $600,000 to the Ohio Republican Party. The couple continues to make large contributions today. Lamont also shared that approximately $3.6 million in political campaign contributions have been made by some of the corporate leaders involved with the Triumph Management Company.

LEADERSHIP STYLES OF PRINCIPALS, TEACHERS, AND STAFF

Bass (1981) stated that many types of leadership styles have been observed and researched and the most common styles are Autocratic, Aarticipative, Laissez Faire, and Transactional leadership styles. According to the principals and teachers at the Duke and Duchess Technology Centers, the Transactional leadership style is the most common style used because the manner and approach is necessary in providing direction and discipline The reason is that disadvantaged children need some form of motivation, personal assistance, and financial incentives to progress towards achieving the required goals (e.g. graduation or a job). Although most of the students expect the transactional and participatory leadership approaches, Bass believes there are advantages and disadvantages that exist within each leadership style (Ibid, 1981). Veronica supports the recommended approach and also stated that any leadership style can be applied if necessary to get the work done collectively.

For example, Veronica has directed the principals and teachers of Duke and Duchess Technology Centers to implement different learning services. The services are displayed on the monitors located throughout the schools. The teachers and counselors also promote the services using transactional and transformational leadership styles to enhance the educational programs, recognizing that services to address real-world barriers to learning resulted in positive behavioral changes and a the learning environment.

Another example, parents are encouraged to take an active role in their child's education, however, their involvement is limited. With the high absentee rate of parents at the elementary, secondary, and high school levels, unique relationships are developed with the students to promote positive behaviors necessary for academic achievement and employability skills. The school leaders and staff develop and maintain value systems that reward outstanding performance while following corporate and state guidelines. Social workers are onsite at the high schools to provide consultative and referral services. The executive team also employs security staff and devices to maintain a safe learning environment in a few schools located in the inner city in which the student population can cross ethnic, racial, gang, and geographic boundaries. To champion the students' academic future, free breakfast and lunch programs are available to elementary and high schools.

Marlon, the CEO with more than 25 years of experience in the field joined the organization because he supported Veronica's vision and leadership beliefs. In year 2012, Marlon revealed that the academic data highlights the challenges faced by some of our schools and leaders requiring a collective leadership approach. He also shared that everyone may need to strengthen their knowledge and expand their focus concerning today's disadvantaged students aligning educational goals using smart technologies with specific career outcomes for each student.

Sougata has more than ten years of technology experience and he shared that, "We are aware of the challenges and we are proud of our work implementing and using technology as a tool to educate. We are especially pleased with our teachers' and administrators' performance levels as they are committed to the academic progress of the students who are enrolled in the schools."

DESCRIPTION OF TRAINING CENTERS

The training centers owned by Veronica were acquired as start-up schools or they were converted from traditional schools into state-of-the-art technology centers. The legal status of either the start-up schools or the converted schools is an authorized institution where the professional staff is dedicated to helping students make their vision a reality. The executive team has implemented innovating tools and strategies offering potential solutions to students most challenging circumstances.

SCHOOL DESCRIPTIONS

1. The Duke and Duchess Online Technology Center: Tuition-free, K-12, program in which students' courses are available online. This is a distance-learning charter public schools located in Ohio, Colorado, and Pennsylvania.
2. The Duke and Duchess Elementary Technology Center: Tuition-free, K-8, traditional learning program. This is a community-based charter public school available to students ages 5 to 15 who are located in Ohio.
3. The Duke and Duchess Adult Technology Centers: Alternative charter school program serving students between the ages of 16 and 22. The program is designed for students who have dropped out, or who may be at risk for dropping out, from a traditional high school program.

COMPANY ISSUES AND LOCAL COMPETITION

Of the many school choice options available to parents and guardians of disadvantaged students, charter schools appear to be the most common choice in the 21st century. However, a compilation of newspaper articles and web blogs about Veronica and her technology centers may have community leaders and parents questioning the company's instability and practices. In December 2010, additional articles were published about Triumph Technology Centers. As the negative articles continue to circulate in Columbus, Veronica is scrutinized by local competitors, political leaders, and other stakeholders regarding the poor performance of the disadvantaged students enrolled in the Duke and Duchess Technology Centers.

Amidst the negative publicity, two community-based schools have emerged and they are being acknowledged as the high-performing tuition-free centers presenting additional challenges for the leaders of The Triumph Management Company as they implement strategies to improve their reputation. The two schools are Jersey Schools and Entrepreneurship School (E Prep).

JERSEY CHARTER SCHOOLS

Jersey Charter Schools are managed by a not-for-profit charter management organization similar to The Triumph Management Company. The schools are located in Columbus, Ohio. The owner operates the schools on the city's north side. Founded in 1999, the tuition-free college preparatory high school also prepares students for 21st century careers. According to data on the website, 95 percent of its students graduate from high school and 100 percent of those students are accepted to college.

ENTREPRENEURSHIP SCHOOL

Entrepreneurship School is another high-tech and high-performing Columbus charter school. The staff is dedicated to providing a premier educational experience to their students. The organization places emphasis on individual educational growth, recognizing above-average test scores, high graduation rates, and students' acceptance to colleges or universities.

REAL CHALLENGES

Veronica's career as an advocate for education reform took root in the late 90's. The Duke and Duchess Technology Centers are registered as a 501(c) (3) tax-exempt firm. Since the Triumph Management Company is a for-profit organization providing technology education and operational management services to the Duke and Duchess Technology Centers, the organization has been scrutinized by local competitors, political leaders, and other stakeholders. For example, Yolanda Zellner, a spokeswoman for Ohio Teachers Advocacy Group has asked the Internal Revenue Service to examine the for-profit status of charter schools managed by Veronica.

Yolanda disclosed in year 2008 that the Columbus-based management company collected approximately $250 million to run charter schools in Ohio for more than 10,000 students.

Recent articles and Internet blogs published by several reporters regarding the Duke and Duchess school board members and the community leaders in which they have voiced concerns about recent layoffs and school closings in Columbus. The community leaders are suggesting a number of the Duke and Duchess Technology Centers in Ohio are failing to meet the academic requirements established by State of Ohio-Department of Education. The concerned leaders stated that the students enrolled in the centers know how to operate the computers, but they do not have the latest software, equipment, and training to compete with students enrolled in traditional schools. Many of the students are unable to pass the OAA and OGT state mandated tests. According to the board members, 75% of the schools are failing and only 40% of the students are passing the OGT state mandated tests.

ORGANIZATIONAL CONCERNS: FINANCIAL DISCLOSURE, LAWSUIT

Financial disclosure has been an ongoing discussion with The Triumph Management Company and several governing school board members. A group of Columbus and Cincinnati board members are in open rebellion against the for-profit management company. The Columbus and Cincinnati school board members filed a lawsuit alleging that a 2006 state law passed by majority-party Republican party is unconstitutional and gives the for-profit company unlimited authority. According to Yolanda, at the center of the lawsuit is The Duke and Duchess Management Company, the for-profit company whose five-year contract to run the charter schools in Columbus and Cincinnati Ohio expired on June 30, 2011. Although the schools are publicly funded, they are privately operated. In the case of Triumph Management Company, 90 percent of the state funding flows directly to the management company.

In the lawsuit filed, the school boards argued the law is unconstitutional because it gives too much power to Triumph Management Company; which is funded entirely with state and federal tax dollars through the Ohio Board of Education. The contract requires the schools to pay 90% of the state and 100% of federal funds to Triumph Management Company. The remaining dollars are split between the schools (5.5%) and the sponsors (4.5%). The suit charges that the owner of The Triumph Management Company lobbied to fire any school board who tried to sever ties with them.

The plaintiffs' contracts with The Triumph Management Company, states that the executive board members of Duke and Duchess Training Center receives about 90 percent of the public money allocated for the school, according to the suit. Although contracts expired on June 30, 2011, the school boards wanted several changes that would give them a better accounting of how the owner spends taxpayer dollars.

The lawsuit also alleges that Triumph Management Company failed to account for how grant money has been spent or to prepare quarterly un-audited financial disclosures required by the contract. It also alleges that the defendants, Triumph Management Company and its subsidiaries failed to promote programs that resulted in the academic success of each school's students, ultimately jeopardizing the charters of the plaintiff schools. The Ohio Department of Education concluded that four of the Veronica's schools where in academic emergency, the equivalent of an F grade on the last state report card. Several were in academic watch, a D grade. A few received a grade of C, continuous improvement. None of the schools received a grade of A or A+, Excellent.

The future of The Duke and Duchess Technology Centers may be questionable depending on whom you ask. Overall, Veronica and her team continue to address the unique needs of disadvantaged students employing alternative technology learning programs. Their hard work can be accurately reflected in the students who attend and graduate from the schools.

The case study was prepared only as a basis for classroom discussions. Not for reproduction or distribution without the written permission of the author.

REFERENCES

Annual Survey of America's Charter Schools. (2008). Center for Education Reform. Retrieved from http://www.edreform.com/Archive/?Annual_Survey_of_Americas_Charter_Schools_2008.

Bass, B. M. (1981). *Stogdill's handbook of leadership*. New York: Free Press.

Chapter 23
Maximizing Employee On–Boarding:
A Study in a Pharmaceutical Company

Shalini Kalia
Institute of Management Technology (Ghaziabad), India

Neha Mittal
Stryker Global Technology Center Pvt Ltd., India

Rohit Arora
Jubilant Life Sciences Ltd., India

EXECUTIVE SUMMARY

A pharmaceutical company faced with the challenge of high attrition of new hires, took the initiative of revamping its employee on-boarding program. The gaps in the existing processes were identified by the HR team and customized solutions were implemented ranging from operational to strategic solutions.

ORGANIZATION BACKGROUND

SNR Group of Companies is a leading pharmaceutical company based out of India. The Company provides pharmaceutical products and services across the value chain serving its customers globally with its ground presence in India, North America, Europe and China. The company has 7 manufacturing units and R&D units across PAN India with about 5000+ employees. The company has been growing at an increased rate of over 10% every year across the globe.

DOI: 10.4018/978-1-4666-4357-4.ch023

Copyright ©2014, IGI Global. Copying or distributing in print or electronic forms without written permission of IGI Global is prohibited.

Challenges Faced by SNR Group of Companies

The scope of this study extends to the Pharma Group in India. The organization was facing critical issues related to high attrition, low engagement and non standard-ization of HR processes including on-boarding. Some of the key challenges faced by the organization particularly with respect to new hires are summarized below:

1. **High Attrition in The First Year of Joining:** On analyzing the attrition data of executives from April 2007 to October 2009 it was observed that of all the employees who left in this duration, 35% left within 3-6 months of joining and 60% left within 6-12 months of joining. The same applied for executives across junior, middle and senior levels. The reasons though could be manifold; the primary ones were identified as poor on-boarding experience and lack of role clarity.

2. **Lower Engagement Level for <1 Year Tenure Employees:** The Gallup en-gagement score for executives with less than 1 year tenure also declined from 40th percentile in 2008 (N=1510) to 30th percentile in 2010 (N=1000). The scores also saw decline in role clarity, managerial effectiveness and alignment to the overall mission/purpose of the company.

3. **New Hire Survey:** In view of the above facts, a new hire survey was conducted in October 2009 with all new hires who had joined six months prior to the survey so as to further validate the issue. Out of 100 eligible employees, 40% completed the survey. New Hire Survey indicated that 35% of new hires were not satisfied with the current on-boarding process. 40% of new hires expressed that their induction was not scheduled in advance while 25% indicated that they did not get complete information on compensation, benefits and other important policies during induction (*Refer Appendix 1 for questionnaire*). Some of the other key issues voiced by the new hires were:
    a. Inadequate information prior to joining
    b. Poor Day 1 Experience – Resource Provisioning (ID creation, Access Cards, Workstation, Computer)
    c. Inadequate/Delayed induction
    d. Delay in getting appointment letters
    e. Inadequate cross functional orientation
    f. Lack of Interaction opportunities with leadership team including Head of Businesses/Function Heads/Site Head

4. **Concerns Voiced by HR and Hiring Managers:** *Somewhat similar con-cerns were voiced* by the HR–Talent Acquisition team and Hiring Managers across sites during discussion with them. 20 Hiring Managers and 10 HR

Talent Acquisition Managers were interviewed on the existing process and the improvements required in on-boarding process. Major concerns voiced by HR- Talent Acquisition team were:

a.   Resource Provisioning (ID creation, Access Cards, Workstation, Computer)
b.   Delay in getting appointment letters from Head Office (HO)
c.   Fixing up manager's accountability for on-boarding a new hire in the department

5. **Top Concerns Voiced by Hiring Managers**

a.   Need for structured and standard induction with information on the Group, businesses, company structure.
b.   Safety, GMP, SOP training should be part of induction for manufacturing units and R&D.
c.   Information about company policies to be more structured.

LITERATURE REVIEW

Research indicates that effective on-boarding can motivate new employees, enhance productivity, reduce new hire turn over and improve new hire performance. As highlighted in the article 'Implementing and Managing On-boarding Programs', an organization's bottom line can be improved by effective on boarding as this leads to 11% improvement in employee Performance; reduces new hire turnover by over 50%; can increase an employee's discretionary effort in excess of 20% and increases employee retention. It has been found that a strongly engaged employee is 87% less likely to leave a company within the next 12 months.

SOLUTIONS AND RECOMMENDATIONS

The key research question addressed in this case study is *'How to revamp the existing on-boarding process in SNR Group of Companies to maximize its effectiveness?'* A detailed project plan of over one and a half years was designed under the supervision of Senior Manager, HR to address the key research question. The project plan designed for the task is highlighted in Table 1 followed by the detailed description.

Table 1. Project plan

	Focus Area	Sub-Activities	Timelines
Phase 1	Process Streamlining with finalization of accountabilities, timelines and Service Level Agreements (SLAs) with stakeholders	1. Study the existing practice to map the As-is Process through meetings with HR Single Point of Contact (SPOCs) at each location and relooking the new hire survey findings	April 2010
		2. Benchmark on-boarding practices with external and internal companies/best practices	

		3. Make recommendation w.r.t. gaps identified to reach the 'Desired State'
		    a. On-boarding checklist
		    b. Resource Provisioning and ID creation
		    c. Induction
		    d. Department Orientation
		    e. Appointment Letters	

Phase 2	Process Enhancements	1. Pre-Hire Communication -On-boarding Portal Design	August -December 2010
		2. On-line Joining Forms	December 2010- April 2011
		3. e-Induction	June 2010 – October 2011
		4. Redesign of Employee Kit	January- October 2011
		5. Launch and Communication	October 2011
Phase 3	Way Forward	1. Integration of online forms with HRIS	December 2011 onwards
		2. Measure effectiveness through HDW Online Feedback Mechanism on process maturity	December 2011 onwards

Phase 1: Process Streamlining with Finalization of Accountabilities, Timelines, and Service Level Agreements (SLAs) with Stakeholders

1. **Study the Existing Practices:** The existing process of on-boarding was mapped by referring to the process documents and by interviewing 10 HR-Talent Acquisition Managers across all locations. The discussions were held primarily on the following aspects:
    a. Existing on-boarding process (Location specific activities included in the on-boarding process, the timelines and accountabilities).
    b. Best practices in the current system.
    c. Challenges involved in the system.

2. **Benchmark On-Boarding Best Practices:** The companies that were included for external benchmarking on-boarding best practices are Dell Inc; Tata Steel Ltd; Genpact Ltd; FreeScale Semiconductor Inc; The Dow Chemical Company; Tech Mahindra Ltd; Dr. Reddy's Laboratories Ltd; Gillette India Ltd; General Motors Company; Novell Inc; Philips Electronics India Ltd; Hewlett Packard Company; American Express Corporation and Daimler AG (*Refer Appendix 2 for the best practices studied in these companies*).

3. **Make Recommendations W.R.T. Gaps Identified to Reach the 'Desired State':** After studying the existing process in the organization and analyzing the best practices in other companies, the following action plans were implemented using STAR (Situation, Task, Action and Result) format pertaining to the concern areas keeping in view the feasibility of implementation at locations:

   a. **On-boarding Checklist:** After studying the 'As-is' process and some of the industry best practices, the 'To-be' process was mapped in terms of the activities to be completed from acceptance of offer till the first 12 months of joining along with timelines and responsibility. This checklist was shared with all HR teams and agreed upon.

   b. **Resource Provisioning on Day 1 and Id Creation:** One of the major pain areas of the new hires and also of the talent acquisition team in HR was the poor Day 1 experience with respect to inadequate availability of working equipments- primarily desktop/laptop and intranet, Human Resource Information System (HRIS) Ids and e-mail Ids. To overcome this challenge, an SLA with the IT team was prepared under which it was agreed that IT will work on hiring projections for next 3 months circulated by HR every month to procure the machines. This will take care of the time being spent on approvals for procurement. It was henceforth agreed that the new employee should get the desktop/laptop on Day 1 and his/her e-mail and other Ids must be created within four hours of generating the employee code.

   c. **Induction:** Timeliness and quality of induction was a major concern of new employees. The induction was delayed till 3 months of joining and also the information communicated across locations in the induction with respect to policies, company, practices etc was not standardized. The new employees were not aware of the bigger group that they were part of. The new hires either did not have detailed cross functional orientation or it was delayed and inadequate. The following action plan was followed to resolve these induction issues:

      i. It was mandated that all joinings take place on Monday as this would help in planning the induction better and for a group of people rather than duplicating it for one-two people joining on daily basis.

ii. The HR Single Point of Contact (SPOC) at each location was made responsible to conduct induction of the new hires on Day 1 in a classroom session where they would share information on company, policies, practices and some standard information about the site specific businesses. Facility tour, mandatory site specific training like SOP, Fire and Safety were also made part of this induction. To maintain standardization of information, the induction presentation was shared by corporate HR team at all locations.

iii. Location HR teams decided to have the cross functional orientation during the first week of joining itself where-in each business/function head would address the new hires about their respective areas. This would help new hires to meet and get introduced to different cross functional heads for better functioning. For corporate office and R&D centres, it was decided to conduct the induction program at the interval of once in 2 months instead of earlier practice of quarterly induction so as to overcome delay in induction. To reduce the time taken in conducting the induction, an e-induction module was proposed to be designed with an objective that this platform would not only help in inducting employees faster but also help in communicating standard information about the company. The e-induction module also aimed to familiarize the employees with the larger group and its subsidiaries within first 2 days of joining which further helps in employer branding. However, this e-induction was not meant to be a replacement of one-to-one induction but an additional platform.

d. **Department Orientation:** Inadequacy of department orientation was a major reason for employee dissatisfaction, disengagement and attrition. This process was also included as a formal process in the on-boarding period. A manager's checklist was designed highlighting the activities that managers are required to do from day 1 till the 12 months of joining. The managers were sensitized of their responsibilities and important roles that they can play in engaging a new employee through small group interactions with them. Auto-generated mails listing down the activities of manager's checklist *(Refer Appendix 3 for Manager's on-boarding checklist)* were activated as per the schedule of on-boarding. This includes extending a warm welcome to new employee, introducing him to team, defining his first assignment, clarifying role and responsibilities, providing performance feedback, development planning and checking with the employee on what's working well and what's not.

e. **Appointment Letters:** Appointment letters across levels and locations were issued from Head Office. It used to take one week to one month to issue the appointment letters. This was also dependent on the availability of signatories which was not formalized in a structured manner. To resolve this, the alternate signatories were assigned and formalized for each business/function. The SLA was made with payroll team that it would prepare and get the appointment letter signed and handover to the Business HR/concerned location HR personnel responsible for new hire. This whole process is required to be completed within 4 days of receiving the documents as per checklist. It was henceforth targeted that the new hire should get the appointment letter within 10 days of joining.

Phase 2: Process Enhancements

1. **Pre-Hire Communication:** In the existing system, pre-hiring communication was limited to only confirming the joining of the candidate. The study of the best practices highlighted that best employers have a well defined pre-hire communication with the candidate that serves the following purposes:
   a. New hire feels welcomed and valued by the organization.
   b. Helps in keeping him/her warm.
   c. More informed about the organization and location he is joining.

In this context, a portal was designed specifically for new hires as one stop to address all their joining related FAQs. This link was part of the career section of the company website and also served as an effective platform for employer branding. The candidate was informed of the portal by means of a welcome mail from HR SPOC on acceptance of offer letter.

Some of the broad areas that this portal addressed were:

- Pre Employment Medical Test
- Documentation for Joining
- Joining Forms both Online and Downloadable
- Relocation Information – on various sites, accommodation, nearby schools, guest houses, tourist attraction etc
- On-boarding FAQs
- Life at SNR Company Ltd.
- Company Factsheet etc

2. **Online Joining Forms (E-Joining):** To expedite the joining time and enhance candidate's convenience; the existing manual forms were made completely

online. These forms could be filled-in and submitted online even before the candidate joins so that on the day of joining the formalities can be completed in lesser time. The subsequent processes linked with employee enrolment would also be expedited.

Auto reminders to the respective stakeholders in the on-boarding process like IT for laptops/desktops and Admin for workstation etc were also activated as additional functionality of this portal.

3. **E-Induction:** The e-induction portal was designed to close the gap with respect to the delay in face to face induction. This module covers exhaustive information on the group, the subsidiaries, HR policies and practices.

4. **Employee Kit:** The employee kit was redesigned including a detailed employee handbook, pen and on-boarding checklist. The employee handbook gives a glimpse of the company, HR processes and policies and information on how to access intranet and HRIS portals.

This helps in enabling new employees with the right information at the right time. The on-boarding checklist is a set of to-do list that helps employees to plan their days accordingly in the first year. *(Refer Appendix 4 for new employee on boarding check list)*

5. **Launch and Communication:** The leadership team and all existing employees were informed of this new process through town-hall meetings and employee communication posters titled *"Helping you with your first step in SNR Company Ltd...."* *including the features of t*he new on-boarding process (e-joining, e-induction, employee kit). The communication was drafted with a view to keep the emotional connect with new hire intact reinforcing the fact that human interface with new hires will not be replaced with automated processes rather, it's a means of facilitating the existing process.

Phase 3: Way Forward

1. **Integration of online forms with HRIS:** In the existing system, the employee details were entered by the HR SPOC on the HRIS. For saving joining time, it was decided to eliminate this activity and integrate the online forms with HRIS.

2. **Measure Effectiveness through Hour-Day-Week (HDW) Online Feedback Mechanism on Process Maturity:** Last but the most important step was to keep track of the effectiveness of the above processes. To capture the new

employees' feedback, HDW Online Feedback mechanism was designed. It is an online feedback mechanism wherein feedback will be taken from the new employees at the end of first day's 7 hours, first seven days and first seven weeks. The questions in each form were designed keeping in view the set of activities that were planned during that time e.g. the 'Hour' questionnaire focused more on resource provisioning, the 'Day' focused on quality of HR, e-induction and 'Week' focused on quality of department orientation. This helps in monitoring the process both centrally and at locations. The feedback mechanism is scheduled to start one month post implementation of on-boarding modules *(Refer Appendix 5 for questionnaires)*.

CONCLUSION

Thus, employee on-boarding, which started as m*erely improving the operational aspects* of the on-boarding process, got extended in its scope including not just the operational but also the strategic aspects of the on-boarding process. Employee on-boarding became an umbrella brand indicating the new revamped on-boarding process including sub brands as e-joining, e-induction, employee kit and HDW.

APPENDIX 1

New Hire Survey Questionnaire

On Day 1 of joining, I was provided

☐   A tour of the area/office/plant
☐   Information on Admin services like time/attendance recording, Access card, Parking, Extension Lists etc.
☐   Induction schedule for the next 1-2 weeks
☐   Contact point for any queries etc.

Within 1 week of joining, I was provided a fair understanding of the company and its operations, specifically about its:

- History and Key Milestones
- Locations and Subsidiaries
- Key Product areas and Markets
- Organization structure, Key Personnel, Culture
- Organization Vision and Core Values
- Compensation and benefits information, conditions of employment, pay, leave, holidays, pay date, bank details etc.
- Standards of Conduct: discipline, grievance, other policies

Suggestions for improvement: ....
....

APPENDIX 2

External Benchmarking

Dell Inc

- Pre-Joining Bouquet at Home
- 2 fixed dates (15th and 30th) every month for joining
- Joining Formalities completed within 2 hours
- **Day 1:** Common 2 Day Induction for all new hires; meeting leadership team; session with IT/Admin/Payroll
  - ◦   Sample Joining Forms shown over projector to help in filling up
  - ◦   Office Walk Through

- ◦ Workstation allotted; Organized desk with complete stationary etc
- ◦ HR SPOC assigned to each new hire for any query (1:25)
- ◦ Lunch with HR person

Tata Steel Ltd

- **Pre Joining Letter:** Welcome, travel Plan, contact person details
- Welcome at guest house
- **Joining Kit:** Employee Handbooks, Induction Plan, Work Sheets and Department Org Structure
- **Department Induction Plan:** 3 Days: Meet all DRs of HOD with Discussion sheet which in turn is finally reviewed by HOD.
- **Discussion on Training Needs and Goal Plan:** 1 Year
- **Detailed Plant Induction for all new hires every month:** They have to undertake that once in 6 months.

Genpact Ltd

- **Separate team for Pre- Hire communication:** Follow up every 2/3 days post offer acceptance.
- **Pre Hire orientation before joining:** About the org, role, manager etc. Try to de-sell the job.
- Outsourced Reference Checks
- Online joining forms (20 pages) followed by generating permanent employee ID
- **New Hire Orientation:** 2 day program across levels within a week of joining, Very closely tracked by HR

FreeScale Semiconductor Inc

- **Online tool:** Redcarpet from Silkroad for onboarding
- Just launch the employee on the site before joining and the trigger mails will go to the concerned.
- All joining forms are online, the Ids are created pre joining.

The Dow Chemical Company

- Welcome at Reception
- HR Representative assigned for all his joining formalities
- Shown a corporate film of 15 mins with HR representative

- **Day 1:** Get all resources (laptop, stationary and workstation).
- Meeting with other HODs
- 2 Days of Cooling Period in which he has to have half an hour discussion with direct manager on KRA and expectations for next 6 months
- Meeting/Call with Matrix Manager within a month of joining
- CEO address once a month
- Discussion on Training in 3 months of joining

Tech Mahindra Ltd

- Joining and Induction every Monday/Wednesday and Friday
- **Resource Provisioning:** By DAY 2
- Mentor assigned depending upon project
- HR SPOC has meeting with new hires within a month of joining
- Intranet has all info on policies etc
- **Resource Allocation Team:** Makes requirements known well in advance

Dr. Reddy's Laboratories

- Fixed Days of Joining (every Monday)
- Buddy Program
- **Day 1:** Resource Provisioning (Appointment Letter)

Gillette India Ltd

- Buddy Program
- Pre Hire Communication

General Motors Company

- New hire accountability checklist to cover all critical tasks through the first year, timelines and roles (1 week to 1 year)
- E-Orientation form

Novell Inc

- **One Click On-boarding:** Novell's automation of new employee outreach puts the tools in the hands of hiring managers. It automatically coordinates with functions across the organization and completes the suite of administrative tasks needed for employees to begin work,

- Hiring managers can monitor new hires' on-boarding status online and in real time, removing the need for continual coordination and communication between managers, recruiting, human resources, IT, and other internal functions.

Philips Electronics India Ltd

- **In Touch:** Personalized pages; Platform for Networking; On-boarding Calendar; Info
- To ensure that the on-boarding process is implemented consistently, new hires complete questionnaires at the end of key stages of the on-boarding process.

Hewlett Packard Company

Hewlett-Packard builds a connection to corporate mission as reflected in the following aspects of its on-boarding program philosophy:

- Giving new hires the opportunity to connect with other new hires, peers, and senior management
- Offering ways for new employees to "feel connected" to the large corporation
- Providing new hires with a solid grasp of corporate traditions, values, and culture
- Making consultants proficient in communicating to the customer what the company or their business unit is about and what makes the company different from competitors

American Express Corp

- American Express begins development at the point-of-hire by leveraging knowledge gained during the recruiting process. The company ensures that relevant assessment data is not lost after selection is made, but instead forms the backbone of a long-term focused development plan put in place within 30 days of the new hire's arrival.

Daimler AG

- DaimlerChrysler Services North America LLC revamped its on-boarding content to include more consistent messages about the newly formed entity.
- The company also ensures that managers fully explain job responsibilities and performance expectations to new hires, with emphasis on how those jobs fit into business objectives.
- In addition, understanding that its initial online approach to information delivery was preventing new hires from establishing critical networks, DaimlerChrysler Services North America LLC altered its delivery channel strategy to include more "in-person" elements in the on-boarding experience; examples include a scavenger hunt and an assigned peer mentor and integration of senior executives into the company's unique innovation-focused on-boarding graduation session.

APPENDIX 3

Manager's Checklist for On-Boarding

Long term retention of any new employee starts at recruitment. Now that you have your new employee recruited with a planned start date, it's time to foster his/her success in the role that he/she has been hired for.

Just like for new employees on-boarding is a critical period during which they form expectations of their job, the company and you during this process, it is equally as crucial a time for a leader.

Research shows that supervisors who shepherd the new employee's first year in the new position can expect these positive results:

- **Reduces Anxiety:** The new employee feels welcomed and a sense of belonging is established.
- **Sets Context:** He/she understands how the new position contributes to the group's mission and goals.
- **Establishes Bonding and Pride:** He/she feels a connection to—and pride in—the work group, which reaffirms their decision to take the job.

The following checklists will help get your new employee, joined in your department under your leadership, off to the best start possible and in establishing a bond with him/her.

Manager's Checklist: The New Employee's First Days (First 2/3 Days)

The purpose of the first day checklist is to help remind you of key areas that should be considered to ensure that the new employee feels welcome and that their first impression and day at work are comfortable and engaging. Getting to know the work group supports a new employee's progress toward both productivity and acculturation.

Welcoming New Employee

☐ Give a warm welcome and discuss the plan for the day.

☐ Introduce new employee to all coworkers in department.

☐ Schedule times for the new employee to meet with key team members helping him understand department's functioning. *This should be scheduled in advance to ensure key staff members have the time available.*

☐ Wherever possible, assign a coworker as Buddy as an immediate resource for any questions and to help the new employee navigate the work place.

☐ Show the new employee his workstation. Ensure that the workstation is assigned to him in advance with basic supplies of stationery, laptop/desktop.

☐ Share some key client contacts, inter-department contacts.

The New Employee's First Weeks (Week 1 - Week 2)

Clarifying departmental organizational structure and communicating your expectations are fundamental during this time period, as is success in the employee's first assignment

Clarify the Job Description and Context

☐ Review job description, key responsibilities and initial job expectations. Explain how the job fits in the work group and department, and how they specifically contribute to the Organization Objectives; Describe success measures for the job.

☐ Review written statements of organizational mission, vision, current goals and priorities, and give the new hire a copy of the current department organization chart.

- ☐ Explain department's strategy for the current and next year.
- ☐ In case of Plant/R&D, reinstate basic occupational health and safety guidelines to be followed at work. Ensure that the new employee attends safety training before entering the work area.
- ☐ Clarify Next Steps: Explain initial assignments that encompasses the first three to six months.
- ☐ Discuss learning and development needs in relation to the initial work plan/ assignment and identify how those needs will be met.

Introduce Performance Management

- ☐ Explain how the employee's performance will be evaluated, including the performance management structure and processes for the work group and department.
- ☐ Establish clear goals (KRAs) and provide regular feedback.
- ☐ Clarify the Review Process and Timelines.

Introduction with Key Clients/Stakeholders

- ☐ Schedule meetings with clients, partners, or other stakeholders within the first month.
- ☐ Introduce him/her with inter-department stakeholders.

The New Employee's First 2 Months (Week 3 - Week 7)

The purpose of this checklist is to reinforce information you have already shared, check progress on the initial assignment and to encourage a conversation with your employee about additional orientation needs/processes. New employees also need progress feedback, and the end of 7 weeks is a good point in the initial review period to give specific feedback to assist the new employee in setting priorities and completing training.

Review Progress and Provide Informal Feedback

- ☐ Meet the employee to review progress on initial work plan. Provide any relevant feedback on performance to date.
- ☐ Check progress on scheduled meetings with other stakeholders/clients to ensure they are occurring.
- ☐ Review and follow through on any learning and development activities agreed to earlier.

Continue to Meet Regularly with the Employee

☐ Meet regularly with the new employee to answer questions if any.
☐ Discuss experiences, concerns if any, and identify any new needs.
☐ Introduce challenges that may emerge in the job and plan how to meet them.
☐ Review the on-boarding process with the employee—is it working well?
☐ Ensure the new employee is becoming acclimated to department and new job responsibilities.

Although the first 7 weeks are critical for any new employee but we understand that the on-boarding cycle typically lasts a year which is also an important time period. The additional checklists below will further help you to settle down during this entire period.

The New Employee's First Six Months

This is a great point to review work expectations, progress and learning needs. It will allow for a check in and to determine what changes, if any, are required for work expectations and learning and development. These items will assist with ensuring the employee is engaged and a valued contributor in meeting organizational goals.

Continue Performance Management and Engagement

☐ Is employee fully engaged, seeing him or herself as a valued contributor?
☐ Assure that necessary trainings are completed (Functional and HR Induction, Safety Training, SOP training etc).
☐ Continue providing regular informal feedback.
☐ Provide formal feedback on the work plan at end of the 6 months.
☐ Review the onboarding process with employee—is it working well? What support he/she would need?

The New Employee's First Year

Continue Performance Management and Engagement

☐ Is employee working at full productivity, seeing him or herself as making a difference?
☐ Continue providing regular informal feedback, and provide formal annual feedback.

Observe the Milestone and Look to the Future

☐ Review the first year; celebrate successes with recognition of contributions (perhaps including a congratulatory note from HOD). Possible additional talking points to discuss with the employee:

☐ Is the job what you expected? How or how not?

☐ Are you having enough opportunities to learn and grow? What are some you would like?

☐ Are you running into any hindrances to your productivity? What are they and how do they affect you?

☐ What's the best thing that's happened to you here this year?

☐ Do you feel recognized for your contributions? How do you like to be recognized?

☐ What suggestions for improvements do you have?

Continue to Meet Regularly with the Employee

☐ Discuss career development and plans for the future.

☐ Offer professional development opportunities.

APPENDIX 4

New Employee On-Boarding Checklist

Welcome to SNR Company Ltd.

The following On-boarding Checklist will facilitate your smooth transition in the new workplace. You may keep this handy as a ready reference to plan your activities accordingly. Please feel free to add activities to the checklist as per your requirement.

We wish you a successful career ahead in SNR Company Ltd.

Day 1

☐ Complete Joining Formalities: Fill and submit to HR all joining forms with supporting documents.

☐ Attend the induction facilitated by location HR on policies, company overview, functional orientation, and other safety/SOP trainings as per schedule. In case of manufacturing locations, Functional Induction is also clubbed with HR Induction.

☐   Initiate to activate your bank account with the help of location HR.

☐   Initiate to activate your mobile number.

☐   Check for your employee code from location HR.

☐   Check for your laptop/desktop, workstation, e-mail ID, HRIS ID and intranet ID and password from IT with the help of HR.

☐   Visit the facility – enquire about facilities like canteen, ATM etc.

☐   Incase of outstation candidate at site, enquire about residential accommodation.

☐   At the end of the day, collect your ID Card from the HR.

Day 1-Week 1/2

☐   Complete the e-induction module available on intranet.

☐   Complete the Hour Employee Feedback Survey as intimated to you through an auto-generated mail.

☐   Get introduced to your Reporting Manager, Head of the Department and co-workers.

☐   Schedule meetings with co-workers to understand department's role/functioning and business priorities.

☐   Meet the Reporting Manager to discuss in detail the job description, key responsibilities and initial job expectations. Understand the department structure and how the job fits in the work group and department.

☐   Understand the department's strategy and goals in the context of organization.

☐   Clarify Next Steps: Understand initial assignments that encompasses the first three to six months.

☐   Discuss learning and development needs or other support required in relation to the initial work plan/assignment and identify how those needs will be met.

☐   Understand how your performance will be evaluated, including the performance management structure and processes for the department; Establish clear goals (KRAs) with your manager.

☐   Get introduced to key clients/stakeholders. Schedule meetings with them.

☐   Complete the Day Employee Feedback Survey as intimated to you through an auto-generated mail.

☐   In case of new salary account, inform the HR of the account number once activated.

☐   Collect your Appointment Letter from HR.

☐   Declare Flexi benefits on HRIS.

☐   In case of outstation employees, initiate to submit the relocation expense claims to HR with supporting documents as per eligibility.

Week 3 – Week 7

☐   Attend the functional induction scheduled by HR with functional Heads.

☐   Initiate to meet/call the Matrix Manager if any. Understand his expectations from the position.

☐   Meet the manager frequently to update him on the progress on initial work plan. Get informal feedback on performance to date.

☐   Complete the Week Employee Feedback Survey as intimated to you through an auto-generated mail.

Although the first seven weeks are critical for any new employee but we understand that the on-boarding cycle typically lasts a year which is also an important time period. The additional checklists below will further help you to settle down during this entire period.

First Six Months

☐   Ensure that necessary trainings are completed (Functional and HR Induction, Safety Training, SOP training etc).

☐   Initiate review with your manager at the end of this period. Get formal feedback. Work out the plan for next 6 months.

☐   Discuss your learning and development needs with your manager.

☐   If below General Manager position, collect your Probation Confirmation Letter from HR.

First Year

☐   Review the first year with your manager. Get formal feedback.

☐   Discuss career development and plans for the future.

☐   Discuss professional development opportunities.

APPENDIX 5

HDW Online Feedback Forms

Feedback Hour Form

Name:
Employee Code:
Department:
Location:

Pre Hire Communication

1. I received Employee On-boarding link and information on the transition/ relocation support from HR prior to my joining

    ☐   Yes
    ☐   No

2. I found the link useful with information facilitating my joining in SNR Company Ltd.

    ☐   Yes
    ☐   No
    ☐   NA

3A. I was provided with the link to fill the joining forms online at least a week before my joining.

    ☐   Yes
    ☐   No
    ☐   NA

3B. I found it convenient to fill the joining forms online.

    ☐   Yes
    ☐   No
    ☐   NA

4. **Outstation Candidate:** I received good support on relocation and transition (e.g. temporary accommodation).

   ☐   Yes
   ☐   No
   ☐   NA

Joining Kit

5. On joining, I received a "Welcome Kit" and found it very informative about the organization and policies.

   ☐   Yes
   ☐   No

Joining Formalities

6. My joining formalities were completed on DAY 1.

   ☐   Yes
   ☐   No

Department Introduction

7. The HR SPOC introduced me to my department team members and HOD/ Reporting Manager

   ☐   Yes
   ☐   No

IT/Other Infrastructure

8. I got my workstation on Day 1 of joining

   ☐   Yes
   ☐   No
   ☐   NA

9.   My desktop/laptop was configured and installed to start my work when I joined

☐   Yes
☐   No
☐   NA

10.   My Log-in IDs (E-mail, intranet and Windows ID) were activated on Day 1.

☐   Yes
☐   No

Facility Tour/Site Visit

11.   I was taken for a facility tour and was shown all the necessary places– like cafeteria, ATM, parking and was explained other location specific norms.

☐   Yes
☐   No

Day 1 Support

12.   I was satisfied with the support provided on DAY 1 by the HR SPOC

☐   Yes
☐   No

13.   I was provided with support in arranging for opening of my Bank Account.

☐   Yes
☐   No

14.   I was informed about safety related guidelines before entering my work area in plant/R&D.

☐   Yes
☐   No
☐   NA

What's Working Well

15. List any 3 things that you liked most about your DAY 1

    1._____
    2._____
    3._____

Areas of Improvement

16. List 3 areas where you think the on-boarding process needs improvement?

    1._____
    2._____
    3._____

Any other comments...

Thank you for your participation. We take this opportunity to wish you a very successful stay with us in our Organization and look forward for a long term association.

Best regards,
HR

Feedback Day Form

Name:
Employee Code:
Department:
Location:

1. Please rate your experience of the first few days of working in SNR Company Ltd.?

    ☐ Poor
    ☐ Moderate
    ☐ Can't Say
    ☐ Good
    ☐ Excellent

Induction

a.   My induction was planned in advance and communicated to me

   ☐   Yes
   ☐   No

b.   I received an induction from HR within first 2 days of my joining

   ☐   Yes
   ☐   No

c.   Induction was informative about the organization and company policies/ HRIS

   ☐   Yes
   ☐   No

d.   In case of manufacturing unit, mandatory trainings like SOP/Fire and Safety were part of my induction.

   ☐   Yes
   ☐   No
   ☐   NA

For DGM and above: My induction with other HODs was also scheduled and informed to me.

☐   Yes
☐   No
☐   NA

E-Induction

2.   I was notified of e-induction link on Day 2 of my joining

   ☐   Yes
   ☐   No

3.   I found e-induction module effective and useful

   ☐   Yes
   ☐   No

Department Orientation

4.   My reporting manager spent time in helping me understand the department structure and its objectives.

   ☐   Yes
   ☐   No

5.   I received good support from my peers that helped me establish networks.

   ☐   Yes
   ☐   No

Support

6.   I knew where to go for help and resources? (like for business cards etc)

   ☐   Yes
   ☐   No

7.   What's working well

   What did you like most about your first few Days in SNR Company Ltd.?

   _____
   _____
   _____

8. Areas of improvement

    Would you like to mention any area where the on-boarding process needs improvement?

    ☐   Yes
    ☐   No

Comments: _____
          _____
          _____

Any other comments..

Thank you for your participation. We take this opportunity to wish you a very successful stay with us in our Organization and look forward for a long term association.
    Best regards,
    HR

Feedback Week Form

Name:
Employee Code:
Department:
Location:

1. Please rate your experience of first few weeks of working in SNR Company Ltd.?

    ☐   Poor
    ☐   Moderate
    ☐   Can't Say
    ☐   Good
    ☐   Excellent

Role Clarity

2. My reporting manager/HOD clearly explained my role and responsibility, set clear expectations in terms of work/deliverables for next 6-12 months.

    ☐ Yes
    ☐ No

3. My Matrix Manager (if any) spent time explaining me the role and responsibility and job expectations.

    ☐ Yes
    ☐ No
    ☐ NA

Cross Functional Induction

4. I received Plant or/R&D or/Business (cross-functional) induction by the respective HODs that helped me understand organization's business better

    ☐ Yes
    ☐ No

Appointment Letter

5. I received the Appointment Letter within 7-10/11-15/>15 working days of joining

HR POLICIES

6. I am clear about the HR policies and procedures that apply to me.

    ☐ Yes
    ☐ No

What's Working Well

7.   What did you like most about your first few Weeks in SNR Company Ltd.?

_____

_____

_____

Areas of Improvement

8.   Would you like to mention any area where the on-boarding process needs improvement?

   ☐   Yes

   ☐   No

Comments:_____

_____

Any other comments.......................................

Thank you for your participation. We take this opportunity to wish you a very successful stay with us in our Organization and look forward for a long term association.

Best regards,

HR

Compilation of References

Abernathy, F. H. (2000). Retailing and supply chains in the information age. *Technology in Society*, *22*, 5–31. doi:10.1016/S0160-791X(99)00039-1.

About university hospital consortium. (n.d.) The University Hospital Consortium's official website. Retrieved from http://www.cancernz.org.nz/reducing-your-cancer-risk/.

Akinci, S., Akoy, S., & Atilgan, E. (2004). Adoption of internet banking among sophisticated consumer segments in an advanced developing country. *International Journal of Bank Marketing*, *22*(3), 212–232. doi:10.1108/02652320410530322.

Alabbadi, M. M. (2011). Cloud computing for education and learning: Education and learning as a service. In *Proceedings of 14th IEEE International Conference on Interactive Collaborative Learning*. Washington, DC: IEEE Press.

Al-Hawari, M., Hartley, N., & Ward, T. (2005). Measuring banks automated service quality: A confirmatory factor analysis approach. *Marketing Bulletin, 16*.

Al-Shammari, M. (2009). Capturing data from customers Customer Knowledge Management: People, Processes, and Technology (169-190). New York: Information Science Reference.

Anand, M. (2011). *Indian luxury car space leadership war persists*. Retrieved from http://newstonight.net/content/indian-luxury-car-space-leadership-war-persists

Anand, T. (2009). *Brand yatra: Fair & lovely-From getting a life partner to getting a life*. Retrieved from http://www.exchange4media.com/brandspeak/brand-speak_FS.asp?Section_id=42&News_id=35377&Tag=31042.

Andreoni, J., & Petrie, R. (2008). Beauty, gender, and stereotypes: Evidence from laboratory experiments. *Journal of Economic Psychology*, *29*(1), 73–93. doi:10.1016/j.joep.2007.07.008.

Angelbroking. (2013). Retrieved from angelbroking.com.

Anita. (2010). Scam hits citibank india; fraud worth 400 crore. *One India*. Retrieved from http://news.oneindia.in.

Annual Report, H. U. L. (2012). Growing sustainably. *Annual Report (2010-11)*. Retrieved from http://www.hul.co.in/Images/HULAnnualReport201011tc-m114268010tcm114268010.pdf.

Annual Survey of America's Charter Schools. (2008). Center for Education Reform. Retrieved from http://www.edreform.com/Archive/?Annual_Survey_of_Americas_Charter_Schools_2008.

ArticlesBase Online. (2009). Fairness creams-For the glowing skin. Retrieved from http://www.articlesbase.com/health-articles/fairness-creams-for-the-glowing-skin-930916.html.

Avkiran, N. K. (2000). Rising productivity of australian trading banks under deregulation 1986-1995. *Journal of Economics and Finance*. Murfreesboro, TN: Middle Tennessee State University.

Ball, D., Coelho, P. S., & Machas, A. (2004). The role of communication and trust in explaining customer loyalty. *European Journal of Marketing, 38*(9/10), 1272–1293. doi:10.1108/03090560410548979.

Banyte, J., Joksaite, E., & Virvilaite, R. (2007). Relationship of consumer attitude and brand: Emotional aspect. *The Engineering Economist, 52*(2), 65–77.

Bass, B. M. (1981). *Stogdill's handbook of leadership*. New York: Free Press.

Begum, S. & Khan. (2011). Potential of cloud computing architecture. In *Proceedings of IEEE International Conference on Information and Communication Technologies*. Washington, DC: IEEE Press.

Benjamin, J. (1996). *Principles, elements, and types of persuasion*. Fort Worth, TX: Harcourt Brace.

Berry, L. L. (2000). Relationship marketing of services–Growing interest, emerging perspectives. In Sheth & Parvatiyar (Eds.), Handbook of Relationship Marketing (149-170). Thousand Oaks, CA: Sage.

Bharat Book Bureau. (2008). *Indian gems and jewelry market*. Retrieved from www.Bharatbook.com.

Bhatia, G. (2002). Cream and added color. Retrieved from http://www.outlookindia.com/article.aspx?214596>.

Bhatnagar, S., & Bhalla, M. (2010). Citibank fraud: Rs 400 cr allegedly siphoned off. *India Times*. Retrieved from http://articles.economictimes.indiatimes.com

Bhattacharjee, A. (2002). Individual trust in online firms: Scale development and initial test. *Journal of Management Information Systems, 19*(1), 211–241.

Bhimani, A. (1996). Securing the commercial internet. *Communications of the ACM, 39*(6), 29–36. doi:10.1145/228503.228509.

Biggadike, R. (1997). *Entering new markets: Strategies and performance*. Cambridge, MA: Marketing Science Institute.

Birtwistle, G., Siddiqui, N., & Fiorito, S. (2003). Quick response: Perceptions of UK fashion retailers. *International Journal of Retail & Distribution Management, 31*(2), 118–128. doi:10.1108/09590550310462010.

Bitner, M. J., Brown, S. W., & Meuter, M. L. (2000). Technology infusion in service encounters. *Journal of the Academy of Marketing Science, 28*(1), 138–149. doi:10.1177/0092070300281013.

Black, N. J., Lockett, A., Winjklhofer, H., & Ennew, C. (2001). The adoption of internet financial services: A qualitative research. *International Journal of Retail and Distribution Management, 29*(8), 390–398. doi:10.1108/09590550110397033.

Booz & Company. (2011). Indian automotive market 2020. New Delhi.

Compilation of References

Brodie, R. J., Whittome, J. R. M., & Brush, G. J. (2009). Investigating the service brand: A customer value perspective. *Journal of Business Research, 62*(3), 345–355. doi:10.1016/j.jbusres.2008.06.008.

Broughton, B. (2001). The global tobacco industry: The real world choice for tobacco regulators., In *Proceedings of World Tobacco International Symposium and Trade Fair.* Hong Kong: British American Tobacco.

Bruce, M., & Daly, L. (2006). Buyer behaviour for fast fashion. *Journal of Fashion Marketing and Management, 10*(3), 329–344. doi:10.1108/13612020610679303.

Bruce, M., Moore, C., & Birtwistle, G. (Eds.). (2004). *International retail marketing: A case study approach.* Oxford, UK: Butterworth-Heinemann.

Business Line. (2010). *Why Citi can never sleep.* Retrieved from http://www.thehindubusinessline.in/2010/12/31/stories/2010123150230600.htm.

Business Standard. (2008). *Brand managers need to connect with rural consumers.* Retrieved from http://www.Business-Standard.com/india/storypage.php?autono=340384.

Business Standard. (2013). *Organised retail jewelry sector growing by 40%.* Retrieved from http://www.business-standard.com/article/companies/organised-retail-jewelry-sector-growing-by-40-111041300065_1.html.

Capgemini and Merrill Lynch Global Wealth Management. (2011). *2011 world wealth report.* Paris: Merrill Lynch.

Carew, E. (1998). *Fast money 4: The best selling guide to australia's financial markets.* Sydney: Allen Unwin.

Cassandra. (2009). *Welcome to apache Cassandra.* Retrieved from http://cassandra.apache.org/.

Center for Macro Consumer Research. (2011). *2011 report: National council for applied economic research (NCAER).* New Delhi: Center for Macro Consumer Research.

Challapalli, S. (2002). All's fair in this market. *Business line: The hindu.*

Chang, I. C., Li, Y. C., Hung, W. F., & Hwang, H. G. (2005). An empirical study on the impact of quality antecedents on tax payers' acceptance of Internet tax-filing systems. *Government Information Quarterly, 22,* 389–410. doi:10.1016/j.giq.2005.05.002.

Chan, S., & Lu, M. (2004). Understanding internet banking adoption and use behaviour: A hong kong perspective. *Journal of Global Information Management, 12*(3), 21–43. doi:10.4018/jgim.2004070102.

Chard, K. (2010). Social cloud: Cloud computing in social networks. In *Proceedings of 3rd IEEE International Conference on Cloud Computing.* Washington, DC: IEEE Press.

Chen, S., Cowan, C. F. N., & Grant, P. M. (1991). Orthogonal least squares learning algorithm for radial basis function networks. *IEEE Transactions on Neural Networks, 2*(2), 302–309. doi:10.1109/72.80341 PMID:18276384.

Cho, N., & Kim, E.-K. (2011). Enhanced voice activity detection using acoustic event detection and classification. *IEEE Transactions on Consumer Electronics, 57*(1), 196–202. doi:10.1109/TCE.2011.5735502.

Chou, D., & Chou, A. Y. (2000). A guide to the internet revolution in banking. *Information Systems Management, 17*(2), 51–57. doi:10.1201/1078/43191.17.2.20000301/31227.6.

Citibank. (2013). Retrieved from http://www.online.citibank.co.in/.

Cockburn, C., & Wilson, T. D. (1996). Business use of world wide web. *International Journal of Information Management, 16*(2), 83–102. doi:10.1016/0268-4012(95)00071-2.

Commodity Online. (2009). *Goldplus from tata banks on rural buyers.* Retrieved from http://www.commodityonline.com/news/goldplus-from-tata-banks-on-rural-buyers-15291-3-15292.html.

Compeau, D. R., & Higgins, C. A. (1995). Application of social cognitive theory to training for computer skills. *Information Systems Research, 6*(2), 118–143. doi:10.1287/isre.6.2.118.

Compeau, D. R., & Higgins, C. A. (1995). Computer self-efficacy: Development of a measure and initial test. *Management Information Systems Quarterly, 19*(2), 189–211. doi:10.2307/249688.

Coner, A. (2003). Personalisation and customisation in financial portals. *Journal of American Academy of Business, 2*(2), 498–504.

Confederation of Indian Industry. (2013). *Gems and jewelry.* Retrieved from http://www.cii.in/Sectors.aspx?enc=prvePUj2bdMtgTmvPwvisYH+5EnGjyGXO9hLECvTuNt+KvFl5tZninrd2RhXtdzu.

Council of Leather Exports. (2011). *Indian footwear industry–A status note.* Retrieved from http://www.leatherindia.org/products/footwear.asp.

Dabholkar, P. A., & Bagozzi, R. P. (2002). An attitudinal model of technology-based self service: Moderating effects of consumer traits and situational factors. *Journal of the Academy of Marketing Science, 30*(3), 184–201.

Dalgic, T. (1998). Niche marketing principles: Guerrillas versus gorillas. *Journal of Segmentation in Marketing, 2*(1), 5–18. doi:10.1300/J142v02n01_02.

Dalgic, T. (2006). *Handbook of niche marketing: Principles, and practices.* New York: The Haworth Press Inc..

Dalgic, T., & Leeuw, M. (1994). Niche marketing revisited: Concept, applications, and some european cases. *European Journal of Marketing, 28*(4), 39–55. doi:10.1108/03090569410061178.

Data Center Knowledge. (2010). *The facebook data center FAQ.* Retrieved from http://www.datacenterknowledge.com/the-facebook-data-center-faq/.

Datamonitor. (2010). *Industry profile, footwear in india.* Retrieved from Business Source Complete database.

Dawar, N., & Frost, T. (1999). Competing with giants. *Harvard Business Review, 77*(2), 119–129. PMID:10387768.

Day, G. S., Shocker, A. D., & Srivastava, R. K. (1979). Customer-oriented approaches to identifying product-markets. *Journal of Marketing, 43*(4), 8–19. doi:10.2307/1250266.

Delaney, J. (1995). Minding your own niche business. *Nation's Business, 83*(5), 56–58.

Compilation of References

Delgado-Ballester, E., Munuera-Alemn, J. L., & Yague-Guillen, M. J. (2003). Development and validation of a brand trust scale. *International Journal of Market Research, 45*(1), 35–52.

Diamond World. (2008). *Reliance jewels targets 10% of india's jewelry market.* Retrieved from http://www.DiamondWorld.net/contentview.aspx?item=1938.

Dinev, T., Bellotto, M., Hart, P., Russo, V., Serra, I., & Colautti, C. (2006). Privacy calculus model in e-commerce–A study of italy and the united states. *European Journal of Information Systems*, 389–402. doi:10.1057/palgrave.ejis.3000590.

Doval, P. (2011). *Mercedes to step up price war with A and B Class.* Retrieved from http://timesofindia.indiatimes.com/business/india-business/Mercedes-to-step-up-price-war-with-A-and-B-Class/articleshow/7776778.cms.

Dyche, J. (2001). *The CRM handbook: A business guide to customer relationship management.* New York: Addison-Wesley Professional.

Eastlick, M. A., Lotz, S. L., & Warrington, P. (2006). Understanding online b-to-c relationships: An integrated model of privacy concerns, trust, and commitment. *Journal of Business Research, 59*(8), 877–886. doi:10.1016/j.jbusres.2006.02.006.

Egger, F. N. (2003). *Evaluating the customer trust experience in business to consumer ecommerce environments.* Retrieved from www.scholar.google.com.

Engel, J. F., Blackwell, R. D., & Miniard, P. W. (1993). *Consumer behavior* (7th ed.). Chicago: Harcourt Brace.

Ernst & Young. (2011). *Wealth-management-study-investing-in-the-future.* Retrieved from http://www.ey.com

Ezzat, S., Gayar, N. E., & Ghanem, M. M. (2010). Investigating analysis of speech content through text classification. In *Proceedings of Investigating Analysis of Speech Content through Text Classification.* Paris: IEEE Press. doi:10.1109/SOCPAR.2010.5686000.

Facebook. (2013). *Facebook newsroom.* Retrieved from http://newsroom.fb.com/News/The-Next-Web-Conference-New-Timeline-Apps-14f.aspx.

Fenton, N. (2000). Trust, confidence, and risk. In: F. Tonkiss., A. Passey., N. Fenton, & L. C. Hems (Eds.), Trust and Civil Society. London: MacMillan.

Fibre2Fashion. (2008). *Tanishq bags retail chain of the year award.* Retrieved from http://www.fibre2fashion.com/news/fashion-news/newsdetails.aspx?news_id=61754.

Financial Express. (2008). Tanishq bags retail chain of the year award. Retrieved from http://www.ibef.org/exports/Gems-and-Jewelry.aspx.

Fitch. (2011). Fraud may impact Citi's wealth management biz, but not short-term rating. *Hindu Business Line.* Retrieved from http://www.thehindubusinessline.in

Flavian, C., Guinaliu, M., & Torres, E. (2006). How bricks-and-mortar attributes affect online banking adoption. *International Journal of Bank Marketing, 24*(6), 406. doi:10.1108/02652320610701735.

Flourishing on Red Tape, Mirza International leaves global footprint. (2009). *The Economic Times.* Retrieved from Newspaper archive.

French & Raven. (1959). *The bases of social power. Studies in Social Behavior.* Ann Arbor, MI: University of Michigan Press.

Fukuyama, F. (1995). *Trust: The social virtues and the creation of prosperity.* New York: Free Press.

Gabriel, I. J., & Nyshadham, E. (2008). A cognitive map of people's online risk perceptions and attitudes: An empirical study. In *Proceedings of the 41ˢᵗ Annual Hawaii International Conference on System Sciences*, 274. Washington, DC: IEEE Press.

Gan, C., Clemes, M., Limsombunchai, V., & Weng, A. (2006). A logit analysis of electronic banking in new zealand. *International Journal of Bank Marketing, 24*(6), 360–383. doi:10.1108/02652320610701717.

Gan, C., Limsombunchai, V., Clemes, M., & Weng, A. (2005). Consumer choice prediction: Artificial neural networks versus logistic models. *Journal of the Social Sciences, 1*(4), 211–219. doi:10.3844/jssp.2005.211.219.

Gardener, E., Howcroft, B., & Williams, J. (1999). The new retail banking revolution. *The Service Industries Journal, 19*(2), 83–100. doi:10.1080/02642069900000020.

Gefen, D. (2002). Reflections on the dimensions of trust and trustworthiness among online consumers. *The Data Base for Advances in Information Systems, 33*(3), 38–53. doi:10.1145/569905.569910.

Gefen, D., Karahanna, E., & Straub, D. W. (2003). Trust and TAM in online shopping: An integrated model. *Management Information Systems Quarterly, 27*(1), 51–90.

Gefen, D., & Straub, D. W. (2003). The relative importance of perceived ease of use in IS adoption: A study of e-commerce adoption. *Journal of the Association for Information Systems, 1*(8), 1–28.

George, J. F. (2004). The theory of planned behaviour and internet purchasing. *Internet Research, 14*(3), 198–212. doi:10.1108/10662240410542634.

GetSatisfaction. (2012). *Get satisfaction anywhere.* Retrieved from http://getsatisfaction.com.

Ghosh, J., & Lele, A. (2010). Citi scam puts wealth managers under lens. *The Business Standard.* Retrieved from http://www.business-standard.com.

Gill, R., Henwood, K., & McLean, C. (2005). Body projects and regulation of normative masculinity. *Body & Society, 11*(1), 37–56. doi:10.1177/1357034X05049849.

Goldplus. (2010). *Goldplus launches diamantine india.* Retrieved from http://www.goldplus.in/goldplus-launches-diamantine-india.

Gong, C. (2010). The characteristics of cloud computing. In *Proceedings of 39th IEEE International Conference on Parallel Processing Workshops* (ICPPW). Washington, DC: IEEE Press.

Gopakumar, G., & Shukla, T. (2011). Citi fraud highlights regulatory gap in wealth MGMT service. *Money Control.* Retrieved from http://www.moneycontrol.com.

Gorpade & Goswami. (2011). After gold prices fall, goldsmiths take to adulterating. *DNA India.* Retrieved from http://www.dnaindia.com/bangalore/1593656/report-after-gold-prices-fall-goldsmiths-take-to-adulterating.

Compilation of References

Gourville, J. T., & Soman, D. (1998). Payment depeciation: The behavioral effects of temporarily separating payments from consuption. *The Journal of Consumer Research*, *25*(2), 160–174. doi:10.1086/209533.

Grabner-Kraeuter, S., & Faullant, R. (2008). Consumer acceptance of internet banking: The influence of internet trust. *International Journal of Bank Marketing*, *26*(7), 483–504. doi:10.1108/02652320810913855.

Grabner-Kraeuter, S., & Kaluscha, E. A. (2003). Empirical research in on-line trust: A review and critical assessment. *International Journal of Human-Computer Studies*, *58*, 783–812. doi:10.1016/S1071-5819(03)00043-0.

Grayson, K., Johnson, D., & Chen, D.-F. R. (2008). Is firm trust essential in a trusted environment? How trust in the business context influences customers. *JMR, Journal of Marketing Research*, *45*(2), 241–256. doi:10.1509/jmkr.45.2.241.

Gronroos, C. (2001). *Service management and marketing: A customer relationship management approach*. Chichester, UK: Wiley.

Grunig & Hunt. (1984). *Managing public relations*. New York: Holt, Rinehart, and Winston.

Grunig. (1992). Excellence in public relations and communication management. Mahwah, NJ: Erlmbaum.

Gulati, R., & Sytch, M. (2008). The dynamics of trust. *Academy of Management Review*, *33*(1), 276–278. doi:10.5465/AMR.2008.27753143.

Gupta, S., & Kim, H. W. (2007). The moderating effect of transaction experience on online purchase decision calculus. *International Journal of Electronic Commerce*, *12*(1), 127–158. doi:10.2753/JEC1086-4415120105.

Gyptra, P., & Dixon, P. (2002). Future of banking expectation. *Global Change*. Retrieved from www.globalchange.com/futurebank.htm.

Hachman, M. (2012). Facebook now totals 901 million users, Profit slip. *PCMag.com*. Retrieved from http://www.pcmag.com/article2/0,2817,2403410,00.asp.

Hamermesh, D. S., & Biddle, J. E. (1994). Beauty and the labor market. *The American Economic Review*, *84*(5), 1174–1194.

Hammermesh, R. G., Anderson, M. J., & Hards, J. E. (1978). Strategies for low market share businesses. *Harvard Business Review*, *50*(3), 95–102.

Hardin, R. (2002). *Trust and Trustworthiness*. New York: Russell Sage Foundation.

Harkonen, J. (2008). Labor force dynamics and the obesity gap in female unemployment in finland. *Research on Finnish Society*, *1*, 3–15.

Heath, C. & Soll. (1996). Mental budgeting and consumer decisions. *The Journal of Consumer Research*, *23*(1), 40–52. doi:10.1086/209465.

Herington, C., & Weaven, S. (2007). Can banks improve customer relationships with high quality online services? *Managing Service Quality*, *17*(4), 404–427. doi:10.1108/09604520710760544.

Hernandez, J. M. C., & Mazzon, J. A. (2007). Adoption of internet banking: Proposition and implementation of an integrated methodology approach. *International Journal of Bank Marketing*, 25(2), 72–88. doi:10.1108/02652320710728410.

Hezar, I., Dalgic, T., Phelan, S., & Knight, G. (2006). Principles of global niche marketing strategies: An early conceptual framework. In Dalgic, T. (Ed.), *Handbook of Niche Marketing: Principles and Practices*. New York: The Haworth Press.

Hill, N., & Alexander, J. (2006). *Handbook of customer satisfaction*. New Delhi: Gower.

Hinchcliffe, D., & Kim, P. (2012). *Social business by design: Transformative social media strategies for the connected company*. Hoboken, NJ: Jossey-Bass.

Hines, T. (2001). From analogue to digital supply chains: Implications for fashion marketing. In Hines & Bruce (Eds), Fashion Marketing, Contemporary Issues (34-36). Oxford, UK: Butterworth-Heinemann.

Hoffman, D. L., Novak, T. P., & Peralta, M. (1999). Building customer trust online. *Communications of the ACM*, 42(4), 80–85. doi:10.1145/299157.299175.

Howcroft, B., Hamilton, R., & Hewer, P. (2002). Consumer attitude and the usage and adoption of home banking in the united kingdom. *International Journal of Bank Marketing*, 20(3), 111–121. doi:10.1108/02652320210424205.

Huang, E. Y., & Lin, C. Y. (2005). Customer-oriented financial service personalisation. *Industrial Management & Data Systems*, 105(1), 26–44. doi:10.1108/02635570510575171.

HUL. (2011). *Hindustan unilever limited-Our brands*. Retrieved from http://www.hul.co.in/brands/personalcarebrands/FairAndLovely.aspx.

HUL. (2011). *Hindustan unilever limited-Know us*. Retrieved from http://www.fairandlovely.in/knowledge_center/about_fairandlovely.aspx.

HUL. (2012). *Hindustan unilever limited-Introduction to HUL*. Retrieved from http://www.hul.co.in/aboutus/introductiontohul/.

IBEF. (n.d.). *KPMG report*. Retrieved from http://www.ibef.org/download/ibef_%20jewellery_06.pdf.

IBISWorld. (2011). Tobacco product manufacturing in australia. *Australian Industry Report*. Retrieved on http://www.ibisworld.com.au/industry/default.aspx?indid=120.

IBTimes Staff Reporter. (2010). India's citibank fraud case: Gurgaon police arrest key suspect shiv raj puri. *International Business Times*. Retrieved from http://www.ibtimes.com/articles/96175/20101230/india-s-citibank-fraud-case-gurgaon-police-arrest-key-suspect-shiv-raj-puri.htm#ixzz1HWv6BVeG.

India Times. (n.d.). Retrieved from http://economictimes.indiatimes.com/tech/software/mobile-internet-startups-to-shine-despite-dim-facebook-ipo/articleshow/13683334.cms.

Indian footwear market has large potential. (2009). *One India News*. Retrieved from http://news.oneindia.in/2009/07/13/indian-footwear-market.

Compilation of References

Indian Jewelers New Service. (2012). *Industries plans to increase number of goldplus, tanishq stores.* Retrieved from www.indianjeweller.in/contentview.aspx/ Titan.

Investopedia. (2013). *High net worth individual-HNWI.* Retrieved from http://www.investopedia.com.

Islam, K. S., Ahmed, H. S., Karim, E., & Amin, A. M. (2006). *The whiter the better, 5*(94). Retrieved from http://www.thedailystar.net/magazine/2006/05/02/cover.htm.

İslamoğlu, A. H. & Altunışık. (2008). *Tüketici davranışları.* İstanbul: Beta Publications.

Jarvenpaa, S. L., Shaw, T. R., & Staples, S. (2004). Toward contextualised theories of trust: The role of trust in global virtual teams. *Information Systems Research, 15*(3), 250–267. doi:10.1287/isre.1040.0028.

Jarvenpaa, S. L., Tractinsky, N., & Saarinen, L. (1999). Consumer trust in an internet store: A cross-cultural validation. *Journal of Computer-Mediated Communication, 5*(2).

Jerga, J. (2011). More info needed on cigarette laws, says opposition health spokesman dutton. *The Australian.* Retrieved from http://www.theaustralian.com.au/news/breaking-news/more-info-needed-on-cigarette-laws-says-opposition-health-spokseman-dutton/story-fn3dxity-1226035388737.

Jha, D. K. (2011). Personal care industry set to grow 15% in 5 years. *Business Standard.* Retrieved from http://www.business-standard.com/india/news/personal-care-industry-set-to-grow-15-in-five-yrs/457480/.

Jones, L. (2012). *Fashion therapy, Daily mail.* Retrieved from http://www.dailymail.co.uk/femail/article-2160686/LIZ-JONES-FASHION-THERAPY--Why-Zaras-step-ahead.html#ixzz1z5C003rV.

JustStyles. (2011). *Indian gems and jewelry market-Future prospects to 2011.* Retrieved from http://www.Juststyle.com.

Kadakia, P.; Nigam, A. & Rao, A. (2009). Outlook for personal care industry: An indian perspective. *Chemical Weekly*, 208-210.

Kahneman, D. & Tversky. (1979). Prospect theory: An analysis of decision under risk. *Econometrica, 47*(2), 263–291. doi:10.2307/1914185.

Kalagiakos, P., & Karampelas, P. (2011). Cloud computing learning. In *Proceedings of 5th IEEE International Conference on Application of Information and Communication Technologies.* Washington, DC: IEEE Press.

Kandampully, J. (2002), *Services management: The new paradigm in hospitality.* Melbourne, Austrailia: Pearson Education.

Kannan, S. (2009). Tanishq hopes to raise the bar for jewelry artisans. *The Hindu Business Line.* Retrieved from http://www.thehindubusinessline.com/todays-paper/tp-marketing/tanishq-hopes-to-raise-the-bar-for-jewellery-artisans/article1066398.ece.

Kantsperger, R., & Kunz, W. H. (2010). Consumer trust in service companies: A multiple mediating analysis. *Managing Service Quality, 20*(1), 4–25. doi:10.1108/09604521011011603.

Karlsson, N., Garling, T., & Selart, M. (1997). Effects of mental accounting on intertemporal choice. *Göteborg Psychological Reports, 27*, 1–17.

Karnani, A. (2007). Doing well by doing good-Case study: 'Fair & lovely' whitening cream. Michigan Ross School of Business, 28(13), 1351-1357.

Kasiran, Z., & Yahya, S. (2007). Facial expression as an implicit customers' feedback and the challenges. In *Proceedings of Computer Graphics, Imaging, and Visualisation.* Bangkok, Thailand: IEEE Press. doi:10.1109/CGIV.2007.40.

Kassim, N. M., & Abdulla, A. K. M. A. (2006). The influence of attraction on internet banking: An extension to the trust-relationship commitment model. *International Journal of Bank Marketing, 24*(6), 424–442. doi:10.1108/02652320610701744.

Kaya. (2005). *Consumer trends report.* Retrieved from www.pilgrim.co.in/images/kaya_report.pdf.

Kendall. (1997). Public relations campaign strategies: Planning for implementation (2nd Ed.). New York: Addison-Wesley.

Kenning, P. (2008). The influence of general trust and specific trust on buying behavior. *International Journal of Retail & Distribution Management, 36*(6), 461–476. doi:10.1108/09590550810873938.

Kerin, R., Hartley, S., & Rudelius, W. (2013). *Marketing.* New York: McGraw-Hill.

Kivetz, R. (1999). Advances in research on mental accounting and reason–based choice. *Marketing Letters, 10*(3), 249–266. doi:10.1023/A:1008066718905.

Kotler, P. (1986). Mega marketing-Strategies to enter blocked markets. *Harvard Business Review.*

Kramer, R. (1999). Trust and distrust in organisations: Emerging perspectives, enduring questions. *Annual Review of Psychology*, 569–598. doi:10.1146/annurev.psych.50.1.569 PMID:15012464.

Krishnan, S. (2010). BMW vs mercedes-Clash of the teutons. *The Business Standard.* Retrieved from http://bsmotoring.com/news/bmw-vs-mercedes-clashthe-teutons/2102/1.

Kulkarni, P. (2011). RBI seeks wealth management details post citibank scam. *India Times.* Retrieved from http://articles.economictimes.indiatimes.com.

Kumar, S. R. (2009). Adapting IMC to emerging markets: Importance of Cultural values in the indian context. *Journal of Integrated Marketing Communication*, 38-42.

Kumar, A., & Paddison, R. (2000). Trust and collaborative planning theory: The case of the Scottish planning system. *International Planning Studies, 5*(2), 205–223. doi:10.1080/13563470050020194.

Kumar, N., & Linguri, S. (2006). Zara fashion sense. *Business Strategy Review, 17*(2), 81–84. doi:10.1111/j.0955-6419.2006.00409.x.

Kumar, N., Scheer, L. K., & Steenkamp, J.-B. E. M. (1995). The effects of perceived interdependence on dealer attitudes. *JMR, Journal of Marketing Research, 32*(3), 348–356. doi:10.2307/3151986.

Kumar, S. R., Guruvayurappan, N., & Banerjee, M. (2007). Cultural values and branding in an emerging market: The Indian context. *The Marketing Review, 7*(3), 247–272. doi:10.1362/146934707X230086.

Lane, R. (2011). *Mercedes benz, audi, and BMW: India war of the German triad.* Retrieved from http://www.bmwownersclub.com/forums/index.php/topic/5645-mercedes-benz-audi-and-bmw-india-war-of-the-german-triad-rush-lane.

Compilation of References

Lasagna, L. (1964). *Evolution of medical ethics: Hippocratic oath modern version.* Retrieved from https://owlspace-ccm.rice.edu/access/content/user/ecy1/Nazi Human Experimentation/Pages/Hippocratic Oath-modern.html.

Leduc, B. (1998). *Target a niche market to increase your sales and profits.* Retrieved from http://www.smithfam.com/news/aug98j.html.

Lee, P. (1996). The cutting edge: So far, online banking is mostly wishful thinking. *Los Angeles Times.* Retrieved from http://articles.latimes.com/1996-09-30/business/fi-48990_1_online-bank-customers.

Lee, M. K. O., & Turban, E. (2001). A trust model for consumer internet shopping. *International Journal of Electronic Commerce, 6*(1), 75–91.

Leistikow, N. (2003). Indian women criticize 'fair and lovely' ideal. *Women's ENews.* Retrieved from http://oldsite.womensenews.org/article.cfm/dyn/aid/1308/context/archive>.

Li, J., & Oussalah, M. (2010). Automatic face emotion recognition system. In *Proceedings of the IEEE 9th International Conference on Cybernetic Intelligent Systems.* Reading, UK: IEEE Press.

Li, E. P. H., Min, H. J., Belk, R. W., Kimura, J., & Bahl, S. (2008). Skin lightening and beauty in four Asian cultures. *Advances in Consumer Research. Association for Consumer Research (U. S.), 35,* 444–449.

Linneman, R. E., & Stanton, L. Jr. (1992). *Making niche marketing work: How to grow big by acting smaller.* New York: McGraw Hill.

Linneman, R. E., & Stanton, L. Jr. (1992). Mining for niches. *Business Horizons, 35*(3), 43–51. doi:10.1016/0007-6813(92)90068-K.

Luarn, P. & Lin, L. H. (2004). Towards an understanding of the behavioural intention to use mobile banking. *Computers in Human Behaviour,* 1-19.

Lyell, D., Crane, R., Crowley, M., & Fraser, I. (1997). *Financial institutions and markets.* Sydney: LBC Information Services.

Lymperopoulos, C., Chaniotakis, I. E., & Rigopoulou, I. D. (2010). Acceptance of detergent-retail brands: The role of consumer confidence and trust. *International Journal of Retail & Distribution Management, 38*(9), 719–736. doi:10.1108/09590551011062457.

Mackay, J., & Eriksen, M. (2002). *The tobacco atlas.* Geneva, Switzerland: World Health Organisation. Retrieved from http://www.who.int/tobacco/statistics/tobacco_atlas/en/.

Magazine, H. U. L. (2012). Doing well by doing good. *Hamara-The Hindustan Unilever Employee Magazine, 8.* Retrieved from http://www.hul.co.in/Images/HUL_75Years_Special_Issue_tcm114-194253.pdf.

Mahesh, R. (2006). Despite volatile price, tanishq gold sales up. *Financial Express.* Retrieved from http://www.Financial-Express.com/old/latest_full_story.php?content_id=136052.

Mail, D. (2012). *Valued at $100bn, Facebook expected to hold record-breaking IPO launch in third week of May.* Retrieved from http://www.dailymail.co.uk/news/article-2087557/Facebook-IPO-date-Launch-expected-week-May.html.

MakeUseOf. (2010). *How does facebook work? The nuts and bolts.* Retrieved from http://www.makeuseof.com/tag/facebook-work-nuts-bolts-technology-explained/.

Marshall, A. (2009). *Principles of economics* (8th ed.). New York: Cosimo Publications.

Mason, K. (2005). How corporate sport sponsorship impacts consumer behavior. *The Journal of American Academy of Business-Cambridge, 7*(1), 32–35.

Massola, L. (2011). Coalition split over cigarette packaging as barnaby joyce backs tobacco companies. *The Australian.* Retrieved from http://www.theaustralian.com.au/national-affairs/coalition-split-over-cigarette-packaging-as-barnaby-joyce-backs-tobacco-companies/story-fn59niix-1226061714807.

Mattila, H., King, R., & Ojala, N. (2002). Retail performance measures for seasonal fashion. *Journal of Fashion Marketing and Management, 6*(4), 340–351. doi:10.1108/13612020210448637.

Mayer, R. C., Davis, J. H., & Schoorman, F. D. (1995). An integrative model of organisational trust. *Academy of Management Review, 10*(3), 709–734.

McCole, P., & Ramsey, E. (2009). A profile of adopters and non-adopters of ecommerce in SME professional service firms. *Australasian Marketing Journal, 13,* 36–45. doi:10.1016/S1441-3582(05)70066-5.

McGee, G. (2011). Cigarette packaging to go ugly olive green under proposed laws. *Herald Sun.* Retrieved from http://www.heraldsun.com.au/news/more-news/cigarette-packaging-to-go-ugly-olive-green-under-proposed-laws/story-fn7x8me2-1226035141689.

McGuire, W. J. (1976). Some internal psychological factors influencing consumer choice. The University of Chicago Press Journal of Consumer Research, 2(4).

McKnight, D. H., Choudhury, V., & Kacmar, C. (2002). Developing and validating trust measures for e-commerce: An integrative typology. *Information Systems Research, 13*(3), 334–361. doi:10.1287/isre.13.3.334.81.

McKnight, H. D., & Chervany, N. L. (2002). What trust means in e-commerce customer relationships: An interdisciplinary conceptual typology. *International Journal of Electronic Commerce, 6*(2), 35–59.

McNeal, J. U., & McDaniel, S. W. (1984). An analysis of need-appeals in television advertising. *Journal of the Academy of Marketing Science, 12*(2), 176–190. doi:10.1007/BF02729495.

Melwani, L. (2007). The white complex. Retrieved from http://www.littleindia.com/news/134/ARTICLE/1828/2007-08-18.html.

Memcached. (2009). *What is memcached?* Retrieved from http://memcached.org/.

Menon, J. (2011). *Mercedes, BMW continue the war of supremacy in india.* Retrieved from http://automotivehorizon.sulekha.com/mercedes-well-set-to-regain-top-slot-from-bmw-in-india_newsitem_2936.

Miles, M. B., & Huberman, A. M. (1994). *Qualitative data analysis: An expanded source book* (2nd ed.). Thousand Oaks, CA: Sage Publications.

Milkman, K. L. & Beashers. (2009). Mental accounting and small windfalls: Evidence from an online grocer. *Journal of Economic Behavior & Organization, 71*(2), 384–394. doi:10.1016/j.jebo.2009.04.007.

Mirza international reports Rs 95.09 crore turnover for quarter ended June, 2010. (2010). Retrieved from www.moneycontrol.com.

Mirza International targets Rs 480-500cr top line this year. (2010). Retrieved from www.moneycontrol.com.

Mirza International. (2009). *Annual report.* Retrieved from http://www.mirza.co.in/annual_report_currentyear.html.

Mishra, A. (2009). *Forbes india: The BMW-mercedes war in india.* Retrieved from http://ibnlive.in.com/news/forbes-india-the-bmwmercedes-war-in-india/100486-25.html.

Mittal, B., & Lassar, W. M. (1996). The role of personalisation in service encounters. *Journal of Retailing, 72*(1), 95–109. doi:10.1016/S0022-4359(96)90007-X.

Module for Hosting. (2013). What is apache HTTP server? Retrieved from.http://www.modulehosting.com/apache.html

Moerman, L., & Van Der Laan, S. (2005). Social reporting in the tobacco industry: All smoke and mirrors? *Accounting, Auditing & Accountability Journal, 18*(3), 374–389. doi:10.1108/09513570510600747.

Money Contorol. (1970). Tata gold plus promises to offer pure gold. Retrieved from http://www.moneycontrol.com/news/business/goldplustata-promises-to-offer-pure-gold-jewellery_190784.html.

Moni, M. A., & Ali, A. B. M. S. (2009). HMM based hand gesture recognition: A review on techniques and approaches. In *Proceedings of the 2nd IEEE International Conference on Computer Science and Information Technology.* Washington, DC: IEEE Press.

Moorman, C., Zaltman, G., & Deshpande, R. (1992). Relationships between providers and users of marketing research: Dynamics of trust within and between organisations. *JMR, Journal of Marketing Research, 29*, 314–329. doi:10.2307/3172742.

Morgan, R. M., & Hunt, S. D. (1994). The commitment-trust theory of relationship marketing. *Journal of Marketing, 58*(3), 20–38. doi:10.2307/1252308.

Mukherjee, A., & Nath, P. (2003). A model of trust in online relationship banking. *International Journal of Bank Marketing, 21*(1), 5–15. doi:10.1108/02652320310457767.

Nager, N. R., & Allen, T. H. (1984). *Public relations managed by objectives.* Lanham, MD: University Press of America.

Naylor, J. B., Naim, M. M., & Berry, D. (1999). Leagility: Integrating the lean and agile manufacturing paradigms in the total supply chain. *International Journal of Production Economics, 62*, 107–118. doi:10.1016/S0925-5273(98)00223-0.

NDTV Profit. (2013). Retrieved from http://profit.ndtv.com/news/show/rs-400-crore-fraud-uncovered-at-citibank-s-gurgaon-branch-132352?cp.

NDTV Profit. (2013). Retrieved from http://profit.ndtv.com/news/show/probe-into-citibank-fraud-to-complete-soon-govt-143568?cp.

New Indian Express. (2009). Unique offers for this akshaya tritiya. Retrieved from http://newindianexpress.com/cities/chennai/article62157.ece?service=print.

Newsonproject.com. (2012). *Tata industries plans to increase the retail presence.* Retrieved from http://www.newsonprojects.com/story.asp?news_code=13254.

O'Guinn, T., Allen, C., & Semenik, R. J. (2009). *Advertising and integrated brand promotion* (5th ed.). Independence, KY: Cengage.

Palmatier, R. W., Dant, R. P., Grewal, D., & Evans, K. R. (2006). Factors influencing the effectiveness of relationship marketing: a meta-analysis. *Journal of Marketing, 70*(4), 136–153. doi:10.1509/jmkg.70.4.136.

Parekh. (2011). Lack of wealth MGMT guidelines caused citibank fraud. *Press Trust of India.* Retrieved from http://www.business-standard.com.

Parrish, E. D., Cassill, N. L., & Oxenham, W. (2006). Niche market strategy for a mature marketplace. *Marketing Intelligence & Planning, 24*(7), 694–707. doi:10.1108/02634500610711860.

Patton, M. A. (2004). Technologies for trust in electronic commerce. *Electronic Commerce Research, 4*, 9–21. doi:10.1023/B:ELEC.0000009279.89570.27.

Pavlou, P. A. (2003). Consumer acceptance of electronic commerce: Integrating trust and risk with the technology acceptance model. *International Journal of Electronic Commerce, 7*(3), 101–134.

Pavlou, P. A., & Gefen, D. (2004). Building effective online market places with institution-based trust. *Information Systems Research, 15*(1), 37–59. doi:10.1287/isre.1040.0015.

Pavlou, P., & Fygenson, M. (2006). Understanding and predicting electronic commerce adoption: An extension of the theory of planned behaviour. *Management Information Systems Quarterly, 30*, 115–143.

PHP. (2013). What is PHP? Retrieved from http://php.net/manual/en/intro-whatis.php.

Pine & Gilmore. (1999). *The Experience Economy.* Boston: Harvard Business School Press.

Pinto, V. S. (2011). Garnier steps on the gas. *Business Standard.* Retrieved from http://business-standard.com/india/news/garnier-stepsthe-gas/430274/.

Popp, A. (2000). Swamped in information but starved of data: Information and intermediaries in clothing supply chains. *Supply Chain Management: An International Journal, 5*(3), 151–161. doi:10.1108/13598540010338910.

Pradhan, S. (2012). *Retailing management text and cases.* Noida, India: Tata McGraw.

Pralahad, C. K., Ramaswamy, P. B., Katzenback, J. R., Lederer, C., & Sam, H. (2002). *Harvard business review on customer relationship management.* Boston: Harvard Business Press.

Prelec, D. & Loewenstein. (1998). The red and the black: Mental accounting of savings and debts. *Marketing Science, 17*(1), 4–28. doi:10.1287/mksc.17.1.4.

Presi, C. (2009). Motivation and values. *LUBS5402 Consumer Behavior. Week Three Lecture, 5.*

Production starts at new unit of the company. (2011). *Press releases of mirza international.* Retrieved from www.mirza.co.in/announce-ments.html.

PTI. (2011) Citi fraudster took exposure of Rs 1.13 lakh cr on nifty:sebi. *One India.* Retrieved from http://news.oneindia.in

Raj, A. (2011). *Mercedes, BMW may miss their yearly targets in india.* Retrieved from http://www.livemint.com/2011/11/09213328/Mercedes-BMW-may-miss-their-y.html.

Ramphal, S. (2006). *Mental Accounting: The Psychology of South African Consumer Behaviour.* (Unpublished Master's Thesis). Pretoria, South Africa, University of Pretoria.

Ratnasingam, P., Gefen, D., & Pavlou, P. A. (2005). The role of facilitating conditions and institutional trust in electronic marketplaces. *Journal of Electronic Commerce, 48*(3), 69–82. doi:10.4018/jeco.2005070105.

Raynor, M. E. (1992). The pitfalls of niche marketing. *The Journal of Business Strategy, 13*(2), 29–32. doi:10.1108/eb039478 PMID:10117142.

Red tape plans 16 more exclusive outlets. (2007). *The business line.* Retrieved from www.thehindubusinessline.com/todays-paper/tp-marketing/.

Reporter, B. S. (2011, March 06). Wealth management under FSDC radar. Retrieved from http://www.business-standard.com

Report, W. (1997). *The financial system inquiry final report.* Canberra, Australia: AGPS..

Rhee, H. S., & Riggins, F. (1999). *GVU's WWW user surveys: High level summary of internet banking survey.* Retrieved from www.gvu.gatech.edu/user-survey/survey-1997-04/graphs/banking/report.html.

Ribbink, D., Riel, A., Liljander, V., & Streukens, S. (2004). Comfort your online customer: Quality, trust, and loyalty on the internet. *Managing Service Quality, 14*(6), 446–456. doi:10.1108/09604520410569784.

Riegelsberger, J., Sasse, A. M., & McCarthy, J. D. (2005). The mechanics of trust: A framework for research and design. *International Journal of Human-Computer Studies, 62,* 381–422. doi:10.1016/j.ijhcs.2005.01.001.

Ruscio, K. P. (1999). Jay's pirouette, or why political trust is not the same as personal trust. *Administration & Society, 31*(5), 639–657. doi:10.1177/00953999922019274.

Sahota, P. (n.d.). *Germany vs germany in india: BMW & mercedes benz.* Retrieved from http://www.indiancarsbikes.in/auto-news/mercedes-benz-vs-bmw-india-sales-4782/.

Sarpila, O., & Rasanen, P. (2010). Personal care consumption in finland: Trends in the early 2000s. *The International Journal of Sociology and Social Policy, 31*(7/8), 441–455. doi:10.1108/01443331111149879.

Sathye, M. (1999). Adoption of internet banking by Australian consumers: An empirical investigation. *International Journal of Bank Marketing, 17*(7), 324–334. doi:10.1108/02652329910305689.

Schiffman, L. G., Kanuk, L. L., & Kumar, S. R. (2010). *Consumer behavior* (10th ed.). Delhi, India: Pearson Education.

Search Enterprise Linux. (2008). *Definition: Linux.* Retrieved from http://searchenterprise-linux.techtarget.com/definition/Linux.

Seddon, J. (2009). *BrandZ top 100 most valuable global brands.* Retrieved from http://www.brandz.com/upload/brandz-report-2009-complete-report(1).pdf.

Seitel, F. P. (2006). *The practice of public relations.* Upper Saddle River, NJ: Prentice Hall.

Sewell, C., & Brown, P. B. (2002). *Customers for life: How to turn that one time buyer into a lifetime customer.* New York: Crown Business.

Shani, D., & Chalasani, S. (1992). Exploiting niches using relationship marketing. *Journal of Consumer Marketing*, *9*(3), 33–42. doi:10.1108/07363769210035215.

Shankar, P. R., & Subish, P. (2007). Fair skin in south asia: An obsession? *Journal of Pakistan Association of Dermatologists*, *17*, 100–104.

Shelby & Nevin. (1974). Power in a channel of distribution: Sources and consequences. *JMR, Journal of Marketing Research*, *9*(1).

Shevde, N. (2008). All's fair in love and cream: A cultural case study of fair & lovely in india. *Advertising and Society Review*, *9*(2). Retrieved from http://muse.jhu.edu/login?uri=/journals/advertising_and_society_review/v009/9.2.shevde.pdf.

Shrivastav. (2009). *Experiential marketing: Buy it or leave it, but try it with pleasure.* Retrieved from www.televisionpoint.com.

Singh, N. (2009). *Youngest user of fairness creams is just 12.* Retrieved from http://timesofindia.indiatimes.com/Business/India-Business/Youngest-ser-of-fairness-creams-is-just-12/articleshow/4371786.cms.

Sirdeshmukh, D., Singh, J., & Sabol, B. (2002). Consumer trust, value, and loyalty in relational exchanges. *Journal of Marketing*, *66*(1), 15–37. doi:10.1509/jmkg.66.1.15.18449.

Sissors, J. Z. (1966). What is a market? *Journal of Marketing*, *30*(3), 17–21. doi:10.2307/1249085.

SmartInvestor. In. (2010). *Rs 400 cr fraud uncovered at citibank's gurgaon branch.* Retrieved from http://smartinvestor.in/market/story-54488-storydet-Rs_400_cr_fraud_uncovered_at_Citibanks_Gurgaon_branch.htm.

Sohail, M. S., & Shanmugam, B. (2003). E-banking and customer preferences in malaysia: An empirical investigation. *Information Sciences*, *150*, 207–217. doi:10.1016/S0020-0255(02)00378-X.

Solomon, M. R. (2011). *Consumer behavior: Buying, having, and being* (9th ed.). Upper Saddle River, NJ: Pearson.

Soman, D. (2004). Framing, loss aversion, and mental accounting. In Koehler, D. J., & Harvey, N. (Eds.), *Blackwell Handbook of Judgment & Decision Making.* Hoboken, NJ: Blackwell Publishing Ltd. doi:10.1002/9780470752937.ch19.

Srinivasan, S. S., Anderson, R., & Ponnavolu, K. (2002). Customer loyalty in e-commerce: An exploration of its antecedents and consequences. *Journal of Retailing*, *78*(1), 41–50. doi:10.1016/S0022-4359(01)00065-3.

Compilation of References

Srinivasan, T. C. (1987). An integrative approach to consumer choice. *Advances in Consumer Research. Association for Consumer Research (U. S.)*, *14*, Retrieved from http://www.acrwebsite.org/volumes/display.asp?id=6661.

Stanton, J. L., & Linneman, R. E. (1991). *Making niche marketing work*. New York: McGraw-Hill Inc..

Subramanian, S. (2007). Golden management lessons from titan. *Rediff Business*. Retrieved from http://www.rediff.com/money/special/titan/20070328.htm.

Successful Product Differentiation Strategies. (2010). *Strategic direction*. Bingley, UK: Emerald Group Publishing Limited.

Suh, B., & Han, I. (2003). The impact of consumer trust and perceptions of security control on the acceptance of electronic commerce. *International Journal of Electronic Commerce*, *7*(3), 135–161.

Sull, D., & Turconi, S. (2008). Fast Fashion Lessons. *Business Strategy Review*, *19*(2), 4–11. doi:10.1111/j.1467-8616.2008.00527.x.

Swagata Gupta And John Satish Kumar. (2011, January 07). Indian Regulators Investigating Citi Case. Retrieved from http://online.wsj.com

Tan, M., & Teo, T. S. H. (2000). Factors influencing the adoption of internet banking. *Journal of the Association for Information Systems*, *1*, 1–42.

TATA Group. (2001). Tanishq in talks with US Group to market jewelry. Retrieved from http://www.tata.in/company/Media/inside.aspx?artid=us2gxa6D+rY=economictimes.

TATA Group. (2008). *The world's biggest gold bangle unveil by the gold plus jewelry*. Retrieved from http://www.IndiaPRwire.com/pressrelease/fashion/2008080711862.htm.

TeachTerms. (2013). *MySQL*. Retrieved from http://www.techterms.com/definition/mysql.

Teo, T. S. H., & Liu, J. (2007). Consumer trust in e-commerce in the united states, Singapore, and china. *Omega–The International Journal of Management Science*, *35*, 22–38. doi:10.1016/j.omega.2005.02.001.

Thaler, R. H. & Shefrin. (1981). An economic theory of self control. *The Journal of Political Economy*, *89*(2), 392–406. doi:10.1086/260971.

Thaler, R. H. (1980). Towards a positive theory of consumer choice. *Journal of Economic Behavior & Organization*, *1*, 39–60. doi:10.1016/0167-2681(80)90051-7.

Thaler, R. H. (1985). Mental accounting and consumer choice. *Marketing Science*, *4*(3), 199–214. doi:10.1287/mksc.4.3.199.

Thaler, R. H. (1990). Anomalies: Saving, fungibility, and mental accounts. *The Journal of Economic Perspectives*, *4*(1), 193–205. doi:10.1257/jep.4.1.193.

Thaler, R. H. (1999). Mental accounting matters. *Journal of Behavioral Decision Making*, *12*, 183–206. doi:10.1002/(SICI)1099-0771(199909)12:3<183::AID-BDM318>3.0.CO;2-F.

Thaler, R. H. (2008). Mental accounting and consumer choice. *Marketing Science*, *27*(1), 15–25. doi:10.1287/mksc.1070.0330.

The Business Standard. (2011). E-paper dated 6th March 2011. Retrieved from http://www.business-standard.com/todays-paper.

The Business Standard. (2011). E-paper dated 3rd December-2011. Retrieved from http://www.business-standard.com/todays-paper.

The Times of India. (2012). *Gold demand falls for 2nd straight quarter.* Retrieved from http://articles.timesofindia.indiatimes.com/2012-08-17/india-business/33248673_1_gold-demand-world-gold-council-investment-demand.

Thrift, A. (2012). *Getting started.* Retrieved from http://thrift.apache.org/.

Tiwari, V. (2011). *The write handed drive: BMW merc audi faceoff.* Retrieved from http://www.themarketers.in/the-write-handed-drive/.

Tobacco in Australia Facts and Issues On line Resource. (n.d.). Retrieved from http://www.tobaccoinaustralia.org.au/chapter-10-tobacco-industry/10-8-the-tobacco-growing-industry.

Toften, K., & Hammervoll, T. (2008). Niche marketing and strategic capabilities: An exploratory study of specialized firms. *Marketing Intelligence & Planning, 28*(6), 736–753. doi:10.1108/02634501011078138.

Toften, K., & Hammervoll, T. (2009). Niche firms and marketing strategy: An exploratory study of internationally oriented niche firms. *European Journal of Marketing, 43*(11/12), 1378–1391. doi:10.1108/03090560910989948.

Trembath, B. (2011). Tobacco industry gets creative to skirt ad bans. *ABC news.* Retrieved from http://www.abc.net.au/news/stories/2010/04/29/2886304.htm.

Tversky, A., & Kahneman, D. (1981). The framing of decisions and the psychology of choice. *Science, 21*(1), 453–458. doi:10.1126/science.7455683 PMID:7455683.

Uniglobe, T. I. (2011). *Nine in Ten business travel clients give uniglobe high marks for service quality.* Retrieved from http://corp.uniglobetravel.com/site/viewhome.asp?aid=39086&sit=314&vty=ARTICLE&tid=21030&sessionid=.

Unnithan, C. R., & Swatman, P. M. C. (2001). eBanking adaptation and dot.com viability–A comparison of Australian and Indian experiences in the banking sector. In *Proceedings of the 11th BIT 2001 Conference.* Manchester, UK: AES Press.

Van Hoek, R. (2000). The thesis of legality revisited. *International Journal of Agile Management Systems, 2*(3), 196-201.

Varadarajan, P. R., Clark, T., & Pride, W. M. (1992). Controlling the uncontrollable: Managing your marketing environment. *MIT Sloan Management Review, 33*(2), 39–47.

Wade, J., & Goodman, S. (2005). Effective marketing of small brands: Niche positions, attribute loyalty, and direct marketing. *Journal of Product and Brand Management, 14*(5), 292–299. doi:10.1108/10610420510616322.

Walczuch, R., & Lundgren, H. (2004). Psychological antecedents of institution-based consumer trust in e-retailing. *Information & Management, 42,* 159–177. doi:10.1016/j.im.2003.12.009.

Wang, Y. D., & Emurian, H. H. (2005). An overview of online trust: Concepts, elements, and implications. *Computers in Human Behavior, 21,* 105–125. doi:10.1016/j.chb.2003.11.008.

Wang, Y. S., Wang, Y. M., Lin, H. H., & Tang, T. I. (2003). Determinants of user acceptance of internet banking: An empirical research. *International Journal of Bank Marketing*, *14*(5), 501–519.

Webopedia. (2013). *Apache web server.* Retrieved from http://www.webopedia.com/TERM/A/Apache_Web_server.html.

Whittaker, R. H., & Levin, S. A. (1975). *Niche: Theory and application.* Stroudsburg, PA: Dowden, Hutchinson & Ross Inc..

Wikipedia. (2013). *High-net-worth individual.* Retrieved from http://en.wikipedia.org.

Wikipedia. (2013). *Scribe (log server).* Retrieved from http://en.wikipedia.org/wiki/Scribe_(log_server).

Wikipedia. (2013). *Mark zuckerberg.* Retrieved from http://en.wikipedia.org/wiki/Mark_Zuckerberg.

Wikipedia. (2013). *Wealth management.* Retrieved from http://en.wikipedia.org.

Winsor, R. D., Sheth, J. N., & Manolis, C. (2002). Differentiating goods and services retailing using form and possession utilities. *Journal of Business Research*, *57*(3), 249–255. doi:10.1016/S0148-2963(02)00324-7.

Wong & Bill. (2008). Determinants of SME international marketing communications. *Journal of Global Marketing*, *21*(4).

World News Service. (2008). *The changing retail formats are changing the way jewelry is sold.* Retrieved from http://wwwdaimond-world.net/contentview.aspx?item=2465.

World, I. B. I. S. (2005). *National and regional commercial banks in australia (k7325).* Retrieved from www.ibisworld.com.au.

Worthington, S., & Edwards, V. (2000). Changes in payments markets, past, present and future: A comparison between australia and the UK. *International Journal of Bank Marketing*, *18*(5), 212–221. doi:10.1108/02652320010356771.

Yousafzai, S. Y., Pallister, J. G., & Foxall, G. R. (2003). A proposed model of e-trust for electronic banking. *Technovation*, *23*, 847–860. doi:10.1016/S0166-4972(03)00130-5.

Yousafzai, S. Y., Pallister, J. G., & Foxall, G. R. (2005). Strategies for building and communicating trust in electronic banking: A field experiment. *Psychology and Marketing*, *22*(2), 181–201. doi:10.1002/mar.20054.

Zeithaml, V. A., & Bitner, M. (2003). *Services marketing: Integrating customer focus across the firm* (3rd ed.). Boston: McGraw Hill.

Zhan, Y., Chen, H., & Zhang, G.-C. (2006). An optimization algorithm of k-nn classification. In *Proceedings of the Fifth International Conference on Machine Learning and Cybernetics.* Dalian, China: IEEE Press.

Zhang, S., Lei, B., Chen, A., Chen, C., & Chen, Y. (2010). Spoken emotion recognition using local fisher discriminant analysis. In *Proceedings of the IEEE 10th International Conference on Signal Processing* (ICSP). Beijing: IEEE Press.

Zhang, Z. Chen, & Huo. (2010). Cloud computing research and development trend. In *Proceedings of IEEE International Conference on Future Networks.* Washington, DC: IEEE Press.

Zhao & Zhang. (2009). The application of experiential marketing in china's real estate. *International Journal of Business Management*, *4*(5), 222–225.

About the Contributors

Vimi Jham is Associate Professor of Marketing at Institute of Management Technology – Dubai, United Arab Emirates. She holds a GCPCL from Harvard Business School, Boston, USA and a PhD from Aligarh Muslim University, India. She has been Visiting Professor to University of Applied Science, Fachhochschule Vorarlberg, Austria and University of Wollongong in Dubai. Her current area of research interest is in customer profitability analysis. She has published books, cases and research papers in refereed journals. She is an active trainer in the area of Customer Relationship Management. She serves on the editorial board of various International Journals. She is the Associate Regional Director for the International Institute of Marketing Professionals, Toronto , Canada for the Middle East region.

Sandeep Puri is working as a faculty in Marketing at IMT, Ghaziabad. He has done his Ph.D. in consumer behaviour. He is Gold Medalist during B. Pharmacy. He has over 19 years of experience in Industry & academics. He has held senior level positions in Marketing and Sales Management in Trident & Novartis. He has 24 publications in various International Journals, magazines and newspapers. He has published seven edited books. His case study is also published with Richard Ivey. He is a visiting faculty at prestigious business schools like S P Jain, Singapore, Fachhochschule Vorarlberg, Austria and Great Lakes His teaching, research and training interests include Customer Relationship Management, Sales Management & Service Marketing. He can be reached at spuri@imt.edu.

* * *

Sujana Adapa is a Lecturer in Management (Strategy & Marketing) in the UNE Business School at the University of New England (UNE), Armidale, Australia. Sujana teaches Introduction to Marketing, Marketing Strategy & Management, Services Marketing and International Marketing units at UNE for undergraduate and postgraduate students. Her research interests relate to the adoption of technological innovations, corporate social responsibility, sales management, destination visitations and branding. She has published research papers in reputed journals and presented her research in national and international conferences.

Salma Ahmed is an Associate Professor at Department of Business Administration, Faculty of Management Studies and Research, Aligarh Muslim University, Aligarh. Salma Ahmed has over 18 years of experience teaching MBA and IMBA (International Business) students. She has authored over 50 papers and research articles which also include cases and case analysis. She has a special interest in developing and also analyzing cases. In fact, 17 of her case analysis have been published in case analysis section of *Vikalpa-The Journal of Decision Makers*, published from The Indian Institute of Management, Ahmedabad. She has also attended over 40 conferences and presented papers at the national as well as international level. She is a faculty member for conducting case workshops at different management institutes. She has also authored a book entitled "How to Write and Analyse Cases."

Li-Minn Ang received the Bachelor of Engineering (1st class) and PhD in Engineering from Edith Cowan University, Australia, in 1996 and 2001, respectively. He is currently a research staff member at School of Engineering, Edith Cowan University. Prior to joining Edith Cowan University, he was Associate Professor at School of Electrical and Electronic Engineering, Nottingham University. He was also the research group leader of research group called Visual Information Engineering Research (VIER) group in Nottingham University, Malaysia campus. He also worked in Monash University Malaysia before joining Nottingham University. His research interests include the fields of video compression, visual processing, wireless visual sensor networks and reconfigurable computing.

Rohit Arora is a Lean Six Sigma Master Black Belt with 14+ year of experience in Business Excellence, Lean Six Sigma, Supply Chain Management, Pharma Quality & Manufacturing Operations. He is an ASQ Certified Quality Engineer, ASQ Certified LSS Black Belt and Certified MOST Assessor currently working with Jubilant Life Sciences. He is a domain expert in setting-up infrastructure for Corporate Quality function, driving improvements towards enhancing plant efficiency, & achieving an increase in productivity while curtailing operational costs & expenses.

Pardeep Bawa completed his Ph.D from Jaipur National University. He received a first class MBA degree in Marketing from Institute of Management & Entrepreneurship Development, Bharati Vidyapeeth in the year 2006. He worked with ICICI Lombard GIC Ltd. for two years before switching to academics. He has got nine research papers in refereed national & international journals to his credit. He is currently working with Lovely Professional University as an Assistant Professor.

Bhavna Bhalla is a qualified faculty member to train and fine-tune the budding managers of the country. She currently holds the position of Senior Lecturer, Business Communication at Institute of Management Technology Ghaziabad, India. Bhalla grew up in Lucknow, graduated from Navyug Girls Degree College (affiliated to Lucknow University) with B.A. and M.A. in English Literature. She completed her doctorate in the year 2010 from Indian Institute of Technology Kanpur, with special focus on Indian Aesthetics. She has published a number of papers in refereed international journals of repute. Gradually making a mark in professional world, she has gained a reputation of being an academician and an expert in the fields of Literature and Communication.

Suresh Chandra Bihari has about 32 years of experience in industry and academics. He is pursuing his academic passion, leaving behind a banking profession for 28 years, including 3 years as a trainer in Allahabad Bank. Presently, he is working as a Professor in Banking & Finance at IBS, Hyderabad, a top ranking business school of India and a constituent of IFHE, a Deemed University under section 3 of UGC Act, 1956. He has more than 100 publications to his credit that includes 11 text books, 6 study materials prepared for MBA students of a reputed University, 8 edited books, and 7 case studies, included in the European Case Clearing House, more than 50 research papers published in reputed and referred International and National Journals bot h in India and abroad. He has also presented his research papers in about 30 International and National Conferences, both in India and abroad that includes those at Northern State University, USA, IIM, Calcutta, MDI, Gurgaon, IMT, Ghaziabad and Nagpur, among others. He is also the winner of Macro Research Award 2009-10 of the Indian Institute of Banking & Finance and one of the prize winners of Micro Research Award 2010-11 of the same Institute. For the year 2011-12, he has won the First Prize under Micro Research Award of Indian Institute of Banking & Finance, the professional body of bankers in India having ISO certification. He is also a reviewer of Text Books, International Journal and is also in the editorial boards of several International Journals. Since October, 2012, he is the Consulting Editor of The IUP Journal of Bank Management, ICFAI University.

Necia Brown-Boone is a senior IT program manager for TaTa Consultancy Services, located in Edison, New Jersey and an Associate Graduate Business Professor for the University of Phoenix for six years. She was employed as the IT Director for the State of New York, the Vice President of Computer Operations and Information Services (COIS) for National City Corporation, and IT Director for Programming Systems Incorporated. She is an Associate Graduate Management Professor for more than 10 years. She is a dedicated leader, consultant, and facilitator providing working adults, students, and military personnel with many opportunities to achieve their professional and academic goals. She has an Associate's degree in Information Systems, B.B.A. in Accounting, a M.Ed. in Adult Learning and Development/Technology, a Ph.D. in Organizational Leadership. She is a certified IT project manager (PMP). She is an active member of Delta Sigma Theta Sorority, Incorporated and an effective leader of community service initiatives that has garnered her many accolades and awards in leadership.

Nidhi Chowdhry is a research scholar at Jaipur National University. She is a graduate in Economics from Delhi University and a post graduate in Economics from Jamia Milia Islamia University. She has published papers in refereed journals of repute. She has a professional span of approx 10 yrs. Her work has spanned from establishing and maintaining customer relations, building appraisal reports and pre-sales/market searches for upcoming ventures, MIS generation within the group/organization with development of reports.

Shreya Dhingra is a research scholar at Jaipur National University. She is working as a Business Coordinator in Ericsson India Pvt. Ltd. Shreya completed her graduation from CSJMU, Kanpur and Post-Graduation in Human Resource and Marketing from IILM, Greater Noida. She is pursuing her Doctorate with research focus on 'Job satisfaction: Exploring the dimension affecting employee satisfaction in Business Process Outsourcing". She has published her two research papers in reputed books as a beginner in the academic field.

Gautam Dutta is a mechanical engineer with Masters in Business Management. He has completed doctoral degree from Indian Institute of Technology (IIT) and presently working as Professor of Indian Institute of Foreign Trade. Prior to that, he served as Director of Indian Institute of Entrepreneurship (An organization under the Ministry of MSME, Government of India), and Professor and Head of the Department of Management Studies, Sikkim Manipal University He has about 29 years of experience in post graduate teaching in management, training, research and project consultancy on SME enterprise development and trade promotion. He teaches International Marketing and Entrepreneurship at campuses of IIFT at Delhi, Kolkata and Dar es Salam (Tanzania). He is actively involved in conducting sponsored research in the field of trade and development both at the national and international level. He is the recipient of UN fellowship and has extensively published research based articles in national and international journals of repute. His recent paper published in Journal for Borderland Studies.

Sonali S. Gadekar is presently associated with Mumbai Educational Trust's, Institute of Management, Bhujbal Knowledge City, Nashik, India, as an Associate Professor. She is heading the Finance Specialization and Academic Division in her college. Her Doctoral Research work is on the topic of 'Valuation and Measurement of Human Capital In Manufacturing Sector'. She has done MBA (Finance) and M.Phil (Management) and has 10 years of Academic Experience of teaching at Post Graduate Level. She has authored articles and research papers in Professional journals and presented papers in various seminars on the topics such as Knowledge Management, Human Capital Management and Corporate Sustainability. Having keen interest in Value Based Management, she conducts guest sessions on 'Management Lessons from Bhagwad Gita' and Vedic Management.

Sushil Gadekar is currently working as Vice Principal at MGV's Institute of Hotel Management, Nashik, India. He had submitted Ph.D Thesis, titled 'Market Segmentation and Effective Marketing Strategies For Tourism in Vidarbha Region'. He has done Masters in Tourism Management (MTM) and Bachelors in Hotel & Tourism Management (BHTM). He has 15 years of Industry Experience in India and abroad in the field of International Desserts, Bakery & Confectionery and Tourism as well as 11 years of academic experience. He used to participate in popular cookery show on Zee Television Channel in 2010. He had participated in the preparation of Longest Cake (3.5 km) in the World at Intercon Hotel in Dubai-an event got recorded in the Guinness Book in the year 1995.

Eric Van Genderen is Professor of International Business and Strategic Management at IMT-Dubai. Van Genderen holds a DBA from Henley Business School in the UK, with further studies completed through Thunderbird, and the Universities of Cambridge and Oxford. He is a lifetime 'fellow' of the Royal Society for the Encouragement of Arts, Manufactures, and Commerce (FRSA). Van Genderen has taught at universities in Europe and the Middle East. He has consulted MNEs including American Express, Citibank, ABN Amro Bank, Mars, Caterpillar, and the World Bank. He was hired as a content expert by the Education Testing Service (ETS; Princeton, NJ) to assist in developing a 'soft skills' exam to compliment the GMAT for business education. Van Genderen has published internationally in books and peer reviewed journals. He has also acted as a reviewer for A- and B- ranked business journals.

S. Jayachandran is Professor of Management in the Department of Management Studies, IIT Madras. He has MA in Economics and MBA in Business Administration from the University of Madras and has Ph.D. in Management with specialization in Marketing Management (1992) from IIT Madras. He has been accorded as Fellow of the Academy of Marketing Science (AMS), USA. Under his supervision and guidance, five Ph. D and two M.S. scholars have been awarded degrees. He has presented research papers in international conferences. He has published more than 25 research papers which include books, reputed journals and conference proceedings, and a text book titled "Marketing Management–Text and Cases" He has organized several short-term management development programs for executives and managers working in the industries. He has served as member in several selection committees and his interaction with other institutions/universities is well-known to the academic community. He has served as senate member in the University of Madras by nomination by His Excellency, the then Governor of Tamil Nadu, Honorable Dr. Chenna Reddy. He has been nominated as Institute delegate to the 80th annual conference of the Association of Indian Universities held in Allahabad, U.P in November 2005. He has served as 'Expert Committee Member' in the committees constituted by AICTE, NBA, MHRD, Govt. of India. He has been conferred the prestigious 'Bharat Jyoti Award' with a Certificate of Excellence for Meritorious Service by India International Friendship Society, New Delhi in Jan. 2006.

Shalini Kalia is an Assistant Professor and Area Chairperson of Business Communication, at Institute of Management Technology, Ghaziabad. With a Doctorate degree in English, Dr Kalia has more than 11 years of teaching experience at the national and international level. Her teaching, training, research, and consulting interests include Business Communication, Soft Skills, Personality Development, Cross Cultural Communication, and Corporate Etiquette. Apart from various courses on managerial and corporate communication, she offers elective course on Advanced Business English to enhance skills required for handling international English language examinations. Dr Kalia is trained to administer Thomas Personal Profile Analysis and has conducted numerous workshops and written articles, case studies, and research papers on various topics in different mainstream publications.

She has travelled far and wide to deliver her talks and workshops and is presently on several councils, including the British Council.

Ali Naci Karabulut is the lecturer and teaching assistant of Marketing at the Muğla Sıtkı Koçman University for 3 years. He received his B.S. degree from the Muğla Sıtkı Koçman University, Faculty of Business Administration, his M.B.A. from the Muğla Sıtkı Koçman University, Institute of Social Science, Department of Business Administration and he is at Ph.D. thesis phase at the Muğla Sıtkı Koçman University, Institute of Social Science, Department of Business Administration. Ali Naci Karabulut has published some articles in a variety of marketing and business journals and made presentations at national conferences.

Pradeep Kautish is Assistant Professor-Marketing Area in Jaipuria Institute of Management, Jaipur (Rajasthan). He is an MBA in Marketing Management and PhD in Consumer and Brand Management. His academic satchel brims with prestigious certifications such as National Eligibility Test (NET) in Management by University Grants Commission, New Delhi and conferred Accredited Management Teacher (AMT) in Marketing Management for his contributions in academics by All India Management Association, New Delhi. His professional experience is of more than a decade now which includes industry, academic research, training, and teaching experience with reputed organizations in India. Kautish has an impressive research credential with research papers, articles, case studies, technical papers, monographs, conference papers, and edited book chapters in national and international referred publications with leading publication houses.

Faisal Mahfooz holds a doctorate in Advertising and Masters in Advertising and Marketing (Leeds University, UK); and has over six years of experience in India and the United Kingdom. His expertise is Advertising, Marketing Communication, Campaign Planning/Deployment, and Brand Management for various brands in tourism, automobiles, consumer durables, telecommunications, FMCG as well as media and fashion. Along with academics, he has completed several consultancy assignments for premium advertising agencies.

Yasser Mahfooz holds a doctorate in Strategic Marketing. He has more than a decade of academic experience in India and abroad and has several international conferences and publications to his credit. His research focuses on multicultural issues, strategy and services; and has received several research grants and project fellowship to travel abroad. Presently he is working as an Assistant Professor in the Department of Marketing, College of Business Administration, King Saud University, Riyadh, KSA.

Neha Mittal is an alumnus of MBA (HR) from Amity University 2007. She has over 6 years of experience in the field of Human Resources. She has worked in the areas of Organization Development, Competency Assessment, Talent & Succession Management, Employee Engagement, Rewards & Recognition and HR Business Partner. She has worked with multinationals in the area of pharmaceuticals and medical device. She is currently associated with a medical device company as Associate Manager – HR.

Rajendra Nargundkar chairs the position of Director at IMT Nagpur and Sr. Dean Academics at IMT Ghaziabad. He earned his Doctoral from Clemson University after completing PGDM from IIM Bangalore. An engineer from Osmania University, he is a keen researcher and an avid writer. His current research interests embrace World-class customer service, G to C Services and Business School Branding. His publications include a number of papers in high order international journals and cases of remarkable distinction. He has also authored and co-authored a number of books in Marketing.

Chandra Shekhar Padhi is currently working with Deloitte Consultancy Private limited as a Consultant in Technology and currently based in Hyderabad, India. He passed his Master's in Business Administration from Great Lakes Institute of Management, Gurgaon in 2012, prior to which he was working with a Major Automotive manufacturer in India. He passed his Mechanical Engineering from Institute of Technical Education and Research, Bhubaneswar.

Jayanthi Ranjan is a Professor in IT Management area at IMT, Ghaziabad. She is also Associate Dean-International Relations, IMT Ghaziabad. She has more than 19 years of teaching experience. She has over 110 publications till date. She has over 53 publications in various International Journals, 15 national conference proceedings and 10 International conference Proceedings till date. She has also published 14 edited books. She has published research papers with refereed publications like in World Scientific, Emerald, Indersceince, ANSINET, GIFT society. She is serving on the editorial board for the international journal "Information Technology Journal", Asian Network for Scientific Information. She is also the editorial member of "Inderscience-International Journal of E-CRM". She is the Editorial member of "Interdisciplinary journal of information knowledge and management", Informing Science Institute, UK. She is the associate editor of "Journal of Applied and Theoretical Information Technology". Her Teaching and Research interests include Data Mining & Building Data Warehouses, Information Systems Design, Information Agents Building and Business Intelligence.

Kah Phooi Seng received a Bachelor of Engineering (1st class) and PhD in Engineering from University of Tasmania, Australia, in 1997 and 2001 respectively. She is currently a Professor at Sunway University Malaysia. She is also the Director of Affective & Assistive Technologies (AAT) Research Centre in Sunway University. Prior to joining Sunway University, she was Associate Professor at School of Electrical and Electronic Engineering, Nottingham University. She and another colleague Kenneth Li Minn Ang formed a research group called Visual Information Engineering Research (VIER) group in Nottingham University, Malaysia campus. She also worked in Monash University in Malaysia, Tasmania and Griffith Universities in Australia before joining Nottingham University. Her research interests include the fields of visual processing, multi-biometrics, artificial intelligence, affective computing, and wireless visual sensor networks.

Bhawana Sharma is an Assistant Director at Jaipur National University. She had done her doctorate from the University of Rajasthan after completing her Masters in Commerce. She has participated in many international and National conferences. Bhawana is also having more than 10 international publications to her credit. She is supervising 8 scholars in their Ph. D. research work. Her Teaching and Research interests include Financial Accounting, Management Accounting, Income Tax, Cost Accounting, and Financial Management.

Lokesh Sharma is an Indian author who has done work over Wireless sensor Network. Lokesh Sharma was born in Mathura (Kosi Kalan) and studied in the Vidya Devi Jindal School at his hometown. He studied Computer Science engineering at GLA University, Mathura and then J. P. university, Solan. He worked as a Sr. Lecturer in MVN University, Faridabad and presently as a Consultant in Laurus Infosystem, Bangalore. Sharma's keen interest to develop their own protocols in wireless sensor network for this he had done his masters in Computer Science, which led to gain interest and develop their own backbone construction schemes. He had published journals and papers over Energy Efficient Schemes in Backbone Construction of Wireless Sensor Network. His writing style tends to be simple, and more elobarative. He is spiritually and intellectually beleive in himself .His philosphy to live life is very simple and always make other's to think in his own way.

Rajeev Sharma is senior academic in marketing within the school of Law and Business of Charles Darwin University. He is a Fellow of the Australian Marketing Institute (AMI) and a Certified Practicing Marketer (CPM). Rajeev is currently a Director of Australian Marketing Institute. Rajeev has researched and published in many international marketing journals and conferences. Rajeev teaches Research Methods regularly for doctorate students at CDU. His current area of research is in 'international market entry options' of developing country organisations. His recent publications have focussed on the motives of IJV formation.

Ooi Chien Shing received the Bachelor (First Class Honours) degree from the Faculty of Engineering, The University of Nottingham (Malaysia Campus), Malaysia, in 2011. He is currently a researcher and postgraduate student of the Department of Computer Science & Networking Telecommunication in Sunway University, Malaysia. He is also one of the members of Intelligent & Visual (IVC) Research Group in Sunway University. He has a background of both electronic engineering and computer science. His research interests include the fields of intelligent visual and audio processing, affective computing, and business intelligence. He has a number of journals and conference papers published in these related areas.

Tulika Sood is an Assistant Professor in Management at Jaipur National University. She is also pursuing her Doctorate from Jaipur National University.

Tugba Ucma is the lecturer and teaching assistant of Accountancy at the Muğla Sıtkı Koçman University for 5 years. She received her B.S. degree from the Muğla Sıtkı Koçman University, Faculty of Business Administration, her M.B.A. from the Muğla Sıtkı Koçman University, Institute of Social Science, Department of Business Administration, and her Ph.D. from the Dokuz Eylül University, Institute of Social Science, Department of Business Administration. Ucma has published many articles in a variety of accounting and business journals and made presentations at national and international conferences. She has also published two books: *Muhasebenin Teorik Yapısı–Genel Bir Bakış (The Theorical Structure of Accounting–From the General Perspective)* and *Kavramsal Çerçeve–US GAAP ve IFRS Yakınsama Projeleri (Conceptual Framework–US GAAP and IFRS Convergence Projects)*.

Ali Çağlar Uzun is lecturer of Marketing at Muğla Sıtkı Koçman University for 9 years. He received his B.S. degree from Dokuz Eylul University, Faculty of Economics and Administrative Sciences, his M.B.A. from Muğla Sitki Koçman University, Institute of Social Science, Department of Business Administration and he is at the Ph.D. thesis phase at Ege University, Institute of Social Science, Department of Business Administration. Ali Çağlar Uzun has published some articles in a variety of socail science journals and made presentations at both national and international conferences.

Fredy Valenzuela is a Senior Lecturer in Marketing in the UNE Business School, University of New England, Australia. Previously he lectured at Universidad de Talca, Chile for 15 years. He completed his MBA degree at University of Ottawa, Canada and his PhD degree at UNE, Australia. His main research focus is on issues related to service recovery, customer relationship management, and online learning and teaching. His industry experience covers several consulting projects for various Chilean companies. Most of these projects were related to measuring customers' satisfaction.

Eric Viardot is Professor of Marketing and Strategy at EADA Business School in Barcelona, Spain. He has a doctorate in management. Before joining academia, he worked in different management positions for Hewlett-Packard, MSF, and Bain and Company in Europe, Asia and North America. He has published various books and articles on strategic management and marketing. He is a reviewer and editorial board member of various international journals, most notably the *International Journal of Technology Marketing*, the *American Journal of Business,* and the *Journal of Technology Management for Growing Economies*. He is also an active consultant and trainer and has worked with several major multinational corporations.

Index

Lightning Source UK Ltd.
Milton Keynes UK
UKOW06n0907060314

227630UK00015B/111/P